# Honest Convictions

Jerry's Rescue from the Fugitive Slave Law

## LOUIS J. VISCONTI

Copyright © 2025 by Louis J. Visconti
All rights reserved.

No part of this publication may be reproduced in whole or in part, or stored in a retrieval system, or transmitted in any form or by any means, electronic, mechanical, photocopying, recording, or otherwise, without written permission of the author, except for the inclusion of brief quotations in a review.
For information regarding permission, please write to:
info@barringerpublishing.com

Barringer Publishing, Naples, Florida
www.barringerpublishing.com

Design and layout by Linda S. Duider

ISBN: 978-1-954396-87-6
Library of Congress Cataloging-in-Publication Data
*Honest Convictions: Jerry's Rescue from the Fugitive Slave Law* / Louis J. Visconti

Printed in USA

*To my mother, Anne, for giving me the joy of writing.*

# Contents

Introduction . . . . . . . . . . . . . . . . . . . . . . . . . . . . . . . . . . . . . . . . . . 1

Chapter One . . . . . . . . . . . . . . . . . . . . . . . . . . . . . . . . . . . . . . . . . 3

Chapter Two (August 1850) . . . . . . . . . . . . . . . . . . . . . . . . . . 13

Chapter Three (September 1850) . . . . . . . . . . . . . . . . . . . . . . . 24

Chapter Four (September – October 1850) . . . . . . . . . . . . . . . 34

Chapter Five (October – November 1850) . . . . . . . . . . . . . . . . 50

Chapter Six (December 1850) . . . . . . . . . . . . . . . . . . . . . . . . . 61

Chapter Seven (January 1851) . . . . . . . . . . . . . . . . . . . . . . . . . 73

Chapter Eight (February 1851) . . . . . . . . . . . . . . . . . . . . . . . . 88

Chapter Nine (March 1851) . . . . . . . . . . . . . . . . . . . . . . . . . . 105

Chapter Ten (March – April 1851) . . . . . . . . . . . . . . . . . . . . . 118

Chapter Eleven (April – May 1851) . . . . . . . . . . . . . . . . . . . . 136

Chapter Twelve (May – June 1851) . . . . . . . . . . . . . . . . . . . . 152

Chapter Thirteen (June – July 1851) . . . . . . . . . . . . . . . . . . . 166

Chapter Fourteen (July – August 1851) . . . . . . . . . . . . . . . . . 182

Chapter Fifteen (August – September 1851) . . . . . . . . . . . . . 196

Chapter Sixteen (October 1, 1851) . . . . . . . . . . . . . . . . . . . . . . . . .215

Chapter Seventeen (October 1 & 2, 1851) . . . . . . . . . . . . . . . . . .230

Chapter Eighteen (October 3 – 14, 1851) . . . . . . . . . . . . . . . . . . .246

Chapter Nineteen (October 15 – 30, 1851) . . . . . . . . . . . . . . . . .260

Chapter Twenty (November 1851) . . . . . . . . . . . . . . . . . . . . . . .276

Chapter Twenty-One (December 1851) . . . . . . . . . . . . . . . . . . . .294

Chapter Twenty-Two (January 1852) . . . . . . . . . . . . . . . . . . . . . .311

Chapter Twenty-Three (January – February 1852) . . . . . . . . . . . .325

Chapter Twenty-Four (March – April 1852) . . . . . . . . . . . . . . . .336

Chapter Twenty-Five (May 1852) . . . . . . . . . . . . . . . . . . . . . . . .354

Chapter Twenty-Six (June 1852) . . . . . . . . . . . . . . . . . . . . . . . . .369

Chapter Twenty-Seven (July 1852) . . . . . . . . . . . . . . . . . . . . . . . .384

Epilogue . . . . . . . . . . . . . . . . . . . . . . . . . . . . . . . . . . . . . . . . . . .399

Acknowledgements . . . . . . . . . . . . . . . . . . . . . . . . . . . . . . . . . . .402

*"How few men there are, at this present time, who have the moral courage to examine the great questions of the day calmly, and dispassionately, and having done so to act upon their **honest convictions**, without regard to what effect it may have upon their popularity."*

— *Ellen Birdseye Wheaton*
*Syracuse, New York 1851*

# Introduction

Despite living in central New York for most of my life, I never heard about the *"Jerry Rescue"* until I turned 55. It's a story from 1851 about men determined to free a fugitive slave, risking a heavy fine, and prison time in consequence. I was fascinated; soon drawn in by the people of the era, discovering what my hometown was like ten years before the Civil War. After fascination, I next felt cheated. Why didn't I already know this? Asking other people about the *Jerry Rescue* only produced blank stares and silence. Ignorance is bliss.

I started reading everything I could get my hands on about Syracuse, the times, and it's people, and I still do. My favorite is the diary of Ellen Birdseye Wheaton, the heroine of this book. *The Jerry Rescue*, by Angela F. Murphy, lit a fire under me, leading me to another book of similar title by Earl E. Sperry, delivered to the Onondaga Historical Association in 1921. Then, a friend pointed me to a great source for old newspapers—FultonHistory.com. I read all the publications of the *Syracuse Star* from the fall of 1849 to the summer of 1852. Looking for an alternative point of view, I likewise read the *Syracuse Standard*. At times, it's not much different than trying to compare the same story on CNN and Fox today. Concerning *Jerry's* release from custody, the *Star* called it a riot, while the *Standard* maintained a rescue. It's just one of the many truths I never understood about the *Jerry Rescue* and those who participated.

I wish that everyone from Central New York (and beyond) knew about the *Jerry Rescue* but most people don't. It's my belief that local history, especially stories of national importance, should be known by the current residents. Far too much authentic history remains unread, hiding in plain sight on library shelves, easily found on-line, seldom, if ever, discussed.

My goal was to put the *'Rescue'* event into a larger story about the Fugitive Slave Law, Syracuse, and the actual news events of the day. The names and occupations of local residents came from the 1851 Syracuse directory. Finding so many *larger-than-life* personalities living in or passing through Syracuse in the mid-1800's, I wanted their names to be heard and spoken again. The abundance of great minds suggested similarities to being in 1776 Philadelphia. Instead of forging a nation, this gathering of courageous Americans railed against the *Fugitive Slave Law* with equal vigor.

When Dr. Alfred Mercer died in August 1914, his will stated a desire

*"To keep green in memory the heroism of the men who rescued Jerry—men who could not look on a slave . . ."*

*Honest Convictions* is my way of honoring the good doctor's wishes. I hope you like it.

**Louis J. Visconti**

# Chapter One

It happened in August of 1850 when I met Jerry Henry at the butcher shop of Caleb Davis in Syracuse, New York. My father, Charles Wheaton, directed me to the establishment, just a few blocks from our home on Genesee Street by the Orphan Asylum on the hill.

*The brand-new city of Syracuse is a happening place to be!* Established in 1848, Syracuse quickly became a convention city in the heart of New York State. Settlers were initially drawn to the area by the springs of salt brine around Onondaga Lake. The opening of the Erie Canal sped development of the salt industry as the Oswego Canal joined the Erie in downtown Syracuse by Clinton Square. Democrats, Whigs, abolitionists, temperance leagues, Union men, and haters of the *Fugitive Slave Law* all gathered at City Hall to make speeches and proclaim resolutions. National politicians and foreign dignitaries visiting Syracuse were welcomed with pomp and ceremony including military parades with brass bands. Syracuse offered a lively array of theatrical shows at popular settings like the National Theater, Malcolm Hall, and Market Hall, among others. All the national headliners played Syracuse, creating a demand for larger venues.

Onondaga County boasted vibrant above and underground railroads, and the first plank roads in the country. Stagecoach teams plied the countryside with omnibus

*Charles A. Wheaton*

lines running daily schedules to the Syracuse House, the popular hotel on Clinton Square. It felt like we lived at the center of the universe with endless barrels of Syracuse Salt pouring down the canals for delivery—who didn't need salt? Knowing the answer, New York State took ownership of the lands around the salt springs and control of the booming industry.

When Pa sent me to the butcher's I felt gratified to be trusted—ever since I turned thirteen in January and claimed to be a man. My mother, Ellen Birdseye Wheaton, was even more anxious for me to grow up; she'd birthed nine children by then, with eight living, needing all the help she could get. I mostly obliged, especially when it took me away from the noise and confusion that accompanies a house full of girls. Lucky for me, little Henry was born in October so now I had a brother again. Tragically, my brother Homer died before he turned one. I was the second child, two years younger than Cornelia. After Homer's brief sojourn on earth, Ma gave birth to Ellen, Emma, Clara, Florence, and Lucia before she finally had another boy at the age of thirty-four.

"Edward, do what your father says!" Ma barked, "And see if there's a special!"

"Don't worry, Ma—consider it done!" I hollered back, banging the screen door behind me.

Before sending me on an errand, my parents were deep in a discussion about the evils of slavery. Both were staunch abolitionists, especially Pa, who turned forty-one in 1850. His cheeks flushed from rehashing the current events.

Pa fumed, "I'm still outraged that thugs were allowed to take over the annual meeting of the American Anti-Slavery Society in New York City, Ellen. Who would have thought that hoodlums from Five Points, led by the notorious Captain Rynders, would be aided by the police?"

"Yes, Charles, but the worst happened when Rynders trotted out a Doctor Grant, who tried to explain how the black person is not the same species as the white man! The doctor quoted Latin in his ruse and used all the medical words that he knew to bolster his claim. He said that black people can't reason like whites, Charles, but only a man of his character would think that."

"That's terrible, Ellen! After that, William Lloyd Garrison had Frederick Douglass step forward, but it didn't matter that he spoke more intelligently than Captain Rynders or Doctor Grant. Instead of giving up, the mob cried out, 'Douglass don't count because he's half white. It's more proof that black people can't reason!'"

Ma replied, "But then Rev. Ward, who's all black, spoke so eloquently that he shamed them. Horace Greeley wrote in the *New York Tribune* that Rev. Ward demonstrated that if anyone was related to an orangutan, it was Doctor Grant, and if there were a cousin to a vicious monkey, that would be Capt. Rynders."

Pa stated, "And if that's not bad enough, the slave powers are intent on liberating Cuba to become the next slave state. Henry Clay didn't like it when President Taylor sent a naval patrol to thwart the filibusterers!"

"I'm not surprised," Ma answered. "Henry Clay's working on the next compromise for national unity, much like he did with the *Missouri Compromise of 1820*, and the *Compromise Tariff of 1833*. Today he leads the committee of thirteen who drafted five bills that are supposed to keep the United States together—*the Great Compromise of 1850!*"

Like many mothers, mine often surprised me with her command of the facts, I didn't expect her to summarize the proposed acts of Congress off the top of her head. She continued,

"The first bill would admit California as a Free State, the second would settle the Texas boundary, and the third bill would buy land from Texas for the benefit of New Mexico. The fourth bill is the vile Fugitive Slave Act, and the fifth bill abolishes selling slaves, but allows slavery, in the District of Columbia."

"True for you, Ellen," Pa answered. "Then they rolled all five together into the Omnibus Bill, but we can all rejoice that the Omnibus is deader than Cock Robbin! Still, it was tragic that President Taylor died last month; the future looks more uncertain than ever," Pa said with reservation.

"President Fillmore's from New York State, but he's not the man that General Taylor was," Ma responded.

"No indeed! That might be why Taylor's entire cabinet resigned, but I'm not a Whig," Pa answered.

Almost at my destination, faint sounds emanated from the Davis Butcher Shop on the corner of Orange Street. Every approaching step brought clarity to a deep, sonorous voice within. A large man of exceptional strength and fiery temperament, at fifty-nine, Caleb Davis remained a formidable person. Davis opposed my father on issues like alcohol and politics, but he disliked the Rev. Samuel J. May of the Unitarian Church even more. I nodded at the two customers at the counter, as several others milled about undecided. Alonzo Ferguson, barkeeper at Clark's Hotel, stood next in line, behind him a muscular, light-skinned black man with a shock of red hair. I overheard Davis call him Jerry as the butcher launched into one of his rants about temperance and the fools who support it. He didn't mind naming names, even paying customers. The act included answering his own questions and laughing at his own jokes.

"I tell ya, Ferguson," Davis began, "I'm leaving town if the *dries* take over. Just yesterday, I was over on Church St. delivering to Robinson's Temperance House, and who's out front chatting away? None other than his lordship of boredom, the Rev. May himself, with his good friend, arid Olly Teall, the dry one. President of the Onondaga Bank and the City Water Works, too, he is—ha! I swear, the sight of 'em together parched my throat. Heard 'em talking about plans for a membership drive and wished 'em both ill. They're the *don't* brothers, they are, as in *don't do this* and *don't do that*. Ha ha ha!"

Jerry laughed, but Ferguson asked, "Then why deliver there?"

Davis bellowed, "Because Robinson pays on time, something you could learn!"

Regular patrons of Davis learned that to speed transactions you kept your mouth shut, smiled, nodded, and never asked questions. Alonzo's unaware that he just pulled the "on" lever. While reloading his repertoire, Davis hallooed when he recognized my face. He must have known half the city by name and affiliation, and that my pa's a member of both the Onondaga County and New York State Temperance Societies. He addressed me with his familiar manner.

"Ahh, a young Wheaton, I see! Wanting a bargain, are you? Sure! Tell your father that I saw his friends at Robinson's and spent their money at the Prospect Hill Brewery—Ha ha! Tell 'im the B'hoys had a good, long drink to his health. Ha ha ha!"

The stranger turned to me and asked, "Is your daddy Charles Wheaton?"

"Yes, he is," I replied.

"Pleased to know ya," he answered, offering his hand. "I'm William Henry, but folks call me Jerry."

"Ed Wheaton," I returned, trying to match his manly grip.

Caleb Davis posed, "William? Never heard you called that."

"Last time was at the watch house after I drank lots of cheap liquor—they needed my name in the ledger," Jerry answered.

My eyes met with the butcher's, which compelled me to greet him but before I could, Thomas Davis, the butcher's twenty-seven-year-old son of a similar build, appeared from the back of the shop. Caleb Davis looked scarier to me, but his son might cripple you. He wiped his apron and smirked as I addressed the elder.

"Good morning, sir. We all enjoyed the stew last week."

Being called 'sir' temporarily caught Davis off guard. A skilled debater, he used my words mockingly.

"Yes, *sir*, it was indeed *last* week, *sir*. Please remind your father, *sir*, that good men of temperance always pay on time."

Thomas Davis thought I was staring. He didn't address me as a gentleman.

"Hey, boy! What you looking at?" he demanded.

"Huh? Uh, nothing."

"Oh yeah, you were, looked to me like you were giving us *the eye!*"

"No, not me, I'd never give you *the eye!*"

"See that you don't, I'll not take it kindly if you try it again!"

I couldn't engage the smile and nod routine and froze up.

"But I didn't . . . er, ah, yes, uh, I mean *NO!* I'd never give you the eye!"

Thomas eased my paralysis, saying,

"Go on, kid, get outta' here."

"Not so fast!" the elder sneered. "We've yet to settle the bill."

Reaching into my pockets, the emptiness rattled me. My mind flashed to where I left the money while I told Ma not to worry.

I stammered, "Uh, I'm deeply sorry, Mr. Davis, but I, uh, left my money at home. I'll run right back and get it, sir!"

"First come, first served," Davis rebuffed, not allowing me to take the goods without paying.

With everyone staring, I wished for spurs to speed my escape. After re-telling the encounter at home, my sisters voiced displeasure with the butcher, but more-so with me for talking to him. Cornelia said,

"What's wrong with you, Edward? Don't ever say anything to that man that you don't want repeated. He doesn't need to know our business!"

Ellen echoed, "Yeah, Edward, what's wrong with you?"

Sometimes, brutal honesty works best. "I'll tell ya what's wrong with me. Ma keeps having girls!" I snarled. They left me alone after that, but I was already running back to the Orange Street butchers to save face.

My father partnered with his older brother Horace, in a thriving business at Clinton Square. Between managing Wheaton Hardware and being on more committees than I could remember, we often

missed Pa at home. His Sundays were particularly busy from attending two or more religious gatherings, his pleasant tenor often in demand. It grieved Ma the most at times when he was present in body, but his mind and spirit were somewhere else. She once remarked that my father couldn't do anything on a small scale; everything had to be magnificent, of a Napoleonic order. This, however, did not extend to the daily operations of our home.

With her family growing rapidly, my mother truly needed help. Without the time or inclination to perform this function himself, Pa's solution was to install George Johnson, *"Black George,"* hired on for room, board, and wages. Of similar age to my parents, George had been born free to a slave mother. Nevertheless, he lived an indentured servant's life until state law freed him for good July 4, 1827.

Black George was always within earshot, ready to put out fires or bring wood to start one. During our frigid winters, he earned heartfelt admiration for keeping the home fires burning. I didn't mind helping, and besides, I liked George from the start.

Ma felt apprehensive when Black George first moved in, despite the stubborn fact that he was there to help her. Still, neighborhood yarns spun around the clotheslines kept her ears ringing.

*"Did you hear about the Wheaton's?"*

*"No, what's Charles out conquering today?"*

*"Hired a black man and moved 'im right in—might be starting a plantation next, knowing him!"*

*"Really? I heard he conducted a railroad, but I never saw one."*

*"You can't see it, Abigail, it's underground, ha-ha!"*

*"Ha! Ya gotta watch those edge-a-ma-cated types—always puttin' on phony airs.'"*

"Black George"
*George Johnson*

*"What? No one ever knows what you're talking about, Abigail—why do I even bother? Put a clothespin on it, would you?"*

Weather permitting, Black George favored outdoor assignments but this one he'd rather avoid, even on sunny days. Escorting the Wheaton children in public could attract awkward glances in the street, or through plate glass windows. Accusatory inferences grabbed tight, twisting under his skin. Worse yet, he suffered with Ma's affliction of ringing ears.

*"There he goes! Wheaton's boy with Massa's chillun."*
*"That darkie's doin' all right for himself, livin' in a big house and all."*
Though expected, passing comments find their mark, the most irksome came from fellow blacks.
*"Bet he thinks he's special, but he ain't!"*
Black George once told me that *"Nobody says nothin' when I walks alone—just the way I likes it!"*

Before working for our family, Black George struggled for security with limited prospects. He resented the house slave implication; he just did the best that he could with the deck stacked against him. Finding opportunity with a good family, he took it, and until something better came along, which was unlikely, he planned to stay put. As long as Pa's fortunes continued, and Ma kept having babies, George had a secure place in a handsome home. And he liked work that kept his favorite foods on the table, doing a stellar job in consequence. I encountered him in our root cellar and felt mischievous enough to provide some friendly irritation.

"So, what is it that you actually do?" I asked with a yawn.
"*You lucky I'm not yo' daddy!* I'd have you over my knee 'bout now, even thou you been foolin' with his razor. Remember what I told ya, boy—safer to put some milk on yo lip an let de cat lick it off!"
"I didn't mean anything bad, George."
"You 'jus hold 'dem lips an I'll tell ya whats I do. I does plenty, boy. Just look 'roun this here root cellar. You think this place filled

itself up? An don't I let yo daddy know when I hear of good product comin' to market? He trusts me to buy what's right. When I hired on at Wheaton's, right off we took the wagon down Genesee to Stanton's farm so I could meet Mr. Rufus and his son, Gardner. Hah! Guess they named 'im right for a farmer's son. Anyways, now 'dat I know'd 'em, dey settled it so's I could trade fo' yo' family. We done the same with Van Ornam's over on Gazelle Street."

I changed the subject to a safer topic.

"That reminds me, George, I wanted to ask you if you heard an update on a story that I read in the newspaper a while back. You remember when Henry Clay was here for the State Fair, in September, right? Well, on the way back to Kentucky, his servant, Levi, ran off near Sandusky, Ohio. Any word on him from the railroad?"

"Prolly' the same you heard, just that he run off again. But callin' him a servant ain't exactly true, is it? When a man quits his job, they don't write it in the newspaper."

"I guess so, but you'll let me know if you hear anything, won't you?"

"Next time I'm down to Loguen's I'll say that Ed Wheaton's worryin' his-self sick 'bout Levi runnin' off!"

The Rev. Jermain Wesley Loguen lived just a couple blocks away at the corner of Genesee and Pine with his wife, Caroline, and their three girls, Elizabeth (8), Helen (7), and baby Sara. At thirty-six, Loguen ran a visible terminal of the underground railroad, openly defying the slave owners. Like the butcher's customer, Jerry, Loguen was of mixed race, born to a slave mother and white master. Pa and his friends in the Liberty Party believed this exposed the immorality of slave owners, having children outside of wedlock, enslaving their own offspring, creating fugitives running for their lives.

At twenty-one, Loguen made his escape from Tennessee in 1834, and eventually settled in Syracuse in 1841, educating himself along

*Jermain Loguen*

the way. He next became pastor of the AME Zion church on Chestnut St., which included a school where he taught black children. Because of Rev. Loguen, his wife Caroline, and the local abolitionists, the underground railroad operated mostly above ground through Syracuse. Pa's generosity helped to feed and clothe the irregular arrivals both day and night.

# Chapter Two
## (August 1850)

Located in the heart of downtown Syracuse at Clinton Square, Wheaton Hardware stood across the street from the popular Syracuse House, and just across the Salina Street Bridge from Rust's Hotel in the Empire Block.

The celebrated Philo N. Rust earned his renown as the best hotel keeper west of Albany from many years running the Syracuse House, now his chief competitor across the street/canal. His forty-one-acre farm on Onondaga Street paired nicely with his patron's appreciation of good food, filling tables with eager customers. Rust would say,

"*There's nothing makes a hungry man hurry like seeing somebody else have a good meal!*"

Before his time at the Syracuse House, Philo kept flies from pestering diners at the Mansion House by installing *punkah* fans. He'd read about their use in India, attached to the ceiling and lowered into position above the dining tables. Rust even had the fans colored green to follow the original pattern. In order to turn, the *punkah* fan required the exertions of a human *wallah* (in another room) to provide the impetus. The fan turned by a series of pulleys, levers, and cables connected to a mechanism turned or peddled by the *punkah wallah*. Rust hired a young black boy for this task, visible from the street but not from the dining room. The sight of spinning *punkah* fans and the peddling *punkah wallah* drew customers like the flies they were meant to keep away.

After exiting the Syracuse House in 1848, Philo couldn't stay out of the hotel business for long, opening Rust's Hotel at the Empire Block in May of '49. Since then, his reputation as the area's premier hotelier spread along both canals and the growing railroads.

Like many of my friends, I dreamt of strolling into Rust's Hotel with the swagger of a packet boat captain surrounded by admirers. I thought about it all week, finding myself standing outside of Rust's on the new stone walk, gazing through the windows. Pa caught me looking and directed me to the 1st Baptist church where Mr. William H. Burleigh was giving a temperance lecture. Pa said that I needed it.

Following his edict, I encountered Parish and Grove Johnson, standing outside the church edifice.

"Hey, Ed!" they both yelled. "You get in trouble, too?"

"Yeah, caught lookin' inside Rust's Hotel again," I lamented.

Parish said, "Our pa said he wants us to know that alcohol's dangerous, and told us we had to go listen to Mr. Burleigh today. He musta heard about us talking with Philo Rust."

"That didn't help none," Grove observed.

Parish Johnson was my age, Grove a few years younger. Both were classmates and ready adventurers, but Parish often preferred to leave Grove behind. He favored steam power to an anchor. For reasons unknown, Parish believed he was somehow related to everyone named Johnson. When he first met Black George, he didn't know what to think.

We entered church late, and all the good seats in the back were taken, forcing us to sit up front. As unattended youth in plain view, Mr. Burleigh frequently glanced at us, which enticed the curiosity of the faithful. We must've presented well as young prodigals ready to be saved. While I listened, everything that he said made sense; how innocent sounding, well-meaning offers of a friendly drink could lead a man to ruin. The devastation left in the wake of an empty bottle. And yet, walking home afterward I still longed to partake in the revery at Rust's Hotel. I imagined cheery friends, outrageous laughter, remarkable food, song and dance, romance and adventure! How bad could that be?

The following week I accompanied my mother to Welch's Coffee House at the corner of Warren and Railroad (Washington) Streets. Pa dropped us off in the carriage at the front door. It was part business, part pleasure for Ma, having Orphan Asylum affairs to discuss with her friend, Mrs. Janet Cook, whose husband, Mr. John Lawton Cook, managed the establishment for old Mr. Welch. The Cook's lived on premises with sons John Jr. (16), Austin (14), Abel (10), and baby Mary (2). The brothers were classmates of mine, though John Jr. now worked full time with his father. I was good friends with Austin and Abel, who worked *almost* full time.

*John Lawton Cook*

George Babcock, assistant to Mr. Cook, greeted us, while barkeeper John McMillan smiled and waved. I never understood how my parents abided non-temperance at Welch's while condemning it at Rust's. Was it that Coffee House patrons could handle their liquor and didn't like dog fights? Welch's also had a special room reserved for the ladies of Syracuse, often filled to capacity. My mother embraced Mrs. Cook, who slipped an arm under Ma's elbow, and they yakked all the way to the ladies' tearoom. I reconnoitered the place for a Cook brother.

Compared with Rust's Hotel, the Syracuse House, and the Globe, Welch's had a different feel than the bigger venues in town. This was a family place, but still a retreat where a man could unwind after a long day's work for a light, tasty meal accompanied by a Havana cigar. Perhaps a glass of Hersey's whiskey, made in Cazenovia, when appropriate. Lawyers, merchants, and other professionals frequented, while ladies of fashion took refuge in their special room. Meanwhile, Rust's Hotel attracted everything from an alley cat to the president.

I headed towards the back to look for my friends when John Jr. entered.

"Hey, Ed!" he said happily. John had his pa's ease of pleasant first exchanges that always made you feel welcome. "What brings you here?"

"Hey John—Pa drove us, and my ma's in the tearoom with your ma."

"Yeah, the ladies are talking business and don't want to be interrupted. Say, Ed, did you go to the dedication of the 1st Presbyterian Church the other day? I heard it was pretty good!"

"Nah, I didn't go—lousy weather, wasn't it?"

"Yeah, overcast but it didn't rain bad. A good-sized crowd watched the topmost stone get placed in the steeple. Two pretty girls accompanied the workmen to the peak and threw flowers to the spectators below. I heard that Philo Rust had a bottle of champagne sent up, but it got broke on the stairs."

"Ha! Maybe Philo's trying to make amends for missing church," I said.

"Don't kid yourself, Ed. Philo understands publicity better than he does the inside of a church, and there must be twenty-five of them around here."

"You sound like my ma sometimes, John. Where you hiding Austin and Abel?"

"They're finishing up now, Ed—Pa just let 'em off to see the *Kentucky Fat Boy!*"

"To see who? You kidding me?"

"Nope—and here they are now, all ready to go!" John said with regret.

"Hey, Ed!" Austin greeted, "You comin' to see the *Fat Boy* with us? He's around the corner at Brintnall's—all 500 pounds of 'im!"

"500 pounds? What they feed 'im in Kentucky? Elephant grass?" I posed.

Austin answered, "When he was a baby they bathed 'im in a tub a' lard, and rubbed his belly like the Buddha. Then the whole village said mystical chants to make him grow."

"You're crazy, Austin!"

"No, I'm not. Heard it from a guy who saw the *Fat Boy* in Utica, so it must be true."

"You believe everything you hear, Austin?" I asked.

"No, but he probably descended from the *Anakims*," Austin said matter-of-factly.

"The *who?*" I asked again. "What's an *Anakim?*"

"Don't you read the Bible, Ed? Remember David and Goliath? Well, Goliath came from a giant race called *the Anakims*. Read it for yourself!"

"Never heard of giant Anakims from Kentucky, Austin. Weren't they from the Holy Land?"

"Well, this one's on exhibit at Brintnall's for a couple days. He's only fifteen and already weighs 500 pounds. Who knows how big he'll get?" Austin asked.

*"He's an Anakim!"* Abel insisted.

"Great! Let's all go see the *Kentucky Fat Boy!*" I said, feigning excitement as we departed to meet the living relic of antiquity. At first glance, Abel appeared disenchanted that he didn't speak Anakim.

"My name's Andy Brand, glad to know ya!" said the young giant, a friendly soul who answered all of our questions.

"How'd you get so big?" Austin asked.

"Not sure, seems I hang onto a little of everything I eat."

"And exactly how big are you?" I inquired.

"Last time they measured me, I was 5'-3" tall and I weighed 537 pounds."

"How'd they figure that? They dunk you in the weigh-lock?" Austin posed.

"I heard that once after I broke a scale," the titan uttered.

"So, where you off to next?"

"Tomorrow, I'm supposed to play somebody named Falstaff at the Fayette Street Theatre. They don't care that I don't know Shakespeare; they told me I was built for the part and said I'd do just fine."

Before we took leave, I asked of his lineage. "Say, Andy, uh, this is kind of personal, but have you ever heard of the *Anakims*?"

"Unfortunately, I have. Been a slingshot target all my life."

Re-enchanted, Abel Cook whispered, *"He's an Anakim!"*

Leaving the happy giant behind, the sounds of Kellogg's Brass Band drew us to Clinton Square where a fire company was once again on parade. A common occurrence complete with music, the uniformed fire companies marched in formation to the sound of brass before catching a train, often to Oswego or Utica, where a warm reception awaited. Syracuse firemen welcomed visiting brethren in return, complete with banquets and more parades. The music made a pleasant distraction, and no-one much cared if the firemen were coming or going, except perhaps the tavern owners and the families left behind.

Following the parade toward the Railroad Depot, we diverted past the Congregational Church where Pa was speaking at a crowded anti-slavery meeting. Hearing his voice drew me to the open door, the Cook brothers followed. Reverends May, Loguen, and Raymond were seated near Mr. Burleigh, all listening attentively.

"It's not all bad news," Pa said. "We can take heart that California will join the Union as a Free State; the Senate has approved!"

"Yes, and there was a parade of black soldiers in New York City!" Rev. Loguen answered. "An entire company marched down Broadway in blue uniform preceded by the American flag and a band."

Rev. May said, "A glorious sight, Rev. Loguen!"

Pa agreed, but now he had bad news. "I was sorry to hear the plight of the President's coachman, William Williams. A slaver abducted his wife, three daughters, and three grandchildren from their home and sent them to Baltimore for transport to New Orleans."

"Williams was coachman to President's Polk, Taylor, and Filmore, but it mattered naught," Rev. Loguen decreed.

The Pastor of the 1st Baptist, Rev. Raymond said, "He purchased his own freedom recently, but his family is still owned by someone in New Orleans."

Rev. May scoffed, "President Filmore felt so deeply that he provided money for the poor man to find his family in Baltimore. The trader said he'd take $3,200 for the lot and the President, Daniel Webster, and other Congressmen contributed to the ransom. Brave men! So far, the coachman's still short $1,500 for the little ones."

Someone said, "Don't forget that Frederick Douglass will speak at City Hall! He's stopping on his way to Cazenovia for the Fugitive Slave Convention."

"That's correct," Rev. May agreed. "I'll be in Cazenovia myself, along with Rev. Loguen, Charles Wheaton, and Gerrit Smith."

I wanted to remain but felt Austin's elbow. "C'mon, Edward, we gotta get back before my brother John has a nervous breakdown," he said.

My mother worried about Pa attending the Fugitive Slave Convention, but of course he went anyway.

"Don't worry, Ellen," he said. "It's times like these for men to stand and be counted!"

"Be careful, Charles, you're making powerful enemies."

"So be it, then. I'll be back in a couple days," Pa said with conviction.

When he returned, we learned that he'd been chosen Vice President of the convention, second only to Frederick Douglass. He was also selected to the committee to free William L. Chaplin from prison. The Liberty Party candidate for Governor of New York had tried

*August 1850 Fugitive Slave Convention*

to flee Maryland with slaves belonging to Congressmen from Georgia, hoping to present them at the Cazenovia Convention. Instead, he landed inside a Southern jail where abolition was highly discouraged.

"Pa, was Rev. Ward at the convention, too?" I asked.

"No, Edward, he couldn't attend but we read a letter that he sent, and another from Mr. Burleigh as well. Then we read the letters that escaped slaves wrote to those still in bondage, offering them encouragement. You should have heard Rev. May and Rev. Loguen—voices of liberty for all mankind!" Turning to Ma, he said, "I can tell that you're still worried, Ellen, but we need to show the slavers what kind of men we are up North."

After the convention ended, Frederick Douglass spoke again in Syracuse at Market Hall, this time with J.C. Hathaway. Both recounted the Fugitive Slave Convention and William Chaplin's imprisonment. People debated whether Chaplin could run for office from jail. When I asked Pa, he suggested consulting with attorney Charles B. Sedgewick for a more learned opinion. Encountering Mr. S., he said there'd be a lawsuit regardless, and being a lawyer, he smiled.

Nearing home at month's end, I spotted my mother conversing with several men in front of our house, soon recognizing three ministers, the Reverends Samuel J. May, Jermain Loguen, and Samuel Ringgold Ward. Rev. Ward introduced me to his son, Sam Jr., who was the same age as me.

I hadn't met Sam before, but had heard Rev. Ward preach back in February when Black George, my father, and I squeezed into the crowded AME Zion Church where Rev. Loguen pastored. I still recall the advice that he offered to young men based on his own experience:

1. Find your own appropriate place of duty.
2. When you have found it, by all means keep it.
3. If ever tempted to depart from it, return to it as speedily as possible.

At the age of two in 1820, Samuel R. Ward fled slavery with his parents, bolting from Maryland to the township of Greenwich in Cumberland County, New Jersey. Escaping slavery didn't always mean going to Canada. A closer alternative was to reach a Free State, and live among the Quakers. The Christian religious sect practiced what they preached, thwarting slave-catchers at every turn while the local black inhabitants encouraged the hounds' speedy return south. The Quakers

*Samuel Ringgold Ward*

could see something of God in everyone, believing that all human beings have unique worth. The populace of Quakers and vigilant blacks around Greenwich made it a safe landing place for fugitives on the run.

In 1826, the Ward's moved to New York City and enrolled their son in the African Free School. Established in 1787 for children of slaves and free blacks, the school was created by the New York Manumission Society, whose members included Alexander Hamilton and John Jay. Connecting with the wealthy abolitionist, Gerrit Smith, Ward joined the Liberty Party in 1840. A speaker on the abolition tour in February of 1841, he lectured in the town of Butler, Wayne County, New York. He was invited to tea following his discourse, and asked to preach the next day at the all-white Congregational church.

As the church had no pastor at the time, several members urged Ward to remain. The young black preacher thought the rest of the parishioners wouldn't approve, advising them to write to him at his home in Peterboro. In a few days, the letter arrived, leading to a return visit to Butler and acceptance of the position in April 1841. The entire congregation was white except for the pastor, his wife and their three-year-old son, Samuel R. Ward Jr. During his few years as their Pastor, which ended for ailing health, the Congregational Church of Butler felt satisfied with the arrangement, grateful to have a speaker of Ward's ability even though only in his mid-twenties. There wasn't racial tension because parishioners in Butler didn't care that Ward was black, nor did they consider outsider opinion. They liked his style of preaching, how he lived, and that was that. If other people had a problem it was *their* problem, not Butler's.

As I stood listening to the men, I noticed that Rev. May held an old newspaper that contained the "Pulpit and Slavery' article written by Henry Ward Beecher. I must have missed that part of the conversation as Rev. May spoke of proposed improvements at the Unitarian Church, primarily an enlargement to accommodate the growing congregation, new pews, and a bell. He rewarded me for not interrupting.

"Well, Edward, what's on your mind? I perceive a question trying to escape."

"Yes, sir, it's about that newspaper you're holding. I wanted to ask you about what Henry Ward Beecher said to the *Journal of Commerce*."

"You're in luck then, my boy, what would you like to know?" Rev. May asked.

Finding myself the focus of three renowned preachers, the curiosity I felt seemed like a hundred years ago as I struggled to find my voice.

"Um, uh, not much, really. I, uh, just wanted to know what you thought of Beecher's article, and if you think it will change anyone's mind," I finally answered.

Rev. May said, "Edward, you should know the most serious obstacle to the anti-slavery cause is the conduct of the clergy and the churches in our country. Influential church members, gentlemen of property and standing too important to be alienated, were permitted to direct the preaching of their pastors about that peculiar institution down south.

They're afraid of upsetting the current system and prefer to keep things the way they are. They fear that agitators endanger the existence of the Union, and even though they oppose slavery it's better to save the union than to destroy it for the sake of liberating the negro."

"So, they think they're playing it safe, sir?" I asked.

"I'm certain that's what they believe, Edward."

Rev. Loguen said, "Edward, the churches and political parties have adapted to slavery, and most are unwilling to be disturbed by it. It took a *steady and persistent struggle* with that idea in the minds of politicians, ministers, and people, to change minds in Syracuse."

Rev. Ward answered next. "Edward, Mr. Beecher touched on an issue even larger than slavery. It's not whether some men have wisely or unwisely pleaded this cause, or whether their measures were commendable or not; nor merely, what shall be done with the Negro? It is, shall religion, pure and undefiled, prevail in the land; or shall a corrupt, spurious, human system, dishonoring to God and oppressive to man, have the prevalence? That is the issue, *before Israel and the sun!*"

With a gaping mouth I stood frozen, the silence broken by laughter when Sam Jr. said, "Don't worry, Ed. Sometimes it's better not to say anything."

I put his advice to immediate use. "You're right Sam—and I don't have any more questions!" I blurted, taking leave of the clergy while saving my foot from my mouth. Talking with Ma afterward, I learned that the Wards were house hunting.

*"Are they really moving to Syracuse, Ma?"* I asked excitedly.

"Yes, Edward, they are—*and perhaps as close as the foot of our garden!*"

# Chapter Three

## (September 1850)

In early September, Black George came home with news of the latest canal drowning, this one happened by the lock in the 1st Ward. Apparently, a twelve-year-old slipped and fell, hitting his head before going into the water. Tragedies like this normally restricted my movements, so I was around to share Pa's grief when he came home. We all could tell that he was upset as soon as he walked in the door.

"Charles, tell me what's troubling you," Ma demanded.

"What's troubling me? Ellen, the Senate passed the infernal *Fugitive Slave Bill!* I thought we were safe when the Omnibus failed, but now it appears that we'll have a Federal Agency for slave catching."

"So, now what?"

"Next the House of Representatives will vote, where it's expected to pass, and then President Filmore could sign it into law."

"Dear Lord!" Ma cried.

"It's not over yet, Ellen—we'll have to wait and see what happens," Pa said.

For many in Syracuse, worse news soon arrived. From the sidewalk, I heard sobs coming through the open windows of our house. I hurried inside to find everyone in tears from Ma down to the baby. Black George and the kitchen maid looked forlorn, while Pa was working at the store.

"Ma, what happened?" I asked, bracing for the worst.

"Oh, Edward," she sobbed, "Miss Bradbury has died!"

Cornelia and Ellen were distraught from losing their teacher, Miss Amelia Bradbury, renowned for her school for young ladies, the Bradbury Seminary, established in 1840. I never heard a bad word about Miss Bradbury, the school, or her teaching methods. She cared more about building her students' characters than in their scholarly achievements. Frankness and candor were encouraged through an appeal to their moral senses. She offered a complete curriculum, but more importantly, she had her priorities in the correct order for the development of wholesome young ladies. Losing the city's best teacher was a significant blow to the community, only ten days into the term!

"I'm real sorry, Cornelia," I said. "You, too, Ellen, I know how much Miss Bradbury meant to you." I hugged them both, but it felt like many more tears would flow before either one felt any better.

The next day at Mr. Weld's School for Young Men and Boys, the misfortune was on everyone's lips. Those of us with sisters at Miss Bradbury's shared details of how the girls found out; where they were, what they were doing, etc.

"My sisters stayed home today with the school closed!" I said.

"How old was she, Mr. Weld?" Parish asked.

"I'm told that she was only 53—and far too young," Weld replied. "To those of you with sisters at the Bradbury School, please extend my sincere condolences. And it wouldn't hurt to buy them a little something on your way home."

"Hey Prentice," I said, "What do you say we slip down to the Knipp Brothers to buy confections for the girls? They'll love it!"

"Good thinking, Ed, maybe a little something for us, too," Prentice replied.

Prentice Cheney and his younger brother, Silas, are good friends who live nearby on Almond Street, not far from the butcher that we all love to hate. Their sister, Frances, goes to Bradbury's along with my sisters. Their father, Mr. Timothy C. Cheney, is a respected builder. His latest project concerns the new Onondaga County Penitentiary up on the hill in the 1st Ward—between Mary and Pond Streets. When the location was first announced, a bunch of us went up there to inspect. The view was incredible, I thought I could see all the way to Liverpool!

After school, we didn't get far before Silas said his mouth was watering for something from G & J Knipp's sweet tooth shop on Pearl Street. The display case in the front window and the wonderful aroma emanating from inside started my juices flowing, too.

*Timothy C. Cheney*

Mr. George Knipp greeted us. "Well, hello, young gentlemen! You look in need of something sweet, but is it for you or someone special?" he asked. "We have something for every occasion!"

"We're here for our sisters, sir, they go to school at Miss Bradbury's, and we want to cheer them up," I said.

"Oh, I heard the awful news this morning—everyone's talking about it! Her funeral is tomorrow afternoon and she's being buried up at Rose Hill. It's hard to believe—she seemed in such good health when I saw her last week."

Mr. John Knipp overheard, joining the conversation. "George," he said, "These young gentlemen deserve a reward for being thoughtful of their sisters, don't you agree?"

"I was thinking the same, John," George agreed, "Especially since they torment the girls most of the time—isn't that so, fellows?"

"Yes, sir!" Si Cheney replied, with me and Prentice nodding affirmation.

"And they're honest, too, George!" J. Knipp offered.

"Step this way to satisfy your desires, gentlemen," G. Knipp directed.

"What a great deal, Ed!" Prentice said excitedly as we departed the sweet shop.

With a mouthful, Silas uttered something unintelligible. I gave him the smile and nod routine, savoring the sweetness going down the back of my throat as we made our way toward home.

The Wheaton's were well-represented at the solemn funeral for Miss Amelia Bradbury. Everywhere you looked, with a long view from atop Rose Hill, were faces of shock, suffering and grief. I sensed that everyone felt the loss. The ceremony lacked the pageantry of President Taylor's funeral, but far eclipsed it by the depth of feeling for the departed. Our community knew and loved Amelia Bradbury for the treasure that she was.

Though Pa provided transport, Cornelia and Ellen decided to walk home, so I joined them. We didn't say much, but I remembered Ma telling me how important *just being there* can be sometimes. Crossing the Erie Canal on the Beech St. Bridge, we cut over on Gazelle to find a big surprise.

*Cornelia Wheaton*

"Cornelia, Ellen, look!" I cried out. "That's Rev. Ward and his family moving in!"

"And right around the block from us, too," Ellen said.

"We'll have to tell Ma when we get home," Cornelia declared.

"Pa must've already told her. He's been anxious for the Ward's to move in," I pronounced. Approaching the loaded wagon in front of the family's new residence, I said, "Say, girls, I'm going to help them unload—tell everybody where I am, okay?"

"We will," Cornelia replied. "You know, Ed, you can be really nice sometimes, did you know that?"

Then Samuel Ward Jr. came outside, so I introduced him.

"Hello, Sam, and welcome to the neighborhood! We live right around the block, and these are two of my sisters," I said while shaking his hand. "Sam, this is my older sister, Cornelia, and my other sister, Ellen—I've got four more of 'em at home, and a baby brother, too. Girls, this is Sam Ward."

"Thank you, Edward," Sam replied. Turning to my sisters he said, "Pleased to meet you, ladies!"

"Thank you, Sam," both girls answered.

"Well, let's get at it, Sam," I said, grabbing a bushel from the wagon.

"Mighty neighborly of you!" he remarked.

"That's the way we are around here, Sam," I answered.

Rev. Ward appeared to shake my hand and introduce me to his wife, Emily (34), and their two young daughters, Mary (7) and Emily (2). They all seemed like nice people. Mrs. Ward said she looked forward to meeting Ma. When I told them where I just had been, Rev. Ward expressed remorse for the loss of Miss Bradbury. He said, "There's ebbs and flows in life, Edward—the Lord giveth, and the Lord taketh away!"

After we finished unloading everyone thanked me again, once more I shook hands with father and son. Walking home from my new neighbors' house, I thought of what Rev. Ward had said, and it felt like the void left by Miss Bradbury began to fill from the Ward's moving in. He was right about life's ebbs and flows, and staying busy when you're feeling down.

It felt like the bottom fell out of the city when President Filmore signed the Fugitive Slave Bill into law. Pa became livid. Like many, he felt uncertain about what to do, but equally determined not to accept it. Rev. Loguen said it was a time for action against the worst law ever made in the United States. A *Meeting of Colored Citizens* was called for two days later, with Black George anxious to attend.

"*Dis here law be makin' it easy for people to get snatched away; we's got to protect ourselves! 'De gov-ment sho' ain't!*" he said with conviction.

Ma agreed, standing in our kitchen by the stove, "It's awful, George, forcing people to help slave owners or be fined $1,000 and jailed for six months!"

"Yes, ma'am, an 'da colored man got no rights to object! There be lots of folks headin' to Canada now, I suspect."

On Friday night, our family saw Black George off to the meeting at the Fayette St. Church. Pa said that he wanted to hear about all the resolutions that they make. George looked determined, nodded his head, and closed the door behind him.

Cornelia, Ellen, and I waited up with our parents for his return, eager to hear what transpired. I'd never seen him so upset as he was after the *Meeting of Colored Citizens*. With all eyes on him, the spotlight only fueled his angst. Ma showed empathy.

"George, we've all been thinking of you and were worried! Are you all right?" she asked.

"Yes, Missus, Ise' all right, but 'dis here slave law sho' ain't!"

"Can you tell us what happened at the meeting, George?" Ma asked.

"And the resolutions!" Pa chimed in while me and the girls offered encouragement.

"Well, suh, we resolved 'dat we ain't done resolvin'. There be another meetin 'dis Wednesday to finish things." George replied. "But I can tell you 'dat we be determined not to let slave catchers steal black folks away!" George avowed with feeling.

Pa replied, "We're determined, too, George—you're not alone! What were folks saying?"

"We thinks the United States gov-ment affords us no protection, and we gots to do it ourselves, even if it means takin' a life."

We were all stunned, and Ma said, "George, that's extreme, isn't it?"

"Why so, Ma'am? 'Dey 'wants to take things even more precious than life from us—'dat be liberty an' pursuit of happiness. 'We's ready to take scalps from gov-ment hounds who dare follow our tracks!"

"But George, are you really that afraid? You're not an escaped fugitive," Pa said.

"No, suh, but I sho' looks like one. 'Dem slavers holds me in contempt fo' my color, an 'dey be comin' 'roun soon fo' 'dey prop-ity! Rev. Loguen a brave man, but I be lookin' over my shoulder if I was him."

"Rev. Ward, too, and he just moved in," I affirmed.

"True for you, Edward," Black George replied.

Ma wanted to know what my father had planned. "Charles, what are all the men saying? Surely there'll be a meeting!" she implored.

Pa answered, "Yes, there will, but I'm not sure when. It'll be soon, though, we're not taking this lying down!"

"We not either," George declared. "And to show respect fo' 'da slave catchin' bill, we's resolved to start wearin' daggers in our belts!"

With Rev. Loguen residing just down the street, the underground railroad rolled right past my front door. I couldn't help noticing the traffic increase since the hated law was signed, and my short leash provided opportunity for close observation. More canal drownings brought the accustomed restrictions on travel. It began with a four-year-old found in the Oswego Canal, then it was poor Billy Pratt, the judge's son, only eleven, who drowned in the Erie Canal by Camillus. The Pratt's lived at Fayette Park, where the heart breaking news unnerved the entire neighborhood. So far, the month had been a shocker for tragedies—first Miss Bradbury and now this.

Lucky for me, the Ward's lived within my allowed range of travel. I found Sam Jr. at home with his mother and sisters, something I knew well. The Ward's lived even closer than the Loguen's. I recalled Ma saying they were moving to the *foot of the garden*, and she wasn't kidding; our backyards touched at the corner. Rev. Ward was out, but the rest were happy to see me, and I, them.

"Hey, Sam!" I said with enthusiasm, "Hello, Mrs. Ward—hey girls!"

"Good morning, Edward," Mrs. Ward replied, "My, you're cheerful this morning!"

"Yes, ma'am, it's good to know your neighbors. Especially when you can't go far from home."

"Were you fussin' with your sisters?" she asked.

"Well, I do that pretty regular, Ma'am, but this time it's more about the drownings. My friends, the Cheney's, are on a short lead, too."

"*Oh, really?*" Mrs. Ward replied, casting an accusatory glance at Sam Jr., who looked at me like I was Judas. I lingered for a while, trying hard not to say anything else incriminating.

After attending the 2nd *Meeting of Colored Citizens* on Wednesday night, Black George returned feeling animated, but not so much as the first time. The resolutions made at the 1st meeting were confirmed, with an important, new resolution made. This one affected the Loguen's hub on the railroad.

"We's against people takin' flight!" Black George said emphatically.

"Why, George?" I asked. "Isn't that the safe thing to do?"

"Fo' three reasons," George began, "First, because we's committed no crime. The second bein' that resistance to tyrants is obedience to God. And third, because liberty that ain't worth defendin' here ain't worth enjoyin' someplace else!"

Pa said the *Great Compromise* was better calculated to inflame the people than to pacify them, and we didn't need a federal agency for slave catching. Fugitives on the run weren't the only ones in the crosshairs.

Pa's business thrived, affording us opportunity for home improvements. Anxious for a change, Ma requested Cornelia and I to accompany her to Ashley & Williston's furniture store on Salina Street. It was unusual for our mother to walk downtown with us, we made the trek almost every day without her. We soon entered the shop where

Charles Ferré Williston stood talking with the black guy, Jerry, whose shock of red hair made him easy to recognize.

Williston moved to Syracuse at seventeen and learned the cabinetmaker's trade. He later partnered with his uncle, Theodore Ashley, soon becoming a leading furniture and undertaking firm in Syracuse. Like Ma, Williston celebrated his 34th birthday in 1850.

Leaving Ma and Cornelia to examine the showroom, I ventured toward the owner, mostly wishing to say hello to Jerry, who remembered me.

"Hello, Mr. Williston! Hello, Jerry!" I said.

"Hello, Edward," Mr. Williston answered. "Tell your mother that I'll be right with her, determined customers are my favorite kind!"

Jerry replied, "Hello, Edward, how ya doin'?"

"I'm good, Jerry! Did you know the Wards found a house over by us and the Loguen's?"

"I heard that," Jerry affirmed. Turning to Mr. Williston, he said, "Well, thanks again, Mr. Williston. You were always good to me."

"No problem, Jerry, stop by anytime!" Williston said cheerily as Jerry departed.

Greeting them both with familiarity, Williston said, "Good morning, Ellen and Cornelia! What can I do for you today?"

"Good day to you, Charles," Ma answered. *"My* Charles said that I should see you directly for a new table and chairs, and anything else of particular beauty."

"Charles said that? Next you'll say he's been drinking with Philo Rust, ha ha!"

"He did just that, Charles! And this set would go nicely in our dining room," Ma replied, admiring the oak table before her.

"Yes, it would," Williston agreed. "Say, Ellen, did you know the man that I was just talking to?"

"No, Charles, but I've seen him."

"He used to work for me, and may have made the chair that you're looking at."

"Well, he does fine work!" Ma said, taking a seat in the said chair.

"His name's William Henry, but everyone calls him Jerry. He once told me that he was the confidential servant of a Missouri senator, born on his master's plantation and carefully educated to become the right-hand man of the estate. I must have had 45 workmen when I hired him, but by week's end a committee told me that *the nigger had to go—it was him or them!* I started asking questions, only to find that Jerry's problem came from being the wrong color. I told the committee that anyone unhappy with the arrangements should come in on Monday to settle accounts, and I would try to run my own business with the *nigger's* help."

"So, what happened next, Mr. Williston?" I asked.

"What happened was that nobody left, and in a short while, Jerry became a favorite. He's well-read, and he knows history, geography, and the slave code legislation. He stayed on for about a year and left for higher wages as a cooper. There's never enough barrels in Syracuse!"

"That's amazing, Mr. Williston," I said. "Jerry's like Rev. Loguen and Rev. Ward, being so smart and a runaway, too."

"Hmm, I think you're right! Well, Edward, I'm told that you're becoming a newspaper man. Did you hear what happened? You won't believe it."

"Not sure what you're talking about Mr. Williston."

"Well, hear this, Philo Rust was arrested—right inside his hotel!"

# Chapter Four
## (September – October 1850)

Mr. Williston's account rang true, police arrested Philo Rust for assault and battery upon Rosanna Kelly, a woman whose fiery temper worsened with alcohol. Officer Ormsby escorted Philo peacefully across Clinton Square from Rust's Hotel to the Police Office where Justice House took $100 bail for his appearance in court. *Mein Host* was back at the bar before the ice melted in his drink, more annoyed than worried. Kelly had accused another man of the same crime a few months ago, whom the judge acquitted. Besides, Rust's Hotel was full with delegates for the State Convention of the Whig Party.

After Ma lifted travel restrictions, I wanted to get as far away as I could, post haste. I asked Sam Ward if he'd like to meet the Willard brothers, friends and classmates of mine from Weld's School. Their father, Mr. William W. Willard, was a partner in the successful Willard & Hawley's Jewelers & Fine Silverware Manufacturing located adjacent to the Syracuse House.

"I sure do, Edward, thanks for asking!" Sam answered.

Mrs. Ward overheard, saying "That's thoughtful of you, Edward, introducing Sam that way."

"That's okay, Ma'am, there's a lots of other guys for Sam to meet around here," I replied, knowing I hadn't given it any thought at all. Sam was the new kid and that's just what you did. Pa taught me that.

Walking north on Chestnut Street we were about to make a left turn on Washington when we saw Rev. Loguen at the AME Zion

Church a block ahead. He signaled for us to come over, giving himself a break from building repairs.

"Looks like double trouble to me!" he said good naturedly. "Where you boys off to?"

"Just down to the Willard's, sir. Sam's meeting my friends," I answered.

"That's good, everyone needs a friend!" the Rev. said.

"Yes, sir!" Sam agreed. "Do you need any help?"

"No, Sam, it's a one man job—now don't be getting shy about meeting new folks," Loguen encouraged. Continuing on to the Willard's, as a train approached us on Washington (Railroad) Street I told Sam about the fun that the brothers had rearranging the china cabinet to make it rattle when a train went by, and how Mrs. Willard stalked them afterward. He laughed and said, "That's funny! You know, I liked Cortland, but so far Syracuse been good, too."

Finding the Willard brothers (aged 14 to 8) at home, they were surprised to see me arrive unannounced with a colored boy, but they welcomed Sam without hesitation. Like me, the Willard's didn't care that my neighbor was black. Mrs. Willard joined us, and asked, "Aren't you going to introduce us, Edward?"

"Oh, yes, Ma'am!" I responded, presenting Sam to the family, including the expected moment of confusion from introducing Florello Willard.

"Sam, this is Mrs. Willard," I began.

"Hello, Ma'am!" Sam rejoined.

"And this is Charlie."

"Hey, Charlie."

"And this one's Billy."

"Pleased to meet ya."

"Sam, this is Florello."

*"Huh?"*

"Oh, just call 'im Flo."

"Yo, Flo!"

A squeaky voice demanded, "What about me?"

"Oh, sorry—this one's Eddie.

"Hey, Eddie," Sam offered.

"Now what?" Charlie wanted to know.

*"Let's git!"* Billy said, and we all jumped at the suggestion.

"I know, let's go by Welch's to check on the Cook brothers, then we can see what's happening at the Square!" Charlie announced with authority, being the oldest amongst us—only by a year, though.

"Hey, Ed," Charlie said as we walked, "Did you know that Jenny Lind drew nine thousand people to her last show in New York? I hope she comes to Syracuse some day!"

Knowing Charlie's infatuation with the singer he'd never heard, I went easy on him. "I'm not surprised, Charlie—but I heard that Barnum said she's only playing the big cities."

"I heard that too, Ed. She's in Boston now where a large crowd waited in the pouring rain to greet her," Charlie answered.

Billy Willard joined in, "Well, they just finished counting heads in the city and we're over 22,000 now. You figure that's enough for Jenny Lind?"

"Maybe next year," I replied. "Barnum has to make his money first."

*"Fuck Barnum!"* Charlie bellowed.

"Hey, Sam—you havin' fun?" I asked, "You hear language like that down by the canal."

"Down Cortland way, too, Ed," Sam replied.

I called, "Hey, Charlie, can you say that in French?"

With a terrible accent he answered, *"Sacré bleu and fuck you, too!"*

Turning to Sam, I said, "He's normally not so excitable."

"Best watch your lips, Charlie," Billy advised. "Pa said he'd wash out your mouth with silver polish from the store!"

"Or he'll have his apprentice Charles Shaver do it for him," Flo added.

Little Eddie quipped, "Yeah, right after he puts on the white gloves."

"I have something for all of you!" Charlie responded while grabbing his crotch.

"I don't know," Billy started, "Looks like Charlie wants to be alone with himself again with a picture of Jenny Lind!"

It took all of us to separate the brothers, but the pair reconciled quickly after another one of their famous brawls. Sam must've wondered what he was getting himself into. The rest of the day passed without incident.

During a break at school, the Willard brothers recounted their meeting Sam Ward when Mr. Weld joined in. He sometimes did, without pretense of eavesdropping—he saw and heard everything.

A middle-aged family man and deacon of the Congregational Church, forty-year-old Stowell L. Weld followed a traditional approach, understanding that results outweigh intentions. Still, he kept his mind open to new ideas, unafraid to try them. This school year would test his courage like no other from including newspapers in the curriculum.

When he first shared his scheme the room fell silent, followed by a burst of surprise as everyone began talking at once. "Newspapers? What's he talking about, newspapers?"

"Does this mean we get to read the newspaper in school?"

"Which newspaper's he talking about? There's a bunch of 'em."

"We use newspapers to clean fish—catches the blood and guts real good!"

"Ha! My pa does that, too. And he likes saving newspapers in the outhouse. Says they're good for readin' and wipin' when 'yer sittin'.'"

Stowell Weld had hoped for this kind of reaction, allowing a moment of uproar and commotion. Though a believer in *spare the rod and spoil the child*, it was rare for him to apply it. He thought that less confident teachers used the method of last resort too quickly. Being called a gentleman, by a gentleman, gave us something to aspire to, or at least it did the real gentlemen. Intent on giving his newspaper class experiment the best chance of success, Mr. Weld recruited local reporter William L. Crandal to pique our interest.

"I'm glad you're welcoming Sam to our community, gentlemen," Mr. Weld began, "His father's a force for good against the tyranny of slavery! Does anyone know where Sam's going to school?"

"He's schooling at AME Zion, Mr. Weld," I replied.

"Ah, that's right! He'll do fine under Rev. Loguen!" our teacher stated.

"His pa's giving a lecture on slavery at the Congregational Church," Charlie Willard said. "Lots of people think Samuel R. Ward's one of the best speakers in the country."

Charlie Pope interjected, "I heard a fugitive from Macon, Georgia, was passing through the other day. He said his master gave him three days for Christmas and it's been Christmas for him ever since!"

"I like that!" Mr. Weld replied. Speaking to us all he asked, "Is there anything else of importance before we begin our next lesson?"

Alex McKinstry Jr., son of the renowned tallow chandler, answered, "Yes, sir, County Judge James R. Lawrence will be resigning to become the next United States District Attorney."

"That's interesting, Alex. If there's ever a fugitive slave rendition around here, he'll be the first person the slavers come looking for," Weld advised.

"I didn't know that, sir," Alex replied.

"Most people don't, Alex—you're not alone."

"There's something else, Mr. Weld," I shouted. "There's going to be a city-wide meeting about the *Fugitive Slave Law*. My pa said everyone's invited and it'll be announced in all the city papers."

Mr. Weld asked, "Is there a date for the meeting yet, Edward?"

"Friday, the 4th, Mr. Weld," I replied.

"That's right after the County Fair, Ed," Will Stoddard declared.

Charlie Pope said, "The Fair starts tomorrow and this year it's on the grounds of the new County Penitentiary. I think they picked that spot for the view, Mr. Weld."

"And General Wool arrives on today's train!" Prentice called out.

"That's right, Prentice," Will agreed. "He's staying at Rust's Hotel."

"Of course he is," Billy confirmed.

Alex McKinstry asked, "Mr. Weld, sir, shouldn't we meet the general's train? It's history, right? General Wool was a hero of the Mexican War with General Taylor!"

"I believe you're right, Alex," Mr. Weld replied, followed by a surprise early dismissal. Everybody liked Mr. Weld, but today we all loved him.

Parish Johnson kicked up his heels on Montgomery Street in the sunshine of freedom. "Hey guys," he said, "there's time before the train gets here—let's see what's doing at the 'Square!'" A bunch of us joined him.

Our arrival at Clinton Square coincided with a runaway span of horses flying down Salina St. pulling an empty lumber wagon. It was clear sailing until the wheels hit the Liberty Pole, ending the wild run much to a fruit peddler's misfortune—once filled boxes and barrels were strewn about from the collision.

"Hey, that's Grasshopper by the Liberty Pole with the canal loafers, and he looks pretty shook up!" Alex cried.

"I hope he's not hurt," Grove Johnson yelped, "Let's go see!"

The well-known, one-armed peddler called Grasshopper lost his forelimb during a 4th of July celebration sometime around 1836 when the gunner failed to properly thumb the piece, causing the cannon to discharge prematurely. Another gunner took a direct hit to the chest and face and died two days later while Grasshopper lost an arm. Although he was most recognized for selling apples, Grasshopper became an opportunist, learning from his mentor, Captain Samuel Larned, about readiness and timing.

Samuel Larned made his fortune (while earning the title of Captain) on the Erie Canal, selling supplies to boatmen from his light craft with the canal boats not having to stop. He began his career in supply during the war of 1812 as a sutler, following the army and selling provisions. Now, instead of the army, he followed canal boats, applying what he learned during the war. He soon opened a floating store that rivaled local grocers and amassed a fortune in the process. Then Larned began buying property.

Meanwhile, the canal loafer fraternity would congregate on the bridges. Intemperate men not seeking employment who issued resolutions repeatedly broken, free to follow their aimless pursuits. Though visibly shaken, Grasshopper narrowly averted disaster.

"That's the second time this year I almost got killed!" he railed, "I've a mind to see Justice House—there oughta be a law against gettin' runned over."

Canal Loafers took up the cry, one yelled, "Yeah, I'll go with ya! Been meaning to lodge a complaint about the vagrancy laws—just got out from another 30-day stretch."

General John E. Wool arrived on the express train, greeted by Syracuse's first mayor, Harvey Baldwin, and current mayor, Alfred Hovey. The entire community was pleased that Gen. Wool accepted an invitation to attend the Onondaga County Agricultural Fair. To the sound of Kellogg's Brass Band, the smartly uniformed Syracuse Citizens Corps, led by Captain Minard, escorted General Wool to Rust's Hotel. We followed in awe, seizing the opportunity to stand up-close to a real war hero. I took my chances following him inside the hotel, hoping that the general's stay might change my parent's opinion of Philo Rust.

*Gen. John E. Wool*

The fair opened with gloomy skies as the rain put a damper on outdoor fun. By late morning it cleared, and General Wool received a military escort from Rust's Hotel to City Hall by the Syracuse Citizens Corps, accompanied by the Mayor, Common Council, and Kellogg's band. During the short march, the Washington Riflemen, one of our German militias, fired a 13-gun salute.

After speeches of admiration for the famous man and his humble response, it was strange that General Wool was next driven to the

Penitentiary grounds, this year's venue for the County Fair. Among the hundreds of agricultural and mechanical exhibits on display, the most observed item was General Wool. Everyone wanted to get as close to him as they could—he was far more interesting than whoever grew the largest vegetable or the fattest hog. All things considered, the view atop the hill along with the man of the hour, made for a memorable County Fair. I enjoyed it much more than last year when I didn't get to go. Who'd have thought that the penitentiary was a great place for a community celebration?

The general departed on Friday with a proper send-off, leaving everyone focused on tonight's meeting about the *Fugitive Slave Law*. Pa was more invested in that than in seeing the general or attending the County Fair. Black George planned to attend, and after a struggle, I gained permission to join him. My mother was dead set against my going.

"But Ma, this is a historic meeting—and Mr. Weld encourages us to keep up with history. I could even write about it in my newspaper at school, Ma."

Surprisingly, my older sister, Cornelia, came to my aide, saying,

"Oh, let 'im go, Ma! Then we won't have to listen to him whine while we're waiting for Pa to come home."

Ellen and Lucia nodded in agreement, tipping the scales in my favor.

With a warning tone, Ma said, "All right, Edward, you can go but make sure that you stay with George, and come back directly!"

"Okay Ma," I quickly agreed, adding, "And this way you'll get the results sooner. You know Pa's always the last one to leave after a meeting."

"Take lots of notes, Edward," Cornelia said with a smile.

When Black George frowned I realized that no one had asked him if he wanted company tonight.

"You don't mind me tagging along, do ya, George?" I asked timidly.

"Well, I s'pose not, but next time you ask a man first!" he remonstrated.

"Sorry, George, I will. Don't you think we should leave now? Pa's already there and he said the hall will fill-up early," I pleaded.

"All right, let's get a move on," Black George replied. Exiting our house he said, "Now don't be wanderin' off when we gets to the hall—I ain't 'bout to answer to yo mamma' fo' comin' home without you!"

Pa was right, we were lucky to find seats in the jam-packed City Hall. He looked surprised to see me there with Black George, but waved to us both. It looked like he was having multiple conversations at the same time. The atmosphere was charged, no mistake. When the proceedings began, Mayor Hovey was chosen as President, with my Uncle Horace selected as one of the eight Vice Presidents.

Pa stood and motioned for a committee to be appointed to prepare business for the meeting, and naturally, he was included along with four others. As the five of them moved off to the side to speak privately, the audience called for Rev. Ward, who stirred the audience with a brief address. Rev. Loguen was called next, and after he made several remarks, both men were loudly applauded. Black George said, *"They done me proud!"*

Then the cry went out for the mayor to speak. His Honor, Mr. Alfred H. Hovey, said that as a law-abiding citizen he should obey the laws, and *hoped* he could, but concluded, *"I am with you heart and soul in this movement!"*

When the business committee returned, Charles B. Sedgwick read a series of stinging resolutions condemning the barbarity of the new law. He described it as a daring assault upon American liberties, and the Constitution, asserting that it was our duty to resist it. He encouraged all citizens to read the law completely to grasp its diabolical spirit and cruel ingenuity. Sedgwick criticized the Congressmen who shirked their responsibilities by not voting, placing most of the blame on Senator Daniel Webster. The most notable resolution was the establishment of a *Vigilance Committee* to ensure that no one was deprived of liberty without due process of law, and he encouraged everyone to aid and sustain them in their efforts.

Pa spoke next, reading an *Address to the Citizens of the State of New York*, urging people to awaken to the degradation caused by the *Fugitive Slave Law*. He said our state is turning into a hunting ground for dealers in human flesh, and we're coerced to help them through heavy fines and imprisonment for refusal. He emphasized that the new law eradicates the right to a trial by jury, and criticized President Filmore for not vetoing it. My father argued that the South has it both ways; slaves are sometimes property, sometimes persons—whichever best suits the slave owners, politicians, and the situation. I thought of Ma when he read, *"We believe this law ought not to bind us to do its bidding, because it violates the law of nature and the law of God. We believe it is also a violation of the Federal Constitution, and that the slaveholding influence has been so controlling in the present Congress as to bring upon us this affliction!"*

Charles Sedwick then read the entire law, highlighting its many problems. Like Pa, he asserted that *good citizens* were under no obligation to uphold it. The audience then called for Rev. Raymond, who delivered a brief yet powerful speech. He declared that as a man of God it was his duty to oppose this most unrighteous law. He drew laughter when he remarked that he was a small man, and Mr. Loguen a large man, but when he saw Loguen in the street he looked up at him and said that he'd protect him. He concluded by stating that his house was open to anyone fleeing oppression, and that all who could fit inside were welcome, to be removed only over his dead body.

Rev. May followed, declaring that his house, too, was an open refuge for fugitives. He warned that if anyone believed non-resistance meant standing still, and quietly observing, then they should come to him and learn better. The audience called for Rev. Ward again, but he declined to make a speech, stating that Rev. Raymond had already covered the entire ground. However, he added that if anyone attempted to take him into slavery, it would be well for him to first perform two acts for the benefit of himself and his own family—*He should first make his will, and then make his peace with his Maker.*

Ward's remark resonated with Black George, who cried aloud, "Damn right!"

Once again, Rev. Loguen was called upon. He shared that he'd spent over twenty years of his life in slavery, and vowed never to be taken back there alive. He mentioned that he had lived in this city for several years, and endeavored to maintain the character of a good citizen, an honest man, and a Christian. He alluded to his family, and said it was his duty to protect them, even at the expense of his life. Then he said to the assembly, *"The strength of this city is here to express their sense of this fugitive act, and to proclaim to the despots at Washington whether it shall be enforced here—whether you will permit the government to return me and other fugitives who have sought an asylum among you, to the Hell of slavery. The question is with you. If you will give us up, say so, and we will shake the dust from our feet and leave you. But we believe better things."*

Rev. Loguen went on to say, *"I don't respect this law—I don't fear it—I won't obey it! It outlaws me, and I outlaw it, and the men who attempt to enforce it on me. I place the governmental officials on the ground that they place me. I will not live a slave, and if force is employed to re-enslave me, I shall make preparations to meet the crisis as becomes a man."*

The meeting concluded with the adoption of resolutions and the *Address to the Citizens of the State of New York*. Most importantly, thirteen citizens were appointed to the Vigilance Committee, including the Reverends Loguen and Raymond, and of course, Charles A. Wheaton. The last order of business was to announce a second meeting, one week from tonight—same time, same place.

Recalling Black George's edict from earlier tonight, I leaned over and asked, "Hey, George, whatcha doin' next Friday?"

My mother and sisters waited up for us, anxious to hear our accounts of the rally. I could see what drove Mr. Crandal towards becoming a newspaper man. Black George and I took turns recounting the best parts, Ma shook her head when she heard about Pa being on another committee.

"And I'd like to go to the meeting next week, too, Ma," I entreated. "I already asked Black George and he said okay!"

"I still need to hear what your father says first, but I imagine you'll be going," Ma answered.

Uneasiness followed the Anti-Fugitive Slave Law Meeting on Friday night. It was *the* topic of discussion around family tables, inside the shops, and on the street corners. Abhorrence of the hated law fueled passions, yet many feared where open defiance would lead—change it certainly, but until then the law is the law. I didn't like it, thinking of Rev. Loguen and Rev. Ward being hunted, especially with rumors of slavers asking about Rev. Loguen in Troy, where he once lived. The hounds could be in Syracuse, now, for all we knew. Charles Sedgwick said that very soon we'll have new state laws to prosecute slavers for kidnapping.

Following the big meeting in Syracuse, the people up north in Oswego held their own gathering to condemn the *Fugitive Slave Law*, achieving similar results. The sentiment was echoed in many other communities across New York State and beyond. The new law riled the spirit of Northerners more than an army of fervent abolitionists ever could. Anticipation began to build for next meeting at City Hall, making time slacken to a crawl.

Black George and I couldn't wait to attend the next *Fugitive Slave Law* meeting on the 11th. Like before, Pa left home well ahead of us.

"Don't worry, Ma!" I reassured her, "We'll be back with the news!"

"You better!" she replied. "And thank you, George, for putting up with Edward."

Tipping his hat, Black George opened our front door and I eagerly followed.

"I can't wait, George!" I said when we reached the corner.

"Me either," he agreed, as we hurried downtown.

City Hall was packed to capacity with hundreds turned away, and everyone anxious for the meeting to start. We ran into Jerry Henry, and exchanged pleasantries. We'd seen him here last week, too. I remembered Mr. Williston telling me that Jerry stayed current on the slave laws.

Rev. May began the proceeding by reciting the resolutions in their entirety, interspersed with applause from the energetic audience. It became clear that slave catchers would struggle in Syracuse. Mr. W.H. Burleigh and Judge Nye of Madison spoke briefly, then Pa stood to read a letter from Senator Seward, expressing his regrets for not being able to attend. Still on-stage, Pa next sang a long solo that somebody wrote for Frederick Douglass while me and Black George exchanged glances.

"I can't wait to tell Ma and the girls!" I said.

"Yo' daddy sho' do love to sing," Black George chuckled.

After Pa sang, Mr. Charles Sedgwick and Rev. Raymond spoke, followed by Rev. Loguen, who said he'd tasted the sweets of slavery and had no desire to taste them again. If the laws of his country would not protect him, he must rely on the law of Loguen.

*"Amen, brother, an 'de law of Johnson, too!"* Black George cried.

After a few more speakers and another resolution or two, Pa made the final motion of the night, which carried, for the military and police to join them. Before Mayor Hovey adjourned the assembly, the Vigilance Committee was authorized to gather the people as best they saw fit.

The audience must've liked Pa's singing, for the next day he was re-elected President of the Syracuse Musical Institute, with Rev. Raymond as Vice Conductor. We joked that they'd be singing abolition songs at the Institute before long. Meanwhile at Clinton Square, Patrick Behan was arrested for assault and battery upon James Riley for laughing at him when he fell in the canal.

Sad news arrived on the train from Albany. Our favorite Anakim, Andy Brand, the Kentucky Fat Boy, had succumbed. I heard about it from Austin Cook in school. His brother Abel took it badly.

"Yeah, Ed," Austin began, "Heard it from a guy who just got off the train from Albany. Poor Andy—he seemed like a nice fella."

"Did the man say what he died of?" I asked.

"No, but he'd read that Andy had been ill for a few weeks," Austin replied.

"Maybe Andy got dunked in the canal after all," Abel Cook suggested. "The water's real nasty and he might 'a caught somethin'."

Austin said, "Sometimes our pa says he'll dunk us in the canal when we're acting up, but not to get us sick—just for a slight drowning is all."

"Right! He needs us to work," Abel confirmed.

Ten days after the second *Fugitive Slave Law* meeting, I heard a story of treachery and horror that chilled me to the bone. I had gone looking for Sam, and found the entire family at home along with Rev. Loguen. Right away I could tell that something was wrong. The two preachers, both large, strong men, showed signs of agitation.

"Jermain, was it really as bad as that?" Rev. Ward asked.

"I'm afraid so, Sam," Loguen answered. It was always strange to overhear either man called by their given names, being accustomed to only hearing them addressed as Reverend and Mister. Mrs. Ward listened with concern, and I whispered to Sam Jr., trying not to disturb the men talking.

"Hey Sam, what's going on?" I asked.

"There was an outrage on the canal, Ed. A colored family was terrorized for trying to escape to Canada!"

"Hush now, you boys," Mrs. Ward commanded. "I'm trying to listen!"

"Tell me again, Jermain—I want to make sure I have this right!" Rev. Ward said.

With a serious look, Rev. Loguen began. "A fugitive slave, William Harris, was trying to take his wife, Catherine, and their three-year-old daughter to Canada after the *Fugitive Slave Law* was signed. In New York City, he bought passage on a canal boat to Rochester, but in Albany his ticket was taken from him and destroyed, forcing him to repurchase their passage. As the boat traveled down the canal, the family was threatened by the crew, who convinced Harris that the sheriff was waiting in Syracuse to arrest them. The husband and wife deliberated their fate, and decided it was better to die than return to slavery. Somewhere near Utica, Harris leaped onto the tow path and slit his own throat, while his despondent wife jumped into the canal with their child in her arms! The mother was pulled from the murky water by the boat crew, but not the little girl. Harris inflicted a serious wound and fainted, but regained his feet and threw himself into the canal right in front of another boat that passed over him for its entire length! The boat captain pulled Harris from the water and carried him to Syracuse where Dr. Hoyt dressed his wounds."

"Lord Almighty!" Rev. Ward said with great feeling. "Does anyone know what became of Mrs. Harris?" he asked.

"Lucky for us, we heard about it right away from Dr. Hoyt, and Rev. Lyles left directly in hopes of finding her! He's a good man, and if anyone can find her, he can!" Rev. Loguen said with confidence of his fellow black clergyman.

The two men stood quietly, clearly moved, as we all were, at the heartless conduct of the human fiends on the canal. Rev. Ward finally noticed my presence, nodding affirmation without saying anything. Unable to remain silent, I said, "I'll tell my pa what happened, sir."

Word spread fast about the outrage, fueled by the sudden return of Rev. Lyles with Mrs. Harris, whom he found aboard the same canal boat near Montezuma, heading west. Police Justice House questioned her, and immediately dispatched Officers Lowell and Kinyon to apprehend the officers and crew.

The next day, I was talking with Parish Johnson at our hardware store when we heard that Lowell and Kinyon had just returned with their prize, including the captain, several of the crew, and a passenger—another fled and got away. Justice House would begin examinations directly, which caused Parish to gaze over at the Police Office. Suddenly, he rushed off to secure a place inside, hollering, "I'll let ya' know what happened, Ed!"

"Okay, Parish, I'll stay here," I said to myself, while Pa laughed and shook his head. Around supper time, Parish reappeared and told Pa what happened, but I was long gone. Later at home, my father recounted Parish's report, saying that so far only Catherine Harris had been examined, but it looked bad for the scoundrels in custody. According to Mrs. Harris, the worst of the lot was a passenger, Jerimiah Cluney. Mrs. H. gave a full account of everything that happened between Albany and Montezuma, the diabolical conduct and threatening language of the perpetrators, the heartbreak of losing her child. Husband and wife were now reunited, William Harris still under the care of Dr. Hoyt.

"Tomorrow we're calling an emergency meeting of the Vigilance Committee," Pa announced with determination.

I rushed to update Sam on the latest developments. Reading the *Fugitive Slave Law* paled in comparison to witnessing its consequences. The law emboldened vile instincts of the worst kind, creating visible fear in runaway slaves and free blacks, especially near the borders with southern States. Canada appeared a better option to many, if only they could make it.

# Chapter Five
## (October – November 1850)

While the Harris tragedy shocked the Syracuse community, reports came from Boston that two slavers were arrested on State charges for conspiracy to kidnap a fugitive slave. I had accompanied Black George to the Loguen's when we heard about it. There were a few others there, including the first black lawyer in New York, George Boyer Vashon, and Jerry, whom I'd seen a few times lately.

"I don't know if the charges will stick, but it's a start!" Rev. Loguen said.

Lawyer Vashon answered, "I can't think of another instance where State and Federal laws conflict like they do over the *Fugitive Slave Law*."

"The new state laws need teeth!" Jerry said with feeling.

Black George replied, "I keeps a club handy to resist 'da kidnappin' law."

"That the club I saw down in the root cellar, George?" I asked.

"Don't you worry none 'bout my club, boy," Black George responded.

"That's right, George," Rev. Loguen said. "If we don't look out for ourselves, nobody will. The good book says to *resist the devil, and he will flee from you.*"

"I'll resist with my last breath!" Jerry asserted.

"Us too," the others vowed.

*George B. Vashon*

Mr. Vashon said, "And one of the richest men in the country is putting his name and fortune behind the abolition movement."

"That's what I keep hearing from brother Ward," Loguen replied. "He's on his way to Gerrit Smith's home in Peterboro now, if he's not there already."

"I'm sure that Smith's watching Cuba," Jerry said. "The island's on alert for another invasion, and thirty, rich Cubans just arrived in Charleston, exiled for supporting Lopez."

Vashon interjected, "The Navy dispatched the steamer, *Saranac*, and Sloop of War, *St. Mary's*, to patrol the Gulf of Mexico around Cuba, under command of Commodore Parker."

"Why's everyone so worried about Cuba, Mr. Vashon?" I asked.

"If Cuba were liberated it could become the next slave state in the Union. Admitting California tipped the scales, so having Cuba join would return the balance."

"But if we liberate Cuba, wouldn't they want to be free?" I posed.

"No, that wouldn't happen," Vashon replied. "There's just over a million people in Cuba, but almost half are slaves. Liberating Cuba from Spain appeals to the rich slave owners in the south—that's why the expeditions are fitted-out almost exclusively by southern men."

"But General Lopez is the leader, right, sir?" I questioned.

"That's right, Edward. Lopez is convinced that Cubans are eager to join him," he answered.

"Then he could run for governor," Jerry added with sarcasm.

During the first week of November, temperatures reached 76 degrees in the shade, a rare occurrence for that time of year in Syracuse. A *Union Meeting* was called in response to the October rallies held in opposition to the *Fugitive Slave Law*, with the aim of guarding against the agitators driving the country toward civil war. Prominent members of Syracuse society attended, choosing renowned lawyer B. Davis Noxon as President, with Moses Burnet, George Comstock,

Miles Bennett, and three others as Vice Presidents. I didn't attend, but heard all about it from Miles Bennett Jr., who sat right up front. From what I gathered, the resolutions made at the *Union Meeting* were far different from the ones we heard at the anti-slave law rally, now already one month ago to the day. This audience opposed open defiance to any law, regardless of the reason. They supported amending the *Fugitive Slave Law*, but believed it must be followed for the sake of the country. Attendees asked, "How could law and order be maintained if people decided which laws to follow, and when?" Folks on the other side agreed, but remained defiant.

With the sun shining on election day, New Yorkers went to the polls to choose our next governor in a race too close to call. I'd guess that most of the people at the *Union Meeting* voted for the Whig, Washington Hunt, while the majority at the *Fugitive Slave Law Meeting* favored the Democrat, Horatio Seymour. We weren't sure when we'd learn the results, but since women couldn't vote, Ma showed more interest in the World's Fair happening in London next year. She also worried about how she'd make it through another Syracuse winter while carrying her 10th child.

"Hey, Ma!" I called across a hectic room of siblings, "I have news for you about the World's Fair!"

"Tell me," she said with interest.

"The Navy's providing the store-ship *Fredonia* to transport exhibits to the Fair!"

"That's wonderful news, son!" she answered. "We'll all be proud of the American displays at the *Crystal Palace*. It's going up quickly, and every nation is invited to the *Great Exhibition!*"

It wasn't a secret that Ma dreamed of the *Crystal Palace*, albeit from the muds of Syracuse. Although we all enjoyed the warm temperatures, it still rained, and by the time you got home you looked like a walking disaster—nothing crystal about it.

"Say, Ma," I began, "Maybe Pa can get invited to a meeting in London during the World's Fair. You could go with him, Ma, and when the men start making speeches you could slip off to the *Crystal Palace* instead!"

"That sounds wonderful, Edward—were you going to watch your brother and sisters for me while I'm gone?" she asked.

"Nah, I figured it best to farm 'em out to the relatives—like when we trade kids sometimes. Then you could bring Cornelia and Ellen with you if you like," I encouraged.

"I bet you'd like that, you and the kitchen maid driving Black George crazy," she teased.

"As your first-born son, I'm ready to prove myself, Ma—should I ask Pa for ya?" I asked, returning her jibe.

"Go ahead!" she shot back, "and remember to say *please*."

Early results from around the State showed the candidates for governor running neck to neck as the Syracuse Common Council stayed busy, creating an ordinance that forbade the drying of wool, sheep, or lamb skins on city streets, under $5 penalty. At school, Austin Cook read us the article he wrote about the new ordinance, creating the *Bleating Hearts Club* for transgressors. Mr. Weld let us all have a good laugh before launching an open discussion.

"Okay, who'd like to get us started?" our teacher asked.

"I will!" Parish Johnson exclaimed. "Officer Lowell got attacked by two women and a man!"

"What happened, Parish?" Weld asked.

"Lowell caught Mary McGurk shoplifting at the Bastable Block and tried to arrest her, but she resisted. Then her friends, Liz McCormick and Denny Kahill, ganged up on him. There was a huge fight, but Lowell managed to land two of 'em in the watch house."

"Can I go next, Mr. Weld?" Prentice asked.

"You may, Prentice," Weld replied. "I hope it's not another tragedy."

"I'm sorry sir, but it is. The steamer *Telegraph* blew her boiler in Delaware and about twenty-four people were killed or scalded, and a bunch of folks were blown overboard!"

Weld replied, "And I'm sorry, too, Prentice. First for those suffering, and second because this will keep happening until someone finds a way to make steam power safe."

"Mr. Weld, I have something!" I beseeched.

"Proceed, Edward," he replied.

"Well, sir, after hearing about the Harris case, I've been reading how the slave catchers are using the new law. There was one in Chicago who arrested a woman and started to carry her south, but a group rallied to rescue her about three miles from there."

"I'm glad it ended well for the poor woman—she must have been terrified," Mr. Weld said. "Is there anything else, Edward?" he asked.

"Yes, sir," I replied, "I heard that Miss Talbot will preach at Rev. Loguen's church on Sunday. That's pretty unusual, isn't it? I didn't think women were allowed."

"That is unusual, Edward, but not unheard of. And yes, in some churches women are strictly forbidden from preaching." Turning to the class, he asked, "Anyone else?"

"Me, sir," Charlie Pope offered. "There's trouble on the plains, Mr. Weld! The Omaha Indians set fire to the dry grass on the prairie and the winds spread the flames for miles around. Crops, fences, and buildings went up in a sheet of fire. They say the Omaha's are dangerous to backwoods farmers and folks heading west. I think that's why some people would rather take the boat to California, Mr. Weld."

"It's a lot faster going by water, Charlie, and better chances of getting there alive," the grocer's son, Larry Sabine, advised. "Disease and accidents kill way more settlers than American Indians do."

"Someday there'll be a railroad that goes all the way across the country, and we won't have to worry about it," Charlie countered.

Alex McKinstry posed, "Speaking of the American Indians, sir, it's the middle of November and it's still Indian Summer. Isn't that something historical?"

"Yes, it certainly is, Alex," Weld agreed.

"Well, sir, since it's *history*, I thought that maybe we should be outside enjoying it, and I hoped you'd grant an early dismissal!"

> THE WEATHER.—The delightful Indian Summer of the present year, is the theme of universal remark. It has now continued for a month, and we never remember it in greater perfection. November in England, is proverbial for its gloom and its suicides. Here, in the year 1850, at least, it has been thus far, as delightful a May.

On the last warm day of November everyone loved nature, history, Mr. Weld, and the American Indians.

The day after Indian Summer it began snowing and it didn't stop for days. Syracuse weather can change in a hurry, usually for the worst. Still, the snow looked better on the ground than the slushy mud that it covered. Until the ground froze, early snowmen resembled

> The Weather.
> The weather for a day or two past has been very disagreeable, and considerable snow fell in our streets on Sunday morning. It had no other effect than to make the mud a few inches deeper.

Chinese panda bears. I once saw a picture of one at the Stoddard bookstore with a round, white body and black arms and legs.

The first snow brought sentimental longings, but intensified our disappointment that Governor Fish declared December 12th as Thanksgiving Day this year. We all thought that was too close to Christmas, and we'd miss a holiday in November—better to spread them around a little more. When different states celebrated Thanksgiving on the same day it was purely accidental, though all occurred on a Thursday. If you lived close to a neighboring State, you could celebrate Thanksgiving twice by making a short drive across the border.

The first Sunday with snow, Grandfather Birdseye surprised us with an impromptu visit after church, accompanied by Grandma and cousins, Julia and Eunice. I asked Grandpa if he'd heard about the Harris case and he said that he had, and that it appalled him. I enjoyed hearing him talk, especially about how things were while he was growing up. All my friends thought I was weird.

My grandfather, Victory Birdseye, was born in Cornwall, Connecticut, in 1782. His father, Ebenezer, owned slaves, including a male named Obed who was about the same age as Victory. In 1794, Grandpa left for schooling in New York, followed by college, while at the same time Obed worked the Birdseye estate whenever not rented out to neighboring farms. Back then, by Connecticut law, slaves born after 1784 were freed upon reaching age twenty-five. Obed was born before then, meaning a life of servitude. While under no legal obligation to free him, Ebenezer did so in 1805. Obed (Hebrew for slave) changed his name to Obadiah (slave of God) Freeman, signing a one-year contract to work the Birdseye farm for wages. Growing up with a slave his own age left its mark on Grandpa, and all the Birdseye's, or Wheaton's, for that matter. He knew Obed as a person, just like anyone else. Still, many around the world, as close as next door, thought differently.

Victory Birdseye served in Congress twice; first from 1815 to 1817, and again from 1841 to 1843. Politically, he was a Whig and staunch supporter of Kentucky Senator Henry Clay, who was Speaker of the House during grandfather's first term in Congress. So much so that in 1826, he named his newborn son, Henry Clay Birdseye, despite Clay owning slaves. Tragically, my Uncle Henry died at twenty-one from typhoid fever in 1847, and this only one year after his older brother Ebeneezer died from smallpox at twenty-seven. I was only nine or ten when my uncles passed, Ma missed her younger brothers terribly. While not in Congress, Grandpa was the local postmaster, a practicing attorney, and held various other elected offices.

*Victory Birdseye*

The change in weather signaled the end of recounting votes for governor. Washington Hunt won narrowly by around 250 votes, carrying Syracuse by a single ballot! Whigs had little to celebrate otherwise. By a great margin, voters chose to keep the Free School Law, much to the joy of Mr. W.L. Crandal. Of more significance to our household, Ma replaced the kitchen maid. She and Black George were pleased with the change, so Pa was happy.

Around this time, the famed British abolitionist, George Thompson, came to speak at Faneuil Hall in Boston but his vocal detractors had none of it. Pa told us about it at dinner one night, saying it was much like what happened in New York City when Capt. Rynders, Doctor Grant, and their followers seized control of the Anti-Slavery meeting.

"William Lloyd Garrison, Wendel Phillips, George Thompson, Abby Kelley, and Frederick Douglass were all drowned out with cheers for Daniel Webster, the Union, and Jenny Lind!" Pa said with remorse. Ma wondered what happened to the police, allowing the riffraff to take over.

Thunderous cheering for Jenny Lind didn't surprise Charlie Willard. He kept us all informed of her movements and many triumphs. Of late, she was back in New York City performing at the Asylum for the Blind, followed by a performance attended by Daniel Webster, whom the audience cheered.

On a late November school day, Charlie came in grinning from ear to ear, unable to contain himself.

"Mr. Weld! Have you heard? *Jenny Lind's coming to Syracuse next spring!*"

We were all skeptical, but Charlie's face said otherwise.

"Is that for certain, Charles, or just wishful thinking?" Weld asked.

"*Oh yes, sir, it's true!* P.T. Barnum gave authorization to say that she's performing here in the spring," Charlie announced. We all believed him now, if Barnum said so it must be true.

"That's incredible!" Mr. Weld rejoined, "Where else is she playing?"

"Mr. Weld, she's performing at Albany, Utica, Rochester, and Buffalo. Then she's off to Cleveland and Detroit," Charlie answered.

Austin and Abel Cook exchanged glances, knowing what Jenny Lind's arrival promised for business across the street from the train depot.

"We'll have to tell everyone when we get home!" Abel said to his older brother.

"We sure will," Austin agreed. "There'll be even more people at the depot for Jenny than for Henry Clay or General Wool. John's gonna start getting crazy ideas about selling Jenny Lind pies or something."

"It's a good thing that Pa built those extra rooms at the Coffee House—we'll need 'em for the Jenny Lind show," Abel remarked.

Austin said, "Excuse me, Mr. Weld, but I think that Abel and I will be working on the day that Jenny Lind arrives."

"And the day she leaves, too, Mr. Weld," Abel added.

"Understood, gentlemen," Weld replied.

Word of Jenny's arrival spread like wildfire on the prairie. My sisters were excited, but Ma didn't care much, knowing she'd be carrying the 1851 edition of our family, #10 and counting. Pa focused on reports from New York about a great temperance meeting.

"There were 3,000 people at the Tabernacle, Edward!" Pa said with enthusiasm.

"Who was the big name speaker, Pa?" I asked.

"Henry Ward Beecher, son," he replied.

Ma showed interest at mention of Beecher's name, both my parents esteemed the famed orator from the Congregational Church in Brooklyn, siding with his positions on temperance, slavery, and gambling. It wouldn't surprise me if Beecher shared their opinions of Philo Rust, and what happened at his hotel.

"But did Rev. Beecher say anything about all the **GOLD** in California?" I asked, exclaiming, "The Crescent City just pulled in with **$1,500,000** in **GOLD DUST!**"

"Alcohol's a bad mix with gold fever, Edward," Ma shot back. "And Rev. Beecher's lecture was about temperance!"

"I just thought of all the fortunes being made, Ma, that's all."

"And for every person who strikes it rich, how many don't?" she asked.

"I don't know, Ma."

"Well, you should read about something other than getting rich quick," she instructed.

"I do, Ma, Will Stoddard told me they're getting Charles Dickens' new book called *David Copperfield* at their store. I have to tell Cornelia—she liked *Oliver Twist*."

"Yes, we all did," Ma agreed. "It's a heartfelt story of orphans and poverty."

"And speaking of poverty, Ma, I heard a good one from Parish about a guy brought in for breaking off the boards from Dr. Hubbard's fence. He said he needed to make a fire for his sick wife. Parish said the man looked so poor that Justice House gave him a coat and let him go."

"As usual, your mind is racing all over the place, Edward. What's your next random thought?" she asked.

"Hmm, well, there's been lots of Scandinavians moving to Minnesota!" I stated with joy, but she wasn't impressed. I thought that reciting an obscure fact would demonstrate intelligence and amaze her, but she went silent, unmoved.

With November waning, having no Thanksgiving made us all anxious for the month to end. Black George asked me to help him by running down to the Davis Butcher Shop for a bargain on chicken. Approaching said shop, I saw many people and could hear Davis's booming voice. Crates of cackling fowls lined the sidewalk outside as I went to get in line. Everyone was talking about the fire at the German Brewery in the 1st Ward, over by the Court House. Cale Davis appeared upset, yet followed the usual script.

His next customers were two Syracuse House clothes wringers, called manglers.

Davis hailed, "Who's this then? Sure, it's my favorite mangless, Annie Rhyan, and the famous mangler himself, Denny Dwyer! As if you don't have enough clothes to wring, now you want to twist chicken necks."

"That we do, Cale," Dwyer answered. "But chicken tastes better in a pot than a laundry vat!"

"Where's Gillette getting his porter & ale with the Germans burnt out?" Davis asked.

"It's early days, Cale—must be a blow to Capt. Pfohl and his partner, Goettel."

"Sure, sure," Davis agreed.

It shocked me, standing in line hearing of the Pfohl's misfortune. My friend George's father was half owner of the brewery, now a total loss. A shoemaker's shop and a two-story house burned with it. I wanted to find my friend to see how everybody was doing, recalling Ma's words about the importance of *just being there*.

# Chapter Six

## (December 1850)

From Maine to Florida, and west to California, great rallies for the Union drew large audiences, with the *Fugitive Slave Law* debated everywhere you went. While Rev. Loguen lectured in Fulton, NY, they were making resolutions in Nashville, TN, at a large Union rally—much like the one held in Syracuse. Union men on both sides of the Ohio River held the southern fire-eaters in the same regard as the abolitionists. The southern Union Men differed from their northern brethren about the *Fugitive Slave Law*, though—they only wanted to stay in the Union with the law enforced, *as-is*. Any changes or non-enforcement were deal-breakers worthy of secession.

>**The South and the Union.**
>
>Baltimore, Nov. 35.

December arrived none too soon with everyone anxious for the holidays, but we still had to wait until the 12th for Thanksgiving. Ma was in good spirits from attending a lecture at the Franklin Institute. She liked the list of speakers booked for the winter session and encouraged me to join her.

"Edward, you should come along sometime, it'll be a treat!" she implored.

"I don't know, Ma, it depends on who the lecturer is. You weren't thrilled with the last guy you saw." My mother always expected much from orators. She was tough, but fair.

"Focus on the topic before you start checking credentials, Edward," she declared. "How privileged you are, and you don't even know it. This is a great opportunity for you to improve your mind and your heart."

"I'll go with ya sometime, Ma," I replied. "I like the speakers that you do, so pick a good one for us. It'll be a good story for my newspaper at school—I could interview you!"

"I'm glad to see you being creative in your writing, Edward—you're giving me ideas that I can use in my new diary book." Just to make conversation, she asked, "So, is your pal, Parish Johnson, still a fixture at the Police Office?"

"Yes, mostly," I replied. "He told me Officer Lowell arrested two guys in Chittenango for the robbery at the Broadway Saloon last week. Lowell was in on the arrests of the boat crew that terrorized the Harris family, too. Parish says they send him out for the all the important cases.

"It sounds like officer Lowell has a fan club at Weld's School," Ma teased. "You could present him with a homemade citizen's award and Parish could cover the story—how's that?"

"You're a great thinker, Ma!" I responded. The next day walking to school with the Cheney's, the brothers liked her idea, too.

"That's great, Ed," Prentice said. "And I know a printer who can help us."

"Who's that, Prentice?" I asked.

"You know, it's Chauncey Crofoot at the *Journal*. He lives just down the street from your favorite butcher. Let's see if he's home!"

Passing the Davis butchery we arrived at the printer's house just a block or so further. Mrs. Crofoot answered our knock, saying, "Sorry boys, but he's left for work. You can find him at the Journal Office—he's the man with black fingernails, ha ha!"

"We will, ma'am, thank you," Prentice replied.

"We'll find 'im after school, Ed," Silas urged.

The school day dragged despite an enthusiastic Mr. Weld and a surprise visit from Mr. Crandal, still joyful that voters passed the *Free School Law*. Upon dismissal, Parish and Grove Johnson eagerly joined, along with Charlie Pope. Parish led us on his familiar trek to the Journal Building, home to the Police Office where the Clinton St. bridge crossed the Erie Canal. The bridge was approached by an inclined roadway so high that the bridge deck was on level with the second story of the Journal Building. The Police Office was located on the 2nd floor on the heel path side of the canal.

*The Journal Building with 2nd floor Police Office.*

"Hey, Parish, is this your first time here for anything besides the Police Office?" I asked.

"Nah, I've run messages from my pa to the editor, before," Parish responded.

"Yeah, I guess everybody around here knows Vivus Smith," Charlie said.

Gaining entry, the *Journal* buzzed with activity. Printers, apprentices, clerks, bookkeepers, paper folders, even the news carriers were bustling about. Pressmen Baptiste Shearer and August Cargy manned the printing presses. Mr. Smith himself greeted us just inside the door.

"Hello boys, what can we do for you today?" the editor asked. But before anyone answered, he recognized Parish, a familiar face at the Police Office upstairs in the *Journal* building. "Ah, I see the junior detective of the Syracuse Police—have you brought a posse to arrest me?" Smith joked.

"No, sir, we came to ask Mr. Crofoot for help with a Citizen's Award," Parish replied.

"And perhaps something for our school newspapers, too," I offered.

"Oh, no—not more competition!" Smith jibed. "Just remember to give the *Journal* free publicity like they do at the *Standard* and the *Star*. Whenever they criticize me we sell more newspapers."

Chauncey Crofoot approached us before a clerk could be dispatched. I'd seen him countless times before on Genesee St., but never noticed his fingernails. Mrs. Crofoot was right.

"I understand that young businessmen are in need of services," the printer said with a smile, directing us to a small, unoccupied office. "What's on your minds, gentlemen?" he asked cheerfully.

Prentice answered, "Mr. Crofoot, we're hoping you'd help us make a Citizen's Award for us to give to deserving people around here. It's part of our Newspaper class at Weld's School, sir, and we want it to look nice!"

"A Citizen's Award, huh? Do I earn one for helping you? Ha ha!"

"Why yes, sir, I hadn't thought of that." Turning to us, Prentice asked, "We can do that, can't we fellas?"

"Oh, yes—sure we can!" everyone joined with feeling.

"Okay, boys, I think I know what you're after—come by in a few days and I'll have something for you," Chauncey Crofoot directed, assuring our return.

Leaving the *Journal* at early twilight, a light snow had sleigh bells ringing all around Clinton Square. Feeling the chill, I hoped that Pa might give us a ride home, but we walked as usual.

***Thanksgiving Day, 1850!*** Our tribe from Pompey descended: Grandma, elder relatives, Aunt Emma and Uncle Frank, same age relative, Aunt Julia, and younger relative, Aunt Eunice. Grandpa Birdseye felt ill, so he stayed home with other offspring and relations. Black George stoked the fireplaces while daring to instruct the kitchen maid, who wanted the intruder gone. Fragrant aromas erupted from the giant stove in our kitchen, transferring heat and delightful whiffs of deliciousness to the adjoining rooms. Whenever Black George was involved, the outcome tasted better, but having achieved a higher station he was adamant about not being called a cook, much to the kitchen maid's delight.

Ma declared with conviction that we're all going to hear Rev. Raymond at the 1st Baptist, and we did. She made the right choice, especially with all the city churches to choose from. Although they were members of the Congregational church, she and Pa were independents, real anti-sectarians. She'd say things like, "it makes little difference by what name people are called, if only they live a Christian life."

Pa had the sleigh brought around, transporting us to a steepled church opposite Clinton Square. Ma loved the sermon—we all did. Afterward she asked, "Those were impassioned, eloquent words, Edward, don't you think?"

"Sure, Ma, he's a good singer, too! You think he's better than Pa?" I answered, teasing Pa.

"I don't think so, Edward. Rev. Raymond's not called to perform solos like your pa."

"I guess so, and Pa's the President of the Syracuse Musical Institute, too. Lots of time for singing, I suppose."

In an instant, I realized my blunder, striking chords better left alone. Skilled in non-verbal communications, Ma's eyes flashed at Pa, who understood instantly. In turn, Pa flashed displeasure in my direction, assuring a fearful predicament. But for the tight proximity in the sleigh, and holiday visitors at our door, I averted disaster.

We enjoyed an incredible Thanksgiving dinner! I could tell that Black George had a hand in it, despite the irate kitchen maid. The room grew loud with merriment, thanks were given for many blessings, especially for the bounty on our table. Dinner conversation moved to the headlines of the day.

"There was another steamship accident!" Uncle Frank said. "This time it wasn't a boiler explosion, but a collision. The little steamer *Mariposa* was run over by the larger *West Point*, bound for Sacramento. The *West Point* picked everybody up from the *Mariposa* before she went down, though—*thank God!*"

"That's right, Uncle Frank," I replied, "You should meet my friend, Prentice—he's the steamer accident reporter at school."

"Then I bet he knows that over 25 people were killed or missing last week when the *Antoinette* burst her boiler on the Alabama River near Mobile," he said. "The *Arkansas* picked up the survivors."

I answered, "And when the *Columbus* burned at the mouth of the Potomac the week before that, nine more were lost including the captain, 1st mate, and three deck hands."

Ma interrupted to say, "All right, that's enough about collisions and disasters!"

With our clan of an abolition bent, the conversation moved to slavery, not the *Crystal Palace* she intended.

Pa said, "Brazil is enforcing their new law against the slave trade! Warships have orders to seize slavers and to hand over the officers and crew for civil trials. Their ships and cargo will be sold at auction, saving $40 expense for each slave returning to Africa. They're dividing the remainder amongst the officers and crew of the ship making capture."

Aunt Emma added, "And the party denouncing the slaver will share in the prize money! No Brazilian ship can leave Africa without giving security that it won't carry slaves."

"They're writing new laws against slavery as piracy, punishable by death," Pa stated.

"Excuse me, Pa," I interrupted, "Do you think Gerrit Smith will post bail for Chaplin? He's still in a Maryland jail for trying to free the slaves of Southern Congressmen."

"Probably so, Edward, I wouldn't be surprised," he answered.

Cornelia joined the conversation, saying, "George Thompson finally got to speak at Worcester. The mayor had to preside to keep everything peaceful."

Ma had the last word. "When I was at Dr. Loomis' last week I had conversation with the ladies about making a donation to Frederick Douglass for his paper, the *North Star*, but most thought we should help Ward with his paper instead."

Grandma Birdseye changed the subject. "I read that the President's Cabinet is worried about the American Indians!" she said, turning everyone's head.

"That's right Grandma, I read that, too," I replied. "The Secretary of the Interior said that our relationship with the American Indians demanded the prompt attention of Congress."

"How do you know all of this, Edward?" Ma asked.

"We talk about it in school, Ma. Charlie Pope keeps us updated on the American Indians, it's his niche."

"So what else did he tell you?"

"Plenty! When we annexed the land from Mexico after the war it included 124,000 Indians, many with fierce dispositions and predatory natures. The Secretary said that we needed more agents to establish friendly relations."

Ma asked, "Is that all that you learned from Charlie?"

"No, Ma—The Secretary of War said what's most important now is the protection of Texas and New Mexico against the Indians. Our small detachments of troops are so far apart that it's easy for Indians to pass in-between and commit depredations. He said we needed a cavalry because the Indians were skillful horsemen. They're not afraid of infantry, but a good cavalry could stop them."

"What's new with the canals, Charles?" Uncle Frank asked Pa.

"They just closed for the season two days ago," Pa replied.

"Leaving the *Canal Boys* scurrying to find work, food, and shelter for the winter," Ma interjected.

"That's right, Ma, I heard from Parish that some of them had courage to report the captains who tried to cheat them of their wages."

Pa said, "Anyone who can give them work will confer a blessing by doing so. As many are saved from idleness, the county would save in poor and prison rates."

It's always about this time of year, after the canals closed for the season, when canal boys found themselves out of work, and in crisis. Unscrupulous captains would cheat them of their seasons' wages, leaving them to shift for themselves however best they could in the cold of winter, compelled to steal or starve.

"Does anyone have anything cheerier to talk about?" Ma interposed.

"Sure, Ma," I said, "the sleighing is sure picking-up, but more outside the city. All the wood brought to market came in on sleighs."

"Your grandma told me all about it—how do you think she got here?"

Before dark, the Birdseye's of Pompey loaded their sleigh to return, taking Cornelia with them, bellies full, sleigh bells ringing. The next day Ma's older brother, Victory Jr., wife, and child arrived and stayed for two days. I was glad Cornelia went to Pompey and wished she had taken Ellen, Emma, and Clara with her to make room.

Having time off from school for the holidays, I snagged the Cheney brothers and together we found Parish and Grove. Everyone wanted to see Chauncey Crofoot at the *Journal* for the Citizens Award he promised. Recent snowfall improved sleighing, and Grove had a near miss with a farmer hauling a load of poultry.

*"Put on sleigh bells!"* an angry Grove shouted.

Down by the Clinton St. bridge outside the Journal building, Si Cheney slipped and lost his feet beneath him. He landed flat on his back and almost bashed his head.

"You okay, Si?" everybody asked. Lucky for him, he was.

Just then outside the Police Office, Officer Shattuck had Thomas Davis in custody! *"I never touched Eliza Appleton! How can you believe her lies?"* an angry Davis shouted.

"That's not my decision to make," Shattuck answered. "She filed a complaint, and you'll have to take it up with Justice House. Make bail and be on your way!"

We were all pretty surprised by the spectacle, Thomas Davis under arrest.

"Hey Ed, what do you make of that?" Parish said more than asked.

We could hear the *Journal's* presses humming from the street outside when I said. "C'mon guys, let's go find Chauncey Crofoot!" Stepping inside we soon connected with our favorite printer.

"Well, boys, how's this?" Crofoot asked, holding out a stack of Citizen's Awards. He must've told his co-workers, for a small group came over to watch.

"It's the moment of truth, Chauncey!" someone said.

"And I risked it printing copies without customer approval," he replied, wary of our reaction.

*We all loved it!* All we had to do now was fill in the names, dates, descriptions, and signatures. Chauncey Crofoot made it all nice and neat with a place for everything and no mistake at the top about it being a Citizen's Award. I liked how it showed that it came from the Newspaper Class at Mr. Weld's School for Young Men and Boys. There was a special place for Mr. Weld to sign, too. Whoever thought of a worthy citizen (meeting class approval) got to sign the award, along with Mr. Weld. A bunch of us signed the first one, as promised, to Mr. Chauncey N. Crofoot of the *Journal*, for unselfish support of young newspaper men at Weld's School for Young Men and Boys. We all thought that Mr. Weld would be happy to sign it after school started back up in January.

The week before Christmas it snowed again, compelling me and Sam to shovel a backyard path between our houses. Sam started on one end with me at the other, connecting somewhere in the middle.

"Hey, Sam, this is pretty good!" I said. "We should build a fort or something."

"Right, Ed, but not today—I'm freezing and I'm going home!" he uttered and disappeared.

That night, Ma took me and Cornelia with her to enjoy society at the home of Courtland & Julia Bates. Courtland's brother, Abner, was there with wife, Electa, and his sister, Esther, came with husband, Ira Cobb, who made his living at silver plating and saddlery hardware. Several other friends of the Bates' joined, but without same aged company, the evening proved dull for teenagers. Cornelia and I resigned ourselves to follow Ma's conversations with her peers.

"Ladies, would you sign a petition for granting the vote to women?" Ma asked.

Mrs. Maltbie said she was in favor, but couldn't sign the petition, while others thought it didn't matter if they were granted equal privileges with men for things of a more vital interest. Abner Bates suggested they should use the example of the early church as a guide.

*Ellen Birdseye Wheaton*

"But should we not follow the example of Christ more-so than the church, Abner?" Ma countered. "As the Gospel is to spread everywhere, for all time, our expression of faith will take new forms across the ages."

"Amen, Ellen!" Julia Bates responded.

With it starting to feel like church inside the Bates' house, I errantly tried to lighten the mood. "Hey, anybody hear about the employees' party at Rust's Hotel on Friday? Philo and Betsey personally served the entire staff. They all said that Philo's white apron never covered a truer landlord."

My good intentions returned unexpected results. The room went silent as I shrank between the cracks of the hardwood floor. Not the best words to offer in a room full of temperance.

*"Excuse me, Edward?"* Ma retorted.

"Well, I, er, ah, yeah, Ma?" I stammered.

Cornelia shook her head and asked, "Ma, are we really related?" Some people laughed but others pitied her. When we arrived home, I sensed that I'd be working around the house a lot, especially after Pa hears about me and Philo. I guess I'll be available to help Black George make another poultry run, there were sleigh loads of chickens, geese, and turkeys arriving daily for the holidays.

***Christmas Day, 1850!*** Having Thanksgiving just two weeks ago reduced the build-up toward December 25th, dampening the excitement for many. Governor Fish is a good man, but he got it wrong putting turkey day so close to Christmas. We celebrated much like on Thanksgiving, with the same cast of characters and a few different guests and relatives, poultry galore on the table. Pa told us about the meeting two days ago for the Syracuse—Binghamton Railroad.

"The weather was so bad that there weren't many people, and I was the only one from the committee appointed in June," Pa said.

"I'm not surprised, Charles. I would've gone myself, but the storm kept me home," Uncle Horace Wheaton replied."

"You see, Charles, your older brother thought it wise to stay indoors—someday you'll heed my advice!" Ma remonstrated.

"Who chaired the meeting, Charles?" Uncle Horace's wife, Aunt Helen, asked.

"The honorable James R. Lawrence did, Helen. He read a report and wanted to hear from the committee that took to raising subscriptions for the new road. Then Harvey Baldwin made a good speech, saying how important the new railroad is to Syracuse."

Ma asked, "Helen, I understand that you had a close call with a sleigh driver, what happened?"

"We were crossing Salina Street when a crazy driver without sleighbells came whipping around the corner and almost ran me over!" Aunt Helen stated with feeling. Uncle Horace and Aunt Helen had five boys, three living. The eldest is James, four years my senior, the next two died young, leaving William (6), and baby George (1).

The near tragedy presented an opportunity to report on a steamer accident that I heard about from Prentice.

"The steamer *Fashion* collapsed a flue near Pittsburgh that killed some of the crew and passengers, and the boat's a wreck!"

Ma stated, "I thought you learned at Thanksgiving that exploding ships and scalded bodies aren't suitable conversation for holiday dinner."

"What should we talk about then, Ma?"

"How about the Donation Visit for Rev. Loguen tomorrow at City Hall?" she suggested. Everyone present supported our neighbor's hub on the underground railroad, the most active one for miles around.

Christmas day and night passed affably, phenomenal sleighing brought cheer. All around Syracuse, every conveyance imaginable was hitched up for a ride. For those without sleighs, boards and wooden crates would suffice. Sounds of singing, laughter, and sleigh bells echoed from the city streets through the countryside. That evening, the ladies of the Second Baptist Society provided entertainment at City Hall that included Kellogg's Brass Band. With permission to attend, Cornelia and I joined some of our older relations there. Encountering Cornelia's friends, the Dickinson sisters, Sarah smiled at me and Harriette looked great! A Christmas kiss seemed appropriate, but I was clueless on how to proceed. A smiling Parish Johnson approached.

"Hey Ed!" he cried, "Saw a good one the other day! Some guy got drunk in the morning, was married at noon, and flogged after dinner! He told Justice House, "*Sir, I'm burdened with increasing cares and prospective responsibilities. Awakening this morning I was sober, and a bachelor. But twelve hours have passed, and here I am, half-seas-over, and a married man. I am, sir, the fabled unfortunate of whom poets write!*" Then he turned to his bride, reminding her that she might attend to the dirty dishes, and not to wait up for him burning candles—McKinstry had advanced the price of tallow 2 or 3 cents a pound."

# Chapter Seven

## (January 1851)

**Bell towers announced 1851's arrival** across Onondaga County and beyond. To start the new year, Ma wished to attend the donation party for Rev. Raymond, but ailing children prevented her. She missed Senator Hale's lecture before the Franklin Institute, too.

Mr. Weld's school reopened on the 2nd to a class anxious to start handing out Citizen's Awards. Parish showed everyone the forms printed at the *Journal*, while Prentice sang praises of Chauncey Crofoot. Our teacher showed his surprise.

"I don't know what to say, this shows much initiative on your parts—the recipients will be delighted! And it's only right that Mr. Crofoot is first."

"We're gonna walk over to the *Journal* building after school and present it, Mr. Weld," Si Cheney said. "But we need your signature!"

With the rest of the class wishing to follow our lead, Mr. Weld cautioned, "Don't be too hasty, gentlemen, the less you award, the more prestige it will carry." To change the subject, he asked, "Tell me, what are people talking about to start the new year?"

Alex responded, "Mr. Weld, my folks were talking about how much has changed in the last 50 years. Ma said that our country was only about 1,000,000 square miles in 1800, and now it's over 3,000,000. And Pa said that back then we only had 5,000,000 people, and now there's over 23,000,000!

Mr. Weld said to Parish, "Yes, Mr. Johnson? I see that you wish to speak."

"Yes, sir, I do, I saw the butcher, Thomas Davis, get arrested again. This time it was by the new police officer, George Green, for another complaint filed by Eliza Appleton. She had him brought in a couple weeks ago on the same charge, and she also filed against Gilbert Haynes, too," Parish answered.

"Did Justice House have any words with Miss Appleton?" Mr. Weld asked.

"Yes, sir, he did, he said that her name's been coming up regular of late, then he cautioned her on the consequences of living fast and loose."

Ma said, *"I want to go!"* after she read that William L. Chaplin would speak at the Congregational church. Me and Pa did, too, so did Black George. Chaplin just made bail after being held in Maryland since July for trying to help two slaves escape. Pa made sure we arrived early to get a seat. I saw lots of disappointed faces turned away, but recognized Jerry in the crowded church. He waved over to us.

Rev. May introduced the abolitionist hero, Chaplin. to the audience, followed by a welcome from Rev. Loguen. Chaplin rose and spoke for about an hour, surprising the audience when he said that in addition to the large contribution from Gerrit Smith, he made bail with donations from slave owners! Chaplin said that, *"No man having the feelings of a man, could resist doing what he did on the occasion."*

Driving home in our buggy afterward, Ma offered a good appraisal.

"I think many liked his simple manner of storytelling, it was touching! He set all doubts to rest for the part he'd taken."

I answered, "You know, Ma, I think it was brave of him to run off with slaves to the North."

"It was, Edward. Let's hope some benefit will come from his incarceration, for the slave and freedom's sake."

The next day an *Anti-Fugitive Slave Law Convention* opened for two days at City Hall. Dr. Clary was chosen President, Vice Presidents included the lawyer George B. Vashon, and our newspaper mentor, W.L. Crandal. The Rev.'s May & Raymond spoke forcefully to a charged audience. Detractors said that nothing good would come from the convention, but there should still be a Union Meeting afterward, to show the world that Onondaga County didn't sympathize with abolitionists bent on destroying the Union to carry out their one idea. The *Syracuse Daily Star* drew Ma's ire when it called Rev. May a fanatic of the New England type, purporting that his resolutions were of the *no-government* school.

The Rev. Samuel J. May pastors the popular Unitarian Church at the end of Burnet Avenue where James and Lock Streets intersect. Unitarians opposed the Mexican war and slavery, while promoting women's rights and temperance. The overflow of fugitives from Loguen's hub on the railroad first led to Rev. May's house, then to Rev. Raymond's, both pastors opening their homes to strangers. Rev. May's singing isn't so pleasant like my pa or Rev. Raymond, but he tried.

My mother asked, "Edward, you've heard Rev. May, do you think he's a fanatic?"

"No, Ma, I don't—but the *Star's* readers do, and they think the convention was just another abolition wrangle."

"Watch your tongue, young man!"

"I didn't say it, Ma, the *Star* did! And they called Mr. Crandal an agitator."

"But I was there and saw for myself. The speech most to the purpose came from Charles Sedgwick. You should have heard him, Edward, he gave an excellent summation of the Fugitive Slave Law—he seems to have thought deeply on the subject."

"Mr. Cheney said that, too, Ma—I heard him telling Prentice and Si."

"What else did Mr. Cheney say?"

"He said that he wanted to bring the family out to see the Swiss Bell Ringers, they're playing at Malcolm Hall for two nights only."

"And how did your friends react? Somehow, I don't see them enthused."

"They weren't, Ma, but Prentice thought it was a good idea for the Bell Ringers to bring the Fox Sisters up on stage and start the spirits rapping to the music. Then Mr. Cheney said, *Keep it up and you won't be going!*"

*The Fox Sisters*

Communicators with the great beyond, the Fox Sisters' fame grew daily. Doubters lined up but couldn't explain how all the knocking sounds were produced. The latest investigation into the sisters' communications with the dead indicated that clairvoyance or a kindred psychological phenomenon was likely involved. The best advice was to see the act for yourself and to draw your own conclusions. Ma felt certain of her convictions, sight unseen, but I didn't share her confidence of deception at play.

"But, Ma, none of the so-called experts can explain how the girls are doing it—*maybe it's real!*" I protested, wishing it were true.

"Listen to your mother, Edward. This isn't real. The Fox Sisters aren't talking to dead people, no matter how many they can deceive."

"Did you see the long article in the newspaper about them, Ma?" I asked.

"Do you believe everything you read in the newspaper?" she answered. Extending one towards me, she asked,

"How about this one? Luke Daley dies of Intemperance! First he drank too much, then instead of taking the bridge he walked into a pond and drowned. That's real, Edward. Should we have the Fox sisters ask Luke what happened? Maybe he watched the men carry his body out."

"Funny, Ma, but he wouldn't be the first tipsy spirit, though, would he? Ha ha!"

"Be careful, young man! I know you've been thinking about Rust's Hotel again," she warned.

Down at the Syracuse House, a big send-off was planned for barkeep Hiram Elderkin, heading west for a temporary change of climate. The topic was discussed at both Willard & Hawley's next door and at Wheaton Hardware across the street. Charlie, Billy, and Flo Willard said that I had to go.

"C'mon, Ed, it's not Rust's Hotel," Charlie urged.

"Yeah, you won't get in trouble so bad," Billy comforted,

"C'mon, Edward—don't be a baby!" young Flo Willard insulted.

"You're right, Flo," I responded. "I can see it now, all of us holding our glasses high at the Syracuse House!"

"Now you're talking, Ed!" Charlie said.

At the appointed hour, I rendezvoused with the Willard's, minus Flo, whose elders arranged to stay home. The Syracuse House was livelier than normal from a gathering for one of its own. The place remained a magnet downtown, despite the crowds at Rust's just over the canal. Home to the General Stage Office and the US Post Office, the Syracuse House was the most referenced building around. If someone asked for directions they were told, *"It's such and such from the Syracuse House."* Boarders included attorneys, reporters, jewelers, and workers from the Oyster Depot across the street.

We arrived in time to hear the landlord, Mr. Gillette, speak kindly of his trusty barkeep, known to the public as *"Speaker"* Elderkin, soon bound for Geneva, Buffalo, Cleveland, and Detroit. All of the *Speaker's* cohorts were on-hand; fellow barkeep Charlie Holt, head waiter Joseph Remlinger, and Fanny Wylie, the housekeeper. Waiters Morris and Bill Doland turned out, as did Joe Steiner, Peter Lanahan, and Freddy Studly the pastry cook. Domestics Marge Hewet and Cathy Slaven gave the *Speaker* a farewell kiss, as did Catharine Stapleton, the chamber maid.

"*Now, that's the kind of send-off I want when I strike out for California,*" an excited Charlie Willard declared. "And I must admit that I'd toast the *Speaker* with a tasty ale, but Pa would kill me if he ever found out."

Charlie was right, my pa would do likewise if he knew some of the things that had crossed my mind lately. Truth be told, I'd tasted the forbidden fruit before—it's hard not to when your friend's father owns a brewery, and a German one at that. We'd heard that German lager paired well with fried walleye, so a few of us tried it at the Pfohl's house. I found the taste not disagreeable, but had the sense to leave it at that.

Billy spied Mr. Crandal across the crowded lobby, greeting him after we made our way over.

"Hello, sir, we saw that you made Vice President at the Abolition Convention!" Billy said excitedly.

"Hello gentlemen!" Crandal responded. "This looks like two Williard's and a Wheaton to me, am I right?"

"Yes, sir. I'm Billy, that's my brother Charlie, and I think you know Ed Wheaton!"

"I do indeed, but it was an *Anti-Fugitive Slave Law*, not an Abolition Convention! Abolition's something more, though a great many there would support it."

"How do you think it went, sir?" I asked, blurting, "My ma said a great opportunity was almost lost!"

"Hmm, your ma's a keen observer, and she's right," Crandal agreed. "But it's not unusual to have heated discussions over the resolutions. It's a good thing that so many people stood together against this infernal law, don't you agree? It sent a powerful message!"

"I guess you're right, Mr. Crandal," I replied.

"Good! I'll see you fellows in class to check on your progress."

Before school began the next day, we heard a good story from the Police Office. Parish said all the officers had a good laugh, even Justice House.

"Two drunks pretending to be police officers went inside the home of Mrs. Thankful Long to arrest Miss Emeline Stephens," Parish began.

"What she do, Parish?"

"Nothing! Her fine figure was to blame—especially her big 'uns. The intruders made sham police markings as disguise to apprehend Emeline for a thorough body search. The ladies were lucky that Officer Lowell was nearby and heard their screams."

> **POLICE.**
> BEFORE JUSTICE HOUSE—YESTERDAY.
> Franklin Hicks and George Hier, were arrested by officer Lowell, charged with pretending to be police officers, and entering the dwelling of Thankful Long and arresting Emeline Stephens against her will. Examined and held to bail.

"So what he do?" someone asked.

"Lowell went inside and discovered the two phony policemen trying to make an arrest. He said he could tell right away they were pretty high on the booze, and one look at Emeline told him what they were after."

"What else you hear, Parish?"

"Down at the Police Office they were all paying compliments to Emeline's figure, and saying how smooth that Lowell was."

"What happened next?" someone encouraged.

"After Lowell tucked his captives aside, he eyed Emeline's endowments, twice to be sure, and said, *'Why, they've ruffled your blouse, ma'am, and frazzled the stitching!'*"

Emiline answered, *"What? Where?"*

*"Why, right there, Ma'am,"* Lowell replied, grabbing some loose threads while the backs of his fingers pressed against her bosom. He said he tickled it with his pinky."

"Oh, yeah? What Emeline do?"

"The police told me that she smiled, and said, *"Why thank you, Officer Lowell!"*

Our interest peaked. "Then what, Parish?" we pleaded.

"That gave Lowell courage, so he seized another loose thread hanging on the other side.

*"And there's another one over here, too, ma'am,"* Lowell said with a wink, repeating the move with his other hand, pinky-tickle, and all!"

"Anything else?"

"Lowell said that Thankful Long was watching, and she said, *That's fine police work, Officer!* The last thing I heard was that Emeline looked sad that he left."

Judging by their intent faces, I guessed that most of my friends would be thinking about Emeline later on tonight, alone with themselves somewhere in the dark.

Mr. Weld called class to order, welcoming W.L. Crandal, who addressed us.

"Good morning, gentlemen! Before hearing from budding reporters, I must congratulate you on your Citizen's Awards. Chauncey Crofoot has one hanging at the *Journal* for all to see, and down at the Police Office, Justice House tacked Officer Lowell's award by the main door."

Parish leaned toward me and whispered, "Yeah, and now we 'gotta make him another one for Emeline!" Lowell had already received the 2nd award presented, just like Ma suggested when the idea first came to her.

Crandal resumed, "Now, to the world of newspapers and reporting! What's the biggest news happening out there? Anyone?" Crandal challenged.

Alex McKinstry shouted, "There's **GOLD**, Mr. Crandal! The *Cherokee* and *Prometheus* just pulled in with *$2,000,000 more,* and the *Cresent City* had *another $1,500,000 in gold dust!* But the specie train crossing the

> **FROM CALIFORNIA.**
> ARRIVAL OF THE CHEROKEE AND PROMETHEUS.
> $2,000,000 more in Gold.

isthmus was attacked by sixteen gunmen, Mr. Crandal. They were after the gold, all right."

"That's big news for sure, young man. Anything else about California?"

Larry Sabine answered, "Yes, sir! The Senate is considering $300,000 for a telegraph line from the Mississippi to California."

"I think it's only a matter of time," Crandal replied. "You there, Prentice Cheney, is there another steamer accident to report?"

"Yes, sir, but this one didn't burn or explode."

"Really? Where did it happen?"

"Mr. Crandal, it happened at Niagara Falls—the *Maid of the Mist* sank to the bottom!"

"Oh, no, I've been aboard her myself!"

"She was moored for the winter, but the last storm left so much snow on one side that she leaned over and started taking on water. It wasn't long before she sank in about 20 feet with her cables still attached, but nobody thinks they can raise her."

"Hmm, that's a loss any way you look at it, but I wouldn't be surprised if they replace her with a new steamer in the spring. Now, I'd like to hear from Mr. Parish. Johnson—attend please!" Crandal ordered.

Parish stood to report on local crimes and criminals.

"Mr. Crandal, there's been some real characters brought in before Justice House lately. A drunk and disorderly person was released after he promised to move to Truxton! The Judge told 'im to stay in Cortland County or he'd send 'em to the penitentiary. That was right around the time that Tommy Dink got picked up again for intoxication.

But sir, the biggest news is that two more *Model Artists* were arrested for exposing themselves! Porter Herriman showed himself to the girls at Miss Palmer's school on Genesee Street until a passing gentleman made him stop. Then Edward Coy showed his privates to Mrs. Steve Reynolds, and Steve had Officer Shattuck arrest him. I don't get it, Mr. Crandal—what makes a man do such a thing? And it's freezing cold outside!"

"I'd call it human depravity," Crandal replied, while Mr. Weld nodded agreement.

The few of us who heard him laughed when Billy Willard whispered a warning about shrinkage. Our teacher's weren't in on the joke.

Then Parish repeated the story about Officer Lowell, Emeline, and the phony police at the home of Mrs. Thankful Long, leaving out the part about the pinky-tickle. Those of us *in-the-know* grinned and winked pinkies at each other while he spoke. Parish tried to pretend he didn't notice, but couldn't stop himself from laughing.

Crandal said with vigor, *"That's what I like about this newspaper class, everyone's always in a good mood!"*

If he only knew.

It's not every day that a man turns fourteen. Repeating last year's ritual, Cornelia observed me eying my reflection in the morning light. I thought that maybe it's time to try growing a beard. Her laughter from the hallway ended further contemplation.

"Edward, if you need a shave I could have the kitchen maid bring up some milk, and ask Black George to get the neighbor's cat! We had a good laugh talking about you, he said, *'da cat be safer fo' him 'den usin' yo' daddy's razor!* Ha ha ha! *Happy Birthday, Edward!*"

"He told me that a long time ago, Missy, but I'm expecting great things from all my sisters today! Whatcha get me?"

"Ha! Same as last year I suppose."

The best gift ever came that night when Ma dispatched me to deliver an important message to Mrs. Dickinson from the ladies at the Orphan Asylum. Cornelia and Ellen objected, but Ma needed their help elsewhere so off I went. On a crisp, starry night, the clear skies made it feel colder. Passing the Cheney's, I wished Si and Prentice could see me traipsing off to spend time with the Dickinson girls after hours. I dreamt of finding Harriette alone, and that she was glad to see me. After all, it *was* my birthday.

Three knocks on the Dickinson's door began the dream come true. Harriette answered, looking better than ever. She even appeared pleased by my sudden appearance. Then she asked me inside.

"Oh, Edward, it's freezing out there, please come in!"

"Thanks, Harriette—don't mind if I do!"

"What brings you here on this cold winter's night?"

"My ma wanted me to deliver a message from the ladies at the Orphan Asylum."

"Well, you'll have to leave it with me—everyone's gone and I'm here alone."

"*Oh, really?*"

"Yes, and I was starting to hear noises—you're my knight in shining armor!"

"*Oh, really?*"

"You'll wait with me, won't you? They'll be home soon; I hope you're not too busy."

"Oh, no! I wasn't doing much, and my birthday's almost over now."

"Your birthday? If that's true then I have something for you." Then she leaned over and kissed me. *"Happy Birthday, Edward!"* she said with a smile.

A true son of Charles A. Wheaton, I began to sing.

The next day I wished it were still my birthday when Prentice stopped over. He thought I was full of it after hearing my tale.

"So, you were there with her alone, and she kissed you? Tell me another one, Wheaton!"

"Yup! Special for my birthday!"

"Oh, boy—next you'll be saying that you gave her a pinky-tickle."

"No, just a love song."

"A what? You? How'd her cat like it?"

"She has a dog, Prentice, but now that you mention it . . ."

"So when you going back for your next rendezvous, Romeo?"

"I'm still working on that."

"Ha! I bet you'll be declaring soon!"

"Funny, Prentice—why do I tell you anything?"

"Hey, Ed—we should go see Madame Blanche, the world famous astrologist. She's here for a week at Brintnall's."

"Yeah? What for?"

"To find out your future with Harriette, dummy! She can tell by how the moon, the stars, and the planets are aligned," Prentice said matter-of-factly.

"And you believe that?"

"Sure, they even offered a $10,000 reward to anyone better at fortune telling."

By now, Ma had heard enough. Neither one of us knew she was listening, and she startled us.

*"Boys, please don't say that you've abandoned the Fox sisters!"* Ma said with fake urgency, a master of sarcasm when required. "And where will you get $1 to consult with Madame Blanche, Edward?"

"Well, I, err, uh . . ."

"That's what I thought," she said, *"I must be psychic."*

Taking our cue to depart, we took the backyard path to the Ward's house that Sam and I kept shoveled. We found Sam Jr. at home with the entire Ward family plus Rev. Lyles and George Vashon, the lawyer. The Ward girls played on the floor while the adults were deep in conversation. Sam was eager to leave with us, but his ma said that he had to finish the job that she gave him first. Prentice and I listened to the men while we waited. The Rev. Lyles was just finishing his recollections about when he found Mrs. Harris on the canal and rescued her from her tormentors.

Rev. Ward said, "A lot of folks appreciate what you did for the Harris family, and the donation visit for your church proved it!"

> **GEORGE B. VASHON,**
> *ATTORNEY AND COUNSELLOR AT LAW,*
> Office in the Empire Block, adjoining the Supreme Court Room.

"Yes, indeed," Rev. Lyles answered, "we're all pleased at the Fayette Street Congregational."

Mr. Vashon asked everyone, "Have you all heard that free blacks in Albany petitioned for legislative protection from the *Fugitive Slave Law?*"

"Yes, and for once I'm hopeful that something good will be done," Rev. Ward answered.

"Charles Sedgwick shares your view," Vashon replied.

Rev. Lyles said, "That's good for New York, but in Kentucky the Legislature just passed a law that prohibits transportation of negroes across the Ohio River, except with their owners."

"It's no surprise that they made this law in Kentucky," Rev. Ward said, "It's the land of Henry Clay and supporters of the Colonization Society."

"That's right," George Vashon agreed. "And Clay just spoke at the colonization meeting in Washington where he advocated creating the *Ebony Line* of steamers!"

"They had themselves a good old time in the Capitol, making toasts and congratulating themselves about how they're helping colored people. Just stick 'em on the first boat to Africa where they won't know anyone!" Rev. Lyles said with warmth.

Rev. Ward said, "The latest news from Congress was about Henry Clay presenting three petitions from Indians who favor removing all free colored people of the United States willing to go to Africa, with provisions made to support them for one year after arrival."

"I read that, too," Vashon answered. "Then Senator Hale spoke next, and he asked for a repeal of the *Fugitive Slave Law*. But, of course, the motion was tabled."

"Did everyone hear the blind, colored man, from Ithaca preach?" Rev. Lyles asked.

### Lecture.

W. F. JOHNSON, of Ithaca, a blind man, will deliver a Lecture at J. W. Loguen's Church in the 4th ward, this (Monday) evening, 13st inst., on the Rise and Progress of the Colored People in the United States. Those who are friendly to the cause are respectfully solicited to attend.

"Yes, I was among the faithful at the AME Zion," Vashon replied.

"He spoke of the rise and progress of black people in the United States. Imagine that, coming from him," Rev. Ward observed. He jokingly added, "And when Rev. Loguen's desperate enough, he'll even allow *me* to speak there!"

Rev. Lyles and Mr. Vashon both blurted, *"Me, too!"* at the same time, and they all laughed.

Sitting there listening, I tried to imagine how a blind, colored man might describe the progress of his people in 1851. Looking around the room, I realized that Rev. Ward, Rev. Lyles, and George B. Vashon were living examples—I sensed that Prentice knew it, too. Then, I considered the recent Donation Visit for Rev. Lyles, reflecting on the white people who supported a black church. Wasn't that progress, too? I felt sure that this didn't happen down south, but then again, I never imagined slave owners contributing bail money for Chaplin. When the three of us left the Ward's house I couldn't wait to tell Parish that we heard about a blind Johnson preaching, and to ask him to explain how they were related.

By the end of January, the canal bridges needed repair. Crossing over on Salina Street, I noticed holes that needed shingles before something, or someone, fell through. Many people wanted to build a new, iron bridge instead of replacing the beams of an aging eyesore. Warming temperatures made the snow *great packing* for snowball fights, but dangerous for skaters on the canal—a boy went through the other day and nearly drowned. Combined with the other narrow escapes, most Syracuse mothers prohibited skating.

The January thaw was short-lived, though, the next storm buried everything, making the unfortunate living in poverty even more desperate. Many *"out-of-work for the season"* canal workers applied to Justice House for accommodations at the new penitentiary, but he'd never heard a request made for an entire family until now.

"It was sad to see it," Parish Johnson told Ma, Black George, and me, standing around a warm stove in our kitchen. "A man limped into the Police Office and begged Justice House to help his family. He was bitten by a dog six months ago, and it must have got infected or something because he hasn't been able to work since then. He said they were cold and starving, but could stay alive in the penitentiary."

"What did Justice House do, Parish?" Ma asked.

"Mrs. Wheaton, right away he sent Officer Shattuck to go see the man's house and his family. It didn't take long for Shattuck to return, and he told Justice House that things were even worse than the man said."

"How did Justice House react, Parish?" I asked.

"He shook his head, and said that he believed this was a case for the Superintendent of the Poor that didn't fall under his jurisdiction."

Black George said, "It be hard for a workin' man to make it without usin' his legs."

"I hope and pray that people aren't allowed to starve in our midst," Ma declared.

"Many have so much and don't appreciate it!"

# Chapter Eight
## (February 1851)

Daydreams of Harriette lingered until Prentice ruined it. Walking to school with the Cheney brothers, he acted like he had a big announcement. Whenever Prentice preceded a thought with, *"I was thinking,"* whatever followed could be anything. I braced for the worst.

"Hey, Ed, *I was thinking,* we all know that Harriette kissed *you,* but *you* still haven't kissed *her!* Have you considered that?" he asked.

I conceded his point, alarmed that others had figured it out. "Sure, wouldn't you?"

"Yeah, I suppose so, but whatcha gonna do now? I'm not the one that she kissed—and you were all alone with her, too. *Boy, you missed your big chance!*"

"Thanks, Prentice, you're a real pal! But I'm hoping to deliver another note to her house."

"Oh yeah? What's the note say? Next time I wanna kiss you back?"

"Nah, just another message from the ladies at the Orphan Asylum."

"That'll never work, Wheaton, somebody else'll snatch her up first!"

Silas said, "Don't worry Ed, we won't tell anyone that you sang and made her dog cry."

When we arrived at school, I desired distance from Prentice Cheney, but there was no escaping him. The school's wood stove kept us all warm, but too warm for the people sitting closest, sometimes they fell asleep. Prentice had everyone laughing as he sat comfortably reclined, head back, mouth agape. When he began to honk like a Canadian goose. Mr. Weld asked Si to assist.

"Silas, restore your brother to the class, please."

*"Yes, sir, Mr. Weld!"* Si responded in word and deed.

*"Hey, Prentice, wake-up!"* he urged, giving his brother a good shake. Prentice mumbled, *"Wha, what?"* to our delight.

*"Wake-up, Prentice!"* Si repeated, *"Mr. Weld wants to hear about the steamers."*

*"Yes, sir!"* a waking Prentice declared, "Sorry for nodding off there, Mr. Weld."

"Proceed, Prentice."

"Sir, it's all bad news again. The *John Adams* hit a snag near Greenville and over 100 people were lost. And it's been over a month since the *Atlantic* left port in England and nobody knows where she is. The *Atlantic* might be at the bottom of the Atlantic, Mr. Weld."

"I'm sorry that we woke you, Prentice. Tell me, is there any good news?"

"Yes, sir, there is. The *Maid of the Mist* was raised, and she'll carry passengers again."

"Ah, finally a glimmer of hope!" Weld rejoiced.

Bill Wallace interrupted, "Excuse me, Mr. Weld, can we talk about the population explosion? In the last ten years, our country's grown by over 6,500,000!"

"We shall, Mr. Wallace, and pay attention, gentlemen—there's a lesson in this," Mr. Weld advised, motioning Bill to proceed.

"Well, sir, the report that I read broke down the population by the total number whites, free coloreds, and slaves, and it talked about the 3/5 law. Can you tell us more about that, sir? I don't quite understand."

**Population of the United States.**

With regard to the population of the thirty-one States, on which representation in the lower House of Congress is based, we believe it will stand nearly as follows:—

| | |
|---|---|
| Whites | 19,876,468 |
| Free Colored, | 500,000 |
| Slaves | 3,100,000 |
| Total | 23,479,468 |

"Great question, William! Was everyone listening? One reason that the report includes the slave population is because that as their numbers increase, so do the number of Southern Congressmen."

"How's that Mr. Weld?" someone asked.

"It's based on population, so the more people there are, the more Congressmen there will be for that particular state. The 3/5 law was a compromise between counting all, or none, of the slaves. But it's wrong, just like the *Fugitive Slave Law*."

"Why, Mr. Weld?"

"It's wrong because the South has it both ways. On one hand, they treat blacks as *property* to justify the *Fugitive Slave Law*. Then, on the other hand, they treat blacks as *people* to gain more representatives. As the slave population grows, the 3/5 law increases the number of Southern Congressmen to keep them enslaved. It's a cruel way to calculate the value of human property for the benefit of slave owners."

"Are you saying that Southern Congressmen should represent the rights of the slaves then, Mr. Weld?" Bill asked.

"That's right, William, but they don't elect abolitionists down south."

A favorite after-school stop, the appeal of Welch's Coffee House only grew with falling temperatures. Will Stoddard and I tagged along with Austin and Abel Cook for a warm-up, wishing to say hello to their older brother, John, the full-time working man.

The enticing aroma of delicious roasts and freshly baked pies enticed us indoors where business was starting to pick-up. I recognized the owner, old Mr. Eliphalet Welch, seated by the door. Austin waved to his pa, signaling his return from school. When John Jr. waved back instead of their pa, Abel insisted that he couldn't wait to put them to work. Austin directed us to a small side-room where staff took refreshment. John Jr. appeared while our hot tea seeped.

"Hello Will, Hello Ed! How are you?" John asked in his easy manner.

"Great, John," Will replied, how's things at the Coffee House?"

"Busier than ever, Will, how about you?"

"I'm busy, too, been working at the bookstore after school, and gathering information for my pa about the fires. He sells insurance and the insurance companies want to know everything. Have you heard about all the fires happening around Utica lately?"

"Yes, I have, Will. Heard plenty from people getting off the trains. Folks say arsonists are to blame, and they want to start a Vigilance Committee to catch 'em!"

"That's what I heard, too," Will agreed.

As I listened, I began to wonder what else people formed vigilance committee's for. I'd read they were springing-up all over in California, especially around the gold mines.

Eyeing his younger brothers, John said, "We have a lot to do, so don't take a long break!"

Austin snapped, "Break? We haven't started yet and already you're cracking the whip!"

Abel looked at me and Will, and implored, *"See, I told you!"*

Austin barked at John, "And Pa even said not to ride us so hard—do you remember that?"

"Yes, I remember," John calmly replied. "And Pa also said that he wants me to be a leader. He told me, S*ometimes you gotta be the bad guy.*"

"You've got that part down pretty well," Abel quipped, as John returned to duty.

The four of us enjoyed our hot drinks longer than John liked, talking about how Mr. Welch reopened his door to firemen and was recompensed $10 by the Common Council. Then after Philo Rust petitioned them for another $10, the Council made a policy that all future bills for Firemen refreshments had to be ordered by a City Alderman or the Chief Engineer, otherwise they wouldn't be paid.

John reappeared for a second prompting, duly ignored as before. Visibly angered, he approached a third time, waving his arms and pointing as he bellowed, so animated that his words became confused. His final command, spoken with authority, didn't come out right.

"*That's enough, now—**I'm in charge!** **What I say, I go!***"

We couldn't stop laughing. Austin eyed John and remarked, "What, you're still here?"

With Valentine's Day falling tomorrow, I vowed that nothing in the world could prevent me from sending a card to Harriette this year. All the bookstores were full of them, this year's edition more colorful than ever. They all looked good to me, but others remarked that many were quite ugly. Finally deciding on one, I headed home with my prize, confident that I'd picked a winner.

Returning home, I heard my sisters from the street outside, and so retired to the quiet of my room to write a Valentine greeting to Harriette.

> *Wishing you the happiest of Valentine's!*
> *Your admirer, Edward Wheaton*

Happy with the result, I said to myself, *"There, that ought 'a do it—short and sweet!"* To make sure, I decided to show Ma and Cornelia, then to make corrections as needed. Getting a word with Ma appeared daunting from the look on her face and the boisterous girls buzzing around her. I began with an innocent question, like, *"How was your day?"*

"Nothing unusual, Edward," she replied, "Just the daily mountain of sewing and needy children calling for me day and night."

"Yes, that's normal but you look kind of sad."

"You're right, Edward. I won't be able to attend the *Ladies Fair* at the 1st Presbyterian Church tonight, and tomorrow I'll miss Ralph Waldo Emerson lecture at City Hall."

Ma looked unhappier than before I started asking questions, so I tried to cheer her up.

"Say, Ma, I heard that Rev. Loguen's church was having a Ladies Fair at the end of the month—maybe you could go to that one."

Her expression indicated that my attempt failed miserably. I beat a hasty retreat, vowing to try again later—there was still lots of time. After a day passed, desperation sank in. I called for Cornelia even though Ellen was with her, and resigned myself for unwanted commentary.

I called, "Hey, Cornelia! Can you come over here for a minute?"

"Sure Ed, what is it?" she replied, coming to my room with Ellen right behind her.

Finding courage, I presented the Valentine for critique. "Well, what do you think?" I asked, extending the card of many colors for a better view. "Do you think Harriette will like it?"

Wary looks and silence foretold impending doom. Cornelia spoke first.

"Edward, you weren't really going to give that card to Harriette, were you?" she asked.

Ellen laughed, *"Ha ha ha! That's gotta be the ugliest Valentine I ever seen!"*

Expecting the opposite, their reaction rocked me. "But it's colorful, isn't it?" I protested.

Cornelia pronounced, "Yes, it's colorful all right but *the colors don't match*. I'm sorry, Edward, but Ellen's right, *that's one ugly card you have there!*" Last word spoken, she departed with the ever joyous Ellen.

I sat there dazed, then stumbled about the house, card in hand, feeling like Grasshopper after the cannon misfired on the 4th of July. Black George inquired.

"What be troublin' you?" he asked.

"Oh, nothing, George. I just picked out the world's ugliest Valentine for Harriette, and it's too late to get another. Besides that, it's all good!" I replied, heavily laden with sarcasm.

*"Hey boy, that lip 'a yours sho' ain't helpin' you none!"* he advised.

Combining Black George's wisdom with my sisters' knowledge, I consigned the abomination to the fire. Then I wailed, sounding not unlike Harriette's dog.

Gloom pervaded the days that followed another Valentine's Day that wasn't. The worst happened when Ma's friend, Julia Bates, passed suddenly at the age of forty! Having just been to a party at her house in December, it came as a shock to us—she didn't appear so close to the end of her life. Ma said that her husband, Courtland, was in despair.

"Is there anything I can do, Ma?" I asked. "Sometimes, just being there is important, right?"

"That's right, Edward, and very thoughtful of you, too! Yes, there is something you can do—you can accompany me to Julia's funeral tomorrow and *just be there* for me. I stopped by the Bates' house earlier today—it's a tragedy for their family."

"Okay, Ma! Mr. Weld says we're allowed to miss for funerals."

The church crowded to overflow the next morning. Rev. Mr. Snow delivered a solemn homily, yet praised the character of the departed. Tearful mourners presented a vision of sorrow—poor Mr. Bates and his children!

Leaving the sad event behind, with the sun shining, and the mud drying, we enjoyed our walk home together. Ma provided critique of the sermon.

"He spoke well, Edward, but I don't like excessive laudation in funeral discourses. If my friends didn't already know my good qualities by then, it's too late to tell them now."

"But it's never too late, Ma, at least not with the Fox Sisters. Professors Flint and Coventry just examined 'em and wrote a report. So far, nobody's proved deception!"

"Don't bother, Edward. If the Fox Sisters come knocking I won't answer," she joked.

"Funny, Ma, but the spirits don't knock, they rap."

"Knocking, rapping, whatever you call it, I have no faith in crazy girls from Rochester."

"Sometimes I don't know what to believe, Ma."

"Really? Well you can believe this—we're invited to the mayor's party tomorrow night at Rust's Hotel and your pa said that you can go! What do you think of that? Sometimes *just being there* is important, right, Edward? This is your reward for coming along with me today."

I had to catch my breath, and finally uttered, "Sure, Ma, I'd love to go!"

"I knew you would!" she said with vitality—funerals added determination to her step. Leaving us behind, she had Black George drive her to Welch's for society with Mrs. Cook and the other ladies in the tearoom. The following day, darkness covered the skies for the Mayor's *"Invitation Only"* event. Rain poured in torrents, streets became rivers of liquid mud. I couldn't have cared less—*the mayor needed me at Rust's Hotel!* I always thought his honor showed great intuition by inviting me—the party would never have been the same.

Streetlamps illuminated a stormy Clinton Square, with Ma, Pa, Cornelia, Ellen, and me, thoroughly soaked for the mayor's gala. Party goers hurried indoors to escape the tempest. My ten-year-old sister, Emma, was to attend, too, but as the time approached Ma declared she was too ill to go. I knew she was really sick when she didn't complain.

Like the unexpected kiss from Harriette, stepping into Rust's Hotel felt surreal. Philo had the place decorated with princely taste, while accomplished ladies greeted the arriving guests with grace and dignity. It all made me feel like I was important, or something. His honor, himself, stood front and center, beaming a great smile that made you glad to be there. Afterward, Ma said that she thought the mayor must have felt lonely, holding his nine-year-old daughter by the hand—it had been less than a year since his wife died.

To everyone's delight, Philo's gifted artisans delivered a sumptuous feast, followed by perfect arrangements for the dance. There must have been four hundred people there from all around central New York and beyond. If anyone needed an introduction to the city of Syracuse, this was it! Young people naturally gravitated to their own spaces in the banquet hall, voluntarily segregating themselves from the elders. Me and the girls were no exceptions.

*I'll never forget the mayor's party!* Up till then I'd never danced so much in my life. After Cornelia and Ellen dragged me onto the floor I just stayed out there. Charlie Pope approached in disbelief.

"Hey Twinkle-Toes, you should audition for the National Theater! Don't look now, but there's a pretty girl staring at you."

I looked anyways, confirming his observation on both counts.

"Yes, she's pretty," I said in wonder, returning her gaze. "Do you know her?"

"Nah, I don't know who she is, but you better go ask her to dance, huh?" Charlie urged.

"You're right, Charlie!"

*"Go get her, boy!"*

*"I will, I will!"*

Entranced, I crossed the dance floor like a Packet Boat Captain. The pretty girl watched my approach while I struggled with what to say. Will Stoddard once told me that you had to show confidence with strangers, but when he tried, *"Good, and you?"* as an opener, the girl just walked away. I tried an alternate version.

"Well, hello there! Great party, isn't it?" I said, using more words than I thought possible.

"Yes, you look like you're having fun!" she replied.

"Oh, I am, would you like to dance?"

"Yes, I was hoping that you'd ask me, Edward."

"How'd you know my name?"

"I asked my friend, 'Who's the handsome guy dancing out there?' and she told me."

"Really? And I just asked who the pretty girl was, too. But I don't know your name."

"I'm Mira," she said, "Mira Barker."

"Say, is your pa Marmaduke Barker the whitewasher? I've seen him at the hardware store."

"That's him alright. He's busy all the time and hardly ever at home."

"I know the feeling, Mira—*let's dance!*"

That night, everything lined up perfectly—no need to consult Madame Blanche for an astrologic reading. There I was, dancing the night away at Rust's Hotel, with parental consent, *and meeting pretty girls who liked me!* Ignoring my friends, I found that dancing greatly increased your chances. Girls I could never talk to became approachable. Mira taught me the steps, and I had the time of my life dancing with her. Holding her hand in-between songs was a thrill. As one of the few young men on the floor, my status improved significantly as the other girls sought a partner. More than once they dragged me away from Mira, I didn't know which way to look. Even both my sisters wanted a turn. Charlie said that the girl I just danced with looked like she was related to Emeline from over at Thankful Long's.

Saying goodnight to Mira, she reached up and kissed me on the cheek, just like Harriette did. This time I was smart, though, and kissed her back, eager to find out where the band played next for a happy do-over. Charlie and Prentice saw me with Mira, and I hoped they both were jealous. *The Polka Kid rides again!*

Mr. Weld attended the mayor's party, but I only saw him at a glance. Not a word passed between us. He surprised me at school, speaking for all to hear.

"Good morning, Edward! You were running at full steam the other night, eh? ha ha!"

"Yes, sir, I was."

"Indeed, you didn't miss a dance." Now addressing the class, Mr. Weld challenged, *"And where were the rest of you? Watching from the back!"* Shaking his head, Mr. Weld continued, *"You missed your chance!"* I looked over at Prentice and grinned when our eyes met, savoring his awareness of despond. Mr. Weld saw it, too, asking, "What's wrong Prentice? Did another steamer explode?"

"No, sir, and the *Atlantic's* been found, too, Mr. Weld. Nine days out, she broke both her shafts and put into Cork, Ireland, sir!"

"That's a relief! Not a word from the *Atlantic* for over a month. Thank you for reporting good news for a change."

"I'm trying, Mr. Weld, but good reporters have to tell the facts."

"Yes, Prentice, and more importantly, good reporters should tell the truth."

"Isn't that the same thing, Mr. Weld?"

"Not quite. People have a great capacity to exaggerate, and to not tell the whole story."

"What do you mean, sir?"

"I mean that if you only focus on facts A, B, and C, but leave out D, E, and F, you'll arrive at the wrong conclusion. And believe me, a deceptive reporter will lie by omission."

"Do editors lie, too, sir?"

"Ha! Especially, editors—but thankfully, not all."

During a routine stop at the Ward's, a dejected looking Sam was slow completing his chores. Seeing my face only made him more anxious to leave.

His ma told him, "If you started when I asked, you'd be done by now. Maybe next time you'll do what I say the first time."

Sam didn't answer, but I think he knew that his ma was right.

"Sam shouldn't be long, Edward, but you're welcome to wait," Mrs. Ward advised.

"Thank you, ma'am, I'll wait," I replied, settling into a living room chair. I could hear the lawyer, George B. Vashon and Rev. Ward discuss the fight against slavery in the next room. I liked listening to them talk, I always learned something.

Mr. George Vashon said, "I was glad to hear that Governor Quitman of Mississippi resigned to face charges for the failed expedition to Cuba."

"And, I!" Rev. Ward responded. "But I don't believe this is the end of it; they're already plotting their next attempt."

"That's true, Sam," Vashon answered. "They haven't given up on Cuba yet, and that General Lopez is fool enough to try again."

"I'm sure of it, but have you heard the news from Iowa?"

"Yes, the Iowa legislature passed a law that prohibits free black people from settling there. If discovered, they must leave within three days' notice or face severe penalties."

Rev. Ward added, "The free blacks already in Iowa can remain, but they're not allowed to buy property."

Mr. Vashon said, "Senator Steven A. Douglass wants us on a boat to Africa! He backs Henry Clay's plan—even for the *Ebony* line of steamers to Liberia."

Suddenly, Rev. Loguen appeared with exciting news. *"A captured runaway slave was freed by force!"* he said with urgency.

I stood up for a better listen, Sam joined me, Mrs. Ward, too.

"Where did it happen, Jermain?" the lawyer asked.

"In Boston, George!"

"Who was it?" Rev. Ward queried.

"Shadrach Minkins, and I pray that he made it to Canada!"

"Was the Boston Vigilance Committee behind this?"

"Yes, they've been the fugitive's friend for ten years now."

*Shadrach Minkins*

"And now you're part of the Syracuse Vigilance Committee yourself, Jermain!" Rev. Ward said proudly.

"That I am," Rev Loguen replied, "and ready to resist the *Fugitive Slave Law*."

"You're not alone!" Mr. Vashon said forcefully.

Rev. Loguen continued, "It's not all good news, though. President Filmore ordered Federal troops to Boston to enforce the law, and the Boston Vigilance Committee is no match for the US Army—it looks bleak for fugitives."

As I followed the discussion, I recalled the former rallies held against the *Fugitive Slave Law*. Rev. May condemned it at the Congregational Church recently, encouraging defiance of the slave catchers, but nobody stuck their neck out further than the Rev. Jermain W. Loguen. Rev. Ward was a marked man, too—black men who spoke eloquently could make white men feel uncomfortable. Still, hatred of the *Fugitive Slave Law* caused Northerners to reconsider what *"All Men Are Created Equal"* really meant. Shadrach Minkins' ordeal vindicated Pa for inviting the police and local militias to join the Syracuse Vigilance Committee last year.

We left the men talking, and stopping home, Ma informed us that she heard about the story from Boston. She looked upset.

"Rev. Loguen told us all about it down at the Ward's, Ma."

"I wonder how long it will be before that happens here. And when it does, will we have courage equal to the crisis?" she asked.

"I guess we'll find out when it happens, Ma."

"I fear for your father. I know his determination, and he'll be in the midst of danger when it comes."

"But Pa's brave—he'll know what's best to do."

"It's a hard lesson, Edward, to learn to labor and to wait."

"To wait for what, Ma?"

"To wait for God's own good time, and to have faith in God, and in truth."

She's a deep thinker, my mother.

George Washington's birthday fell on a Saturday in 1851, perfect for a military parade. Two companies turned out, the Syracuse Citizens Corps, led by Capt. Minard, and the National Guards, a new company of Irishmen led by Capt. Prendergast. A bunch of us wanted to check it out, undeterred by lousy weather.

Sam knocked at my door; together, we picked up the Cheney's to walk downtown, finding the Willard's, Johnson's, and Charlie Pope down by the liberty pole. Before the parade began, the cold, gloom, and rain had us all rethinking outdoor fun.

"What time's this thing supposed to start again?" Parish asked.

"Yeah, anybody know what time it is?" Prentice inquired.

Charlie Pope said, "I wish they'd hurry-up and install the new town clock!"

"They approved $500 for it in the steeple of the 1st Presbyterian Church," Billy commented.

"Hey—there's the new Irish Company!" Prentice remarked.

"Nice uniforms!" Charlie Willard observed. "Now the Irish and the Germans both have their own militias and fire companies."

"Are the ones with Irishmen *and* Germans the *American* militias?" I asked.

"You think too much, Ed," Charlie answered.

"I'm thirsty," Flo declared.

"Me, too," Grove agreed.

"Here we go again!" Parish complained.

Looking skyward, Billy said, "Someday I'm 'gonna move where it don't rain so much."

"Me, too," Prentice agreed, "Three steamers just pulled in with more **Gold** from California!"

"Hey, Sam, you wanna go to California?" I asked.

"Been 'thinkin on it—I hear the sun shines out there, too," Sam replied.

"Hey look, the parade's starting!" Si Cheney proclaimed.

"They march pretty good—look at 'em all stepping in time," Billy said.

"It's good for the military to turn out for Washington's Birthday," Charlie Pope stated.

"That's not what they're saying in Boston, Charlie!" I jested.

The parade had barely started when the weather splintered us. Were we older, we might have followed to Scott's Hotel in the 1st Ward where Capt. Prendergast secured goodwill by supplying free food and drink. An auctioneer by day, it was easy to pick out his voice in a crowd.

By the end of February, Parish Johnson had accumulated a multitude of stories from the Police Office. He told Mr. Weld that he renamed his newspaper the *Watch House Chatter*.

"There's sure been a lot going on at the Police Office, Mr. Weld. I thought I should start grouping cases together to make it easier to report." Parish said.

"That sounds reasonable, let's hear it," Mr. Weld replied.

Parish rose, cleared his throat, and started to read. "Ah hrmm, *The Watch House Chatter*, by Parish B. Johnson. Headline: 'Dancing Vagrants and Poor Folk'—Parish B. Johnson, reporting.

"Another case of suffering came before Justice House when Hugh Riley asked the Judge to lodge his family in the County Pen. He claimed illness prevented him from working and they all were starving, but the Judge said he couldn't help him because no crime was committed. Then John Hardy, the apple peddler, died a vagrant, locked in the tombs. Grasshopper said they'd all miss him down at the bridge.

"Two more vagrants were picked-up by Officer Ormsby, who arrested Joseph S. Graham and Mary Snay after they loafed around the city for days. Half Joe's age, Mary was all dressed up like a man and making trouble. Standing before Justice House, Graham testified they were both professional dancers bound for National Theater, asserting,

*'That proves we'll have money soon!'* The judge wanted a demonstration, but when they refused he booked them both at the penitentiary; Joe for thirty days, Mary for ninety.

"In related arrests, Officer Lowell apprehended Samuel Forman, an Indian, for being drunk and disorderly, and Catherine Harvey, for selling liquor to an Indian. Justice House released them both; the Indian, once sober, and the girl, because she was only twelve."

Parish sat down, and I had to admit that he did a nice job. Mr. Weld said, "I wonder what the girl's father said about her selling liquor."

Parish answered, "She didn't have a father, Mr. Weld."

"That explains it," Weld confirmed.

Dreary weather had my mother in the dumps. We had a strange conversation sitting by the front window, watching it rain and blow. Pa was gone, as usual.

Ma said, "It's another dark, dreary day, Edward."

"You're right, Ma, do you think it'll ever end?"

"It rains, and rains—oh, how I wish it would stop!"

"And it's not easy getting around out there."

"The streets are great channels of liquid, brown mud—it's slow going for anyone trying to move about."

"A few days ago the sun was shining!"

"Edward, did you hear about the Temperance Meeting this week?" she asked.

"Not much—only that it was at City Hall and a lot of people went. And Pa was on another committee again."

"That's right. He's on the committee to pick delegates for the State Convention."

"Wasn't Pa's name in the paper for something else, too?"

"Yes, they said he's qualified for mayor, and I'm thankful he's not interested."

I could tell that Ma was troubled, and tried to distract her from worrying. "Ma, did you hear that Congress approved a bill to fund a Military Asylum for wounded and disabled soldiers? That's good, isn't it?"

"Yes, but please don't tell your father or he might form a committee and start planning a convention," she sighed.

# Chapter Nine
## (March 1851)

Election day dawned during the first week of March, 1851, drawing Syracusans to the polls. The *Friends of Temperance* had nominated Pa for mayor at Robinson's Temperance House, much to Ma's dismay. The Whig Party nominated Mr. Cheney for 4th Ward Supervisor, and Mr. Pope for Alderman. George Pfohl's pa was running for Inspector of Elections, and a German Ball was planned for election night at Graff's Hotel at the corner of Salina & Lock St.

Consistent with everything he'd said for the past two years, Major Moses D. Burnet declared that he had no interest in becoming mayor. He discouraged his nomination, insisting that if elected he would refuse to serve. No-one listened. The Democrats nominated him, and the voters chose him by a wide margin. Then he refused to serve, just like he said.

The Cheney's were distraught that their pa lost the race for County Supervisor by three votes. Prentice and Silas both took it hard.

"There's treachery involved, all right!" Prentice asserted at my house the next day. "Pa was sure to win—*everybody* likes him! Some of the Whigs betrayed him for the *Higher Law* candidate."

"That's right!" Si harmonized behind two red eyes. "The *Star* and the *Journal* both said it."

I tried to cheer them up, or at least to provide a distraction. "Charlie Pope's father won the seat for Alderman, though," I said, "and Mr. Pfohl won his race, too."

"Good for them!" Prentice retorted bitterly.

"Yeah, good for them!" Si echoed. They both looked about to cry.

"Hey, did you guys hear what happened at Graff's last night?" I asked.

"Who cares?" Prentice replied.

"Well, Parish Johnson would. It's a great story for the *Watch House Chatter*. C'mon, let's go find him! I bet Sam will go with us and we'll probably run into some of the other guys."

The Cheney's looked undecisive but I didn't relent. *"Well, that's what I'm gonna do. C'mon, let's go downtown!"* The brothers followed in silence, we found Sam anxious to join us. This time we didn't have to wait for him to finish his chores.

Heading west on Genesee St., Sam said, "Everyone's excited about the Anti-Slavery convention that's starting today! The Englishman George Thompson will speak, and Frederick Douglass, too. My pa would've spoke, but he's out of town."

"My folks are excited, too, Sam," I replied. "I probably won't see my pa 'till it's over."

"Who cares?" Prentice growled again, still bewildered by three votes.

Approaching the corner of Orange St., the butcher Davis's voice announced his presence before we could see him. He saw me first and started right in.

"Ah, it's young Wheaton and the abolitionists," Cale Davis boomed. Looking right at me he asked and answered his own question. "Did the *Friends of Temperance* candidate for mayor win the election? *No, of course not!* Ha ha ha!"

I wanted to say something but wasn't sure what. Davis turned his attention to the Cheney's.

"I voted Cheney for supervisor, and was sorry of the result," he declared, then pointing at Sam he bellowed, *"It's all his fault!"*

Sam looked down and didn't reply. I couldn't keep quiet.

*"What?* How's it Sam's fault? He's too young, and black people can't vote anyway!"

Davis responded in typical fashion, answering a question with a question.

"Who's agitating for dis-union and spoiling the elections? The damned abolitionists! The city's full of 'em now for their blasted convention. If you see the Rev. May, tell him I said they can take their whining somewhere across the Atlantic. Maybe a boiler will blow, who can say?"

Prentice avowed, "We don't want your vote, Davis!"

"No? then your pa would've lost by 4 votes instead of only 3. Now run along and remind him that his bill is due."

I nudged Prentice discreetly to continue our journey. His strong desire to throttle the butcher eased, but it took him a few blocks to unclench his teeth. Sam looked sorrowful from Davis's rant.

"Don't worry, Sam—our pa's not blaming you," Si Cheney said.

"That's right, Sam, don't be sad—we all know Davis is a blowhard!" I offered.

"Yeah, his son, too!" Prentice joined. "I should've said something about him being arrested."

"It wouldn't matter, Prentice—Davis has an answer for everything," I replied.

Downtown Syracuse filled in anticipation of the Anti-Slavery Convention at City Hall. We encountered the Willard brothers at the Liberty Pole, who joined our search for Parish and information. From a distance we saw Alex & Charlie McKinstry at the Johnson's door on Church St., with Parish and Grove both coming out.

I called, *"Hey there!"* and they all hollered back when they saw us. We halted our approach, thinking Parish would direct us back to the Police Office, not far behind.

"What brings you guys here?" Parish asked good naturedly.

"You!" I answered. "We thought you'd know about the election night arrests."

"And I do! *What-cha wanna know?*"

"Just the short version—what happened?"

"Well, it was 'kinda like what happened on New Year's in 1844. There was a German Ball at Graff's and around thirty uninvited Irishmen showed up. The rowdies forced their way inside, but the Germans stopped 'em before they got into the ballroom. So they started fights in the dining room and the barroom, and they knocked over a whole bunch of tables & chairs. After the Germans finally evicted them, they threw rocks and broke a lot of glass! A bunch of people got hurt, and one guy pretty bad. I heard that a couple pistol shots went through a window, but nobody got hit."

"You're right, it sounds just like 1844 except there wasn't a talking parrot, and they didn't call out the militia," I said.

"Hey, there's George Pfohl down the street—let's ask him if his pa was involved," Billy Willard proposed.

Prentice agreed, "Yeah, his German militia would know how to handle rowdy Irishmen."

George Pfohl lived on Salina Street, not far from the Johnson's just over the Oswego Canal. Crossing the bridge always gave me a feeling of entering Bavaria; German culture pervaded the north side of Syracuse with many ethnic taverns and inns drawing a loyal patronage. Active in society, German immigrants provided Syracuse with many firemen, craftsmen, businessmen, and two uniformed militias, complete with Samsel's brass band.

*Jacob Pfohl*

A few years ago, George's younger sister, Mary, died, aged three. Last year, his other sister, Maria, also succumbed at three, along with his mother, Anna, who was only thirty-one! That left Jacob Pfohl a widower at thirty-three with two boys aged eleven and four.

George looked uneasy from seeing all of us coming at him at once. "What did I do now?" he asked with a nervous smile.

"No worries, George. We just want to know if your pa cracked any heads at Graff's Hotel," Parish replied.

"No he didn't, Pa was home with us the whole time. Good thing, too—candidates shouldn't be out brawling on election night."

"Yeah, and we heard that he won, too. Now that he's the *Inspector of Elections*, you think that he'll make any rules about parties on election night?"

"I doubt it. Pa wished our brewery didn't burn down—we lost a lot of election business."

"I heard they celebrated the brewery fire at the Temperance House," Billy remarked, quickly adding, "But they were all glad that nobody got hurt."

Parish said, "Look at all the people coming downtown! C'mon guys, let' see what's happening at the Anti-Slavery Convention!" We all agreed and quickly traversed the few blocks to City Hall where people were trying hard to get inside.

Alex said, *"Hey Ed, there's your parents! They're walking in now with Rev. May and the Englishman."*

Sure enough, it was them, but the doorman had started to turn people away. As disappointed adults departed, boys with marbles filled their places on the dry spots outside, while others commenced a hotly contested game of two-old-cat. Pleasant hours passed, I think we enjoyed the convention more than the conventioneers who packed City Hall for two whole days. I couldn't wait to hear Ma's assessment—she'd said how much she wanted to hear the British orator and statesman, George Thompson.

"*Oh, You should have heard him!*" Ma said to me, Cornelia, and Black George after the convention had ended. "I think he is without exception the most fascinating public speaker I have ever listened to."

"Really, Ma? That's saying a lot, coming from you," Cornelia remarked.

"Do you think he changed any minds about slavery, Ma?" I asked.

*George Thompson*

"It would seem so, Edward. The people listened intently, and surely, no one who heard him could afterwards ill-treat, or abuse him."

"No one, Ma?"

"Well, perhaps the witty editors of the political papers. Their business is to abuse all who don't serve their purposes. They don't hear him themselves but slander him entirely upon the reports of others."

"I heard they picked Mr. Wheaton for vice president of the Convention," Black George said.

"That's right, George," Ma answered with a sigh. "Gerrit Smith was chosen President, and Rev. May and Dr. Clary were on the business committee with Frederick Douglass."

"Tell us about it!" Cornelia urged.

"Well, it started with Rev. Miner offering a prayer, then we were informed that William Lloyd Garrison was too ill to attend. Frederick Douglass spoke briefly, and suggested that as George Thompson came here from England, we should send Gerrit Smith to speak over there! Mr. Thompson then entered the hall to thunderous applause. Gerrit Smith announced his arrival, but he had Rev. May introduce him."

"What he say, Ma?" I asked.

"I can't tell you everything, but at the beginning he said that the slaveholding tyrants hunt him down because he advocates for freedom. He declared that he's testing his right to speak in the land of liberty."

"What do you mean?"

"He told us what happened to him in Boston at Faneuil Hall when 3,500 people showed up for a peaceable meeting, but a couple of hundred rowdies broke it up. He said the police stood by indifferent because the mayor ordered them not to interfere unless life or property were in danger."

"That's right, Ma, I remember reading about that when it happened."

"Thompson said we should look at how Northerners are treated in the South. He said, 'Once, it were enough for a Roman to say, "I am a Roman citizen."' Then he dared us to try it, and see if being Americans would save us from tar and feathers, or the whip and branding iron if we dared utter a word against slavery."

"Who else spoke, Ma?" Cornelia asked.

"Mr. Burleigh gave a fine speech against the *Fugitive Slave Law*, and Frederick Douglass spoke of the oppression of slave power, and about the collision that he saw approaching. Stephen Foster, Abby Kelley Foster, and Rev. May spoke, too."

"What about the second day? I heard there was some excitement!"

"Mr. Thompson discussed Henry Clay's Colonization scheme in detail, and he had everyone laughing! Then Rev. May stood to present five fugitives, just arrived from the South, and he said, *Men, matrons, and maidens of Syracuse! You see these victims of tyranny before you, and one of them a woman. Say, now, shall these fugitives be taken from Syracuse?*

"And Everyone answered ***No!***

"Then he asked, *Citizens of Syracuse, will you defend with your lives, if need be, these defenseless and hunted children of God?*

"And everyone answered ***Yes!***

"Then he asked if anybody would furnish them with employment, and in fifteen minutes, they were all comfortably provided for, even though it's a penal offence for any man to harbor a fugitive."

"What about Pa? You haven't said anything about him yet," Cornelia protested.

"Your pa was called upon to sing a few songs of freedom."

"Oh, I wish I was there," Cornelia lamented, she sang with Pa at the Musical Institute. I could never get up in front of a crowd and sing, even with Pa's voice. At convention's end, many resolutions were passed, some more irksome than others. The abolitionists struck all the nerves that they could.

The following week the Common Council met for a changing of the guard. Mayor Hovey was thanked for his faithful service along with departing Aldermen, as new members were sworn in. They postponed what to do about the vacancy for mayor.

The *Syracuse Star* criticized the Anti-Slavery Convention, it's resolutions, and especially, George Thompson. They wanted the pompous Brit to take his agitations down South where it was more needed. To their credit, the paper printed Rev. May's rebuttal, including his assertion that the *Star* must wish Thompson dead. May claimed that Southerners only allowed free speech if they agreed with it, and he honestly believed that Thompson would be lynched.

In the middle of March, Billy Willard revived his popularity at Weld's School with his reports on mysteries from the great beyond, including anything strange or unusual.

"Excuse me, sir, I have a story about a great discovery in Texas!" Billy implored.

"What has you so excited, William?" Mr. Weld asked.

"Mr. Weld, they caught *The Wild Woman of Navidad!*"

"The *who?*"

"*The Wild Woman of Navidad*, sir," Billy repeated. "For fifteen years she's lived in the wild, wandering around the settlements. Sometimes she stole food when she couldn't find acorns, or other nuts and such."

A voice rang out, "You're the nut, Willard!"

Another asked, "Who was she?"

"Nobody knows," Billy answered. "A party of hunters came upon her camp and captured her. She doesn't speak English, but can talk to the Africans on the plantations. For years, her wild looks and strange manner threw a scare into all the white folks around there, and more than a few slaves."

"Hey Billy, you think the spirits rap on tables down where *the Wild Woman* was caught?"

"I don't know, but Mrs. Tamlin from Auburn is here for a few weeks to make spiritual communications. She said that if she does well in the 1st Ward she'll take rooms closer to downtown."

**St. Patrick's Day, 1851,** was like no other in Syracuse. The city now boasted a brand new, *All-Irish* militia named the Syracuse National Guards. Capt. Prendergast led them on parade with their attractive uniforms presenting a striking contrast against the dismal weather. After marching through the city, the troop landed at *Scott's Hotel* in the 1st Ward for the first stop on a 3-hotel itinerary. Food, drink, and entertainment at *Scott's* was generously provided by Capt. Minard of the Syracuse Citizen's Corps to welcome a brother militia. After a sumptuous feast, the Guards departed, stopping shortly at the *Syracuse House* to again partake in refreshments, then traversed one block to the *Globe* for an evening banquet. The day transpired to become a testimony of Irish pride and perseverance well into the evening hours. The men toasted like it was the 4th of July.

The following day, I broached the Irish holiday with my mother, who reminded me that Pa was nominated for mayor by the *Friends of Temperance*. Earlier that week the *"dries"* filled Market Hall with calls for legislation to prohibit the sale of alcohol in New York State. As I pondered her words, horrific news came through the front door. A distraught Cornelia announced that Mrs. Dickinson had died unexpectedly.

Ma and Ellen rushed to embrace her, Cornelia trembled with sorrow for Harriette and Sarah. Everyone loved Mrs. Dickinson. Ma said, *"Dear Lord! She was such a beautiful person. My heart breaks for Pliny and the girls!"*

Two days later we all attended a solemn funeral at the Dickinson home on Mechanic St., and Mrs. D. was quietly buried at Oakwood Cemetery. That was another time when the benefit of *just being there* was felt. Teary-eyed friends proffered support in silence.

I recalled reading about how sad and mournful a funeral train moves along, but now I better understood. It reminded me that we're all mortal, someday to breathe our last. Most people never pay any mind to the thought, nor show concern when a funeral procession passes by, thinking little of the mourners and their sorrows. Today friends are buried, tomorrow we're left with their memory. Not long after the funeral I learned that Harriette was moving away to complete her education.

Suspicious fires continued to ignite in the neighboring city of Utica, just east of Syracuse. Will Stoddard kept our class informed of how the police and citizen groups were determined to apprehend the arsonists.

"Mr. Weld, people are starting to feel like Utica is doomed from all the fires! A couple of guys were arrested, but they weren't the arsonists." Will announced.

"What happened, Will?" Mr. Weld asked.

"Two men were picked up walking away from the back of a building near where a fire broke out, sir, but it was only two Dutchmen. They said their only interest in *sparking* was for the girls who lived there, and the police let 'em go."

"I see," Weld replied, grateful that Will's report didn't stray further.

During recess, Will lit a fire under me about all the money he was making. It wasn't like striking gold in the mines, but Will explained how he turned a steady profit selling chickens. He'd buy birds in the rural districts at no more than 20 cents each, sometimes as low as 10, then sell them in town for 25 cents or more. He said it was all a matter of how many you could carry.

I couldn't wait to tell Sam when I got home, hurrying him to a proposed location for a chicken coop. I quickly relayed my scheme.

"Sam, the best part was how he convinced his pa to lend him money for everything he needed to start his business!" I said excitedly.

Sam appeared doubtful. "How'd he do that?" he asked, "I never heard of anybody gettin' a loan from their pa," Sam retorted, narrowing his eyes with skepticism.

"Will said he'd seen enough business at the store to know what his pa would ask him for. *Sam, Will made a plan and he wrote it all down on paper!* He made a list of everything he needed, what it cost, and then he showed his pa how he long he figured it'd take to pay him back. I think he called it a *schedule of profits. Ha!* That's a mouthful just 'sayin it! I can't wait to see my pa's face when I show 'im a schedule of profits—ha ha ha."

"Could you help me with mine, Edward? I never made one before."

"Sure, Sam—it's the first time for me, too. We can get Will to look it over before we show our fathers."

After a few rounds of scribbles and cross-outs, Will made a couple corrections, and soon we stood before Rev. Ward, business plans in hand, ready to present. I thought that writing our plan was painful, but learned that trying to sell it was worse. Rev. Ward sat at their dining room table, Sam and I trembled before him. If we managed to convince Rev. Ward, we'd go down to the hardware store to get Pa's approval.

"I understand that you two have a business proposition for me, are you partners?" Rev. Ward asked with a smile.

We both nodded and said *"Yes, sir!"* in unison. I threw in, *"And we split everything right down the middle!"*

"Then I'm ready to hear your proposal, boys, what do you have for me?"

"Well, sir, you know that me and Ed been 'thinkin 'bout 'gettin into the chicken business, and we figured it be good to write it all down," Sam replied.

"I see," Rev. Ward answered.

Unsure of what to say next, Sam looked over at me. The silence was deafening, I had to speak.

"That's right, Rev. Ward, we had Will Stoddard help us, too, sir. He showed his pa how he could make money in the chicken business, and his pa gave him a loan!"

*Will Stoddard*

"A loan? I'm intrigued! Now, what are you two holding onto? Come closer, and walk me through your plan—I promise to be as reasonable as Mr. Stoddard was," Rev. Ward said.

We followed the Stoddard business model and pretty much copied Will's plan intact, no need to reinvent the wheel. We both liked the written version better than trying to remember how Will explained it.

"You see, sir, right over here is all the things we need to build a coop and everything for feedin' and tendin' the birds," Sam advised.

"And, Rev. Ward, we wrote down how much we figured everything would cost, too," I offered. "If we get your approval we're going to talk to my pa about the supplies and all the stuff we need."

"That's good, boys, what's next?"

We stayed on Will's script, following the plan on the table.

I offered, "Yes, sir, and next we wrote down all of the places we can sell chickens and eggs to."

"And Will said he could always find more!" Sam added.

"Then we wrote how much we'd sell things for and how much we'd clear, sir," I declared.

"Right! And we even guessed how soon we could pay you back, Pa," Sam imparted.

"Yes, sir, and Will said this was Mr. Stoddard's favorite part!"

Sam and I exchanged nervous glances not knowing what to expect. His pa remained seated examining our plan, nodding his head, and murmuring to himself. I thought I heard a positive sounding *mm-hmm*. Finally, he looked up to address us.

"Well, gentlemen, I must congratulate you, and especially your friend Will Stoddard. His willingness to help his competitors validates a vibrant chicken market."

I mostly followed his answer, but wasn't sure we'd secured the 1st half of our loan until he signed his name at the bottom and reached into his pockets.

"I wish you success in your new endeavor," Rev. Ward said. "And tell Mr. Wheaton that you have my support!"

Next bound for the hardware store, we stopped to tell Ma and she directed us to the livery; Black George might not have left for downtown yet. Things transpired as she suggested, and on the ride into town Black George enjoyed hearing Sam's recollections of our *business meetin'* with his pa.

"That be good, you writin' it all down, shows you been thinkin' on it," Black George said. "And don't worry none 'bout Mr. Wheaton—he's 'sho to like it, jus' like Rev. Ward."

Black George was right. Our 2nd presentation went easier from having experience. We weren't standing before Pa for long, both of us smiled when we departed with his signature and some coin of the realm. He even gave us a rate for materials—our prospects were looking up.

A few days later, Sam and I were in front of my house unloading building materials from the Wheaton Hardware wagon. We hauled everything through the backyard and staged it for an early start in the morning, both itching to cut boards and pound nails. During the night, mother nature reminded us that March isn't a great month for outdoor projects in Syracuse. My heart sank to discover that a heavy snowfall had buried our supplies.

Black George reminded me that the snow melted quick this time of year, but what I remember the most about our construction job was freezing my tail feathers, and how numb my hands and feet were. *But we got it done!* It wasn't the greatest looking, but there weren't any gaps for the birds to escape. The next day the sun came out so we hit the countryside with tips on where to find birds on the cheap.

# Chapter Ten
## (March – April 1851)

We were eager to show Black George our chickens, but he showed more interest in our carpentry skills than the birds. He inspected the coop thoroughly, poking and prodding at everything, then he went inside and did likewise. Surprisingly, he mostly liked it.

He said, "It's good you gots da floor so's they can scratch and dig, but you gots ta keep it clean." Then he laughed when he told us, *"You gots ta keep da poop 'out de coop! Ha ha ha!"*

We must've both looked surprised, somehow we left chicken poop out of our plan. Black George continued.

"But ya done right 'makin the doors open in, 'an keepin' the air movin' so's they can breathe."

"Thanks, George," I answered. "Do you have any other tips for us?"

"'Make sho you counts 'em every night, an' keep the dogs away—don't trust 'em just because theys someone's pet."

Sam said, "That's a good one, George—I've seen dogs go crazy around chickens!"

"Yeah, thanks again, George," I agreed. "And we found the farmers, too, just like you said."

Sam said excitedly, "Hey, Ed—we gotta show my pa! Let's go have 'im come see it!"

"Okay, Sam, we can show 'im how we been followin' our plan," I answered.

"Tell your pa where you got dem birds, and what you paid for 'em," Black George advised.

"We will, George!" I yelled back as we headed over to Sam's place.

Noisily bounding through the Ward's back door, we encountered Rev. Lyles deep in discussion with a concerned looking Rev. Ward.

"That's right, Sam," Rev. Lyles was saying, "Judge Kane in Philadelphia remanded the fugitives to their master, and he had sixty officers accompany them to prevent a rescue."

"It's tragic to see our government in league with the slave holders, John. I'm against sending people back to Africa, but is it wise to remain in this country?"

"The New York Colonization Society just sent two families to Liberia, and they expect a hundred more in September!"

"I believe it. Have you heard that Chaplin didn't appear for his trial in Maryland?"

"Yes, and he forfeited his bail—all $19,000!"

"I heard the government decided to drop all the charges against Gov. Quitman and his co-defendants for the expedition to Cuba!"

"That's bad, Sam," Rev. Lyles responded. Motioning our way, he said, "But there's a couple of boys here who look like they have something to say."

"We do, Rev. Lyles," Sam answered. "Me and Ed want Pa to see the chickens in our coop!"

"That's right, sir, and George told us where to get 'em," I added.

"George said that he liked how we built our chicken coop, Pa—can you come see it?"

"That I can, son," Rev. Ward replied.

"Can I come, too?" Rev. Lyles asked.

"Yes sir, Rev. Lyles!" Sam answered with enthusiasm.

A sudden thought occurred to me. "Rev. Ward, if you like, could you please bless our chicken coop? We want to have the Lord on *our* side."

"I think you mean that you want to be on the *Lord's* side," Rev. Ward corrected.

"Yeah, that too, sir."

"Then let's go see it," the big preacher said. Sam and I jumped to lead the way, the elders followed. On location they appraised our coop much like Black George did, showing more interest in construction than the birds.

Rev. Lyles said, "You boys need to keep the birds warm so they keep laying eggs. Walls need insulation, crumple up some newspapers."

"That's what the Canal Loafers do to keep warm," I said.

"And you need to get the food and water off the ground so they're not scratching it all over the place," Rev. Ward directed.

"And keep the feed and water fresh!" Rev. Lyles added.

Sam asked, "What about the chickens, Pa? Do you like 'em?"

Recalling advice from Black George, I said, "We got 'em for twelve cents each just a couple miles from here, Rev. Ward, heading toward Fayetteville. We figure to make a dime a bird, not counting the eggs."

"They're beautiful, Sam! Well done, boys. I commend you for your efforts," Rev. Ward said smiling.

"Yes, and Edward's right that we offer a prayer," Rev. Lyles suggested.

"I agree, John," Rev. Ward said. "Let us bow our heads to thank the Lord for His many blessings. We thank you Lord, for bringing us together here today, for our families and friends who strengthen us, and for your ultimate blessing in our Savior. We ask you, Lord, to bless these boys as they embark in business, and that their chicken coop become a monument to honesty and integrity. We ask this in Jesus' holy name, Amen."

"*Amen,*" we echoed.

As March neared its end, the New York State Government made two big announcements: First, the canals were to re-open on April

15, and second, that ex-Governor Hamilton Fish would become the next US Senator, replacing Daniel S. Dickinson. Around Central New York, the talk was more about the Common Council appointing my uncle, Horace Wheaton, as the next Mayor of Syracuse. Uncle H. was the chosen substitute for Major Burnet, who declined to serve though elected. For my family, the event of most importance was the upcoming concert for the Syracuse Musical Institute. Cornelia and Pa both sang, and Pa was the president.

> **DAILY STANDARD.**
>
> TUESDAY MORNING, MARCH 25.
>
> OFFICIAL PAPER OF THE CITY.
>
> Appointment of Mayor.
>
> Hon. HORACE WHEATON was appointed to the office of Mayor in place of Major Burnet, who neglected to qualify. Upon the result being declared he was conducted to the chair, and delivered a brief and appropriate address.

One night at dinner, I had to ask Ma what she thought about Uncle Horace becoming mayor. Pa was at rehearsal with Cornelia, so I felt emboldened.

"Ma, everybody's talking about the Common Council appointing Uncle Horace as mayor! What you think about it? Neither you nor Pa has said a word."

Everyone at table awaited her response, the kitchen maid craned her neck from the next room.

"Well, we were just as surprised as everyone else in town," Ma began. "but no-one more than your uncle."

"Miles Bennett's pa voted for Uncle Horace at the Council meeting, and he told Miles about how shocked Uncle looked when they told him he was the new mayor," I replied.

"Your uncle informed the Council that he received his appointment from them, and to them he felt responsible, but all the previous mayors received their appointment from a *Higher Power*, the people. Horace said that like everyone else he regretted Major Burnet's decision not to serve."

"But now that Uncle Horace is the mayor, will we get any stuff for free?" I joked.

Ma didn't see the humor. *"Certainly not!* Where do you get such ideas? Did Parish hear something at the Police Office?"

"No, Ma, but I've seen how VIPs get treated at the hotels."

"Ah, now it's becoming clear—you want Philo Rust to throw a banquet for the new mayor!" she said with a ring of certainty.

"Hey, that's a great idea, Ma. And speaking of Parish, he said that he wants to ask Uncle Horace about the Police Office being investigated. Justice House was accused of giving keys to people who shouldn't have 'em, and for outsiders doing police work. Somebody even complained about Parish running errands for them."

*Horace Wheaton*

"Did he get into trouble at home for that?"

"No, because it was his pa's idea for him to be useful at the police office. He said his pa shrugged his shoulders and declared that *no good deed goes unpunished.*"

Two nights later, the Syracuse Musical Institute performed at City Hall. Pa sure could sing, so could Cornelia. I enjoyed the show, but would rather have been dancing with Mira at the Cotillion Party happening at Shamrock Hall. Charlie Pope saw her the other day when a span of runaway horses crashed a lumber wagon into the Grey Hound Tavern and a little girl was almost killed. Mira was amongst the crowd who ran to the girl's aid. Charlie said Mira told him that she was going out dancing again.

"And she asked about you, Wheaton!" Charlie gushed. "She wanted me to say hey to you for her, and she asked if you'd be at the Shamrock tonight."

"And what did you say?" I asked nervously.

"I said that I'd tell you, but gave her the bad news about your pa leading the Musical Institute at City Hall."

"And then?"

With a mischievous smile, Charlie said, "She looked kind-a sad, so I said, Cheer up, Mira—I'll be glad to fill in for Ed while he's at the concert!"

"And then?"

"Then she smiled and said, Oh, thank you, Charlie—I'll see you there!"

During the concert, I pondered Charlie's last words with my stomach twisted into knots. On the drive home, Ma gave us her assessment of the night's performance.

"The show was well-attended, and I thought the music was very good," she began. "However, I don't think that Syracuse audiences appreciate the loftier styles of choruses that were sung tonight. I think they more prefer songs and ballads."

"And dancing, too, Ma—some people are more into that," I mumbled.

"Meaning what, Edward?"

"Oh, nothing. You know I can't sing, is all."

"And yet, I perceive the wheels turning in your head. I wonder what's coming out of your mouth next."

Ma was right, but I had sense to keep it shut, especially with Pa giving me the hairy eyeball.

※

On Saturday after the concert, the Wilkinson's threw a party at their palatial home on James Street. It seemed like everyone in town knew them, and where they lived. Theodosia Wilkinson was my age, and being a friend of Cornelia's we gladly accepted her invitation. Mr. John

*John Wilkinson*

Wilkinson was President of the Syracuse and Utica Railroad, credited with giving Syracuse its name when the city was still a village, and he its first postmaster. Mr. Wilkinson was a convert to opposing slavery, but now he freely gave railroad passes to fugitives, earning him favor amongst my clan of Wheaton's, Birdseye's, Marsh's, and all.

Fresh from her recent singing engagement with Pa and the Musical Institute, several voices called for Cornelia to favor the party with song. Like Pa, she wasn't shy about singing, and with a little encouragement she soon began. Happy voices joined the chorus while I smiled and hummed along. I remember getting along great with my sister all night long, almost like we were friends! But for the lateness of the hour, we tore ourselves away, the merriment still going strong.

Arriving home, Ma's stern look contrasted our joyful spirits. She expected her 10th child in June, which didn't help our cause. I wrongly assumed that Cornelia had secured a late curfew for us.

"Do you know what time it is, young lady?" Ma demanded.

"Yes, Ma, I'm sorry, I know it's late," Cornelia replied.

"Yes, indeed, I've been sitting here wondering where you were!"

I couldn't keep my mouth shut. "Cornelia was safe, Ma, I was with her."

"And who do you think you are, then?" she challenged.

"I've been fourteen for a couple months now, Ma, I could protect her."

"And who's protecting you?"

"Huh?"

"Go to bed, Edward," she said.

"Can I get something to eat first? I'm starving!"

"Didn't the Wilkinson's feed you?"

"Yes, they did, Ma," Cornelia answered, *"and Edward ate like a horse!"*

*"What?* And I almost thought we were friends—*Ha!"*

"Make it quick, mister," Ma conceded.

I began to graze, listening to her tell Cornelia about writing in her diary while she waited for us. She wondered if her diary was of any use, but said that it made her heart feel lighter. Cornelia wanted Ma to keep writing, and so did I. Writing lifted her spirits.

The next morning our mother said that she slept poorly, but a cold bath had refreshed her.

"Ma, I'll never understand how you and Grandpa like taking cold baths. Someday, you'll ask Black George to fill the tub with ice," I remarked.

For once, all of my siblings agreed, even the baby it seemed. Ma had none of it.

"You children mind your own business and start getting ready for church. It *is* Sunday, just in case you forgot!"

Ma had planned to attend several services, but after the first one ended she wanted to go home to rest. Lucky for me, I was allowed to accompany her provided that I watched little Henry. The quiet of our home felt surreal with just the three of us there. Black George and the kitchen maid were gone, too.

As Henry amused himself, I grabbed a newspaper off the sofa where Ma sat comfortably.

"Anything good in the paper?" I asked.

"Oh, yes! I've read many good reports about the preparations being made for *World's Fair* in London. Don't you think it will be great, Edward?"

"Sure, Ma, but probably not as great as you do."

"Why not? Just think of the swarms of different people from all over the world. Think of the contrasts! A polished Frenchman beside a calculating Yankee, a turbaned Turk next to a stolid German, the lowborn thrown together with the wealthy!"

"Yeah, I suppose that'll be something, but isn't that kind of what's happening now in California, Ma? Everybody in the world wants some of the *gold* out there."

"We're not talking about gold, Edward, this is the *Crystal Palace*, filled with wonders from around the world. It'll be like seeing the fairy creations of Aladdin's magic lamp!"

"Wow! I hope they hired enough policemen like they did for the State Fair."

"I'm sure they have, Edward—law and order will reign and the great public protected."

"What do you think will come from the *Great Exhibition*, Ma?"

"I believe it can provide a world-wide benefit. Having so much diversity of nation and language together in one place will impart a general intelligence to everyone—it can soften habits and manners more than the natural progress of civilization would do in many years."

"I don't quite follow you, Ma."

"The natural bonds of brotherhood will be strengthened by all this intermingling, and men will go away surprised at finding so much that is admirable, and wonderful, in men of other climes and colors. People once regarded as barbarians will be found praiseworthy!"

"That's a mouthful, and with you saying it, it must be true."

With feeling she said, "I pray that Heaven will grant smiling skies and favoring gales to those who venture to visit the *World's Fair*. And that no disastrous accident or fearful shipwreck will be associated with it—the *Great Exhibition of 1851!*"

With Henry cooperating and the others still in church, Ma and I were able to pray together in peace. Besides the *World's Fair*, we prayed for health, family, and prosperity. Then I remembered what Will Stoddard told me, and we prayed for the fires to end in Utica—the last one left the community in despair.

"Should we pray for the Utica Vigilance Committee to catch 'em, Ma?"

"I want the fires to end, Edward, but remember that the arsonist will be hung. For what are you praying?" she asked.

I answered truthfully, but it didn't feel right, especially not on Sunday.

"Hmm, both, I guess."

"Vengeance is mine, sayeth the Lord," she retorted.

"You're right, Ma, I've heard all the Reverends say that you'll get into trouble whenever you try to play God. But the law says that if you start a fire on purpose, and you don't care what happens, then you don't deserve to live."

"That's true, the law was written to deter crime. But praying for a person's demise is something else. Don't become obsessed with vengeance, Edward!"

While I pondered her words, a knock at our door broke the silence. It was a poor woman that I didn't know, asking for help. My Mother overheard and immediately came to the door, motioning her inside.

"Oh, you poor dear!" Ma said to her. Marks of want and sorrow were evident on the stranger's face. She told us that she had six children at home and neither herself nor her husband could find any work.

"Come sit by the fire, dear," Ma said. "Edward, please fix a plate of something good and bring it here—and look out for your brother!"

After I supplied refreshment, Ma told our visitor that she'd be happy to give her some work, and soon returned with a stack of clothes that needed mending—an endless task in our house. Ma looked revitalized herself. Our large family didn't leave her with much opportunity to help other people, but when she did it made her feel good, much like writing in her diary did. I went upstairs to read Henry a book, and he surprised me by falling asleep. With commendations from Ma and the lady, I slipped out back to count chickens in the cool sunshine.

Without a joke, April brought tidings of great fortune to our friends, the Cook's. Down at the Coffee House, old Mr. Welch announced that he was moving on, selling his interest to Mr. John L. Cook and Mr. Emilus Gay. Ma couldn't wait to congratulate Mrs. Cook, and asked me to accompany her.

"Edward, I'm going to Welch's, would you mind coming along to provide protection? I think you're old enough now," she teased.

"Sure, Ma, I'm ready when you are!"

Courtesy of Black George, we soon sped off in our buggy, passing a quiet butcher's at Orange. Celebratory sounds from inside of Welch's

Coffee House trumpeted welcome as we approached. Austin Cook waved from the front door.

"Hello Mrs. Wheaton—Hey, Ed!" he greeted, smiling ear to ear. "My ma just told me to keep an eye out for you. How'd she know you were coming, ma'am?"

"That's what friends are for Austin!" she replied.

"She's right," I said, shaking Austin's right hand while he held the door open with his other. Welch's was filled to capacity with well-wishers, the atmosphere felt charged. John Jr. beamed while the crowd pressed to touch Messrs. Cook & Gay. Abel Cook joined us, and together we protected Ma all the way to the Ladies' Tea Room. Austin advised that John Jr. was already getting crazy ideas.

"Wait and see, Ed—John's gonna do something that's never been done here before!"

"Oh yeah? Like what?"

"I have no idea—and neither does he!" Austin said while Abel nodded affirmation.

Shocking news eclipsed the happy start to April. **Philo Rust was dead!** I couldn't believe it. *Could Philo really be dead? He wasn't even sick!* His tall, manly frame looked strong as ever.

Hot off the wire at their Salina St. office, New York State Telegraph operator, E.D. Benedict, became the first person in Syracuse to learn of Philo's demise. Word traveled fast through the city, the story urgently repeated. Philo's death was one of those rare events when everyone remembers where they were when they found out, making it personal. Still, I won't forget that Friday afternoon when Pa came home and announced that Philo Rust had died.

"What happened, Charles?" Ma entreated.

'The telegraph dispatch said that Philo was staying at the Astor House in New York, Ellen. His wife left him in fine spirits getting into a carriage for a short drive to consult his physician, and when the driver opened the door he found Philo having a fit of some kind. He was carried inside and left with the doctor, but he expired before the driver could return with Mrs. Rust."

I stood in shock, *"this can't be real,"* I kept saying to myself.

Ma responded, "What a surprise—I had no idea he was ailing. What happens now?"

"All I know is that his remains will return on tomorrow's train, and that the funeral will likely be on Sunday," Pa replied.

In the morning, the Cheney brothers were anxious to walk downtown with me—we all wanted to hear what people were saying about Philo. Passing Orange St., we heard Cale Davis lament that the city had just lost its foremost citizen. Stopping at Welch's Coffee House, we found the Cook boys hard at work with the entire staff. There wasn't an empty seat in the house from all the mourners waiting to receive Philo's remains at the train depot across the street. Abel Cook told us that he thought this was one of their busiest days ever.

A subdued crowd received the remains of Philo Rust at the Syracuse Station, smartly dressed attendants placed the casket into the dark hearse of an undertaker. A makeshift procession formed to accompany Philo's remains back to his famous hotel. We took our places in line, nobody said anything. Arriving at Rust's Hotel, a murmur of voices soon overcame the pervading quiet. Everyone spoke of Philo. Most were complimentary, but a darker side was revealed as well. I recall Captain Larned telling Grasshopper about being with Philo on the night of the great powder explosion in 1841, and what a help that Philo was.

Overheard voices informed us that all the Syracuse Fire Companies were turning out in dress uniform for tomorrow's funeral, as were other civic groups. I suggested that we form a contingent to join the procession carrying Philo to his final resting place. Why not? We could jump in at the end, one and all.

"I'll start getting the word out, Ed," Prentice said. "I bet that everyone shows up!"

"I will, too, Prentice—everybody that I know liked Philo, except at home," I replied.

Sunday morning felt like it never would end. After an early morning service, Ma ran a Bible study at home, then she had us all sing! Sour faces showed dismay at my continued ruining of harmonies. I thought of Harriette's dog, ne'er to be seen again. After an eternity passed, Ma released me to join the Cheney's for our familiar trek downtown. Like most establishments, the Davis Butcher Shop was closed, not much was open that day—least of all during Philo's funeral.

Approaching downtown our progress slowed as the crowd size grew. At Clinton Square, people stood elbow to elbow as far as you could see in every direction. We stopped outside the closed Wheaton Hardware store, looking across the Salina St. bridge at all the people standing outside of Rust's Hotel jostling for position.

Si Cheney said, "They'll have to rename the place now, I suppose."

"It's just the Empire Block again—can't be Rust's Hotel without Philo," I declared.

Prentice avowed, "This had to be the biggest funeral that there ever was around here! There's no way we'll get inside for the service."

"How we gonna find everybody?" Si Cheney asked.

"We'll find 'em when the square clears out after the procession starts," I answered.

We tried to get close to the hotel but weren't successful. None of us could hear him, but the Rev. Mr. Ashley delivered an affecting eulogy over Philo's remains in the jam-packed hotel. The funeral procession formed immediately afterward, led by the uniformed Fire Companies with each man wearing a black crepe on his left arm. Carriages containing old residents, family, and friends followed, then came the hearse carrying the body. Last, but not least, over 2,000 mourners on foot joined the funeral procession to Oakwood cemetery. The burial service was read at the family plot, and all that remained of Philo N. Rust was consigned to the earth. Ceremony complete, Philo's mourners felt the need for drink, causing Rust's Hotel to have another banner night in consequence. Philo would've been proud.

*Mein Host* was still fresh in the ground when the sell-off began at Rust's Hotel. Furniture of the best description, horses, carriages, harnesses, crockery, and all the utensils were up for sale. When a dispute arose over the hotel's lease, rumors began that called Philo's finances into question. Typical of human nature, everybody had an opinion of Philo Rust, and most couldn't keep it to themselves. I had no interest in listening. Philo's death left me feeling the loss of dreams that would never come true, like someday being old enough to stroll into Rust's Hotel whenever I wanted to. Countless times I replayed that scenario over in my mind, and now it was over before it even began.

Further darkening the skies, the Messrs. Burr effectively demonstrated how the Fox sisters and the mediums were fooling everyone. I wanted to have the ultimate *"I told you so"* moment with Ma, and now, that was dead, too. I decided to concede defeat, desirous to get it over with.

"Excuse me, Ma, but we need to talk!" I stated.

"Of course, dear, you look like you have a lot on your mind."

"I do, Ma, it's about the Fox sisters being exposed."

"Yes, the Burr's entertained the audience with a demonstration of the sisters' act, complete with an explanation of how they did it."

"That's what everybody's saying, Ma."

"Did you hear that Capt. Teall polled the audience after their last show? Nearly everyone agreed that the Burr's had given a satisfactory explanation."

"Yes, I heard that, too. The rapping noises that the Burr's made sounded just like the spirits knocking for the Fox sisters."

"Ah, at last you see the light!" she exclaimed. "I hope this monstrous delusion is finally over with. But I think there's something else that you'd like to talk about, Edward. You've been pretty quiet about Philo Rust dying."

"Yeah, Ma, it's weird thinking of him being gone. Mr. Willard said that Philo left a big hole downtown, and he's right! Why else would so many people show up for the funeral?"

"Well, there certainly was considerable parade and show at the funeral, and much adulation was lavished upon his character. But don't you see how hollow and heartless this was? Why does the world praise the character of a man after death, whose life had been one unbroken tissue of profligacy—whose utmost influence was exerted to lead the young and unwary in the way of ruin! He had no scruples, and trampled upon all obligations of order and decency, in his pursuit of indulgence."

"But you overlook all of his good points, Ma."

"It's true, Edward, that he had some good qualities, but who doesn't? He was kind and generous to the poor at times, though he undoubtedly gave from the impulse of the moment, rather than from any settled principle. His other good traits were obscured and almost lost in the profusion of vices that he nourished, and strengthened in his character for years gone by."

"What do you think happened to Philo, Ma? You think he's in heaven now?"

"He's gone, Edward. We leave him in the hands of an all wise, and merciful God,—who doeth all things well."

"I heard something like that at the funeral from a lady wearing bloomers. I forgot to tell you about all the bloomer ladies out there saying goodbye to Philo."

"Ha! I can only imagine. The last time the new fashions came up at the Ladies Tearoom, one woman became absolutely angry because her sister wanted to try it out. And another thought it perfectly ridiculous and shameful."

"Is that what you think, too, Ma?" I asked.

"No, I don't see why it's any more ridiculous or shameful to adopt a Turkish costume, than a Parisian, if it is more convenient, or more rational. These very persons, are just as much interested in following every new fashion as fast as it appears, as if their very lives depended on it!"

"I bet the bloomers are easier to keep clean than the long dresses, though," I countered.

"Yes, and that reminds me that I have to pay our washerwoman. You can come with me and carry another load."

Following orders, I gathered dirty laundry and slung the bag over my shoulder for the short walk to Miss Rachael Watkins' home, nearby on Fayette Street—Black George found her for us. Miss Rachael was a colored lady, and I suspected that George was sweet on her.

"Hey, George!" I began, "We're dropping a load down at Miss Rachael's—want me to put in a word for you?"

"I already done told you to watch dem lips, boy," came the stern reply.

"Hurry along now, Edward," Ma directed. "After the laundry we have to pick something up for your sister, Clara. Did you forget it's her birthday? She's turning eight on the eighth!"

"It feels like it's always somebody's birthday around here," I answered.

Back in newspaper class at Weld's School for Young Men and Boys, everybody wanted to hear from Billy Willard about the latest ghoulish happenings.

"All right then, Mr. Willard. Please address the class so that we may continue."

Billy rose, anxious to begin with headlines on the ready. He started with the familiar clearing of his throat.

"Ah hem, Well, Mr. Weld, last Sunday some boys were fishing the creek near the pump house when they saw a floating box. They pulled it to shore, and when they opened it up there was a human body inside! One of 'em ran for the police, who came and took the corpse to the dead house."

"Do they know who the unfortunate person is, William?" Weld asked.

"No, sir, all they know is that it was a young woman. I heard that the body must have been in the water for a long time because it was so decomposed. The top of her head was sawed off, and they never found the missing scalp!"

"Do the police have any suspects?" Mr. Weld asked.

"No sir, not yet. The box was weighed down with a large stone, but it wasn't heavy enough to keep it down. Dr. Hoyt was examining the body and that's all I know."

"Thank you, William, was there anything else?"

"Yes, Mr. Weld, there is. Miss Rosa Allmar was walking home the other day when she was attacked by a cow."

Great laughter ensued, Mr. Weld included.

"Was this by chance one of the missing cows that Austin Cook is trying to find?" Weld asked.

"No, sir—this one got away from a butcher leading it to slaughter. The cow had Rosa up on its horns for some distance, and it gored her in the side."

"Thank you, William," Weld repeated. "Who's next? Will Stoddard, you look anxious."

Will stood, wearing a somber look that contrasted the jovial atmosphere.

"Mr. Weld, I have news that you won't believe," Will said with emotion. "They arrested two arsonists in Utica, sir, *and they were both firemen!*"

Will's news stunned the classroom. How could a fireman be an arsonist?

"What details can you provide, Will?" Mr. Weld asked.

"About half past one on the fourth, a fire broke out in the stables of the National Hotel and spread to a couple of warehouse buildings that were destroyed. Mr. Butterfield ran the National, and he lost thirteen horses, a cow, three carriages, and lots of grain and hay."

"How'd they catch 'im, Will?" Charlie Willard asked.

"The Vigilance Committee was on alert, and they arrested a young man walking away from where the fire started. It turned out to be James Orcutt, a Utica fireman! Orcutt confessed, then he informed on a fellow fireman, Horace B. Conklin."

Si Cheney asked incredulously, "So they got two firemen in jail for arson?"

"That's right," Will remarked. "The Recorder of Utica already examined Orcutt and found him guilty of arson in the first degree."

"That's a death sentence!" Charlie Pope cried.

"It sure is!" Larry Sabine agreed.

All of a sudden, I recalled my recent prayers with Ma, and started to feel guilty for wanting to see the arsonists hung. Will I have blood on my hands if they swing? During break, Will was pressed for more details about the Utica fires, but by the time I had a turn, he said that he'd rather talk chickens.

"C'mon over after school to see everything, Will!" I said with conviction, and he did.

# Chapter Eleven
## (April – May 1851)

Being friends with Mrs. Stoddard, Ma was happy to see Will come home with me after school. I told her that I had asked Will to look over the chicken coop, and maybe give me and Sam a few pointers. Ma brought us up to speed.

"You boys just missed Sam—he was here looking for you not ten minutes ago! He said to tell you that he'd be at the Loguen's if you were looking for him."

"Thanks, Ma—we'll do that," I answered. "Do you mind, Will? I want Sam to hear this."

"Sure, Ed—but let's go if we're going."

Traversing the short distance to our destination, we found Sam standing outside with Rev. Loguen, the lawyer George Vashon, and another black man that I didn't know. Rev. Loguen greeted me with his usual friendliness, and I introduced him to Will.

"Pleased to meet you, Will," Rev. Loguen said cheerily. "I'm glad that your friends came looking for you, Sam, now they can meet Mr. William G. Allen! Boys, this gentleman is a professor at the New York Central College in McGrawville."

"That's right, boys, he's the second black professor in New York State, following Charles Reason!" George Vashon added with enthusiasm.

*William G. Allen*

"Spoken by our first black lawyer," Rev. Loguen quipped at Vashon.

"I heard you speak at church last week, Mr. Allen," Sam said.

"I hope you liked it, Sam," the newcomer replied. "I couldn't say no when Rev. Loguen asked me to speak—he's a lot bigger than I am—ha ha!"

"Me, too, William. He's got me down for this Sunday!" G.B. Vashon declared.

"You should have a good-sized crowd, George—I had to compete with Philo Rust's funeral," Allen joked.

"That's great, Rev. Loguen, guest speakers for two weeks in a row! Who's next after Mr. Vashon?" I asked.

"Well, Edward, Rev. May will be next when he returns from Canada in a week or two. He wanted to see for himself how black folks are getting-on up north."

> **Address by Geo. B. Vashon, Esq.**
>
> George B. Vashon, Esq., of this city, will give an Address, adapted to the present crisis, at the Church of Rev'd Mr. Loguen, in Syracuse, on the evening of next Sabbath.
>
> Mr. Vashon has just enough of African blood to be discernible. He is a Scholar, Lawyer and Orator, of accomplished person and education, and high endowments. Go and hear him.

Will Stoddard interrupted, "Excuse me, Rev. Loguen, I heard a little about the fugitive slave case in Boston. Can you tell us anything about that, sir?"

"My two friends can tell you more than I could, Will. What do you say, gentlemen?"

Mr. William Allen began, "Well, I suppose you know that Thomas Sims was taken under the Fugitive Slave Law, and that the local, state, and federal authorities don't want him to become another Shadrack Minkins."

"Especially not in Boston!" Mr. Vashon added. "At first, Sims didn't know they were taking him as a fugitive—he thought they picked him up for drunkenness. But as they approached the courthouse the truth came out, and bystanders raised the alarm with cries of, *Kidnapper!*"

W.G. Allen continued, "When Sims realized his situation, he drew his knife, but couldn't escape. Then an abolition lawyer started yelling at a deputy marshal with such fervor that they made him sit in the watch house for an hour to cool down! And to prevent any attempts at a rescue, the military companies were in readiness at the armories."

"Did Sims' lawyer defend him, Mr. Vashon? Sam asked.

George Vashon answered, "After the claimants showed proof of ownership, Sims' lawyer, Mr. Rantoul, took the ground that the Fugitive Slave Law by itself was unconstitutional. He argued for an hour that Sims should be granted a writ of habeas corpus—that's your right to stand before a judge, face your accusers, and be protected from unlawful imprisonment."

"That's true, George, but this vile law says forget all that, and the accused have no rights." Rev. Loguen interjected with feeling. "I don't have to guess what your daddy thinks about all this, Sam. When's he coming home?"

"Hard to say, Rev. Loguen—we expect him back before long, though. He's down in Philadelphia now, sir, preaching about the religious duties of black men," Sam answered.

"That's a hard sell to men trying to lose their chains, Sam, but your pa's the man to do it! We're all proud of him, you know," Mr. Vashon stated.

"Thank you, sir," Sam replied.

Rev. Loguen expounded, "If I know Rev. Ward at all, his preaching will include something about colonization—another forty-five people just took passage to Liberia on the barge *Baltimore*."

"Yes, sir, I think you're right," Sam answered, "But I've heard him say how frustrating it can be, and sometimes he wishes for his own farm in Jamaica."

"Hey Ed, I have to be back at the store soon—let's go see your coop," Will reminded me, and at that we took our leave.

The following week, Thomas Sims was remanded to his owner in Georgia, creating great excitement outside the courthouse. The southern witnesses were followed to their hotel by about one thousand jeering persons, but the military guard prevented an attack. A government detachment of 150 men armed with clubs and hooks were assembled near Court Square while the police force, armed with short swords, formed by the side entrance to the courthouse. After all was readied, Sims was brought down, appearing in good spirits. During procession to the brig *Acorn*, no attempts at violence were made, though many loud, angry voices poured down disapproval. One called for thunderbolts from heaven to rain down on their heads! Another recited the events of the Boston massacre that occurred on that very street. At the wharf, the *Acorn* was found ready and the steamer *Hornet* alongside with steam up. The singing of hymns erupted when four officers boarded to accompany the prisoner to Savannah. Northerners railed at the government's effort, and expense, to return one slave to his master while Southerners rejoiced.

Happening the same time as the Sims transport to Georgia, it was announced that Syracuse would host the annual convention of the American Anti-Slavery Society. After last year's interruptions by Capt. Rynders, Doctor Grant, and the mob that followed them, the AASS opted to vacate New York City for Syracuse. Scheduled for May 7 – 9, the convention would feature renowned abolitionists George Thompson, Edmund Quincy, Parker Pillsbury, and the society's founder, William Lloyd Garrison.

By mid-April the entire community was primed for the opening of the Erie and Oswego canals. Boatmen were busy fitting out while droves of canal horses arrived daily. Squatters living along the canal were about to lose their homes and scant belongings. The first boat to pass through on opening day brought a shout from the ever-present loafers. With Grasshopper nearby hawking his wares, the b'hoys on the bridge offered a hearty salute as the first boat disappeared beneath them. The scene repeated on scattered bridges all the way to Buffalo.

The longed-for tinkle of packet bells and the omnibus driver's horn announced that spring had finally arrived. Everyone was busy and in a hurry! Housekeepers pounded their carpets, whitewash brushes flew off the shelves, happy chaos ensued. Then word came down the canal that the Mayor of Utica had disbanded the fire department, fully supported by the local residents. After the firemen/arsonists confessed that they had started the fires only to partake in free refreshments afterwards, his decision was easy. Mayor John Hinman provided a fresh start that began with a thorough house-cleaning of the entire department.

Right before Easter, Ma complained that if she had time to be unhappy, she believed that she would be, for want of time to herself. But the holiday cheered her, doubly so with my sister, Lucie, turning four on Easter Sunday.

Ma said, "The weather was not so pleasant as some days we'd seen, but being the anniversary of the resurrection of the 'meek and lowly Jesus,' our splendid churches were well-filled with devout worshippers."

On Tuesday night after Easter, I went to the AME Zion with Black George to hear Rev. May's report on the condition of colored people in Canada. A full congregation heard his upbeat description of life at the other end of underground railroad.

"With very few exceptions, I found them living comfortably," Rev. May began, "but they all were rejoicing in their liberty! There had not been a single instance of intoxication or of any disorderly conduct, and I found them all contented, happy, and enterprising. Several did confess to me that they had never suffered such hardships as they had experienced since they came to live in Canada. The severity of the cold had sometimes tried them to the utmost, and clearing up their heavy-timbered lands had been hard work indeed, especially for those who had been house servants in Southern cities. But not one of them looked back with desiring eyes to the leeks and onions of the Egypt from which they had escaped. They seemed to be sustained and animated by one of the noblest sentiments that can take possession of the human soul—*the love of liberty, the determination to be free.*"

Walking home afterward, I asked Black George what he thought.

"So what do you think, George, would you ever want to move to Canada?"

"No suh! I'se a free man and Syracuse be cold enough," he answered.

On the last day of April, Mr. Weld got us started with the monthly wrap-up in newspaper class.

"All right, Prentice—what's the latest with your niche?" he asked.

"Yes, sir," Prentice replied, "The steamer *Pacific* set a new record for crossing the Atlantic! Took her only nine days and twenty hours, Mr. Weld. But the *Comet* exploded up in Oswego, and that's all that people are talking about. My pa said he can't imagine the pain from getting burned so bad!"

"The blast took three lives instantly, Prentice, and left others in agony, barely alive," our teacher lamented.

I raised my hand. "Mr. Weld, I read a good one about Miss Bradbury, sir! A writer from the *NY Herald* said he knew her well, and he thought that during the twelve years she taught school in Syracuse that nobody did more to improve education in the city. The Teacher's Institute paid tribute to her, too—they're raising money for a monument."

"Ah, yes—she truly was a gem, Edward. The teachers resolved that with her death the Institute and the community suffered a loss beyond repair," Weld responded.

"The *Herald* writer liked Philo Rust, too, Mr. Weld. He said Philo's reputation went all the way from Quebec to New Orleans," I included.

"And speaking of reputations, it's time for Charles Willard to report on Jenny Lind's tour of America!" Mr. Weld stated.

Charlie rose to speak. "Mr. Weld, Jenny recently sold-out in Cincinnati, just like she has everywhere. And she did it again in Pittsburgh, too, but then some lowlife's threw stones into the windows of her carriage, and then again through the windows of her dressing room! ***They insulted her***, Mr. Weld," Charlie bellowed, "O*nly an evil person could throw rocks at Jenny Lind!"*

The diva's number two fan, Larry Sabine, spoke up. "Yeah, I bet they were probably *Canal Boys*. I heard they're even worse on the Pennsylvania Canal between Pittsburgh and Philadelphia," he said with warmth.

"Jenny was so mad that she cancelled the show and left for Baltimore," Charlie said.

Larry added, "They say that only in a city where Joe Barker was elected mayor would you find miscreants capable of insulting the benevolent Queen of Song!"

"All right, that's enough about Jenny for now," Mr. Weld declared, Mr. Wallace, tell us about the President's proclamation on Cuba."

Bill Wallace rose to answer. "Mr. Weld, on April 25th the president issued a proclamation saying there was reason to believe that a military expedition was going to invade the island of Cuba. He said that Cuba is a colony of Spain, a country that we're at peace with. President Filmore said the expedition was started by foreigners who dared use our soil to launch a hostile attack against a friend."

"I see, and what about the southerners who flock to the expedition's banner?"

"The president thinks they were tricked by falsehoods and misrepresentations, sir, but he said there'd be heavy fines and long imprisonments for anyone caught as part of an expedition to Cuba! He said that anyone who attacked Cuba shouldn't expect the protection of the United States, no matter what extremities they faced."

"Very interesting, William—thank you!" Mr. Weld said.

"Hey Bill, do you think the president's proclamation will stop the expedition?" Alex McKinstry asked.

"Nope! Those southern boys think they'll be welcomed home as heroes," Bill answered.

May began with a cold start. I helped Black George carry wood inside while my mother smiled her approval. With Henry, Lucia, Florence, and Clara competing for attention, Ma yelled upstairs to Emma, Ellen, and Cornelia to come down and help her. Turning to me, she said excitedly, "The World's Fair opened in London, Edward! Queen Victoria must have been at the Crystal Palace to make it official." Then she added dreamily, *"Oh, how spectacular it must have been!"*

"I'm sure it was, Ma," I answered. "In a few weeks we should start seeing reports in the newspapers—maybe sooner if the *Pacific* is running."

"I can't wait to read the accounts, I wish there were a telegraph line from New York to London!"

"Don't see how that's possible, Ma—I don't think anybody knows how deep the ocean is, not to mention hungry sea monsters chomping on the wire."

"Ha! You're funny, Edward. Sea monsters? Where do you get such ideas? Don't tell the opponents of the canal enlargement bill—they're already seeing monsters in the Erie Canal."

"Especially not with Pa on the committee in favor of expansion. But nine million dollars is a lot of money, don't you think?"

"Yes, and that's what the State Legislature is fighting about in Albany. But the fight in Syracuse is finding lodging for visitors attending the anti-slavery convention."

"It's like the State Fair, isn't it, Ma? All the hotels are full and the only open beds are in people's houses."

"You're right son, and your pa's on the committee to help direct visitors where to go."

"All the big name abolitionists are here for the convention, Ma. George Thompson, Gerrit Smith, Lucretia Mott, Frederick Douglass, Parker Pillsbury, Abby Kelley Foster, and a whole lot more!"

Ma said, "Many people have already heard William Lloyd Garrison speak. Yesterday, it was standing-room only yesterday at the Unitarian Church, I would have liked to have heard him—I understand he delivered a thoughtful lecture about peace."

"Yeah, he's against fighting wars for any reason, but I don't think there's many people who like hearing him talk bad about our country fighting the Mexicans."

"I suppose you're right, but those feelings only lead to more conflict—just look at Cuba!"

"But, Ma, the biggest conflict around here lately was Justice House and officer Hollister rescuing a horse that fell in the canal by the Police Office. Parish told me all about it."

"That's not what we were discussing, Edward, stay on topic," she asserted.

"Sorry, Ma, I read in the *Star* about George Thompson stirring up trouble in Rochester, and they're pretty much saying that he's not welcome here. They call him the absent itinerant and say we don't need an Englishman to tell us how to live. How's that for conflict?"

"I'd say that's more than enough—and the convention hasn't begun," she concluded.

Before Wednesday's start for the gathering of abolitionists in Syracuse, a *Southern Rights* convention began that Monday in Charleston, South Carolina. Forty associations were represented, with four-hundred and thirty-one delegates present. The convention's president considered that Southern institutions could not last twenty years under the existing circumstances. Many wanted to limit deliberations to when, where, and how resistance should be made.

Day two of *Southern Rights* brought a resolution to the effect that South Carolina could not submit to her wrongs without dishonor and ruin, and that if necessary she should relieve herself, whether other states joined her or not. On day three another resolution came forward, pledging the convention to abide by the action of the Legislature of the State, as to whether secession shall take place with or without the co-operation of the other Southern States. Those against considered that if South Carolina separated from the Southern States, it would be final, and detrimental to the institution of slavery. In closing, the convention of Southern men adjourned with a prayer.

On Wednesday in Syracuse, the abolitionists began their convention with prayer; being allowed to attend with Pa answered mine! William Lloyd Garrison opened the proceedings with a portion of scripture, then Rev. Raymond offered a prayer, followed by a hymn written by Maria W. Chaplin that was sung by the audience. Garrison related that, "the society had met annually in New York but were not permitted by a power greater than liberty in our land. Not a meeting house or a hall could be obtained in New York," he said.

Garrison stated "There are brave men and brave women in our land, but is there one brave enough to go to South Carolina and uphold anti-slavery doctrines? There are also thousands of pulpits in the land, but there is not a man in them, who dares to grapple with the slavery system on the spot, because they would perish in the attempt. Such is our condition at present."

*William Lloyd Garrison*

The society's president continued, "True, the Anti-Slavery Society is branded as disorganizing, and all that. So was primitive Christianity. But that noble band of martyrs were not infidels; the Puritans were not infidels, and we, making ourselves one of them, claim to be not infidel. Those who cannot walk with us because we are so disorganizing, can associate with Rynders' and that class of men. They are the deadliest enemies of the country, who are for putting down agitation. We are patriots in the broadest sense of the word. We do love our country. The Abolitionists are not animated by any ill will against those who hold slaves. It is because we wish to save and bless them that we take the position we do.

"We do not get up mobs, but those who oppose us. We desire to gag no one. We say let truth and error meet. We are for free speech. At our last annual meeting in New York, we had the mob howling around us for the space of three days. So in Boston. These men are horrified because the fugitive slave bill is opposed. I want the slaveholders to see how much better it would be to set their slaves free, than to bow down to Moloch."

Gerrit Smith spoke next, saying, "We welcome you to this city of free discussion. You have referred to the proceedings in New York; does the city of Syracuse contrast with New York, in this respect? Yes, sir, we welcome you to Central New York; to our homes, and to our hearts; and not only the Anti-Slavery Society, but George Thompson!" At this, great cheering broke out in the hall. Smith continued, "I say then, to you, George Thompson, to you, Frederick Douglass, Samuel J. May, Henry C. Wright, Francis Jackson, Edmund Quincy, and others, we tender to you the hand of fellowship and affection."

Smith's latter words drew animated cheering from an audience that included a great many women, the latter reported with scorn by the opposition press.

Rev. May followed, saying, "Mr. Smith has welcomed you to Central New York; I now again welcome you to Syracuse, the city of salt. I do not believe that throughout the country there has been a more enthusiastic condemnation of the Fugitive Slave Law, than here. Sir, I do not say that we are all Anti-Slavery men here; but I do say, we are in favor of the liberty of speech. Sir, I welcome you to this Hall, which has resounded again and again with Anti-Slavery sentiments which would have done your soul good."

At the session's end, Rev. May was named to the finance committee along with Charles A. Wheaton, who never missed a chance to be on board somewhere.

The afternoon assembly saw Edmund Quincy defend George Thompson coming here from England by saying, "Thompson was right in coming to this country and fighting against slavery. What would this country have been without foreign interference? But we never heard complaint of foreign interference until a foreigner appeared to wage war upon that plague spot upon our institutions!"

Garrison enraged his antagonists with detrimental remarks about the nation's founding fathers. "You may speak of the efforts of Washington, Jefferson, and Adams in framing the Government, but they were fallible men, and I know they were criminal men, for they held human beings in bondage. We need not be told that a dissolution is a startling doctrine, for it is not. The American Union is the only God which this nation recognizes or serves, and we idolize it. Whence is it? Is it from Heaven or from men? If I take it that our fathers made it precisely as they do hats and boots. A single breath made it, and thank God a single breath can overthrow it. There is a great deal of veneration expressed for our Fathers, but I say in regard to that, it is mere sham. Why, I say they were men like us; they were dis-unionists; opposed to a union with the mother country, and here the analogy is perfect."

On day two of the convention, President Garrison called the convention to order in the crowded hall, filled mostly by out-of-towners.

Mr. Ritchie of Oswego rose to say he'd visited the new arrivals to Canada twice, and claimed that 5,000 more had crossed since passage of the Fugitive Slave Law. Abby Kelley Foster offered an amendment to not only take cognizance of the fugitives in Canada, but in other places as well. She then spoke in favor of no union with slaveholders in church or state.

"The masses of the north must be convinced that it is as wicked to associate with slaveholders as with horse-stealers. Until they are so convinced, the principles of anti-slavery will not prevail!" she asserted.

Parker Pillsbury boldly followed, "We are in the midst of a revolution. We are engaged in dashing to pieces, one of the proudest governments that ever existed. Our warfare is not against slave extension, nor against slavery, but against the Government of the United States, and we mean to dash it to pieces as a potter's vessel!" He closed by comparing Daniel Webster with Benedict Arnold.

William Lloyd Garrison scoffed at the slaveholder's doctrine, saying, "We are told that the slaves are furnished with religious knowledge. *Property* receiving religious instruction? *Property* praying to God? *Property* asking tor eternal salvation? What an awful paradox!"

During the evening session of the second day, Edmund Quincy of Boston asserted, "The great end of civil government is to protect the weak. The rich do not need it. How does the constitution of the United States perform this highest, holiest feature of Government? It does not protect the poor, defenseless slave. We dare not go in a slave state and aid the oppressed. Go into Georgia and $5,000 will be offered for your head. The government does not protect you!"

Three cheers were given for George Thompson, who spoke at length. "You ask the world to look at you, but what do they see ? Why, 3,000,000 slaves held in perpetual bondage. Pile up 3,000,000 pebbles; go home and count them in your sleep, and recollect that each represents a human soul that will rise up against you in the day of Judgment! When I look at the recreant conduct of the ministers in this land, I stand aghast. When slavery exists no more, and peace and good will obtain among men, then will this society be remembered as one of benefit to the race, and men will look back upon the Garrison's, the Quincy's, and the Smith's as benefactors of the world."

At the convention's third, and final day, AASS President Garrison called the Society to order at ten o'clock . Following the singing of hymns, attention was called to an article in the *New York Herald*, in reference to the annual meeting of their society, stating that a bond of $10,000 was given as security before the hall could be procured of the city authorities, and also that the society pledged themselves to make good all damages to the building, by mobs and other means.

Rev. May rose to denounce the assertions as base libels, affirming that no one had anything to do in securing the hall but himself. He said that he had received a communication from New York stating that Capt. Rynders was coming here to re-enact the same abomination he did in that city, and this may have given rise to the false assertions.

Syracusan William H. Burleigh made some eloquent remarks upon slavery, and the Anti-Slavery doctrines of the Bible. He deprecated any religion that sanctioned slavery, and maintained that God and the Bible did not sanction it.

Following the singing of the hymn *"Come Join the Abolitionists,"* fireworks erupted at the evening session. The fuse was lit by Syracuse lawyer Charles B. Sedgwick, who said, "It is well understood that the chairman knows I disagree with him, in many of the principles of the Society, over which he presides. But there is one fundamental principle on which we can all agree, which is that man has no right to hold property in his fellow man."

The crowd cheered, then Sedgwick took an opposing view to "no union with slaveholders."

"If instead of disenfranchising themselves, we had some Garrison's, Quincy's, and Gerrit Smith's in the Senate their influence would be used to much more advantage than it can be in their present situation. If they would do this and not take the position of "no union with slaveholders," much more would be effected by them."

Garrison then read a resolution denouncing the colonization society, calling it a friend and ally of slavery. Frederick Douglass arose and said that although the colonization journals uniformly speak of the success of colonization, he very much doubted it.

"I not only object to our being colonized to Africa but also to Canada," Douglass said. "I believe in remaining here, and deporting ourselves in such a manner as to gain the esteem of all. I speak as a colored man, for I am determined for one, to fall or flourish with my colored brethren in the United States."

The audience responded with cheers as Douglass continued. "I know we are the victims of prejudice, base, and malignant prejudice. I feel this. But there has been a time when it was much more inveterate than now. Thirty years ago, you could hardly find a colored man who was intelligent. How is it now? In Boston, they are becoming lawyers, in Rochester editors, in Philadelphia physicians, and in Syracuse you have a colored lawyer. As the negroes become intelligent, they will understand their rights, and then all will be wielded against slavery. Friends, I mean to remain!"

Douglass went on to say that he rejoiced to be like the white folks, and he despaired of those who refused to associate with the whites.

"We ought to imitate the white people for the purpose of overcoming prejudice," he said.

George Thompson followed, saying, "A slaveholder knows not what he is, until you tell him. The only Society in the world which pleases the slaveholder is the Colonization Society! Father and daughter are slavery and colonization.

In regard to the question of what shall be done with the colored people, I would answer, *let them alone!* Of one thing I am sure, the American people must make up their minds to dwell upon this continent with the colored people forever," Thompson said.

Thompson then denounced portions of the remarks by Charles Sedgwick in a severe manner.

Sedgwick rose and said he did not believe that a slaveholder ever was, or ever will be converted by epithets. "The human heart is melted only by kindness," Sedgwick said, then spoke more at length, creating agitation amongst the society members.

William Lloyd Garrison rose in reply to vindicate the course and remarks of Mr. Thompson, who denied that he intended to offer any offence to Mr. Sedgwick. The audience both cheered and hissed when Thompson said of Sedgwick, "Still, that gentleman who could find no harsh epithets for the slaveholders, has applied to me harsh epithets, and has publicly insulted me to-night!"

The excitement grew with Thompson's remarks and those present began to array themselves on the respective sides. Rev. Raymond said, "I do not rise here sir to vindicate the character of my fellow townsman, Mr. Sedgwick. It does not need it. We have known him longer than we have known George Thompson!"

My pa was involved in further discussion between Messrs. Garrison, Thompson, Sedgwick, Burleigh, and others, but the noise and confusion made it impossible to hear. The session commenced with harmony and good feeling, but the close was characterized by confusion, recrimination, and waste of time.

Adopted by a hearty aye, A resolution of thanks was given to the citizens of Syracuse for the hospitalities extended to the members of the Society, and to the authorities for the use of the Hall, and for their efforts to uphold free discussion. Three cheers we're given for Syracuse, and three for George Thompson and Charles B. Sedgwick.

In closing, two young colored ladies sang a song, after which the audience sang a hymn. After Rev. May's benediction, the convention adjourned at 11:30 p.m. on Friday night.

With so many abolitionists in town, there was no shortage of guest speakers for Rev. Loguen at the AME Zion church. He already had some booked for Sunday.

## Chapter Twelve
### (May – June 1851)

Conflicting emotions surrounded the Anti-Slavery Convention, particularly on the second day. Inside the crowded hall, Garrison and others were denouncing war and conquest, while outside, a military parade was held to commemorate the battle of Palo Alto. Kellogg's Brass Band accompanied the Syracuse Citizens Corps and National Guards as they marched in uniform to celebrate the anniversary of the American victory in Mexico. Most Americans, except for the abolitionists and a few others, supported the country's significant land acquisition from the war.

Pro-slavery interests capitalized on this sentiment in their plans for Cuba. Despite the President's proclamation, there were rumors from Maryland of young men gathering for mischief, likely bound for the island, and reports that three-to-six-hundred men were encamped near Jacksonville, with others on the St. Johns and Satilla Rivers of Florida, awaiting transport to a secret rendezvous with the expedition.

New York City's notorious Capt. Rynders had supporters in Syracuse who welcomed the false rumor of his arrival to disrupt the convention like

*Capt. Isaiah Rynders*

he did last year. Contributors to the *Syracuse Star* didn't hold back in their denunciations of the late convention, nor in their low regard for agitators determined to tear the country apart. A great many in Syracuse wanted the abolitionists gone on the next train, stage, or packet boat out, with a front-of-the line pass for George Thompson.

Many abolitionists, who also opposed the consumption of alcohol, stayed for the temperance meeting on Monday night. Organized by my pa, Rev. May, and William H. Burleigh, supporters were called to gather in opposition to the city granting licenses for the sale of ardent spirits. The Common Council had scheduled a special session to address the issue, giving local businessmen two weeks to apply for licenses or face stiff fines for non-compliance. However, when the Aldermen canceled the special meeting at City Hall, the temperance supporters reconvened at the nearby Congregational church. My father was on the committee that resolved their abhorrence of the trafficking of intoxicating drinks, deeming it the source of incalculable evil and urging city leaders to refrain from legalizing sales. Later that week, Mr. Thomas L. Carson started a new temperance organization and periodical called the *Carson League*. His membership drive welcomed support from women, and he advertised for all dealers of intoxicating liquors to cease their sales immediately.

Predictably, butcher Cale Davis took exception to Thomas L. Carson and his band of crackpots, as Davis called them. While walking to school with the Cheney's, we suspected that a missing cow might have wandered too close to the butcher's lair. Despite the ordinance that restricted meat sales to the city market, the scattered butcher shops hadn't closed entirely.

"Look at that, Ed," Prentice said, "Folks are lined up for another one of Davis's lightning sales!"

"Ha! That's one less missing cow to worry about," I jested.

"Yeah, that or Davis and his boy clubbed some vagrant swine—I ain't seen any round here lately." Si Cheney supposed.

"Hey, that looks like Jerry in line over there!" I cried.

"Who's Jerry?" Prentice asked.

"You know, he's the black guy with the red hair that I told you about—you see him?"

"Oh, yeah—he's the runaway you were talking to at Loguen's, right?"

"That's him. He's a nice guy, too. C'mon, I wanna go say hello," I urged.

As Cale Davis bellowed epithets against Thomas L. Carson and his damnable league, we walked over to say a quick hello to Jerry, standing in line amongst a group of salt manufacturers waiting to place their orders. Jerry's skills as a cooper were known to the people who needed barrels—as we approached, it seemed that many knew him. From what I'd heard from Will Stoddard, Jerry's views on temperance were more aligned with Cale Davis than my pa—he suggested that Jerry had seen the inside of the watch house a few times from over-indulging.

I waved when our eyes met, and cheerfully called, "Hey, Jerry!"

"Hey, Edward!" Jerry answered, "You here for the special?"

"Nah, just on our way to school—I saw you and wanted to say hello is all."

"Well now, I'm glad you did," Jerry replied. Then glancing at the men around him, he said, "Yes sir, there be some friendly folks around here!"

In reply, salt maker Latham Avery remarked, "The superintendent of the salt works isn't very friendly, though, is he?"

"Not lately," fellow manufacturer Patrick Cooney replied. "We have to get Robert Gere to assess the strength of the brine he's pumping."

"That's right! Everybody knows the quality keeps getting worse." said Napoleon Van Slyck while salt boiler Jacob Clink, salt packer Christian Wingle, and inspector Michael Gleason nodded affirmation.

Another salt maker, Voltaire Newton, took exception to our friendly overtures and turned to his neighbor in line. "Hey, Jerry! Nobody came over to say hello to *me*—you special or somethin'?"

"Ha! You'll have to ask them," Jerry answered, gesturing towards me and the Cheney's. Another salt boiler, Pears Cargy, pressed the matter.

"What's all this? You think Jerry's special or what?" he asked with envy.

I recalled some of Ma's wit to respond. "I suppose so, sir; there's only one of 'im, so that makes 'im unique!"

"Oh yeah? How old are you?" Cargy demanded.

"Fourteen now," I replied.

"Hmmm," he mumbled. I could tell he was thinking, but the butcher spoke first.

"Fourteen, all right," Cale Davis interjected, "and training to join the Carson League. But don't get too chummy, boy. You'll make your pa jealous, then he'll have to start the Wheaton League, ha ha ha!"

I felt a nudge from Prentice's elbow, and he whispered, "C'mon Edward, we're gonna be late."

"We'll see ya later Jerry," I said, flashing a smirk at Pears Cargy and Voltaire Newton as we left in haste. When Mr. Weld rang the bell, we were already seated, listening to Parish tell us how the mayor could assign police constables at the train depot. Parish looked me in the eye and declared, "Your uncle wants a policeman on duty every time there's a train comin' or goin'!"

"That's not what the pickpockets said," Billy Willard joked.

City leaders were ecstatic that President Filmore was expected on the afternoon train for an impromptu visit, accompanied by Secretary of the Navy, William Graham, and Attorney General John J. Crittenden. It wasn't every day that the President of the United States came to town, so a dignified reception was planned. Capt. Yard from the penitentiary was selected as honorary Marshal and under his command were city firemen, the Syracuse Citizens' Corps, the National Guards, and artillery from the Washington Riflemen. Mr. George Saul, now Capt. Saul, commanded the Germans who comprised the artillery company.

Informed that the President would be delayed until nearly midnight, the disappointed welcoming committee postponed, rather than canceled the reception. As darkness fell, bonfires illuminated the downtown streets. Just before midnight a cannon fired from Prospect Hill to announce the approaching train, hearty cheers erupted from the steadfast supporters gathered at the depot. The uniformed, torch carrying men who lined Salina Street created an exciting spectacle!

My uncle, Mayor Wheaton, with the Common Council, awaited the President at the Syracuse House to officially welcome him and the cabinet. Due to the lateness of the hour, Uncle Horace offered only a brief salutation to which the President responded with thanks before retiring for the night. Had Philo Rust survived, the President would have likely opted for Rust's Hotel instead, happily recalling his stay there during the New York State Fair in '49.

The next morning, every young man and boy at Weld's school petitioned the schoolmaster for an immediate release to see the President.

In one voice we cried, "Please, Mr. Weld! It's history!"

"The President of the United States is here, Mr. Weld!"

"Can we go, sir?"

To everyone's delight Mr. Weld agreed, and dispatched us on our next historical mission. Times like these made history everyone's favorite subject, at least for the day. The classroom emptied like magic. On the way out, Bill Wallace yelled back, "If we see Mr. Crandal we'll say hello for you, Mr. Weld!"

Our teacher replied. "Thank you, William—I'm sure he'll be there."

Standing outside on Montgomery St., it was only a quick hop to the Syracuse House where we encountered Crandal as expected.

"Good morning gentlemen," the reporter said in greeting.

"And to you, sir," I answered.

"Mr. Weld sends his regards!" Bill Wallace said.

"And mine to him!" he replied.

"Are you covering the president's visit, Mr. Crandal?" Parish asked.

"Absolutely, we can follow together if you like. I know their route—we can head them off on foot."

Staying ahead of the President's entourage, we began by taking the view from outside the penitentiary—over by where Milo lived. The city's northsiders became alerted to the President's imminent arrival and gathered enmasse to see him up close. Not a popular president, some hoped he'd catch a whiff of Freeof vinegar blowing up the hill from Catawba St., while his more severe detractors wished he'd choke on bullhead down at Welch's. Nevertheless, the tour continued peacefully, stopping at Fayette Park where the president addressed a gathering of public-school children.

Returning to the Syracuse House, President Filmore was introduced to our distinguished locals, including numerous ladies. A large gathering in the street called for the president to speak, and he favored them from the overlooking balcony.

"I am truly grateful for the attention and respect shown to me in your beautiful and flourishing city!" the President began, "I am well aware, however, that the respect awarded to me for the high office came

*The Syracuse House*

by a dispensation of Providence, and not for merits of my own. I shall endeavor to discharge the duties of this office with a single eye to the public good, and shall continue to do so—relying upon the patriotism and good sense of my fellow citizens to sustain me in my efforts to promote the prosperity of the country, and to preserve inviolate, the Constitution and the Union."

The applause that followed masked Filmore's precarious hold over the country, or even his own political party—the Whigs. The Democrats in attendance were respectful, but quiet.

President Filmore then retired back inside the Syracuse House where he, Secretary Graham, and Attorney General Crittenden continued to be introduced, with each responding to calls for them to speak. A magnificent meal was provided, presided by the mayor who offered the first toast, followed by others from US District Attorney, James R. Lawrence, former mayor, Harvey Baldwin, and attorney D.D. Hillis. Secretary Graham offered one in return, saying,

"To the modern city of Syracuse, unlike the ancient city of that name, inasmuch as the latter was ruled by a tyrant, while in the former twenty-five thousand sovereigns have an equal sway!"

Harvey Baldwin responded with a toast, "To Mr. Crittenden, the State of Kentucky, and it's noble inhabitants!"

Crittenden acquiesced with remarks that included a tribute to Henry Clay that drew three hearty rounds of applause. At 3 p.m., the president and his suite were escorted to the cars by the Mayor, Common Council, and the reception committee. When the President's train departed at a quarter past three, Capt. Saul ordered a thirty-one-gun salute that echoed through the countryside.

Arriving home I couldn't wait to tell Ma about my day of Syracuse history, but she showed more interest in a newspaper account of the *Great Exhibition* in London. I took a risk and ignored her late stage of pregnancy.

"C'mon Ma—he's still the President, like him or not!" I protested.

"It didn't sound to me like a very triumphant demonstration, Edward," she said. "There's not much enthusiasm felt here in his behalf."

"But I was there, Ma! People made a lot of noise for the President."

She remained stoic, "Yes, but only by his own particular partisans—and they are not very numerous."

Ma's assessment proved evident the next day. During newspaper class at school, accounts of the President were eclipsed by Parish's story of the pickpockets who worked the crowd, including a slight of hand that relieved Alderman McKinstry of thirty dollars for listening too attentively to the Presidential address.

A leading rival for the Whig nomination, Secretary of State Daniel Webster followed behind the president in his travels across New York State. Arriving at Canandaigua in the western region, Webster accepted an invitation to speak in Syracuse, hand delivered by Maj. Burnet, and signed by a substantial number of Onondaga County residents. Local Whigs prepared for his welcome while Democrats displayed everything from indifference to disdain, dreading what he might say about the Fugitive Slave Law. Both sides would hear his address scheduled for 3 p.m. on May 26, outside of City Hall.

For the second time in less than a week, Mr. Weld cut us loose to experience history. Democrats in class softened their condemnations—anybody who could get us out of school early couldn't be that bad—these Whigs were alright!

Will Stoddard said with conviction, "Let's get there early for a good spot!" And we did.

The area surrounding City Hall bustled with people awaiting Webster's train; everyone excited to hear the great expounder.

Compliments of Daniel Webster, my friends, the Cooks, were busy at the crowded Coffee House by the station. Much like Henry Clay, Syracuse was more inspired by Daniel Webster than it was the President. People of all shapes, sizes, and beliefs crammed together outside of City Hall, where Webster would address them from a balcony across the street. Seats were arranged in the shade outside of Frazee Hall to accommodate the ladies. Webster's train arrived on time, and he was promptly carried the short distance to where he would speak. A vortex of noise surrounded him—the sounds of his brass band arrived far before the man did.

When I first spied Daniel Webster, I yelled to Will Stoddard, "Hey, Will! Here he comes!" Parish saw him, too, and said, "Yeah—with the Syracuse Citizens Corps providing escort."

The Secretary arrived at the speaker's stand in a handsome carriage, greeted by an honor guard formed by the militia. As Thomas T. Davis (no relation to the Orange St. butcher) introduced him, I had a long, hard look at the famous statesman. The crowd grew eager seeing him in position, ready to begin.

"So whatcha think, Will?" I asked.

"Well, I've seen pictures of him before," Will replied, "But that dark gaze of his goes even deeper in person."

Parish barked, "Be quiet—he's starting to speak!"

"Fellow citizens of Syracuse, Ladies and Gentlemen!" Webster began, "I thank you cordially for the pains you have taken to assemble this afternoon, forming so broad an assemblage, to welcome me to your important and growing city of Syracuse!"

Somehow, it made me feel important to hear the great expounder. I can't explain it, but the longer I stood there listening, a couple of hours for sure, the more I understood the weight of his words. I didn't like much of what I heard, but it's better to know where you stand, I think. Friend and foe alike could appreciate Webster for saying what he really thought, seeking neither favor nor agreement. He drew hearty cheers when he spoke of patriotism, the Constitution, and our future prosperity. Then he turned to more dangerous grounds.

"Ladies and Gentlemen! I know very well that on the agitating questions of the present day, I do not have the happiness to concur with all the people of Syracuse, or the county of Onondaga, or other parts of the State of New York. I know there are varieties of sentiments, and I know the sources of that disagreement. Some of them are very justifiable, and some of them, I am sorry to believe, are not capable of much defense.

*Daniel Webster*

"But since I am requested to address you, you must take from me the honest sentiments of my own heart, the convictions of my own conscience. I lay no claim to your approval of my views, and I ask no favorable reception of them, farther than you see the suggestions I make to you are worthy of your regard."

Webster claimed to be anti-slavery, citing his public record as evidence, yet it was his opinion that, "Since the abolition societies were formed in New England, they have done nothing but mischief—they have riveted the chains of every slave in the Southern States—they have made their masters jealous and fearful, and postponed far and far the period of their redemption. This is my judgment—it may not be yours."

Webster went on to state that he had always opposed the admission of Texas as a slave state while the representatives of New York voted in favor, and he drew laughter when he spoke of references to himself as being a fit associate of Benedict Arnold. Then came the most contentious part of his address.

"We hear of persons assembling in Massachusetts and New York who set themselves over the Constitution—above the law—and above the decisions of the highest tribunals—and who say this law shall not be carried into effect. You have heard it here, have you not? Has it not been so said in the County of Onondaga?"

Cries from the crowd answered, "Yes! Yes!" Webster continued.

"And have they not pledged their lives, their fortunes, and their sacred honor to defeat its execution? Pledged their lives, their fortunes, and their sacred honor? For what? For the violation of the law—for the committal of treason to the country—for it is treason and nothing else!"

Great applause erupted from Webster's supporters, while at least an equal number stood frozen. A line had been drawn from which there was no turning back.

"I am a lawyer," Webster said, "and I value my reputation as a lawyer more than anything else—and I tell you if men get together and declare that a law of Congress shall not be executed in any case, and assemble in numbers to prevent the execution of such law—they are traitors and are guilty of treason, and bring upon themselves the penalties of the law.

No! No! It is time to put an end to this imposition upon good citizens, good men, and good women. It is treason, treason, TREASON, and nothing else!"

As the Secretary spoke, I couldn't help thinking of Pa, Rev. Loguen, and the other members of the Vigilance Committee.

"Who and what are these men? I am assured some of them are clergymen, and some, I am sorry to say it, are lawyers, and who the rest are, God only knows!

They say the law will not be executed—let them take care, for those are pretty bold assertions. The law must be executed, not only in carrying back the slave, but against those guilty of treasonable practices in resisting its execution.

Depend upon it, the law will be executed in its spirit and to its letter. It will be executed in all the great cities—here in Syracuse—during the next Anti-Slavery Convention, if the occasion shall arise; then we shall see what becomes of their lives and their sacred honor!"

For the abolition minded, his words were a bolt of lightning. Many appeared dumbstruck by the threat, while Webster's supporters cheered with vigor. It felt like we were heading for disaster, full steam ahead.

After Webster finished and the band was struck, I turned to Will Stoddard and asked, "So, *now* whatcha think, Will?"

"I'll tell ya what," he said, "I think Webster had no idea he was making a proclamation of war, and that hundreds of people were accepting it!"

"You really think so?"

"I do, and I think an untellable amount of mischief has just been done."

"They're taking Webster down to the Globe now for supper, you wanna go?" I asked.

"Nah, but I'll walk with ya," Will replied.

"What do you think, Prentice?" I asked. "Did you like Webster's speech?"

"Yes and no, Ed. He was fascinating to see and hear with that deep voice of his. He's probably got the darkest eyes I ever seen! But I was hopin' that he'd say a word about the steamer Webster that just burned to the water's edge above Vicksburg—around forty people died, including the captain and his wife."

"What's a steamer burning got to do with the Fugitive Slave Law, Prentice?"

"I thought it mighta been named after him," Prentice observed. Then, with genuine concern he asked, "You think Kellogg's band will play the Syracuse City March on the way to the Globe?"

Daniel Webster's speech resonated deeply in Syracuse and beyond. The Fugitive Slave Law was enforced in Boston with trials for the rescuers of Shadrach Minkins, a locality where the populace nominated the great expounder for president. In Philadelphia, a George Thompson lecture was canceled for an expected riot. Meanwhile, the colored citizens of New York announced a state convention to discuss colonization, suffrage, public education, and the Fugitive Slave Law.

At the annual meeting of the Unitarian Association in Boston, Rev. Theodore Parker and Syracuse's Rev. S.J. May proposed that fellow Unitarians, including President Filmore, Daniel Webster, and Edward Everett, be expelled from the church for supporting the hated law. The resolution narrowly failed to carry.

After reading a report in the *Syracuse Star* that Rev. Loguen was among the fugitive slaves heading north, I hurried down the street with the newspaper to show him. We shared a laugh, and he said, "I'm sure there's folks who wished it were true—and I'm happy to disappoint them!"

"Me, too, Reverend. Syracuse needs you!" I replied.

"Ha! That's a good one. Did George Johnson tell you to say that?"

"No, sir, but after livin' with him for so long I'm pretty sure he'd agree."

"Fair enough, Edward, I thank you for the thought."

"Say, Reverend Loguen, are you and my pa celebrating the Maine Law? He came home smiling like when they killed the Omnibus Bill."

"Yes indeed! Rev. May and Charles Burleigh most of all. Now if only the other states would follow Maine's example and make alcohol illegal."

"Pa said that too, Reverend, but he's worried that the working class will revolt, them and the immigrants, he said."

"No need for a revolt around here—the city council decided to issue licenses and started handing them out. Your pa read the resolution stating that the league was mortified with the city for doing it. I'm not sure how he squared that with his brother, the mayor, though."

"Me either, Rev. Loguen. But my friend George Pfohl's pa just got his license, and they were pretty happy about it. And Parish Johnson told me that the watch house was full up from Indians sleeping off their annual stipend, them and anyone caught sellin' 'em liquor."

"That's a shame, Edward."

"My pa gets worked up every year around this time. You think he'll bring it up at the State Convention later this month, Reverend?"

"More than likely, but I can't imagine what good it will do. Have you ever heard of preachin' to the converted, Edward?"

"I think so—is that when folks agree about the things they already know?"

"Hmm, there's truth in that," Rev. Loguen said.

# Chapter Thirteen

(June – July 1851)

One day before school in the middle of June, Charlie Willard looked about ready to explode with excitement. He couldn't wait to share a hot story with everyone in the newspaper class. Once again, Mr. William L. Crandal was present, and after an opening prayer, Mr. Weld relieved Charlie of his distress.

"All right, gentlemen, Mr. Crandal is here so we'll start with the news! Mr. Charles J. Willard, I believe you have an announcement."

Charlie stood tall, face aglow, "That I do, sir. Mr. Weld, Mr. Crandal, everyone, it's official—*Jenny Lind is coming to Syracuse!*"

After a chaotic outburst, Crandal remarked, "That's great! How much are tickets going for?"

"Mr. Crandal, I heard they're gonna be around three dollars," Charlie replied, crestfallen at the unreachable price.

"What made her decide to play Syracuse, Charles?" Mr. Weld asked.

"Jenny wants to see Niagara Falls, Mr. Weld, and she'll hit Syracuse coming or going there, but Jenny Lind will be in Syracuse next month, sir."

"Where's she gonna sing, Charlie?" Larry Sabine asked.

*Jenny Lind*

"Not sure yet, Larry—I suppose whatever place can fit the most people."

Austin Cook quipped, "Ticket prices are a little steep, eh, Charlie?"

*"Don't remind me!"* Charlie snapped angrily, "But I'll be there listening alright—one way or another!"

Mr. Weld interrupted to change the subject. "Mr. Stoddard, I see you're anxious to be next."

"Yes, I am, Mr. Weld. It's about the Utica fires, sir—the fireman, James J. Orcutt, was convicted of arson in the first degree!

"What can you tell us about him, Will?" Mr. Crandal asked.

"He's pretty young, sir—maybe in his late teens, and he worked at one of the Utica iron foundries."

"What did the judge say, Will?" Charlie Pope asked.

"I have it right here, Charlie," Will replied, holding up a paper, "Judge Allen talked to Orcutt for ten or fifteen minutes then he said, I sentence you to be taken from jail on the first Friday in August next, between the hours of nine and four, between the rising and setting of the sun, and taken to some convenient place in the county of Oneida, and hung by the neck until dead, and may God have mercy on your soul."

Someone yelled, "That's fast work—convict 'im in June and hang 'im in August!"

"Yup—that's what an arsonist should expect!" another answered.

"Hey, Will—was anyone else charged?" I asked.

"Yes! Another fireman named Horace B. Conklin."

Mr. Crandal changed the topic by asking, "Excuse me gentlemen, would anyone care to accompany me this afternoon? I'm going to see the Aztek Children at Malcolm Hall!"

Our curiosity intensified, questions flew from every corner of the room, nobody waited for an answer. Crandal made us all anxious to examine the human oddities on display.

"They were discovered last year, deep in the jungle, at the ancient city of Iximaya!" Crandal began, doing his best P.T. Barnum imitation, pausing in-between phrases to let his words sink in. "A boy and girl,

Maximo and Bartola, were found squatting on an altar of idols, and they're both shorter than a yard stick," he pronounced, trying to be serious but unable to conceal his humor.

After school, many of us accompanied Mr. Crandal to Malcolm Hall to see the famous *Aztek children*. They were even smaller than I imagined, and very childlike. Purported as the last two survivors of the Aztec race, Maximo and Bartola were running around and touching everyone. Abel Cook became enthralled, much like he did in believing the *Kentucky Fat Boy* was an Anakim. With a twinkle in his eye, he pronounced their authenticity and proclaimed, *"They're Azteks!"*

Austin said, "They must only weigh twenty pounds each, but I ain't so sure what they look like—maybe, they're not human!"

Mr. Crandal overheard, to say, "They look like each other, Austin, and nothing else, living, dead, or imagined."

"They're the last of an ancient race never conquered by the Spaniards, Mr. Crandal," Abel Cook said with resolve, repeating the pitchman's words.

Austin replied, "That's what they want you to believe, Abel—after this they'll be in Barnum's museum next to the bearded lady."

"He's right, Abel," Charlie Pope said, "And right by her sister, the tattooed lady, can you believe it?"

*The Aztek Children*

"I can," Parish Johnson answered. "The Police Court's been full of women lately—Mary McGurk, Mary Jacobson, and Elizabeth McCormick were brought in for kicking up a row, and Matilda Cady, Thankful Long, and Emma Sullivan were accused of keeping a disorderly house."

"Hey, Parish, wasn't it at Thankful Long's house where Lowell gave Emeline the pinky tickle?"

"That's right, you should've been there when the judge heard the disorderly house case. Lots of their friends showed up, and witnesses were sworn, but they didn't prove the house was disorderly, so the judge let 'em all go. Then everyone in the courtroom cheered!"

I laughed, "Ha! Looks like Thankful Long's living out her name."

"Yup, let's ask your pa to get her into the State Temperance Convention!"

My pa, Charles A. Wheaton, might have been the driest man in town, even up against the likes of Rev. May, William H. Burleigh, Oliver Teall, and a host of others. His considered views on abolition, temperance, and religion were well-documented in the newspapers and lived out openly in his day-to-day life. His peers understood him. Pa lived by doing more than he said, and saying what he believed. He was never afraid to speak or act as the situation required.

Pa was known for his kindness, too. Through his friendship with Rev. Loguen he became a great enabler of the underground railroad, his generosity provided immediate, albeit not permanent, relief for the many fugitive slaves who arrived in Syracuse.

As a member of the executive committee, the convention for the New York State Temperance Society commanded his attention. At the opening, chairman Burleigh read a report that summarized how dreadful things were ever since Gerrit Smith had quit. Funds were tight with the loss of their largest contributor, prompting cancelation of the publication, the *Temperance Protector*. Lucky for the society, the new *Carson League* periodical filled the void.

Pa read several letters from friends unable to attend, then others presented resolutions for a vote. Mr. Miller said there weren't twenty men in the State Legislature who didn't drink liquor, and with such men to make laws, they shouldn't expect temperance legislation.

Dr. Wisner said they can do comparatively nothing without political action. He thought their society was like a steam-boiler filled with steam, which must blow off or burst the boiler.

During the convention's second day, Rev. May proposed a resolution to prevent the election of Daniel Webster as President.

*"Resolved, That the intemperance of the Hon. Daniel Webster, so notorious, that his most unscrupulous adherents will not soberly deny it, is a sufficient reason why all true friends of our country, and of humanity, should exert themselves to prevent his election to the Presidency, without any other consideration of his qualifications for that high office."*

Rev. May's call met with considerable opposition, especially from fellow clergymen. In the final, approved version, Webster's name was replaced with the words, *any candidate.*

Then Pa offered a resolution.

*"Resolved, That the influence of the members of the Cabinet of this nation, in their late tour through this state, to say nothing of other states, is very disastrous to the cause of Temperance; participating, as some of them did, at all of their public dinners, in the use of intoxicating liquors—thus giving the influence of their high example to the perpetuation of such drinking customs and habits in the community, as we are laboring to extirpate and destroy."*

After a lengthy debate, the resolution was laid on the table. A prayer concluded the proceedings, and the convention adjourned. Pa wasn't smiling when he came home.

Ma wasn't smiling either. She was thirty-five, with her tenth child late arriving. Preparing for Ma's confinement, Black George readied her a quiet, resting place. Little Henry protested, so they shipped him off to the relatives.

The day after the temperance convention, my seventh sister was born. Ma named her Mary Haskal Wheaton in tribute to her longtime friend, but everyone called her *Minnie.* Our new addition seemed happy and healthy, and she was quiet, too, which endeared her all the more. Family friends and relatives called to pay their compliments and to pass Minnie around for hugs. Everyone remarked at her beauty, the ladies struggled to let her go. My sisters could have led a parade. I soon achieved my fill of cuteness and sought Black George in the root cellar to talk about anything unrelated to childbirth.

The following week I managed to have a private conversation with Ma, our first since Minnie was born. Seated comfortably, newspapers and magazines scattered on the sofa—she still couldn't get her fill of the *Great Exhibition* in London.

"Come sit next to me, Edward!" she directed. I want to hear what you've been up to."

"Well, Ma, I don't know how much you heard about the State Temperance Convention—everyone was talking about it."

"Yes, your father shared his frustrations with me."

"Yeah, Ma, but did you know that a fireman from Utica was sentenced to hang for arson? He told his pastor that he blamed it on the alcohol—said he deplored the weakness that made him the victim of criminal excitement!"

"I can believe that, Edward," Ma replied, then holding up a newspaper she said, "I was just reading that Horace Greeley gave a temperance lecture in London with the Black minister Henry Garnet. With the World's Fair happening, the reporter said that he'd never seen so many drunks in one place in his life!"

"Did Pa tell you about the notice that Uncle Horace put out? He gave fair warning that the police would enforce the liquor laws, and that violators would be prosecuted. It's in all the papers, Ma. Just the other day John Honor was arrested on complaint of Pitkin Butler."

"You've been with Parish Johnson, haven't you?" she asked, not waiting for an answer. "What else have I missed?"

"Well, I probably shouldn't tell you, but an eight-year-old drowned in the Oswego Canal. He must've slipped and fell in, and nobody suspected anything till they saw his cap floating in the water."

"That's terrible—the poor boy and his family!"

"And a nine-year-old German boy was found wandering the streets, he said his name was George Peet and he came from Albany—they got 'im at the Orphan Asylum now."

Sensing I was finished, she asked, "Is that it? How are you and Sam doing with your chicken business?"

"Oh, me and Sam are doin' good, Ma, we're gettin' lots of advice and makin' money! We'll have Pa and Rev. Ward paid back in no time."

"That's great, but I wonder why you haven't mentioned this year's Rose Festival—are you ready for Thursday night? Your sisters are!"

"Yeah, Ma, I'm ready—all I have to do is get dressed up and sit in the crowd."

"And cheer!" Ma added. "The girls are counting on your support—and your friends, too!"

"We'll be there, Grove wouldn't miss a chance to be near Miss Ellen." He had a thing for my sister.

As promised, a bunch of us arrived early to get seats for the annual Festival of the Rose. Decorative placards announced a *pleasant assemblage of youth, beauty, music, and flowers*, while we read it as an opportunity to ogle our favorites, and all their friends. Miles Bennett celebrated that his popular sister, Lucy, had outgrown the pageant, and a Miss Stevens was crowned Queen. Towards the end, Grove became entranced by a solo from *Miss Ellen*, so I asked him when he'd be declaring again. He happily replied,

"I do declare she got the best pipes on stage!"

North and south, and now west to California, Americans celebrated our nation's 75th birthday on Friday, **the 4th of July 1851!** The thirty-first state in the union celebrated its first Independence Day from Pelican Bay to San Diego and everywhere in-between. The mines were

still producing with abundance, headlines of steamships filled with gold continued to capture imaginations around the world.

Inexplicably, the festivities in Syracuse left much to be desired. Throughout the month of June, city papers increasingly complained that no arrangements were being made. The *Standard* featured a comedic devil making his own plans. People feared a mass exodus of the Syracuse fire companies, along with the local militias and their bands, leaving the city parade-less on the Fourth of July. Samsel's German Band had already accepted invitation to Cazenovia, and the Syracuse Citizens' Corps and National Guards, accompanied by Kellogg's Brass Band were booked by the Village of Baldwinsville. The contingent hoped to return in time to parade in our city, but a long afternoon of ardent toasting stood in the way.

Direct appeals were made to the city council, but as the date approached without movement, people called their own meeting to take action. Nevertheless, the holiday arrived without official arrangements from city leaders, but the ban on firecrackers was paused for a few days, and an excellent display of fireworks was launched. Some took consolation that the famous Italian opera soprano, Teresa Parodi, would arrive in a couple of weeks.

Sam Ward asked me to go with him to hear his father speak at the Congregational Church on the Fourth of July. I gladly accepted, and my own pa didn't need convincing. I helped Black George bring the horse and carriage around, and Pa drove us all downtown. My sisters stayed home with Ma and the baby, while I piled in back with Mrs. Ward, Sam, and his sisters. Rev. Ward sat up front with my father—I could tell that Pa liked him.

Crossing Orange St., Cale Davis recognized us, and we him, without an exchange of friendly greetings. Pa remained a contender on Davis's favorites list, right up there with Rev. May. The butcher didn't think much of the Rev. Samuel R. Ward either. As our carriage rolled past, Davis mused, *"Who's he thinks he is? Darkie don't know his place!"*

Arriving at the Congregational Church, many were eager to shake hands with Rev. Ward and to greet Mrs. Ward and the family. The atmosphere was charged with patriotic feelings from people who longed to celebrate. I scanned the crowd for familiar faces, quickly recognizing Mr. George Vashon, Rev. Loguen, Rev. Lyles, and Jerry. Then I saw Rev. May and Mr. Williston, too.

The speaker's reputation filled the seats of the Congregational church with people of all colors, shapes, and sizes, all anxious to hear the Rev. Samuel Ringgold Ward. Several babies cried, making me glad we left Minnie behind, snuggled up at home. Having been promised an oration in the spirit of 1776, the attentive audience awaited his address. Rev. Ward took command of the podium and spoke with his accustomed eloquence, his words founded by the Bible and the Declaration of Independence.

He said, "The Whigs deny the faith of their revolutionary fathers, whose Whiggism was but another name for self-sacrificing love of liberty. The Democrats claim Jefferson as their father and boast of his having written the Declaration of Independence, but they hate nothing so intensely as Jefferson's writings against slavery—and that very Declaration of Independence, when, among "ALL MEN" in it declared to be entitled by God to the unalienable right to liberty, Negroes were said to be included.

What the abolitionists demand, and now contend for, is the simple application of the principles of the Declaration of Independence to the black as well as the white, and that the former should share the benefits secured by the constitution as well as the latter. Believing just what the Declaration of Independence says that the right of man to liberty is unalienable, they hold that no enactments, no constitutions, no consent of the man himself, no combinations of men, can alienate that which is by God's fiat made unalienable."

Rev. Ward spoke for a good hour, captivating his listeners. After the church service, we waited outside while he exchanged pleasantries with a long line of well-wishers—I felt important sitting near him in our carriage. Cale Davis couldn't have cared less, but I figured that was *his* loss.

In the days following the holiday, Syracusans learned that our city was outperformed from every direction; by Cazenovia in the east, Baldwinsville to the west, Cortland to the south, and perhaps the most telling from Oswego in the north. Although Syracuse and Oswego both became cities in 1848, this year's 4th of July celebration at the harbor on Lake Ontario put Syracuse to shame. A grand procession formed in front of the city hall that stretched for half a mile, moving through the streets to the public square where the Genesee poet, W.H.C. Hosmer, delivered the oration.

After the fireworks display and the consumption of a significant amount of liquor, the usual number of fights occurred, but things never got out of control. The worst incident of Oswego's celebration happened in the morning when a drummer from Company F was seriously injured by the premature discharge of a cannon—the same cannon that misfired last year and took the right hand of another unfortunate gunner, much like what befell Grasshopper in Syracuse many years ago.

On the fifth of July, Parish Johnson told me about the lively business at the police office.

"With all the comings and goings, they ought to just take the door off the watchhouse, Ed! I never saw so many long faces and aching heads in my life, but they're more lenient with drunks than with illegal liquor sales."

"That happens every year, Parish—did anything unusual happen?" I asked.

"Well, yeah, there was a tragedy when a little girl died after she ate a poisoned cracker left in the street!"

"*Oh, no!* It must've come from the same people who're poisoning the watch dogs."

"Yeah, that's what everyone's sayin' at the police office," Parish confirmed.

"Don't get worse than that," I lamented.

A few nights later, at one in the morning, Pa woke me with a determined shake.

*"Wake up and get dressed, Edward! The store's on fire and we've got to get down there fast!"*

I sensed our house awakening from the sounds of my parents moving about. Pa lit candles to illuminate the darkened rooms, Black George stumbled past my doorway.

"Get ready, Edward!" Ma encouraged me. "Your pa needs you!"

"Okay, Ma—gettin' my shoes on now!" I responded.

With worried looks, Cornelia and Ellen joined Ma to see us off, then Pa, Black George, and I hustled to the nearby livery, soon galloping down Genesee St. to save our store if we could.

"How'd you know about the fire, Pa?" I asked.

"Someone at the Syracuse House saw it first—then Norman Gillette sent a boy here to tell me," Pa answered. "Did you hear a knock at the door?"

"No, Pa—I didn't hear anything until you woke me up."

"Me, neither," Black George agreed.

The fire illuminated Clinton Square like I'd never seen it before or since. We arrived to find our building very far gone like the others around it. The old wooden block was entirely consumed—the brick walls of Wheaton Hardware and E.B. Wicks were the only structures to stand against the flames. The surrounding streets were haphazardly piled with a myriad of contents hastily removed just ahead of the blaze.

Syracuse firemen performed admirably! Were it not for their actions the inferno would have continued down the street, fed by an extensive line of wooden buildings. Still, many spectators stood idle, hands in pockets, not lifting a finger to save property, nor to assist the firemen despite their obvious signs of exhaustion. I couldn't help but notice the irony in that most of the volunteers came from the working class—people who seldom owned property of their own. Much was saved and much was lost.

Pa spoke with Orsamus Van Der Voort, our building's resident tinsmith, to thank him for saving what he did for us. I overheard Orsamus tell Pa he was glad that he boarded nearby on Warren St. and got there early. Capt. Edwin R. Prendergast of the Syracuse National Guards lost his auction house amongst twenty other businesses burnt to the ground.

Despite the great material loss, the next day city pulpits rang with gratitude that not a soul was claimed. At home, tales of the ensuing chaos, combined with seeing Pa highly agitated, made Ma unwell to the point of sending for the doctor who extended her confinement for the rest of July.

Over the following days, a great number of laborers were hard at work clearing away the charred remains of what was now being called the *Burnt District*. Teamsters were in high demand; Orson Brown, Peter Deyo, and Dudley G. Carrier made repeated hauls of debris, as did Hezekiah Goodrich, Lyman Hemsted, Casper Huller, and Milton Kain. Business operated on a first-come, first-served basis, regardless of race or nationality, for individuals such as the German Adolf Mutte, the Irishman Davey Myers, or the teamsters John Jackson and Frank Lando. Black George introduced me to Frank as we stood together on Clinton Square, eyeballing the former Wheaton Hardware. The property owner, Mr. Townsend, vowed to have the corner rebuilt in six weeks!

Parish Johnson was thrilled that Pa made arrangements to temporarily locate our store in an open corner of the Journal Building. Now we'd be downstairs from the Police Office, where they were busy with the poisoning investigation—the latest victim was the old watch dog at the Onondaga County Bank. For me, being in the Journal Building meant that I could check on my favorite printer, Chauncey Crofoot, to see how black his fingernails were.

During the last two weeks of July, Syracuse played host to three songbirds of world acclaim. My friend Charlie Willard was ecstatic.

"Hey Ed! Did you know that Madame Anna Bishop will be at Malcolm Hall on Monday, and that Jenny Lind will sing in Utica on Tuesday? *This means that Jenny should be here on Wednesday, Ed!*" Charlie exclaimed.

"Everybody in town knows that, Charlie," I replied.

Undeterred, he answered, "Oh, yeah? Well don't forget that Mademoiselle Parodi is still coming here, too!"

July 15, 1851, was an incredible day with the announcement that Jenny Lind would perform in Syracuse the following night. Ticket sales would commence in the morning, creating a buying frenzy never seen before. Exactly 1,100 seats would be sold to fill the First Baptist Church, selected for its acoustics and seating capacity. Tickets priced between two and four dollars were no deterrent to speculators poised to turn a hefty profit.

Charlie Pope, the Cheney's, and I were surveying the *Burnt District* when Clinton Square began to fill with people determined to get inside the former Rust's Hotel for a ticket to the Jenny Lind show. I wondered if Philo was watching, and what he'd think about the mob fighting to get inside his old place, anxious to part with their money. The Salina St. bridge clogged to a standstill, the Empire block was surrounded.

Turning our backs to the Burnt District, we watched the spectacle unfold. Bright sunshine increased the temperature, souring temperaments as the crowd pressed for entry. Suddenly, Prentice yelled,

"Hey, did you see that? A fight's gonna break out!"

"Over on the left side, there? Yeah, I saw it too!" Charlie Pope answered.

"I just saw a lady get knocked over!" Si Cheney cried.

"Me, too, Si!—People are going nuts for tickets!" I hollered back.

"If I had the money, I'd hire a blacksmith to fight his way inside. Looks like the only way to get a ticket," Charlie suggested.

"Great idea, Charlie," Prentice confirmed. "That Enoch Lacy's a real bruiser!"

"Right, and Squire Deer could elbow his way inside with those big arms of his," I agreed.

As chaotic as things were in the street, it was even worse inside from the heat and lack of ventilation. We watched as fainted bodies were passed overhead to the fresh air outside, where the sun felled others packed together like fish in a barrel—bodies wiggling hard and going nowhere.

"Man, can you believe it?" Prentice observed.

"I never seen people go crazy like this before!" Charlie agreed.

Si Cheney spotted the Johnson brothers, and called across the sea of humanity. *"Hey, Parish! Hey, Grove!"* he yelled, summoning them with his waving arm.

"Hey there, fellas!" Parish said as the pair approached. Grove echoed, "Hey everyone!"

"Hey, Parish, you all on special assignment from the Police Office?" I joked.

"Ha! They could use some help with all the pickpockets. Officer Green just caught this guy all dressed up in a fancy suit with a bunch of pickpocket tools on 'im. Shattuck, Lowell, and the rest are out tryin' to catch more of 'em, too."

Ticket madness continued through dinner time, hawkers made enormous profits on Genesee Street, and all around the First Baptist Church by the corner of Franklin. Even at exorbitant prices, there just weren't enough tickets to be had. To satisfy the desperate, an ingenious homeowner next door to the church sold rooftop seats at the bargain rate of one dollar each. *Jenny Mania* caused people to spend their money like they all had plenty to burn.

The early summer heat didn't relent with the approach of evening. When doors opened at 6:30 p.m. the church filled quickly, increasing the temperature indoors considerably. Having all the windows opened wide proved a blessing to everyone inside and out. Scanning the crowd, I noticed that Charlie Willard had secured a position outside an open window. He didn't see us approach.

"Hey, Charlie! You got a great spot to hear Jenny," I remarked as we came up behind him.

"Oh, hey yourself, Ed," he answered. "You're darn right I did!"

"Hey, Charlie—you here alone? Where's Billy and Flo?" Grove Johnson asked.

"They're off taking a wee somewhere, Grove—you guys are all staying for the show, right?" Charlie asked with obvious excitement.

Grove nodded, but I answered remorsefully, "I wish I could, but Ma said she'd close the chicken coop if I did."

"What are you talking about, Ed?"

"Blame my sisters! Cornelia and Ellen both wanted to see Jenny, but Pa said that his daughters weren't allowed anywhere near the debauchery in the streets. Then Ma told me the same thing goes for me, and she'd skin me alive if I came home with Jenny Lind stories."

"But you're here now, Ed! Ain't you in trouble already?"

"Yeah, but way less than if the girls whine to Ma that I got to hear Jenny Lind, and they didn't."

"Us, too, Charlie," Prentice added while Si nodded somberly. "Pa kept our sister, Frances, home, too."

Charlie Pope announced, "Well, I don't have any sisters so I'm stickin' around!"

"Sorry you guys gotta leave," Grove reflected, "But tell Miss Ellen hello for me, would you?"

As soon as we departed, Si Cheney protested, "This ain't right! I'm older than Grove, and he gets to stay."

"Yeah, but Grove only lives a block away on Church Street, Si." I said to no avail—the three of us were pretty glum walking away from where all the action was.

The next day we heard about all that we missed. The show began at 8 p.m. sharp with a solo by the Italian tenor, Signor E. Belletti, then the audience erupted when Jenny rose to sing *"Come unto Him"* from

Handel's *Messiah*. For two hours she wowed the crowd, closing with a stunning rendition of the "Echo Song." From what I heard, everyone left satisfied, including a thousand people in the streets, but none more, I think, than Charlie Willard.

## Chapter Fourteen
### (July – August 1851)

With her memory firmly entrenched in our community, the "Swedish Nightingale" departed for Niagara Falls, performing several concerts enroute, including shows in Rochester and Buffalo. She sang in nearby Auburn the following evening, coincidently on the same night as Madame Anna Bishop. Typical of every stop on her American tour, multitudes of followers sang her praises—most entranced by her rendition of the "Echo Song." Still, differing accounts of the songbird began to resonate, not all of a flattering nature.

Despite her reputation for philanthropy, some had it that Jenny's mood could swing from sweet and charming to utterly disagreeable in a flash. To be fair, I gave allowance for the endless demands on her immediate attention. But still, Harvey Baldwin took the brunt of it. Unbeknownst to the songstress, Syracuse's first mayor and a small group took a buggy to meet Jenny's approaching train where it stopped at nearby Chittenango, intending to greet her and to provide official escort to Syracuse. When the nightingale desired her privacy, non-angelic tones emanated from inside the train.

"*I don't care who they are, tell them to get out of my car!*"

All poor Harvey could do was tuck tail and beeline for the buggy. Upon her arrival in Syracuse, I heard that the diva had refused lady callers at the Syracuse House, ordering a hammer and nails for the doors and windows of her room. I could understand her nailing the door, but it was way too hot for the windows.

Two nights after Jenny Lind sang, Madame Anna Bishop filled Malcolm Hall before another appreciative audience. By all accounts she sang great, but Jenny proved a hard act to follow. With the city still on fire for Mademoiselle Lind, a real blaze ignited on West Street that consumed a block of wooden buildings adjoining the freight depot of the Syracuse and Utica Railroad. Syracuse firemen earned the undying gratitude of railroad president, John Wilkinson, who expressed his appreciation with tangible practicality. This conflagration wasn't as large as what became the *burnt district*, but amongst the losses were the uniforms and equipment of the Irish militia, the Syracuse National Guards, who could ill afford it.

He'd never admit it, but it's my belief that it was the culmination of all the excitement from the Jenny Lind show, and the fires, which inspired Pa to call another temperance meeting at the Congregational church. While keeping the faithful from falling off the wagon, the society could mend their constitution and transact other business according to propriety. Pa said that he still wanted to do something more for the Indians.

Parish Johnson said that he agreed with Pa after he and Grove knocked at my door, fresh from their latest visit to the Police Office. Parish told me how Officer Kenyon brought in Jemima Solomon for being drunk and disorderly, and that Officer Shattuck had arrested another Indian, Charles Crowfoot, for giving Jemima the liquor.

"How bout that? Even if you're an Indian you can't give liquor to an Indian!" Parish exclaimed. "You think your pa can get 'em to join the temperance society?"

"I doubt it, Parish—they follow Indian law and the society's more about trying to change New York State laws."

"Yeah, I guess you're right—and they mostly keep to themselves at *the Castle*."

"That ain't what they're doin' out west—especially in California!" I pronounced.

"You been talkin' to Charlie Pope, Ed?" Parish asked.

"Oh, I see you have, too," I answered, laughing. We both knew Charlie's proclivity for the wild west.

"Yup, Charlie said that he read how large movements of Indians could make people feel leery, especially with reports of Indian raids on the settlements."

"Right, and 130 men rode out to confront 'em!"

"The next war could be with the Indians, Ed."

"Well, I'm glad they ain't like that around here, Parish."

"Me, too, I'd hate to be out huntin' or fishin' and have to run back to circle the wagons!"

"You been drinkin' Mr. Freeof's special batch, Parish? Milo showed me the jug that his pa hides in the closet."

"Ha! I seen it too, Mr. Freeof could do a toast for the latest Anakim in town. Don't tell Abel Cook, but this one's called the Nova Scotia Giant!"

A bunch of us turned out for Circus day. It began with a solar eclipse that commenced at seven o'clock in the morning and lasted for an hour and a half. With only about one tenth of the sun obscured, it was still eerie—like a harbinger that something unexpected would happen. Brightly colored circus boats and the promise of entertainment drew the community to watch their slow approach on the Erie Canal.

Always the showman, Dan Rice made his typical grand entrance, pitching a massive circus tent on the corner of Salina and Jefferson. Dan made at least one stop in Syracuse every canal season, last here in September. His troupe of horse performers always put on a great

*Dan Rice*

show, but the audience tired of his constant airing of grievances. His former employer, Dr. Spaulding, had heard enough, he recently had Dan arrested in Rochester for slander. The showman made bail to salvage the season.

I joined the sea of people yearning for the afternoon performance, but looking around I began to notice a growing number of unhappy faces in the crowd. Happening directly across the street, a solemn vigil was in process at the home of Gardner Lawerence. The late Police Justice and City Alderman had died on Saturday morning, his funeral being today. Esteemed for his steady, honorable character, a great number of Syracuse society were visible paying their respects, including both my parents.

And yet, *the show must go on!*

With the circus boats arrival, the bustle began opposite the house in mourning. By noon the work was done, complete with cake, beer, and rum stands on the sidewalk. By 2 p.m. the loafers descended, along with many Indians and squaws eager to see the show. At 3 p.m. the funeral exercises commenced, at times drowned out from the audience cheering for Dan Rice and his troupe. When the afternoon show concluded, the uproar and profanity of the crowd spilled into the street outside, permeating the home in lamentation.

That evening, Dan Rice held a second performance before another excited audience, even louder than the first. The revelry lasted to a late hour, adding to the grieving family's angst. Ma didn't mince words after I got home.

"Edward, I'm sorry we let you participate in that downtown disgrace!"

"Huh? What do you mean, Ma? I only went to the circus with my friends."

"Sure! Part of the crowd that paid no heed to what was happening across the street. A weeping widow and orphaned children subjected to the chorus of inebriated roughs. We're a Christian society, Edward, and the circus incites heathen drunkenness and lewd behavior!"

"But we only went to see the trick riding, Ma. You shoulda seen the *Sprites of the Silver Shower!*"

"You can just *trick* yourself up to bed, mister!" Ma growled, and I wisely complied. I didn't understand why she railed against the circus, even when there *wasn't* a funeral happening across the street—the entire police force was there! When we saw Officer Lowell talking with Emeline and Thankful Long, Prentice said he wished that Lowell would find an errant thread on Emeline's blouse to demonstrate his famous pinky tickle, drawing circles around one of her large nipples, and smiling.

Well, perhaps Ma was right about the lewd behavior, but at least we didn't drink.

July of 1851 ended with a bustle of activity in Syracuse. Ladies in favor of reforming the dress code *for the health and happiness of females* met at Mr. Burleigh's house on Madison Street. The gathering was called to discuss the alternatives to the traditional *street sweeper* variety of dress including tips on how to make them. Following speeches, discussion, display, and handling, a resolution was made stating that *the General adoption of the American costume is well worth the effort, as well as an example of intelligent American women, who know and feel not only the dignity of their sex, but its obligation and capacity to improve the condition of society.*

Near month's end, New York State Governor Washington Hunt granted James Orcutt respite from his August hanging for arson, now scheduled to swing on October 24. Most people surmised that Orcutt's postponement was granted in hopes of discovering other incendiaries. So far, only the Utica firemen, Orcutt and Conklin, had been charged.

On the last day of July, one of the best opera singers in the world, Mademoiselle Teresa Parodi, sang before a sell-out crowd at Malcolm Hall—tickets moved quickly after prices were reduced to a dollar. Like Madame Bishop, the audience loved her, but she didn't turn heads like Jenny Lind. I witnessed heartfelt debates around our dinner table about the singing talents of the recent performers, but no amount of passionate argument could change any minds. When I asked Pa why the Syracuse Musical Institute (that he ran) never sang back-up he sent me down to the root cellar to help Black George. I told George what happened, and he said he was hoping that Elizabeth Taylor Greenfield, the *Black Swan*, would come to Syracuse.

"Whenever she sing, ever-body stop to listen—she dat good!" he said.

"I believe you George, you were right about the *Nightingale's*. Cornelia still says that was one of her favorite shows!"

"Oh yeah, when she right, she right!"

"Hey George, you gotta bring anything down to the Loguen's? I'll help you, George—we can check the coop for eggs first!" I urged.

Following my plan, we encountered Sam Ward Jr. at the coop with the same idea.

"Ha! Funny meetin' you here, Sam—great minds think alike—right George?" I jested.

"You boys be two jokesters I thinks," Black George countered.

Sam affirmed it. "That what my pa says, too, George—he's down to Loguen's now."

"We can bring some eggs with the vegies that George gathered—lots of cucumbers and some huge squash," I said excitedly.

"No dillydallyin' now!" Black George ordered, "I gots things to do."

"Yes sir, Mr. George!" Sam responded.

Mrs. Caroline Loguen smiled when we presented her with a bushel of fresh vegetables and a basketful of eggs. The underground railroad kept steady pressure on her pantry, so she hugged us all, and she kissed Sam on the head.

"Thank you kindly, Mr. George! And make sure to thank your folks for me, Edward, you hear me now?" Mrs. Loguen directed. "The men be out back makin' high talk and fussin'."

"What they fussin' bout, Mrs. Loguen?" Sam asked.

"They was *discussin'* the colored folk's convention and the slave law, but then they gots to *fussin'* over invadin' Cuba. I told 'em they can't do nothin' bout it—plenty nuff to worry bout right here in Syracuse!"

Black George agreed. "Sho is, Missus, I be steppin' out back now to pay respects, ma'am."

Sam and I followed Black George past the screen door to join the backyard gathering. Mrs. Loguen yelled to her husband.

"Jermain—you thank Mr. George and the boys for the stores they brung over—the good Lord musta sent 'em!"

Rev. Loguen smiled and hollered back, *"Yes, ma'am—directly!"*

The party laughed; everyone shook hands in greeting. Men of high morals, intelligence, and courage (who happened to be black) had gathered in the Loguen's backyard on the corner of Genesee and Pine, including Rev. Loguen, Rev. Ward, George Boyer Vashon, Rev. Lyles, several newcomers direct from the underground railroad, and Jerry Henry with his red hair.

Rev. Loguen said heartily, "I thank you, Mr. George, Mr. Edward, and Mr. Samuel Ward Jr. for helpin' fugitive slaves to embrace liberty."

"Startin' with a full belly!" Rev. Lyles added.

"We thanks yuh sirs," the newcomers offered.

Gesturing toward us, George Vashon said, "We should send these gentlemen to the next convention to give practical advice on helping runaways."

"What be that?" Black George asked.

"There was a Colored People's State Convention in Albany, George," Vashon answered, "but mostly folks from around New York and the capitol attended."

"What dey say in Albany, George?" Black George asked the lawyer.

"Plenty," Vashon replied. "They debated colonization, the voting laws, and having equal use of the common schools of the State."

*"And they condemned the Fugitive Slave Law!"* Jerry Henry declared with feeling.

"That they did, Jerry, a most heinous act straight from Hell's ruler," Rev. Lyles affirmed.

Rev. Loguen said, "We were just tellin' the new folks about the Vigilance Committee in Syracuse, and how the church bell will ring a certain way to signal that a runaway's been captured. So far, there's only been a false alarm."

"That bell got my heart a poundin' though—didn't it?" Rev. Lyles remarked.

"Well, at least the people of Syracuse made a stand against the Slave Law! Advertising that we have a Vigilance Committee should make the slavers think twice—we can only hope," George Vashon offered.

"We need more than hope, George—I mean to face it as a man!" Rev. Loguen said defiantly.

Observing the group, Jerry said, "Most of our heads would bring a price."

With his hand on Sam's shoulder, Rev. Ward answered. "Truly said! The slavers believe they own your children along with your soul. Someday, I want to live without looking over my shoulder."

"Yes, suh," a stranger said. "Dats what we done all de way from Carolina."

"Buts we made it!" a companion said.

"We sho did, we hear dat Syracuse be kind to niggers runnin'!"

"Yessum—we told to look for Rev. May and Rev. Loguen."

Rev. Lyles spoke with angst, "But the damned *Fugitive Slave Law* says that black men be property, and all the white folk have to turn 'em in!"

"Yeah, we hear lotta talk bout dat round da border with free States."

"'Tis an ill wind that blows nobody good, and silent pulpits embolden the Negro-catchers," Rev. Ward declared.

"And they're gettin' bolder all the time—goin' after Cuba now!" Jerry said.

Rev. Lyles affirmed, "There's great unrest on the island from an expected invasion. And in New York and New Orleans they're makin' demonstrations to free Cuba. They're cryin' *Lopez, Quitman, and Liberty!*"

George Vashon said, "If the Cubans truly desire freedom from Spain, and show a willingness to fight it out, Americans from every State would flock to their banner. But Spanish and American war ships patrol the Gulf for invaders, and I don't believe the people have the courage or desire to overthrow the Spanish soldiers."

"Nor I," Rev. Ward agreed. "It's ironic that the filibusterers think themselves freedom fighters in Cuba, yet they keep Black men enslaved at home! Still, it's good the president dispatched a naval deterrent."

Rev. Loguen said, "Yes, and here in New York they created the 51st regiment to align the militias. But I hope the new regiment is never called out like they were in Boston."

*"Never! We gotta keep soldiers outta slave catchin'!"* Jerry cried.

Rev. Lyles jested, "Who runnin' the 51st? He'll have to make the Germans fall in with the Irish—Ha! Lotta Germans don't like *those people*."

George Vashon answered, "Colonel Origen Vandenburgh was appointed, John, and I heard that he's meeting the local commanders."

Having watch house experience for over-drinking, Jerry said, "it'll take more than the 51st to keep a drunk Irishman outta the canal. They found one floatin' by the first lock at three this mornin' until a German fished 'im out."

All the talk of Germans reminded me that I hadn't seen George Pfohl in a while—now as good a time as any, I took leave of the party. Before I left, Rev. Loguen thanked me again, and he told the strangers that my pa was a good friend to the railroad.

In early August 1851, headlines rang with another invasion of Cuba! Heavily laden with men and arms, the steamers *Cincinnati* and *Pampero*

departed from New Orleans with General Lopez aboard the latter. A spontaneous mass celebration erupted at the expedition's launch, with high hopes to elude the sloops of war *Preble* and *Plymouth*, on patrol with orders to intercept.

To gain a military view of the invasion, I again sought George Pfohl to ask what his father, Captain Pfohl, had to say. Enroute, I encountered a bored looking Charlie Pope, now excited to join me.

*Gen. Narciso Lopez*

"I'll go with ya, Ed, I ain't missin' nothin' round here," he declared. "Maybe we'll see the Ojibway Indian Chiefs on their way to Washington!"

"Yeah—I saw 'em the other day with their faces painted with streaks of red, black, and yellow, and they wore headbands stuck full-a-feathers."

"Ed, I heard the Chiefs saw Jenny Lind in Rochester on their way here."

"Word has it that she's sweet on some guy in her group," I countered.

"No matter, the Chiefs liked her just the same."

"Maybe they'll get a Jenny Lind ornament to wear along with their other ones. I liked how they fastened bells at the bottom of their leggins' to make 'em tinkle whenever they moved!"

Charlie said, "I heard they were just at the Council House of the Onondagas, and a great dance was held in their honor."

"I heard that, too, Charlie—but the folks who saw 'em perform at Malcolm Hall said they can dance way better than they can sing."

"Speaking of Indians, Ed, did you hear there's gonna be a massive gathering at Fort Laramie? A whole bunch of tribes want to make treaties with each other and with the United States—they're expectin' about twenty thousand braves to ride in!"

Not waiting for an answer, Charlie continued, "Hey Ed—you heard the latest from California? The steamers are still comin' back with gold, but theft, murder, and lynchings are rampant."

"I did, Charlie, and how some people like crossing Nicaragua better than Panama when they're goin' to California."

"The *lynch law* is what's rulin' the west, Ed, and they're dispatchin' justice by whippin' or hangin' the guilty."

"Do innocent people ever get let go?" I asked.

"Hmm, ain't heard that one, but David Hall from Cortland County got strung up by a mob at Sonora. He was charged with robbery, and they took 'em from the law officers who had 'im in custody—and now he's dead," Charlie gasped.

> **Arrival of Steamship Prometheus.**
> **Fourteen days later from California!**
> Half a Million of Gold Dust!
> MORE MURDERS AND LYNCHINGS.

I said, "I read that out in San Francisco, a Judge Campbell charged the Grand Jury against the dangers of vigilance committees. He got the city all excited when he accused the members of being murderers and nothing else."

"And the Sacramento Vigilance Committee tried to get four prisoners outta jail to hang 'em."

"Hey, Charlie—I'll have to ask George what his pa thinks of the Syracuse Vigilance Committee. I'd hate for the militia to be fightin' against my pa, Rev. Loguen, and the rest."

"Let's hope not—wouldn't be much of a fight!"

We surprised George Pfohl by our sudden appearance—the timing both good and bad. Finding Mr. George Saul conversing with Jacob Pfohl was fortunate, now there were two militia captains to consult. It was bad, however, that we arrived at a somber moment. The men were discussing their friend, John Graff, suffering from the loss of his son,

Jacob, only eight years old. It wasn't a drowning, but many attributed the boy's sudden demise to the toxic canal water that he sometimes swam in. Jacob Pfohl well knew his friend's anguish.

Not the best time to ask about war and killing, I stood silent. When George wondered why we were there I pulled him outside.

"George, I was gonna ask your pa and Mr. Saul about where our Vigilance Committee stood with the militias cause sometimes out west they're not on the same side. And I wanted to ask 'em about Cuba, too, but not after hearin' 'em talk about Jacob Graff!"

"Good thinkin' Ed—They were both startin' to get teary eyed before you came over. Jacob Graff dying must have made Pa think of when we lost our little Mary and Maria."

George's words surprised me because Captain Pfohl had remarried, and earlier this year his wife, Wilhelmina, had given birth to their daughter Mina. "Sorry to hear that, George," I said, "I thought your pa was happy again since the wedding and the new baby."

"Yeah, Pa loves my new ma and baby Mina, but he says that he'll always miss my mother and my sisters."

To our wonder, a moment later both men appeared in the sunshine looking more their usual selves.

Mr. Saul said, "Hello young fellows—a beautiful day, yes?"

"Yes, sir," Charlie Pope answered. "Say, Mr. Saul, Ed Wheaton has some military questions for you and Captain Pfohl."

I gave Charlie a look for putting me on the spot but managed to relate my concerns to the heads of the LaFayette Grenadiers and the Washington Riflemen. They both laughed when I compared Syracuse with what was happening out west.

Mr. Saul asked, "The Syracuse Vigilance Committee isn't planning to lynch people, are they, Edward? That makes a substantial difference—Ha!"

"I suppose not, Mr. Saul, but the Vigilance Committee asked the police and militias to join, and they all said no."

"That's right," Mr. Pfohl answered, "We swore an oath to follow orders—now we report to Colonel Vandenburgh in the 51st regiment."

"Pa, you wouldn't really help the slave catchers, would ya?" George asked anxiously.

"We'll act when we're called upon, son, that's our duty."

"But I know that you wouldn't like it, Pa!" George answered with certainty.

Equally convinced, Captain Pfohl answered, "So what?"

Parish B. Johnson liked having Wheaton Hardware in the *Journal* Building. He'd run down to tell me whenever he heard a good one at the Police Office upstairs, today was no exception.

"Hey Ed, you gotta hear about the triple hanging in Baltimore!" he said eagerly.

"Do I have a choice?"

"No, Ed—you gotta hear this. Taylor, Murphy, and Shelton, the Cosden family murderers, were hung together in front of thousands of people! All of 'em denied their guilt right to the end, and Murphy said, "Murderers, now do your work, but bear in mind that you do not hang murderers!""

"Wow, what happened next?" I asked.

"Ed, you won't believe it. The gallows were twenty-five feet high, and the fall was supposed to be six feet, but when they tripped the spring, the knot on Murphy's rope broke! He hit the ground with his throat all a wreck, laying there unconscious while the other two swung over 'im. There was a great commotion, but after twenty minutes they took the dead men down, and Murphy was starting to recover. He claimed his innocence again, and when he saw the two dead bodies he said, "My God, two innocent men sacrificed!" But they marched him back to the top with his neck drippin' blood, and this time he swung for good."

"That's shocking, Parish, I bet some ladies fainted."

"I think he must-a been innocent, Ed—the way he kept sayin' it right till the end. *There's an ill wind blowin' from this—and it's headin' straight to Syracuse!*"

"I heard Rev. Ward mention ill winds—but why Syracuse?"

"Because there's a *real* murderer named Murphy here—Justice House just charged Edward Murphy with takin' an axe to Patrick Finnell! A *real* killer with the same name will attract a tortured soul, especially an innocent one that got hung twice."

"You sound like Billy Willard, Parish—you're as nutty as he is."

Crooking a finger upward, Parish said, "Go ahead and laugh, Ed, just wait and see what happens."

My friend's forewarning arrived on Saturday with a hailstorm that wiped out most of the tobacco crop. Lightning struck a barber shop in Baldwinsville, while another bolt hit a barn in Lysander that killed several cattle in their stalls. In the town of Clay, another barn was struck, claiming the life of a $400 horse. In Syracuse, the rain poured in torrents not witnessed for many years, while driving winds ravaged the area's roofs and windows.

On Sunday, the storm subsided, but misfortune continued with the death of an eight-year-old, drowned in a pond near McKinstry's Candle Factory. The boy was swimming with his friends but went over his head and sank to the bottom, sadly pulled out too late. Meanwhile, the grand jury indicted axe murderer, Edward Murphy, for taking four chops at Patrick Finnell's head and neck—three of which were fatal by the coroner's account.

Dark clouds persisted with the passing of ninety-six-year-old Peter Sky, Warrior Chief of the Onondagas. Sorely missed by his clan, neighboring tribes mourned his passing. A final harbinger of doom arrived from Cuba with the reported defeat of Lopez and the filibusterers, but I didn't attribute their misfortune to Murphy's curse.

# Chapter Fifteen
## (August – September 1851)

The ill winds departed mid-August, blown away by a military parade with anxious spectators looking for a good time. H.A. Kellogg kept the party going with a "Grand Promenade Concert" of his Sax Horn Band at Malcolm Hall. Pa was happy, too—he just bought Philo Rust's 41-acre farm on Onondaga Street for $17,500 at auction.

The next day at the County Temperance Convention, Pa's friends surmised correctly that he'd divide the property into lots and make a handsome profit. The convention itself did little to slow demand for alcohol, though. Robert Mackechnie expanded operations at the Syracuse City Brewery, then advertised for a partner in all the papers.

With the convention in progress, Cale Davis increased the frequency (and volume) of his verbal attacks on the temperance movement, keeping his favorite target, Rev. May, in the crosshairs.

"An abolitionist teetotaler—just what the world needs!" butcher Davis bellowed.

"He cries about women's rights, too," his son Thomas sniped.

"Aye, better fit for an apron, he is," the elder growled.

Thomas enjoyed sparking his old man's temperament, but held a different opinion of Rev. May. Both opposed the minister on temperance, but Thomas leaned more toward abolition than Cale. He recognized May as a man who got things done whenever he put his mind to it. And Thomas thought the little shit was brave, too, for standing up to his pa when confronted.

At convention's end in Syracuse, word arrived from Buffalo of its first case of the *Fugitive Slave Law*—a national headline that prompted an emergency meeting of the *Syracuse Vigilance Committee*. A somber looking Pa and Rev. Loguen exchanged words about that peculiar law in front of our house.

"We have to be ready, Jermain—what happened in Buffalo can happen here," Pa said.

Rev Loguen agreed, "Yes, Charles, poor Daniels didn't have a chance."

"True, the slave owner's son snuck up from behind and felled him senseless."

"The slavers had a hard time dragging him to the courthouse, though—many citizens were outraged, but others helped the police to follow the vile *Slave Law*."

"I think the military was called for the size of the crowd," Pa said. "I should ask Colonel Vandenburgh how the 51st Regiment would respond."

"Yes, and don't forget Federal Commissioner Sabine! The law's written for a commissioner to decide a fugitive's fate."

Pa stated with confidence, "I know Joe Sabine—he accepted the position right before the law was passed—don't think he'd have taken it afterward!"

Rev. Loguen said, "They only called one witness, but when Daniels didn't deny that he was once a slave, Commissioner Smith in Buffalo followed Satan's law to send him back to Kentucky."

"Smith offered to subscribe towards purchasing Daniels' freedom, though," Pa replied.

"Too little, too late, Charles—but Daniels' lawyer appealed to Judge Conkling for writ of habeas corpus. It's his last hope!"

"At least his assailant was arrested," Pa said with optimism. "Justice Gold fined the slave owner's son fifty dollars for assault."

"There's still a great many who stand by this hellish law, claiming it's to preserve the peace," Rev. Loguen lamented.

"Hellish indeed," Pa answered, "I'd call their preserving the peace a good intention on the road to hell."

*"All the way to Georgia, Charles!* Last week their governor pardoned a black man down in Columbus, but a mob broke open the jail and hung him from a tree."

Near the end of August, Murphy, the axe murderer, attempted suicide in the penitentiary with a gruesome razor cut to the abdomen. Dr. Hoyt attended while the accused man clung to life, and the community wished him gone. We all wondered how long it would be until Billy reported that a local medium had summoned Murphy's raps from beyond the grave.

Despite their initial success, ever-worsening accounts of the Cuban Expedition began to arrive—*fifty captured Americans executed*, with Lopez and his battered force under hot pursuit somewhere in the mountains. Passions ignited nationwide when news from Havana confirmed that outrages were committed on the dead bodies of the massacred. Spontaneous protests broke out north and south, with riots erupting

> **GREAT EXCITEMENT IN HA-VANA!**
>
> FIFTY PATRIOTS CAPTURED AND SHOT!
>
> **THE FALCON FIRED AT!**
>
> *LOPEZ DEFEATED AND FLED.*

in New Orleans and New York targeting Spanish interests. In New Orleans, two Spanish printing offices were destroyed, with the Spanish Consul forced to flee for his life to the city prison. It required an armed militia to prevent the mob from exacting vengeance. Pa thought that people were wasting their sympathy.

"I'm against vile desecrations, Edward," Pa said to me at home one afternoon, "But it's clear that the people of Cuba have no desire to break free. Lopez misread their intentions twice, yet he still convinced hundreds of men to follow him to their graves!"

"How bad do you think it'll be for the rest of 'em, Pa?" I asked. "Do you think the soldiers will shoot all the captured men?"

"Not if they're smart, son. President Filmore dispatched the Saranac out of Norfolk with Commodore Parker aboard—they're steaming to Havana now to investigate the summary executions."

"Pa, it sounds to me like everybody in New Orleans is ready to attack Cuba—I read that all the Spanish businesses were destroyed during the riots. I wouldn't want to be a Spaniard these days, Pa—you ever met one?"

My father laughed, "A Spaniard? Yes—but not too many!"

"Any in Syracuse, Pa?"

"I suggest that you introduce yourself to Mr. George Mendez at his store on Salina Street."

"Oh yeah, I've seen him, but never thought about him being a Spaniard—kinda fits right in, sneaky like."

"What do you mean, sneaky?" Pa asked.

"Well, if we got into a war with Spain, how'd you know who the spies were? He looks like everyone else."

"Hmm, you think he did that on purpose?"

"No, Pa, I'm surprised that an abolitionist like you would say that."

Pa had heard enough. "I think the Cheney's are looking for you, Edward—go find 'em!"

As directed, I rendezvoused with Si and Prentice, who suggested we find the Cook brothers to go see the Giant Boy at Brintnall's Hall, and we did. Abel Cook was thrilled to meet another Anakim. The tallest specimen we'd ever met hailed from Nova Scotia, an amiable giant named Angus MacAskill who told us that he wanted to see the Dan Rice Circus when they returned.

"Dan'll be in Fayetteville, Liverpool, and Phoenix before he's in Syracuse again," Abel advised.

"Yeah—too bad the circus is coming on the first day of school," Prentice observed.

"Is there anything historic about it?" I asked, "maybe we could get Mr. Weld to postpone the opening day of school—ha!"

"It's Dan's first shows since he was arrested for libel, and his manager got stabbed up in Oriskany," Prentice suggested.

"And it's his last show in Syracuse this year," Si Cheney said.

"Forget it, Ed, Mr. Weld already announced our school's opening in the newspapers," Austin stated.

"I suppose you're right. Say, I gotta get back—Sam and I are still rebuilding our chicken business that got blown away in the storm. My pa told us that we just learned why it's smart to have insurance!"

Accompanied by the Cheney's, we trekked back, stopping momentarily at the hobbled coop.

"It's not so good like before," I acknowledged.

"It ain't so bad—not as big as the other, though," Prentice observed.

"We used everything left from the storm," I answered.

Si looked unimpressed. "Let's find Sam!" he said with conviction, and we did.

The Ward's were home along with the Loguen family. Elizabeth and Helen Loguen were good friends of Mary Ward, everyone looked happy.

I blurted, "Hey Sam! What's everyone smiling about?"

"The Loguen's came by to tell us about the slave case in Buffalo, Ed. Judge Conkling ruled for the fugitive over the slave catchers!"

Rev. Loguen overheard, and directed, "You make sure that your pa hears about this Edward, you'll see him before I do."

"Yes, sir, I will!"

"There's bad news, too. Tell him there's another slave case in Poughkeepsie for a man named Boulding, and the New York Colonization Society is shipping another forty souls to Liberia in September," Rev. Loguen stated.

Rev. Ward remarked, "And the newspapers blame the abolitionists that free blacks aren't welcome in Indiana—ha!"

"Why'd Judge Conkling let 'em go, Rev. Loguen?" Prentice asked.

"The Judge ruled that the Fugitive Slave Law only applies to slaves who escaped after September 18, 1850, and Daniels ran off in August. He said that whenever there's a question between liberty and slavery, the presumption should be for liberty," Loguen answered.

"That's why he granted Daniels a writ of habeas corpus," Rev. Ward agreed. "Judge Conkling rightly claimed this to be a universally acknowledged principle of jurisprudence."

Sam heard enough and hurried us to the door.

At the end of summer, Ma looked sad sitting by herself holding a newspaper, so I asked her what was wrong.

"Hey Ma, is there something bothering you? You look upset."

"I'm fine, son—just a little down from reading the final letters home from the condemned men in Cuba. Unfolding the paper, she said, "Listen to this, Edward," and began to read:

*"My Dear Mother—*

*I have but a few moments to live. Fifty of us are condemned to be shot within a half hour. I do not value life, but deeply regret the grief it will cause you to hear of my death. Farewell then, my dear mother, sisters, and all; we may meet again in another world. Think of me often; forget the cause I have given you for grief; remember only my virtues. Farewell again, dearest mother, and believe me to be, your affectionate son.*

*J. Brandt"*

When I didn't say anything, she asked, "How do think his mother felt, huh?"

"She musta felt pretty lousy, Ma."

"That, and more, Edward, here's another one":

*"My Dear and Affectionate Sisters and Brothers,*

*Before I die, I am permitted to address my last words in this world.*

*Deceived by false visions, I embarked in the expedition for Cuba. We arrived, about four hundred in number, last week, and in about an hour from now, we, I mean fifty of us, will be shot. I was taken prisoner after an engagement, and, with fifty others, am to be shot in an hour.*

*I die, my dear brothers and sisters, a repentant sinner, having been blessed with the last rites of holy religion. Forgive me for all the follies of my life, and you, my dear and affectionate sisters, pray for my poor soul.*

*H.T. Vienne"*

"*How tragic!*" Ma gasped. "Edward, promise me that you'll never write a letter like that!"

"Don't worry Ma, I'm no filibusterer. Is there anything else bothering you?"

With deference to the recent passing of my great Aunt, Lorain Wheaton Bostwick, she answered, "I'm not bothered, just thinking about Aunt Bostwick, God rest her soul."

"They'll miss her in Pompey, Ma—it's hard to believe that she died last week."

"Me, too, Edward, but she lived a full life in her seventy-four years. What a great example she was with her good sense, energy, and untiring perseverance."

"And she loved to help people, too—everybody knew that! What do you think you'll remember about her the most?" I asked.

"Well, there's a lot, Edward. She was a consistent Christian all her life. One of the last times I spoke with her she said that she'd read the Old Testament through fourteen times, the New Testament at least thirty times, and she still wasn't tired of it!"

"I'll never beat her record, Ma, anything else?"

"Once, when I shared my frustrations with her about my unruly children, she said,

"You think you have many cares, but in a few years, your little circle will be grown and gone. Then you'll be left alone, old and gray, to look back on those years and wonder what you were thinking, for they will now seem to have been the happiest days of your life. *Mothers are never so happy as when they are surrounded by their little ones,* and have them under their own eye, exerting an influence such as only a mother can do!"

I found Aunt Bostwick's wisdom troubling.

"I want you to be happy, Ma, but does this mean I gotta stay home? School starts on Monday and the boys are waiting!"

At fourteen and three-quarters, the school year commenced at Weld's School for Young Men and Boys, September 1, 1851. Sporting irregular patches of facial hair, I gazed across my realm, trying hard to exude the persona of command. Nobody noticed except Mr. Weld, who acknowledged with a smirk and several shakes of his head. Playing the history card, Prentice moved for dismissal.

"Excuse me, Mr. Weld, sir, but before we get started, can we have the day off for history? Dan Rice won't be back till next year!"

"Good morning, Prentice, ready for the new year, I see," Mr. Weld replied, ignoring the request. "Who else can tell me what's going on around here?" our teacher asked.

Parish answered, "I can, Mr. Weld. Murphy, the axe murderer, finally croaked after he sliced his guts open at the penitentiary! Dr. Hoyt sewed him back up, but the grim reaper took 'im anyway. Some of the police said they wanted to avoid the grave robbing and consign his corpse to the medical college."

"That's a good example of how violence begets violence," Mr. Weld answered, "Any good news, Parish?"

"Yes, sir. Officer Lowell recovered a couple of expensive horses, and he went all the way to Palmyra and Corning to get 'em."

"Officer Lowell again?" Mr. Weld asked. "You've mentioned him before."

"Yes, sir—Lowell and Shattuck are two of the best—Way, Dodge, and Hollister, too," Parish replied.

Charlie Pope said, "Mr. Weld, there's gonna be another military parade next week, but this time all the companies are turning out, not just the Citizens' Corps."

"But not before Barnum's Menagerie is here on Friday. They're bringing elephants, Mr. Weld!" Larry Sabine offered.

"Mr. Weld, the Fakir of Siva is here this week, too, sir," Alex McKinstry added. "He's the great magician and ventriloquist."

Weld replied. "Excellent! I'd like to see that show myself. Gentlemen, this should be an exciting year!"

Mr. Weld was right. The next day advertisements started going out for the Onondaga County Agricultural Fair, beckoning the countryside to Syracuse on Wednesday, October the 1st. This year's event would be held at the Bastable block in Hanover Square, with the livestock and heavy articles exhibited on the Bastable farm by the Orphan Asylum.

Coinciding with the county fair, the State Convention of the Liberty Party was scheduled to occur at City Hall. We all expected another excitable gathering of abolitionists, including Gerrit Smith, who stopped by the hardware store to talk with Pa about how the runaway Boulding was remanded to Carolina.

"There wasn't a Judge Conkling in Poughkeepsie, Charles, so Boulding returned to slavery. All it takes is a word from the commissioner, and the accused has no rights!" Smith exclaimed.

"I read that efforts are being made to pay a $2,000 ransom—$1,500 for the slave, plus $500 for his recovery," Pa answered.

Smith remained stoic. "But the runaway Daniels just crossed over from Buffalo! If he gets to Montreal he could visit Shadrach, the famous ex-fugitive from Boston."

"Ah, but Shadrach keeps a bar there, and alcohol is no friend of the downtrodden," Pa grieved. "I pray that he doesn't trade one set of shackles for another."

Pa's fellow in temperance, Gerrit Smith, agreed.

Before the first week of school ended, Mr. Weld made a somber announcement.

"Gentlemen, I have terrible news! I've just learned that Herman Saul, the five-year-old son of Captain George Saul, has died, and the military parade on Monday will be postponed by order of Committee."

Hearing that triggered memories of Capt. Saul and Capt. Pfohl grieving over their friend, John Graff, losing his own young son. Now, it's George Saul's turn, despairing over the death of his child. A well-attended funeral for Herman was held on Thursday at the family home on Hawley Street. On Friday, the newspapers printed a Card of Thanks from Capt. Saul to his many friends for their support, and his desire that Monday's parade would not be postponed. Three cheers broke out in newspaper class after Charlie Pope read it. After school let out, everyone who could went to see Barnum's Menagerie.

Led through town by live elephants, P.T. Barnum's traveling wonder show created a rush for tickets not seen since the advent of Jenny Lind. The spectacle included great white bears from the frozen north, lions from the jungles of Africa, colorful canary birds, and the greatest collection of living curiosities since Noah's Ark. Pickpockets were out in force, competing with the ticket booth and a myriad of food vendors to separate the public from their hard earned cash. Abel and Austin Cook sold every slice of their ma's pies, and when Abel saw the tiny General, Tom Thumb, he wondered if he might be part Aztek.

Still hungry for entertainment, Malcolm Hall filled to capacity for the Fakir of Siva, who astonished the audience with his marvelous exploits and illusions. Tonight, he'd cut off a man's nose and suspend him in mid-air without using a wire! Austin called him the Faker of Shaker.

Visitors flocked to Syracuse during the second week of September for the state conventions of both the Democrats and Whigs. City hotels were their busiest since the State Fair of '49. Horace Greeley was back from Europe and came to report on politics, while my troop was more interested in the grand opening of Doan's Ice Cream Saloon on Washington St.

National concerns over Cuba charged the atmosphere from Maine to California, evidenced by the glow of the aurora borealis in the northern sky. Steamships carried the accounts from Havana of more captured Americans, and the demise of Narciso Lopez—garroted before a crazed public.

*Execution of Lopez*

Closer to home, the craziness was exhibited by a man from Cazenovia who paraded the downtown streets wearing red bloomer trousers. Worse yet, a stabbing occurred outside the Pfohl's establishment on Salina Street. An altercation between two Germans began inside the Pfohl's tavern, with the combatants promptly ejected by Capt. Pfohl. The affray escalated in the street outside, a knife was pulled, and its recipient died a few days later. Although Capt. Pfohl had supplied the spirits, George said that his pa attributed the crime to a combination of drinking too much with an over-reaction to a perceived slight.

It was around the middle of September when I encountered a gloomy Sam Ward at our backyard chicken coop.

"What's got you down, Sam?"

"I'm worryin' bout my pa, Edward—he's lecturing in Ohio and sent word there's trouble in a place called Christiana."

"Never heard of it—where's Christiana, Sam?"

"Just west of Philly—I could show ya on Pa's map."

"So, what did your pa say?" I asked.

"Pa said that every month or so, somebody gets dragged off from a free Northern town to the South and slavery—but this time the free blacks and abolitionists helped the slaves to make a stand!"

"What happened, Sam?" I implored.

"The slave owner, Edward Gorsuch, tracked his runaways to the home of a free black man named Parker, and he brought his son and the federal marshals to help take 'em back. Somehow the black folks around there got word that the slavers were comin,' and they all went to help Parker—them, and the white abolitionists. But Gorsuch didn't flinch, Ed. He pointed his gun and declared that his slave was in the house and he'd have him, if he went to hell after him! Then he tried to intimidate people and fired on the house with his rifle. They shot back, and Gorsuch dropped a corpse with his son, Dickinson, barely alive."

*Dickinson Gorsuch*

"How close did your pa get to Christiana, Sam?"

"Close enough, Ed—and way too close to the Mason-Dixon line. My ma says there's lots of rich slavers who want to see my pa shut up for good."

"I can see what's got you worried, Sam."

"Yeah, but I know that he can take care of himself. It's somethin' else, Ed—I don't wanna move to Canada!"

Sam's proclamation struck home, this option would end many of his family's worries. The uncomfortable silence got the better of my lips.

"Sam, your pa's too important to move to Canada—there's people all over the country who wanna hear him speak!"

"But he's still a fugitive, Ed. Pa said he's waiting to see how the Fugitive Slave Law gets enforced, then he'll decide if it's worth staying. He wrote that after the slave catchers were driven off in Christiana, they came back with lots of lawmen! Around thirty people got arrested, and they're expecting charges for murder and high treason."

"What are the folks around there sayin' about it, Sam?"

"Pa said that most of the town was against the slave catchers makin' arrests, but in Philadelphia there was a large gathering of people who support the law—and that's scary, Ed!"

It worried me, too, especially when the headlines rang of the Negro riot, and how more blacks were apprehended as fugitives. All the white people who helped the runaways in Christiana were arrested, too. Sam wouldn't rest easy until his pa came home again.

The Christiana Affair, as some called it, became a lightning rod for the Fugitive Slave Law. Across the country, passions differed in the extreme with no middle ground. Half believed the law was an abomination, and returning anyone to slavery was wrong, no matter what. But the other half said that the law is the law and must be followed, no matter what. Around Christiana, the number of arrests approached fifty.

Events in Cuba furthered the divide. Although the Island's Governor General pardoned four captured officers, about one hundred and sixty of their comrades were transported to Spain to serve ten years at hard labor. Many Americans fumed at the result, but just as many felt indifferent, claiming the filibusterers were warned of the consequences, and decided to ignore the president's proclamation that no assistance would be rendered.

When it appeared that nothing could bridge the chasm, a tragedy proved otherwise when the Dan Rice Circus boats were lost on Lake Erie! Dan's popularity on both sides of the Mason-Dixon line unified Americans through a shared concern for his fate. The tragedy at sea happened near Sturgeon Point, when a gale separated the canal boats from the steamer Empire State. Initial accounts were filled with dead bodies floating in the water and wreckage strewn upon the shore, but, thankfully, Dan and his company survived.

Ma said she thought it was astute of me to recognize the great divide but reminded me that most of us prayed to the same God, too.

Though it ended well for Dan Rice, the same could not be said for Aaron Stookey, hanged for murder in New York for stabbing a Black man through the heart without provocation. Holding a newspaper, Ma put me in touch with the facts.

"Edward, I want you to hear what this man said right before his life ended with six hundred people watching. It should make you think twice about drinking alcohol!"

I recognized Ma's conviction, and said, "Sure Ma—what he say?"

"My dear fellow citizens—I now stand here before you to die, and I hope and believe my soul will be saved. I trust my God has forgiven me. You must all beware of rum; for rum has been the cause of placing me here to meet this awful fate. I warn you all not to touch the intoxicating bowl, for it will eventually get advantage of you. I am sorry to die under the gallows, but the laws must be carried out, and die I must.

"Remember what I say, rum has done it all, and I hope all who are here will take warning. God bless you all, may God have mercy on my soul, and receive me into his kingdom! Goodbye, God bless you, and my friends."

"So, what do you think of that?" she asked.

"I hear ya, Ma—drinking alcohol will get me into trouble! But reading the last statements of condemned men can't be good for you either. You read all them letters from Cuba and James Fennimore Cooper just died, too—I know how much you liked *The Last of the Mohicans*."

"Just mind your place, Edward!" she answered curtly.

I tried to change the subject.

"Say Ma, uh, how's Aunt Charlotte like running the Bradbury School with Miss Bowen? They started late this year, but that didn't bother Cornelia, Ellen, and Emma none."

Ma wasn't fooled. "All right, Edward, go see your friends!" she directed, and the door banged shut behind me.

I knew something was off when Thomas Davis said hello to me for the first time in my life. His big, ugly pa didn't know what to make of it either, nor did any of the customers in line at the butcher shop unrenowned for friendly overtures. I mumbled something incoherent while the elder gave me *the eye,* which kept my feet moving.

Then I recalled recently overhearing Parish Johnson mention the younger Davis, but wasn't paying attention—now seemed a good time for a retelling.

"Hey Parish!" I hailed, finding him outside of his house with brother Grove. "Tell me again what you heard about Thomas Davis—he just said hello to me."

"Really? Wonders never cease!"

"Well, he did, Parish—I ain't makin' this up so remind me what you said, okay?"

"Okay—relax! So, I was down by the Police Office when Officer Dodge brought him in for assault and battery," Parish said.

"Oh—Did he get in trouble with Eliza Appleton again?"

"Nope—he's done with her and set his sights on Charlotte Terpenny, a widow lady. Her husband James just died, and she has three little boys, too."

"Thomas Davis fell for a widow lady with three kids?"

"Yup—and he assaulted a man for speaking unkindly to her! Davis has been boarding at Terpenny's for a while now—since before James Terpenny died, but that's not the best part. After Davis told his side to Justice House about the assault, he started askin' questions about becoming a policeman, can you believe it?"

"No, I don't, Parish—tell me another one," I sneered.

Grove Johnson settled the dispute. "Yes, he did, Edward—I heard him, too!"

"Oh yeah? I'd love to know what his grouchy pa said after he found out."

"I say the old brute didn't like it," Parish answered. "They musta had it out, and Thomas' sayin' hello to you was really a message for his pa."

"Hmm, you might have somethin' there, Parish! What do you say, Grove?"

"Ed, he seemed intentional how he was talkin' to Justice House," Grove replied.

"Intentional, Grove? That words longer than you are. You still intentional for my sister?"

"Just leave Miss Ellen outta this, she didn't do nothin'," a defiant Grove Johnson retorted.

Parish said, "He still loves her, Ed—ain't you the lucky one!"

"Great! Just don't tell anyone at school, Parish," I urged.

Grove sounded like Ma, bellowing, "You just mind your business, Edward."

Mr. Weld made our class erupt on Tuesday, the last day of September.

"Gentlemen, the Onondaga County Agricultural Fair starts tomorrow—who'd like time off from school?" he asked.

Arms waved overhead as voices rang, *"I do!"*

"All right, on one condition."

"Anything, Mr. Weld, anything! Tell us, sir!" screamed the classroom.

"Come Monday morning every one of you will have a professionally written account in your newspapers about what happened at the fair—no excuses! We can talk about it more on Friday, I don't expect you to complete the assignment overnight."

The mid-week break sounded great, but quickly made us want Friday off, too. Some of the guys felt cheated and we had to shut them up before they ruined everything.

"All right, gentlemen, settle down!" Mr. Weld ordered. "Let's talk about the news—Prentice Cheney, has there been another boiler explosion?"

"Yes, sir! The *James Jackson* exploded as she left Shawneetown in Illinois—they think at least thirty-five people were killed or wounded. But two other steamers brought more gold from California, Mr. Weld," Prentice replied.

Alex McKinstry joined in, "That's right, Mr. Weld. The Steamers *Illinois* and *Brother Jonathan* brought another two and a half million in gold—I'd leave today if I could!"

"You're not alone, Alex. The population out west is exploding faster than all the boilers," Mr. Weld replied. Looking at Charlie, he asked,

"Mr. Charles Pope Jr., I understand that your father is to be congratulated for his election as President of the Franklin Institute. You should be proud of him, Charles—how did your family celebrate the occasion?"

"We had a nice dinner, sir, and afterward Pa wanted to go hear Mrs. Coe at the Unitarian Church," Charlie replied. "Mr. Weld, Pa said it was a most interesting lecture on women's rights. I heard that she spoke eloquently about how women aren't permitted to hold property and live outside the control of a husband."

"Ha! I bet Mr. Coe wasn't in the audience when she said that," Austin joked.

"Yeah, and I know a butcher who thinks Mr. Coe wears an apron," Billy added.

Charlie Pope wasn't finished. "Mr. Weld, I wanted to say that there's a new Chief of the Six Nations!"

"Please do, Charles—and the rest of you pay attention," Weld directed.

"Yes, sir, out near Buffalo in Tonawanda the Grand Council of the Confederacy of the Six Nations—the Mohawks, Onondagas, Oneidas, Cayugas, Senecas, and Tuscaroras met to hold funeral rites of their fallen leader, John Blacksmith. He was the Grand Sachem, Mr. Weld, the head Chief."

"Who is the new leader?" Weld asked.

"Ely S. Parker was chosen as the next Grand Sachem, Mr. Weld, but in Indian they call him *Do-ne-ha-ga-wa*. They gave him the silver medal that General Washington gave to Chief Red Jacket, that he wore till he died."

"Excellent, Charles!" Mr. Weld replied. "Mr. Wallace, what's happening in Cuba?" he asked.

"Mr. Weld, it's been quiet lately, but Lt. Stevens surrendered after hiding in the mountains for a month. He jumped overboard and swam to shore when the Spanish steamer was chasing his boat. That's what saved his life, Mr. Weld—the other fifty men were captured and shot!"

"That's incredible, William—I hope that Stevens can tell what happened to the thirty men still missing. Mr. Wheaton, have you any news on the abolition front?"

"Yes, sir—there's a few things to report. First, they started legal examinations in Christiana, and both sides brought an army of lawyers. There's a lot of excitement around there, Mr. Weld!"

"I'm sure there is, Edward, but you look like you're not finished reporting."

"Well, sir, the legislature of Jamaica sent a representative to America to see how to get the free colored people to emigrate."

"So now there's an alternative to Liberia!" Weld exclaimed.

"Yes, sir—and it's a lot closer than Africa. The Jamaican official said that blacks would be welcomed on the same footing with whites, and I've heard Rev. Ward say good things about Jamaica, too, Mr. Weld."

"Thank you, Edward—was there anything else?"

"Well, sir, in the *Syracuse Star* they said they hoped that the Liberty Party would behave at their convention tomorrow. Do you think there'll be any trouble, Mr. Weld?"

"Oh, nothing unusual," my teacher replied.

# Chapter Sixteen
## (October 1, 1851)

The Cheney's found me waiting when they banged at my door in the morning. Black George laughed at our speedy departure while my sisters whined that they felt cheated.

"You boys behave now!" Ma shouted.

"Yes, ma'am!" we echoed back.

Cutting through our backyard, Prentice said, "Okay, Ed—let's get Sam and see what's happening at the fair!"

"Right, Prentice—let's go, Si!" I answered with glee.

Passing the rebuilt chicken coop, Silas said, "Say, Ed—the coop looks better than last time."

"Thanks, Si, just tell Sam, 'cause he did most of the work."

"Okay—here he comes now!" Si exclaimed.

Sam saw us first and came running before his ma remembered a delinquent chore. He shouted, *"C'mon fellas—time to see the giant hogs!"*

"And monster cows!" Prentice added.

"And watch where yer steppin'!" Si warned.

"It's just over the hill," I cried. "We'll be there in a minute or two!"

Growing noise emanated from the fairgrounds erected at the Bastable farm. At the crest of Asylum Hill, we saw columns of people and conveyances converging from all directions toward the biggest Onondaga County fair ever, with the promise of even more exhibits at Hanover Square. The wind announced the presence of farm animals and their excrements.

"Ha! Smells like the fair, don't it?" Si remarked.

"Yeah, it do," Sam agreed.

"Hey Sam—is your pa bringing the family later on?" I asked.

"He still ain't back from Ohio, Ed—but maybe yet this mornin'."

"I know he wouldn't want to miss the convention; I'm sure they asked him to speak."

"Yup, Gerrit Smith told Pa to keep agitatin'."

Gaining the fairgrounds, we began our examination of agricultural curiosities, starting with Sam's giant hogs. Standing beside a behemoth, Sam remarked, "That's a lotta bacon there!"

"Yeah, an apple would look like a grape in that mouth," Si Cheney said.

"How long you think it'll take to roast him, Ed—maybe a week?" Prentice joked.

"Almost, but even longer for that cow over there," I replied.

Si Cheney detected the scent of barbeque. "Don't that smell good?" he asked.

"Whatever they're cookin,' I want some!" Sam affirmed.

"We'll get some before we leave," Prentice answered, "Got lots to see first—like all the new inventions."

Adjacent to the livestock, machinists from the Phoenix Foundry exhibited their contributions to agricultural progress. Hezekiah Davis, Lorenzo Hudson, Harvey Snow, and the Dunk brothers, Al, and Harry, proudly displayed their mechanical ingenuity. Not to be undone, the Syracuse & Utica Railroad dispatched Andrew Spike and Newcomb Ketcham to demonstrate their creations, while Jonas Hobert represented his own machine shop.

After a time with animals and farm equipment, I felt ready for Hanover Square.

"C'mon guys, let's head downtown—we've seen everything up here," I said with conviction, and we did.

We hadn't gone far when a bell began to chime in an unusual way, no mistaking the warning knell from the *Syracuse Vigilance Committee*.

"That's the bell at my church!" I said with urgency. "It's the Congregational!"

"Let's get down there!" Sam responded.

We showed great intention, but the multitudes stymied our progress. Crowded streets hindered us more than distance. A louder peal rang from the bell of the First Presbyterian church, followed by a different tone from another church, then another, until all the bells in the city proclaimed the taking of a fugitive slave—*it was a sound that I'll never forget!*"

We encountered the large figure of lawyer George Boyer Vashon outside the Congregational where the street buzzed like a beehive. I hailed him to halt his progress.

"Mr. Vashon! Mr. Vashon! Can you tell us what happened, sir?"

He turned, and replied, "Federal marshals have arrested a fugitive and they've taken him before Commissioner Sabine. Your father brought the news, Edward, and the convention adjourned."

"Do you know who got arrested, Mr. Vashon?"

"Yes, Edward, **it was Jerry Henry!**"

We stood in surprise as G.B. Vashon vanished in the crowd. I wasn't aware that Alex and Charlie McKinstry were standing behind us close enough to hear everything.

"Hey Ed, you asked the right man what happened—Vashon was chosen as secretary of the convention!" Alex exclaimed.

"Yeah, but we outta follow the crowd to see what happens," I retorted.

"Well let's go then!" Alex directed, and we all fell in line.

Just a few blocks distant on Water Street, upstairs in the Townsend block at Clinton Square, Federal Commissioner Sabine's office quickly filled beyond capacity. Staircases, corridors, and doorways were jammed with bodies pressed toward the hearing in progress.

Amongst the sea of faces were Parish and Grove Johnson, who managed to secure a good spot in front of the building. We nudged toward their location after I saw them wave.

"Hey Ed!—Hey fellas!" Parish greeted.

"Hey yourself! So what's the story, Mr. Reporter?" I challenged. If anybody knew, he did.

Parish answered, "Well, me and Grove were up on north Salina when we saw Officer Lowell and a few other men making an arrest, so we got closer to watch. Ed, it was the black guy with red hair that you know—what's his name?"

*"Jerry!"* I answered emphatically.

"Oh yeah, Jerry. Anyways, it was all peaceful, except I saw your pa across the street watchin' it all real serious like. Then all of a sudden he starts movin' pretty fast towards downtown."

Grove uttered, "Your pa wasn't gone two minutes before the bell started ringin'."

Parish stated matter-of-factly, "Right, but we weren't surprised 'cause I recognized Federal Marshal Allen—and so did your pa."

Prentice followed the thread, and proclaimed, "Daniel Webster's threat came true—a fugitive's been captured during an abolition convention!"

Knowing Jerry's position on the *Fugitive Slave Law*, I demanded, "Did you say that Jerry went peaceful? He never would!"

"He did, Ed—but he didn't recognize Marshall Allen like me and your pa. I heard Jerry's been arrested before, but never for anything serious like he was a thief or a robber. He might a thought he was gettin' brought in for something else. The police had a carriage waiting, and it was all calm when Lowell, Allen, and the other men loaded Jerry for transport."

As we stood listening to Parish Johnson, Rev. May approached, determined to get inside the crowded Commissioner's Office.

I greeted him anxiously, "Hello Rev. May, I can't believe this is happening!"

"Nor I, Edward, and we're not alone! There's many people infuriated that a man among us would be carried away into slavery."

"Will you be able to get Jerry out, Reverend?"

"It's a one-sided process, Edward, one in which the agent of the claimant alone is to be heard in proof. Jerry won't be allowed to state his own case, nor refute the testimony of his adversary, however false it might be."

*Rev. Samuel J. May*

Recognizing Sam, Rev. May shook his hand, and said, "Stand tall like your father, Samuel Ward Jr.—I'll see what can be done!"

For a man of peace, the Reverend Samuel J. May was adroit at maneuvering through a crowd. I watched as he repeatedly said *excuse me*, but never stopped moving. I followed his trajectory and remarked, "I wonder if my pa's in there—and there goes Rev. Loguen, too!"

"And I wonder if my pa ever made it back," Sam replied. "We sure need him!"

The swarms continued to pack Clinton Square, summoned by the tolling bells. My heart ached for Jerry—shackled, and not allowed to speak in his defense. Most, not all, voices sided with the fugitive, indignant at his apprehension. We watched and waited for over an hour when word came down that they were taking a half-hour break. Suddenly, a loud commotion issued from the commissioner's office. In the next instant, Jerry Henry tumbled down the stairs and staggered onto the sidewalk. Still handcuffed, he appeared dazed, uncertain which way to go.

Sam yelled, ***"Run, Jerry, run!"*** and began to follow when Jerry started toward the Syracuse House. His flight attracted friend and foe alike. Prince Jackson, a colored man that I once met from Black George, had hold of a deputy marshal near the foot of the stairs. The lawman struggled violently to get away, but Jerry's self-appointed guardian held fast.

"Hey, there's Mr. Crandal!" Prentice alerted, drawing everyone's attention. There stood our class advisor, William L. Crandal, highly animated, yelling at Jerry's pursuers to stay back and let him go. Then I heard someone say that Crandal rang the bell at the First Presbyterian.

We followed the panicked flight down Water Street, skirting Hanover Square and City Hall. Jerry hesitated at Mulberry Street, then turned left for the Lock Street bridge going north over the Erie Canal.

I recognized Caleb Davis standing there, watching the spectacle approach. The manacles on Jerry's wrists rattled as he passed him by. They exchanged a knowing glance but neither spoke. It was then that Officer Lowell closed in, soon followed by Officers Way and Green.

"Stop right there!" Lowell ordered.

"Never!" Jerry answered. "I'll never go back!"

Lowell collared him and shouted, "I have orders to bring you in!"

"Never!" Jerry repeated, fighting back with all his might. He landed several blows and a few hard kicks that had the policeman reeling, but when Officers Way and Green arrived, Jerry's fate was sealed. While his captors restricted Jerry's movements, the fugitive lashed out with his voice. Anguished cries for life and liberty stirred the crowd—anyone there couldn't help but to be moved. Though the shackled man stood no chance against three able-bodied policemen, he continued to fight for all his life was worth.

"I won't go back to slavery!" Jerry roared as the struggle progressed. He still had the strength to inflict injury, striking his kidnappers as best he could. Conversely, Jerry's captors applied overwhelming force to secure him. An ugly scene ensued, Jerry's cries echoed from the bridge while the crowd screamed angrily at the police. A few burly men helped commandeer a horse and cart to transport the captive back to the Police Office. What remained of Jerry's clothes were a tatter, his face and body marked by the one-sided struggle. I thought that some of his ribs must be cracked, if not broken. After he was thrown face-down in the cart, Jerry's telltale splash of red hair was the only visible means of identification. One officer sat across his legs and another on his body, both holding him down, but Jerry never stopped his struggle for liberty.

The sight unnerved the crowd behind the backdrop of clanging church bells and the heartfelt cries of a fugitive.

Jerry screamed, "Don't send me back to slavery! I'd rather die!"

Scores of maddened citizens including many blacks circled the spectacle at close quarters, screaming in protest that began to escalate to violence.

Lowell barked at his fellows, "All right, let's get moving!"

Cart with captive turned to retrace the route just followed, as hateful epithets rained down on the police. Officer Ormsby arrested a white man for striking Officer Lowell, the assailant an attendee of the Liberty Party Convention from Madison County.

"They're just doing their job!" Parish protested.

We lagged the eerie procession back toward Clinton Square, leaving an ailing Cale Davis in position on the Lock Street bridge. I thought the butcher looked green enough to hurl lunch into the canal. Ma raised me such that I wanted to ask him if he was alright, even though I never liked him.

Returning the way we came, Jerry was carried past the Commissioner's Office to the Police Office, upstairs in the Journal Building. Will Stoddard stood outside the double door on level with the bridge when the waiting lawmen fettered Jerry's legs.

"Take these chains and let me fight like a man!" the fugitive raged in fury.

A spirited crowd had followed Jerry's plight from start to finish. While his friends cleared a pathway or hindered police, the opposite was true of those more attuned to law and order. Parish Johnson was torn—he didn't want Jerry returned to slavery, but still defended his policemen friends.

"What are they supposed to do, Ed?" he asked incredulously. "It's the law, and they're following orders!"

"Then maybe they should follow a higher law, Parish," I protested, coincidentally timed with the reappearance of Rev. May.

"Are you gonna try to get Jerry out again, Rev. May?" Si Cheney asked.

Rev. May laughed in answer, "Ha! I was just approached two or three times by men who said, Mr. May, speak the word, and we'll have Jerry out!"

"What did you tell 'em, Reverend?" Sam asked.

"Boys, I simply asked, What will you do with him when you get him out? You've just seen the bad effect of one ill-advised attempt at rescue. Wait until proper arrangements are made!"

Painful wails from the fugitive continued to be heard from inside the Police Office, further stoking the abolitionists fresh from the convention. Out-of-towners joined the locals in voicing their displeasure. Angry cries of, "Send him out!" echoed off the Journal building.

Taking his leave, Rev. May said, "I'd best go inside to stand with Jerry now—this travesty has the whole city on edge."

"That's right, Rev. May," I replied. "I thought Cale Davis was gonna retch!"

The hurried minister stopped, turning to eye me with great intent.

"Oh, really?" he asked profoundly. Somehow I got his wheels turning, but didn't know what for.

Alex urged, "C'mon guys—let's go talk to Will!"

Prentice remarked on our growing number, "Hey Will, did ya see anyone else from Weld's school out there? Pretty soon our whole class will turn out."

"I bet they do," Will Stoddard replied, "The Cook boys are working again, but I'm surprised the Willard's ain't here."

"So tell us what ya seen, Will!" I implored, with everyone listening for his response.

Will answered, "For starters, I got inside the Commissioner's Office and saw it all go down! Deputy Marshal Allen had a warrant to arrest Jerry—a John McReynolds of Missouri claimed that Jerry was his escaped slave, and sent a man named Lear to get him. Allen had help from other US Marshals from Canandaigua, Auburn, and Rochester."

"But Lowell was there, too!" Parish said.

"Yeah, Allen asked the whole city police force to help him, and they couldn't say no. They brought Lowell to make Jerry think that he was under arrest for something minor. Around one o'clock the examination began. The abolitionists wanted Charles Sedgwick to represent Jerry, but Mr. Leonard Gibbs of Washington County was at the convention and volunteered. Gibbs said he didn't think the Marshal had any right to handcuff Jerry, and he didn't like the claimant sitting in Court with a revolver."

"What they say to that, Will?" Alex asked.

"The US District Attorney, Mr. Lawrence, said the prisoner was in custody of the Marshal, and that he had a right to take every precaution to prevent his escape. Gibbs didn't agree and asked the Commissioner to remove the irons, but Mr. Sabine said that he had no authority to do so. He advised the Marshal to take the irons off, but Allen refused."

Prentice remarked, "We should give you a Citizen's Award for getting inside the office, Will! What happened next?"

"The Commissioner read the application of Mr. McReynolds who claimed Jerry as a fugitive from service. Then Gerrit Smith and Rev. May came in to sit beside Jerry, with Rev. Loguen standing behind him.

Jerry looked heart-stricken, and asked, "You ain't Gerrit Smith, are you?"

Smith replied, "Yes—and I mean you shall have the best counsel, and to stand by you with my fortune."

Grove Johnson asked, "How you remember so much, Will?"

"I don't know, sometimes it scares me!" Will laughed. "Then James Lear of Missouri was called to testify as a witness, but before he could, Mr. Gibbs asked the Commissioner to disarm him! Sabine said that he had no right to presume that the witness was armed, and he wouldn't do anything so long as Lear didn't exhibit a weapon. So then Gibbs asked for proof that slavery was legal in Missouri, and he spoke on it for a while before Mr. Lawrence said the question was irrelevant and asked the Commissioner to proceed."

"I bet they did, too," Sam remarked.

"Yup—Lear stated that he was a resident of Missouri and knew John McReynolds since 1820. Then he testified to the signatures and seals on the documents, and swore that he was acquainted with Jerry since he was a boy. He said that he knew Jerry's mother when she lived with Jerry's former owner, Mr. Henry."

"That's incredible!" I cried, "I'm surprised that Jerry didn't recognize Lear right away."

Will replied, "You're right, but the noise in the office got so loud that you couldn't hear yourself think. The Commissioner called for a half-hour break and that's when Jerry bolted."

"Tell us, Will!" Si Cheney entreated.

"It happened so fast that I didn't see it all clearly. I saw Jerry being hurried out toward the stairs and then somebody closed the door so I couldn't see where he went. There was a great rush to the door, but Jerry's friends blocked the pursuit. I tried to follow, but there were too many large bodies in the way. By the time I gained the street, I saw all you guys in the distance following Jerry, with the police right behind him! I figured they'd bring 'im back to the Police Office, so that's where I went. I stood here on the bridge and watched the crowd surge back the same way they ran off. When they got near the Commissioner's office I saw that several men were kneeling on Jerry to keep him down, while others kept the crowd back with cart stakes."

"Wow, you had a front row seat! What were the police doing at the office?" I asked.

"Justice House had the officers busy in strengthening their defenses. They expected a possible storming party and spiked heavy wooden bars across the windows."

Jerry's mournful wails from inside the Police Office interrupted Will's account. We overheard Justice House entreating Rev. May to assist. "Jerry is in a perfect rage, do come and see if you can quiet him!" House implored.

Chaos enveloped Clinton Square around the Journal Building, the sound of bells made it all surreal. Will Stoddard surprised us with an impromptu speech on the Clinton Street bridge.

"You know, while I watched Jerry being held down in the cart, all the devilishness of human slavery went through my mind like a red hot flash, and I'd been taught all I needed to know of it. Jerry was guilty of no crime except for being a black man, but on that account he must be seized as a criminal, convicted of his color, and sentenced to lose his freedom! Burglars get let out after a while, but the black man's sentence is for life."

Will paused, then concluded with, "And I don't care two cents for Daniel Webster and the Compromise!"

A familiar voice answered with, *"Well spoken, young man—you should join me on the lecture circuit."*

Sam Ward Jr. leapt for joy. *"Pa! You're back!"* he cried, rushing to embrace his father. We all circled Rev. Ward like a retuning hero, his large presence emanated hope and courage.

"What's gonna happen now, Pa?" Sam asked with his arm around his father's waist.

"I'm going to find Rev. May and try to see Jerry, Sam!"

"Rev. May's already in there, Pa, can I go with you?"

"I don't know if they'll let us inside, but we can try!"

"I'll get you inside, Reverend—they all know me," Parish asserted.

Si Cheney begged, "What about us, Rev. Ward—can we come, too?"

"No, we need you boys to stay on alert in case there's more trouble. Who knows where this will end," Rev. Ward replied.

While the trio stepped toward the door I pled, "Please let me know if my pa's in there, Reverend—I haven't seen him all day!"

"I will, Edward—just wait here, it shouldn't be long," he directed.

Parish gained his accustomed entrance, posing no threat to the Police Office under siege. Rev. Ward and Sam followed—all three were admitted to see the prisoner.

Prentice asked, "You really think your pa's in there, Ed?"

"Maybe, he's not one to stay home and play it safe," I answered with certainty.

Time slowed as we waited. People poured into Clinton Square, a couple thousand at least, with everyone pressed toward the Police Office on the western end. A surprising number of ladies attended, their bonnets easy to pick out in the crowd. After what seemed an eternity, our spirits were lifted by the sight of Rev. Ward, followed by Sam, Parish, and Rev. May.

*"Your father's not inside, Edward!"* Rev. Ward informed.

Rev. May added, "He went to retain counsel at the Court House after he gave notice at the convention."

Rev. Ward sent me and Sam on a mission.

"Sam, I need you to run home to let your mother and the girls know that I'm back. Keep your head like we've taught you, Sam—there's mischief afoot!"

*"Yes, sir—I will!"* Sam replied.

"Edward, you do likewise for your mother. Let her know what's going on, I doubt that your pa's been home today," Rev. Ward directed.

"I will, sir!" I affirmed.

Rev. May announced, "I'll walk with you boys, there's someone that I need to see."

Vowing to return, the three of us departed. We hadn't gone far when the printer, Chauncey Crofoot, happened along to offer us a ride in his conveyance. So far, it was the best thing that happened all day, not counting the barbeque.

"I was glad to get out of the Journal Building," Crofoot announced, "that crowd looks ready to storm the gates!"

"But hopefully not until sufficient plans are made," Rev. May replied.

"Will there be a meeting, Reverend?" I asked.

"Certainly, Edward, several I would think—and I'd be surprised not to see your father."

"So tell me what happened in there, Sam!" I begged.

"Ed, Rev. May was already with Jerry in a little room in the back, trying to get him to calm down. It's a tight space, so Parish went to talk with the policemen. I felt bad seeing Jerry all beat up and fettered! He was so excited he couldn't stand still, pacing up and down in that narrow room as best he could with the manacles. Pa surprised me when he said that he'd never seen a chained slave before."

Rev. May said, "Sam's right, Edward. Jerry begged us to break his chains, and give him that liberty which the Declaration of Independence promised to every man. He asked, *'Am I not a man like yourselves? Do you not suppose that I feel as other men feel?'*"

All I could think was, *poor Jerry!* "Sam, what did Jerry say about his arrest?" I asked.

"Jerry said they accused him of a crime, but he was eager to prove his innocence. That's why he let that little Marshal put handcuffs on him. It wasn't until after that they told him he was being taken as a runaway slave!"

This confirmed that Parish was right about why Jerry went peacefully, at least at first, so I asked,

"And what about when he broke outta the Commissioner's Office?"

Rev. May answered, "Jerry said that because they took him deceitfully, he thought it wasn't wrong to break away when he saw a chance. He ran for his freedom, but they caught him and brought him back like a wild beast, chained, and caged!"

While I pondered this intelligence, Chauncey Crofoot pulled up at his house. We all jumped out to complete our journey on foot when Rev. May surprised us.

"And this is where I leave you, boys," he began, "I'm worried about the butcher, but please don't tell anyone!" he said with a serious tone as he crossed the street to visit his nemesis, Cale Davis.

Sam and I stood perplexed. Of everything we'd seen today, this was the most peculiar. Given half a chance, Davis would berate Rev. May at every turn, yet here the preacher went out of his way for him while a real struggle raged against the *Fugitive Slave Law*. It didn't make sense.

"Oh, Rev. May knows what he's doing," Sam said as we walked. "Let's just do what we're told and get back down there."

"You're right, Sam—I'll meet you at the coop after I talk to Ma!"

Everyone but my father was home when I arrived with the exciting news. The toll of bells easily reached our house, and much further, the warning clangs were felt as much as heard. My family wore its effects like all the people downtown, Black George and the kitchen maid, too.

"Tell us what you saw, Edward!" Cornelia demanded with urgency.

"Yes, Edward—we were all sent home from school!" Ellen followed.

"Come in here and tell us, Edward!" Ma ordered.

Without much interruption I related the day's events. Ma had that worried look on her face that usually meant I'd be staying home. Black George's blood was up after hearing the part on the Lock Street bridge.

"I be leavin' now Missus!" he announced, determined to join the fray.

Ma knew there was no stopping him. Seeing his dagger, she cried, "You be careful now, George—I don't want you to get into trouble with the law!"

"Not me, but at the Colored Folks convention we swore to fight back, and I'se goin'."

"I'm going with you, George—Rev. Ward's back, and he said that he needs us." Then looking directly at Ma, I continued, "And Pa needs us, too!"

We left before my mother had time to think, but she yelled, "Stay together!" from our front door. We found Sam waiting at the coop, and the three of us hurried downtown to try and save Jerry. I looked for signs of Cale Davis and Rev. May at the butcher shop, but the place looked deserted.

# Chapter Seventeen
## (October 1 & 2, 1851)

Rushing back to the Police Office at Clinton Square, we saw Rev. Lyles standing amongst a great assembly of colored people. When Black George steered us over, two men stepped forward with familiarity. Observing the crowd, one said,

"Hey, George! Never seen dis many niggers in one place before!"

"And we be one more when Jerry gets freed!" his companion assured.

Black George shook their hands along with Rev. John Lyles, pastor of the *Second Congregational* on Fayette Street near Almond. "What da plan, Reverend?" he asked.

"Waitin' on Loguen, George—told everyone to sit tight till after the meetin' they's havin'!"

"Alrighty then, that's what we do I s'pose," he replied, looking resigned to wait.

"Your daddy's gonna address the crowd, Sam," Rev. Lyles said.

"You haven't seen my pa, have you, Reverend?" I asked.

"Well, yes—a couple times—and lookin' mighty intent, he was!" Rev. Lyles answered.

"I wonder where he is now," I replied.

Sam reassured me. "Somebody'll know—we'll find 'im!"

"Yeah, but your pa said, there's mischief afoot, and my pa's in the middle of it."

"C'mon, Ed—let's find my pa so I can tell 'im that I done what he said," Sam said urgently. Turning to our companion, he said, "We'll find you later, George!"

I agreed. "Right, George—we'll keep an eye out for ya. Let's go, Sam!"

"You boys think sharp now!" Black George advised as we departed.

We found our friends almost where we left them, along with other faces from Weld's School that increased our number. Sam ascertained that his pa had left the police office for a meeting somewhere, likely with Rev. Loguen.

"So, what happened after we left?" I asked urgently.

"Plenty!" Will Stoddard answered.

Prentice said, "I heard the Marshal say he was expectin' all hell to break loose."

"And when the County Sheriff arrived, Marshal Allen asked him to get the military ready in case they're needed," Alex stated.

"And did he?" I asked.

"Yes, and no," Parish answered. "Charlie Pope can tell you more—and he saw your pa!"

"That's right, Ed—I was down at the armory when I saw him," Charlie began. He was on friendly terms with the militia like Parish was with the police.

"The Citizens' Corps, National Guards, and the Washington Artillery were assembling when your pa came walking in with Colonel Vandenburgh. Captain Prendergast showed his colonel the sheriff's order, but the colonel told him that he didn't have to obey it!

Prendergast said that he wasn't a lawyer, but that he was ordered out by the sheriff and that was enough for him. Then the colonel told him that he'd seen the sheriff and requested him not to call the men out."

"So, what about my pa, Charlie?"

"Well, Vandenburgh left right after that, but your pa stayed. He asked Prendergast if he were going out with the men today, and when he answered yes, your pa said that there wasn't a man among them who wouldn't be sued to the end of the law if they turned out. Prendergast told him he should obey the sheriff, but your pa said the sheriff had no right to order them out. Soon after, the captain received a written order from Colonel Vandenburgh directing the militia to disband. Prendergast called everyone together, and after both orders were read, the soldiers decided to follow the orders of their colonel.

And that's the last I saw of your pa, Ed—he left right after that."

"Thanks, Charlie! Now I gotta figure where he mighta gone next," I replied.

Sam pointed to the Rev. R. R. Raymond slicing through the crowd with determination.

"I bet he knows—let's follow 'im!" he cried. The clergy of Syracuse weren't shying away from this one.

Will Stoddard encouraged us to hurry back as the growing crowd grew restless. "The hearing's supposed to start again around five thirty—you don't wanna miss it!"

As the sun faded, Sam and I left our friends in pursuit of the fast-moving pastor weaving through the crowd. We both thought he was headed for the Congregational church, but he walked right past it for a right turn on Warren Street.

"Where you think he's going, Sam?" I asked.

"Not sure—hey, ain't that Dr. Hoyt's that he's going into?"

"It sure is, let's see if our pa's are in there."

Stern faces inside the crowded office of Dr. Hiram H. Hoyt showed a surprise that almost equaled our embarrassment from being eyeballed. A quick glance identified the doctors Hoyt and Pease; Gerrit Smith, Abner Bates, and the Reverends May, Loguen, and

*Dr. Hiram Hoyt*

Ward. There were a bunch more of them packed in the office—Pa saw me before I saw him, quite alarmed by my presence.

"What are you doing here, Edward?" Pa demanded.

"I was worried about you, Pa—with everything going on I thought you might-a been in trouble!"

"Thank you, son—but what would you do if I was?"

"Uh . . . I don't know, Pa," I quietly replied.

Rev. Ward directed, "You boys wait for me outside. I'll walk back to the police office with you."

Heading towards the door, I overheard Gerrit Smith say that the Commissioner would probably release Jerry, but a forcible rescue would have a stronger moral effect. After a short wait outside, Rev. Ward emerged and had us moving again.

"Are we gonna rescue Jerry, Pa?" Sam asked as we followed his lead.

"We're going to try, Sam!"

Thinking of Parish Johnson, I asked, "Do you think any policemen will get hurt, Rev. Ward?"

"I pray not, Edward—we all agreed not to intentionally injure the police. Gerrit Smith pressed this caution urgently, and Rev. May said he hoped that if anyone's injured, it'll be one of us."

Sam asked, "Pa, did you all make a plan?"

"Yes, Sam—but for now it's none of your business."

The growing darkness created a demand for tar barrels like it was the 4th of July. Street corner fires began to pop up everywhere in the crowded downtown area. As we approached the Police Office, we saw that someone addressed the crowd from the Clinton Street bridge. There had to be a few thousand people at Clinton Square, maybe more. "I'm going back inside with Jerry," Rev. Ward said. "You boys stay out of trouble now, you hear me?"

"Yes, sir!" we both replied.

When the hearing resumed, the Rev. Charles C. Foote came out to speak.

"C. C. Foote? That name sounds familiar," I queried.

"Ed, he was the Liberty Party candidate for Vice President in '48—right beside Gerrit Smith," Alex clarified.

"Oh, right—he must've been at the convention."

"He was, the whole convention crowd's out here somewhere."

*Rev. Charles C. Foote*

"Right—and everyone from the fair, too," I replied.

"They were gonna have speeches from the balcony of the Bastable building tonight—bet it's canceled now," Prentice said.

Sam asked, "Who's in there with Jerry?"

Larry Sabine answered, "Messrs. D. D. Hillis, Hervey Sheldon, and Leroy Morgan are helping Mr. Gibbs. You're Sam, right? I've heard Ed talk about you."

"That's me," Sam replied. "Anybody else we know helpin' Jerry?"

"Parish Johnson and Will Stoddard!" Si Cheney answered.

A loud voice shouted, *"Bring him out!"* Another yelled, *"Give him up!"* The call repeated with intensity from the restless crowd.

Grove Johnson alerted, *"Hey! Somebody just broke a window!"*

Everyone felt the growing excitement as more stones were thrown, most of them bouncing off the brick walls of the Journal building. It made me consider what Chauncey Crofoot said about storming the gates. Then I spotted Pa standing on the elevated road, having tense words with Black George. I quickly informed Sam.

"Hey Sam, there's my pa with George over there—it looks like they're arguing!"

"Let's go listen, Ed," Sam urged.

We approached with a clear view of them going nose to nose, both equally determined.

"I'se a free man, Mr. Wheaton, and I'll stand with my brothers to get Jerry out!" Black George voiced with feeling.

"I know you are, George, I know, but try to see reason," Pa answered.

"I'm not runnin' away from this, suh!"

Pa's reply brought truth to Chauncey Crofoot's prediction. He implored, "Nobody's asking you to, George, only not to storm the building."

"Why not? If dey's goin' in, den so's I!" Black George responded.

"George, listen to me—I know I'm asking a lot, but please hear me out. I expect to be arrested for everything I've done and am doing now. If we're both in jail, life will be twice as hard for Ellen and the children!"

"Is I gonna lose my situation over this, Mr. Wheaton?"

Pa beseeched, "No, George—but I'm asking you."

I never heard or saw either of them like this, which made the day even odder than it already was. *What next?* I thought. Both men stood fast, Black George spoke first after a moment's pause.

"Well, suh, when you puts' it dat way . . . I sho' don't wanna make life hard, *but I gots to do somethin'!*"

"You will, George, you will! You can start right away if you come with me now," Pa gushed as the two hurried off somewhere, neither one aware of our presence.

"C'mon, Ed—let's get back with the others!" Sam exhorted.

The crowd's impatience grew as the minutes became an hour while the hearing progressed inside the Police Office. Broken glass tinkled down that narrowly missed Rev. Ward when he stepped onto the platform to shake hands with Rev. C. C. Foote, of Michigan, who'd just finished speaking.

Voices called for Jerry's freedom. ***"Bring him out! Bring him out!"*** they chanted. Then others called for Rev. Ward to address the crowd. Sam's face lit up when his pa stepped forward with a commanding voice that entranced the angry spectators.

"Fellow citizens! We are here in most extraordinary circumstances. We are witnessing such a sight as, I pray, we may never look upon again. A man in chains, in Syracuse! Not a felon, yet in chains! On trial is this man, not for life, but for liberty. He is arrested and held under a law made by *'Us the People'* pursuant, we pretend to a clause in the constitution. That constitution was made 'to secure the blessings of liberty to ourselves and our posterity.' Here is a man one of 'ourselves'; and the color he bears shows that he belongs not altogether to my race, but that he is one of the 'posterity' of those who framed and adopted our federal constitution. So far are we from 'securing' to him the 'blessings of liberty,' that we have arrested him, confined him, and chained him, on purpose to inflict upon him the curses of slavery.

"They say he is a slave. What a term to apply to an American! How does this sound beneath the pole of liberty and the flag of freedom? What a contradiction to our *Declaration of Independence!* But suppose he be a slave: is New York the State to recognize and treat him as such? Is Syracuse the city of the Empire State in which the deeds which make this a day unfortunately memorable should be perpetuated? If he be not a slave, then, he is the most outraged man we ever saw.

"What did our fathers gain by the seven years' struggle with Great Britain, if, in what are called Free States, we have our fellow citizens, our useful mechanics and skillful artisans, chained and enslaved? How do foreign nations regard us, when knowing that it is not yet three short months since we were celebrating the Declaration of Independence, and today we are giving the most palpable denial to every word therein declared?

"But I am told that this is a legal transaction. That it is wrong and unwise to speak against a judicial proceeding, not yet completed: I admit it all. I make no pretensions to speak wisely. I have heard a speech from Jerry. I feel for him, as for a brother; and under that feeling, I may not speak quite so soberly as I ought. *'Oppression maketh a wise man mad.'* I feel oppressed in a twofold sense. Yonder is my brother, in chains. Those chains press upon my limbs. I feel his sufferings and participate his anguish. I feel, and we may all feel, oppressed in another sense. Here there are certainly five-and-twenty hundreds of us, wild with excitement on behalf of our chained brother, before our eyes, and we are utterly powerless to help him! We hear his strong, thrilling appeals until our hearts sicken and our heads ache; but there is none among us that has the legal power to lift a hand in his defense, or for his deliverance. Of what advantage is it that we are free? What value is there in our freedom, while our hands are thus tied?

"Fellow citizens, whatever may be the result of these proceedings—whether our brother leaves the court, a declared freeman, or a chained slave—upon us, the voters of New York State, to a very great extent, rests the responsibility of this Fugitive Slave Law. It is for us to say whether this enactment shall continue to stain our statute books or be swept away into merited oblivion. It is for us to say whether the men who made it, and those who execute it before our faces, shall receive our votes, or shall by those votes be indignantly rebuked. Tell me, ye sturdy working men of Onondaga, shall your votes be consecrated to the latter, or prostituted to the former? Do you swear fealty to freedom this day? Do you promise, so help you God! so to vote, as that your sanction never more shall be given to laws which empower persons to hunt, chain, and cage, MEN, in our midst?"

The crowd roared, *"Yes! Yes!"* as Rev. Ward concluded.

"Thank you, fellow citizens, in the name of our brother in prison! Thank you for your bold, manly promise! May we all abide by it, until deeds of darkness like the one we now lament shall no longer mar our institutions and blacken our history."

His final words were, "I bid you goodnight—you will have a long night of it!"

After he finished, an eerie stillness fell. The crowd caught its breath while his poignant words sank in. I turned to Sam, and said, "I never thought about it like that before—a white man's son carried off a slave!"

Sam answered, "Rev. Loguen's a white man's son, too, Ed, Pa's tryin' to change people's minds!"

The moment quickly passed, chants of ***"Bring him out! Give him up!"*** resumed in earnest as the rock throwers continued their assault. A large projectile shattered a window that adjourned the hearing until morning.

David D. Hillis, the lawyer, addressed the crowd, stating that the fugitive would likely be released through due process of law. He advised everyone to disperse and let the law take its course. Rev. Ward echoed Mr. Hillis's advice, followed by my uncle, the mayor.

Police Justice House, among others, tried to disperse the crowd without success. The people cheered the speeches, but nothing short of Jerry's freedom would suffice. We watched as Rev. Ward departed arm in arm with Gerrit Smith towards City Hall, followed by the Commissioner, whom we assumed had left for home.

Just when I thought it was over, a tight contingent of able-bodied men armed with clubs, axes, and rods of iron ascended the stairs of the Police Office—none of them spoke, their actions did the talking. Many were men of color led by Rev. Loguen, whose eyes blazed with determination. He looked impossible to oppose. I couldn't help but notice that some men had black faces with white necks, or black hands with white wrists.

Prentice cried, "Hey look, some of 'em used burnt cork to hide their faces!"

"I see it, Prentice, must be twenty or thirty of 'em trying to get Jerry out!"

Someone shouted, *"Here comes old Oswego!"* as a long, solid beam was used as a battering ram against the stubborn locks and woodwork. Though our view inside was unclear, we heard the chaos as the rescuers swiftly accomplished their mission. Windows shattered, casings were chopped, doors were battered with the heavy ram. The sounds of wooden casements being ripped from studded walls filled the air. A shot rang out, someone leapt from a second-floor window on the canal side, staggering down the heel path.

*"Holy shite!"* Si Cheney cursed in Irish.

We caught fleeting glimpses of Rev. Loguen who seemed to be everywhere, moving with determined purpose and forcefully applying his will. A deafening cheer erupted when the manacled Jerry appeared on the platform, held aloft by his rescuers who carried him down to the street. After placing him on his feet it became obvious that he was in no condition to run, even without the fetters. We followed the impromptu procession that carried him eastward in a victory march down Water Street. Outside the Syracuse House, Alex remarked,

"I wonder what all the pro-slavery men in there think of Jerry now!"

City Alderman Benjamin Higgins attempted to impede the rescue by ordering everyone to halt. That's when Moses Summers, editor of the *Syracuse Standard*, intervened, pushing him on the chest and telling him not to interfere. Higgins persisted and ran around to get in front of Jerry, but Summers caught him by the lapel of his coat and grounded him. We followed Jerry's entourage down Warren Street to Brintnall's Hotel, where they placed him in a light buggy that sped away—I overheard someone say that he took the *Canada Express*. With Jerry safely away, Sam and I called it a night.

I didn't know what to expect, walking in alone after hours on the most exciting night that Syracuse ever had, but the only trouble came from not being able to talk fast enough. After relaying the night's adventure, I waited up with everyone for Pa and Black George to come home. None of us could sleep until they both returned unharmed. Cornelia manned the look-out post by the window, soon announcing their arrival.

"Here they come, Ma!" she cried.

We all rushed to greet them at the door. Ma and the girls hugged them both as soon as they walked in.

"*We were all worried!*" Ma exhorted.

"I'm sorry, Ellen, but it couldn't be helped," Pa answered.

"Edward told us that he saw the assault on the Police Office, and how the crowd carried that poor man to Brintnall's!" Ma exclaimed.

"And how they had a fast buggy waiting!" Cornelia added.

I felt relieved to detect the familiar calm between my father and Black George, glad their differences were behind them—but even gladder that I hadn't said anything about me and Sam listening in on a private conversation.

Ma urged, *"Charles, please sit down and tell us about it! You too, George!"*

With Ma at his side, Pa reclined to tell us the day's adventure. Black George took a comfortable chair, all us kids gathered around.

Pa began, "There's so much to say we could sit here all night, but I'll keep it short."

*"Tell us, Pa!"* Ellen pressed.

"Alright then, it all started when I recognized the US Marshal, Henry Allen, arresting a black man. Everyone on our *Vigilance Committee* knew that only a US Marshal could arrest a fugitive slave, so we made sure to recognize these men. He wasn't a stranger to me. I knew it was him right away."

"Whatcha do then, Pa?" Cornelia begged.

"I hurried to tell everyone at the convention what happened, but on the way, I grew angry thinking of Daniel Webster and his threat. I knew that we'd prepared for this moment—now was the time for action!

"The convention adjourned, and many started for the Commissioner's Office. Someone mentioned ringing the bell at the Congregational, and others volunteered to get the other churches, too."

"We heard the bells, Pa!" Emma said.

"That's right, honey, I hoped that the other churches would join in, but I didn't expect it."

"It was a glorious sound!" Ma said.

Black George found his voice. *"It sho was, Missus! Never heard anythin' like dat before!"*

Pa continued, "When attorney Leonard Gibbs offered to represent Jerry, I went to the courthouse to find Charles Sedgwick to file a complaint."

"What do you mean, Charles?" Ma asked.

"We exercised the State law on kidnapping, Ellen. Tonight, the slave owner's agent, a man named Lear, was arrested for kidnapping Jerry."

Pa confused me. "I don't get it, Pa. Are you saying Jerry was arrested for being a fugitive slave, then Lear was arrested for doing it?"

"It's like this, Edward—Lear used *Federal law* to have US Marshal Henry Allen arrest Jerry, then we used *State law* to have Lear arrested for kidnapping."

Ma said, "And you're the one who signed the complaint? Don't expect to make any friends down south!"

I asked, "Pa, does this mean that Marshal Allen is next?"

"One step at a time, son," he replied.

"What happened next, Pa?" Cornelia posed.

"With all the people flooding downtown we feared the militia might be called out like they were in Boston. After I heard the rumors, I went directly to the armory to see for myself, only to find Colonel Vandenburgh heading there for the same reason! The companies were indeed turning out, but like me, the colonel questioned the sheriff's authority. He requested that Captain Prendergast not send his men out, departing to draft the official order in writing. I witnessed the captain receive the order from his colonel, and watched as the companies stood down."

"Whatcha do next, Pa?" Ellen asked.

"After that, it was time for the meeting at Doctor Hoyt's. We met at early candlelight to decide how we'd rescue Jerry."

I blurted out, "Who was there, Pa?" I wasn't inside long enough to see everyone."

"No, you weren't supposed to be there at all, Edward. Everyone risked their necks to oppose the *Fugitive Slave Law!*"

Ma shuddered at this, but quietly took it all in. Pa surprised us by dropping names.

"You'll find out eventually, but keep this to yourselves. Besides Doctor Hoyt were Doctors Fuller and Pease; Gerrit Smith, the Reverends May, Ward, Loguen, and Raymond, Montgomery Merrick, Abner Bates, Jason Hoyt, Peter Hallenbeck, *and there were others, too!*"

"What did Gerrit Smith say, Charles?" Ma asked.

"Ellen," he said, *"It is not unlikely the Commissioner will release Jerry if the examination is suffered to proceed—but the moral effect of such an acquittal will be as nothing to a bold and forcible rescue. A forcible rescue will demonstrate the strength of public opinion against the possible legality of slavery, and this Fugitive Slave Law in particular. It will honor Syracuse and be a powerful example everywhere!"*

"Did everyone approve this measure?" she pressed.

"Not at first, Ellen, but with Rev. May as spokesman, a plan was finally adopted. *At a given signal, the doors and windows of the police office were to be demolished at once, with the rescuers rushing in to fill the room. They were to overwhelm the officers with their numbers, not by blows, and so soon as they were confined and powerless by the pressure of bodies about them, several men were to take Jerry out!* Strict injunctions were given, and it was agreed not intentionally to injure the policemen. Rev. May, Gerrit Smith, and several others pressed this caution very urgently. The last thing that Rev. May said was, *'If anyone is injured in this fray, I hope it may be one of our own party!'*

"From there, we'd have a bold and skillful driver waiting in a strong buggy, with the fleetest horse to be had in the city, stationed not far off to receive Jerry. Edward saw as much, and that's all I can tell you for now."

"And what can you tell us, George?" Ma asked.

"Well, Missus, I holds wit ever-thing Mr. Wheaton said, 'cept he didn't know dat I saw Rev. Loguen right after he come out da meetin'! He say dat black men should take part, and when I knowed deys goin' in to get Jerry, I thought to help bust 'im out da Police Office!"

"And did you?" she asked anxiously.

"Not direct, Ma'am, I be on da *rear guard*, handin' out crowbars and axes. An ready to give warnin' if da *law an order* crowd start makin' trouble!"

"That bunch would have, too, if it took longer to get Jerry out," Pa affirmed.

My mother ended the long day's vigil. "All right children, everyone to bed now—it's late!"

"Okay, Ma, but can I ask Pa another question, first?" I posed.

"Yes, but make it quick."

"Pa, where's Jerry?"

"I really don't know, Edward, but *wherever Jerry is, he's free!*"

It seemed that no-one knew where Jerry was, and if anyone did, they weren't talking. Everybody else went downtown to start rumors—clusters formed on street corners to discuss yesterday's excitement. Impromptu debates evoked strong feelings where two positions emerged; some called it a rescue, while others deemed it a riot—with no middle ground to be had.

Most people on both sides believed that Jerry caught the next boat to Canada across Lake Ontario or the St. Lawrence River, but others weren't so sure. The law-and-order crowd remained vigilant for the whereabouts of a fugitive who might have never left town. From horseback, Major Moses D. Burnet, the man who could have been mayor, led a sizeable group of outraged citizens. With all city exits closely watched, it wasn't a leap of imagination to suggest that things would have ended differently for Jerry had Major Burnet been the mayor. People would say something like that right before launching into personal attacks on Uncle Horace, Colonel Vandenburgh, and my father.

Day two of the Liberty Party convention was the hot ticket after Jerry's rescue, competing with people curious to see the Police Office. My sisters, Cornelia and Ellen, both woke up eager for a guided tour of Syracuse history, and the County Fair had a full lineup as well. Major Burnet led the Agricultural Society behind the annual fair each autumn. Black George had business there but detoured the wagon to drop us off at Clinton Square. The butcher shop still looked closed, but I caught a glimpse of Thomas Davis milling about. I couldn't wait for a chance to ask Rev. May what happened.

"Thanks, George!" Cornelia said, echoed by me and Ellen jumping out at the Square.

"Have fun at the fair!" I called.

George answered, "More bout business than fun, but I plans to enjoy it. We's all glad Jerry done gone north!"

The police office wasn't surrounded like last night but continued to draw spectators. We had to wait our turn to get up close, only to find Will Stoddard examining the remains.

"Hey, Will! Didn't you get enough last night?" I joked.

"Hey yourself, Ed—hello Cornelia, hello Ellen," he replied.

"Hello, Will—I heard that you saw everything," Cornelia said.

"Yes, I did—but I had to see the Police Office in the daylight. It reminds me of buildings that I've seen after a fire, only without the flames." Looking around, Will said, "They cleaned it out proper, right? Not a partition, desk, or window sash left!"

"What happened to all the doors?" Ellen asked.

"The battering ram, Ellen," Will replied.

"Did they miss anything?" Cornelia asked in surprise.

Parish Johnson suddenly appeared to say, "No, they didn't!" Brother Grove emerged from behind the rubble.

Parish cried, "Come here and see the little room where they had Jerry—they ripped out the partition walls!"

"Not much left, is there?" I pondered.

"Nope—looks like they gotta start over," Grove replied.

Will said, "Hey, Ed—remember when that big rock crashed through the window and almost hit the Commissioner? That was the last straw, and he adjourned for the night!"

Cornelia interrupted, "C'mon Edward, let's go to the convention now; it'll be good from everything that's happened."

Following Cornelia's lead we departed as Grove smiled from walking close to Ellen.

It was standing room only at City Hall for the Liberty Party Convention where cheerful abolitionists celebrated the rescue of a fugitive slave. Rev. C.C. Foote opened with prayer, Gerrit Smith spoke at length, resolutions were offered by Leonard Gibbs, Timothy Star, and the Reverends Ward and Loguen, subsequently approved.

My favorite was, "Resolved, therefore that we rejoice that the city of Syracuse, the Anti-Slavery city of Syracuse, the city of Anti-Slavery Conventions, our beloved and glorious city of Syracuse, still remains undisgraced by the fulfillment of the Satanic prediction of Satan's Daniel Webster."

Being at City Hall that day felt like the 4th of July, with its promise of life, liberty, and the pursuit of happiness! At least for today, we all felt part of something much larger than ourselves. Everyone prayed for Jerry.

At the convention's end we had one more surprise. Responding to requests from the audience, Pa took the stage to belt out a solo that drew a hearty round of applause.

Somebody said, "He sho got a purdy voice!"

## Chapter Eighteen
(October 3 – 14, 1851)

We were among the last people to see Jerry when the escape buggy sped away from Brintnall's Hotel on Wednesday night. Without knowing his fate, the authorities did the only thing that they could—they offered a liberal reward for information and kept looking for him. But this only fueled speculation, soon clues and sightings were reported all over town by eager residents.

Walking to school with the Cheney brothers that Friday, we were no different than anyone else in Syracuse—the topic of conversation being, Where's Jerry? Approaching Orange St. we heard Cale Davis pontificate the matter.

"The world's gone crazy over one colored man! All thanks to that abolitionist, Unitarian preacher!" the butcher railed. "No one's above the law, not even Samuel J. May. Lock 'im up, I say—there's ways to loosen a man's tongue!"

*Wait a minute!* I thought to myself, Rev. May just went out of his way for Davis. Now I *really* needed to question the Pastor! As the diatribe continued, I was glad not to live as close as Chauncey Crofoot, who hailed us from his door.

"Hello fellows," the printer cried. "I expect to see lots of Citizen's Awards for the rescuers!"

Si Cheney yelled back, "Yes, sir, we're havin' newspaper class directly, Mr. Crofoot."

"Make sure to include the police as well—they saved the building, if not their office. But I'm glad the attackers were focused. Aside from the broken windows, they confined their actions to the Police Office—what's left of it!"

"Were the presses damaged, Mr. Crofoot?" Prentice asked.

"Not at all! In fact, they're working overtime," he answered in departure.

As the butcher's voice trailed off with distance, Prentice remarked, "My pa told me that the abolitionists are incensed that Davis keeps shooting his mouth off. He's been louder than usual."

"Yeah—they wanna make it warm for him, but they ain't sure how," Si pronounced.

We heard our classmates from the street outside Weld's School for Young Men and Boys, everyone excitedly sharing stories of what they'd seen.

All four Willard brothers met us at the door, eager for us to join the conversation.

"Half the town's happy for Jerry, and the other half wants Colonel Vandenburgh's head!" Charlie Willard announced.

"And Mayor Wheaton's, too—they say he's controlled by his brother," Billy said.

"They want your pa's head, too, Ed!" Flo Willard informed, "People are sayin' that he wouldn't be against the militia turning out if a mob attacked his store."

Nine-year-old Eddie smiled, nodding his head in agreement.

"Thanks, guys!" was all I could say.

Mr. Weld restored order amidst the chaos of everyone talking at once.

"All right, gentlemen, take your seats and be quiet—one at a time, please! You there, Parish Johnson—how are the police taking the demise of their office?"

Parish stood to answer, "Mr. Weld, they're taking it pretty well, considering . . . Justice House said he wanted to move anyways."

Mr. Weld agreed. "Yes, a first floor Police Office would be more appropriate. I know you're familiar with the local police, Parish, but what can you tell us about the US Marshals?"

"Our local US Marshal, Henry Allen, brought in help from Marshal Swift from Auburn, Marshal Bemis from Canandaigua, and Marshal Fitch from Rochester. Fitch got his arm broke, but nobody's sure if somebody broke it or it happened when he jumped out of the second floor window."

"I saw him jump!" Si Cheney yelled.

Parish continued, "Fitch stuck his arm outta the back room to fire a shot, and somebody mighta broke it then. When Marshal Allen realized that the Vigilance Committee knew his face, he put on a disguise to get through the crowd; he was already gone before they stormed the building."

Mr. Weld replied, "It doesn't seem right that he left others to guard *his* prisoner."

"Especially since the Marshal's asked all the police to help them and they couldn't afford to say no, like they had an extra thousand to pay the fine! But, to be fair, Mr. Weld, when the commissioner adjourned the hearing, I think everybody thought that Jerry'd be transported to the penitentiary."

Larry Sabine called out, "Hey Parish, who arrested the slave owner's agent?"

"That would be officer Hollister, Larry—with help from Ormsby and Dodge. Ed Wheaton's pa signed the complaint for attempting to kidnap a citizen of Syracuse with intent to carry him out of the state, then Judge Pratt took bail money and let 'im go back to Missouri!"

Alex McKinstry asked, "Mr. Weld, have you spoken with Mr. Crandal since the rescue? We saw him in action and were hoping that he might have been here today."

"Yes, Alex—but briefly. He said how exciting it was to ring the bell at the Presbyterian church, but the best part was standing on the belfry door with people pounding from below trying to get in."

"Can he still hear, Mr. Weld?" Grove Johnson asked.

"His ears are working fine, Grove, and so is his pen! He's keeping the printers busy."

Charlie Pope stood up, holding two newspapers. "Mr. Weld, it's amazing how the *Standard* and the *Star* can tell completely different versions about what happened. It's like they watched two different events, and the only thing they agreed on was Jerry's name!"

"Charlie's right, Mr. Weld—was it a rescue, or a riot that we had?" Austin Cook asked.

"That's a great question, Austin. The answer is, it all depends on your perspective. There are conflicting values at play—what's more important, liberty or following the law?"

Bill Wallace stood to deliver news that shook me. "Mr. Weld, I think it's safer to follow the law for now—I just read that the Grand Jury of the US District Court charged treason against thirty-four people in Christiana!"

Billy Willard answered, "And you know where that can lead . . ."

All I could think of was Sam Ward telling me that he didn't want his family to move north. Although my pa faced risks, it wasn't as dire as that for the Ward's and the Loguen's. He wasn't a fugitive slave, escaping to Canada never crossed his mind.

I spent much of the day worried over the looming charges of treason, and the bad effect it was having. I really needed to talk to Sam, though I dreaded what he might say. Walking home with the Cheney's, Prentice remarked that there must have been *jail break fever* in the air on the first night of October. While events were taking place in Syracuse, in Utica, the young, convicted arsonist, James Jasper Orcutt, failed attempting to escape from his date with the hangman. The conversation carried us a few blocks until we again heard Cale Davis, loud as ever, at Orange Street. I wished that Rev. May had Rev. Loguen's size and might gag him.

When I visited Sam, I found the Ward household in turmoil.

Rev. Ward said, "The government considers opposition to the Slave Law as treason, and one of the consequences drawn after treason is a hempen rope!"

President Fillmore's decree to arrest and charge the Syracuse rioters with treason, coupled with accusations that Rev. Ward had incited the attack on the Police Office, only worsened the situation. All of Rev. Ward's closest friends urged him to leave the country immediately. Speaking to his wife, he expressed his burning dilemma.

"Emily, I feel hopeless that I can do more in my native country; you as well—both of us were already determined to go to Canada. But now, matters are urgent. *I could die; but is it my duty?* I can't remain here without repeating my connection with, or participating in such an affair as I'm guilty of. If I do my duty by my fellow men I must go to prison or even to the gallows. If I do not, I must go to perdition. Between the two, my election is made.

But then, what must become of my family? If I leave, what of your needed bread, and what liberty would you have in a country like this— one that's growing worse? Judge Nelson of Oregon decided that the testimony of Indians is not admissible against whites!"

Mrs. Ward answered, "You must save yourself! We'll be ready to follow when you send for us."

By then, Sam and the girls were crying.

Me, too.

Call me a glutton for punishment. After I left the Ward's, my next stop was the Loguen's where I witnessed a similar scene, only more chaotic. Caroline Loguen echoed Emily Ward's plea for her husband to flee while he still could. The Loguen girls were upset just like the Ward sisters, while Rev. Loguen vented his growing angst.

"Jerry committed the heinous crime of flying from bondage, and for that, the government of the United States seeks to remand him to a fate worse than death! Half the country would rejoice, grateful for an opportunity to display their mock patriotism, and their devotion to the Constitution!"

Hardly able to speak, I asked, "When are you gonna leave, Rev. Loguen?"

"Sometime this weekend, Edward," he replied demurely, which meant the next two days.

Although the streets were peaceful again, former slaves felt even more threatened after the "Jerry Rescue," as it was being called. Living in proximity to the Loguen's, we saw droves of fugitives in tattered clothing that provided clues of their identity. I watched from our front window with my mother and Black George.

"Here comes some more, Ma!" I observed.

"Yes, I see them, Edward—the Loguen's must be running out of everything!" she replied.

Black George agreed. "That's what I be thinkin,' Missus—I should gets down there to see."

"Well, bring something with you, whatever it is," Ma answered.

"I'll help him, Ma!" I cried.

"No, Edward—I might need you here from all the people coming over," she responded.

After the rescue, our abode became thronged with visitors, each bearing a new twist on the exciting topic of conversation. Ma cringed whenever treason came up, while Pa confidently expected to be arrested. I suspected that he looked forward to it.

"Charles, whatever they can prove against you will be of no account, unless they get perjured witnesses—but it won't be difficult to do that!" Ma stated.

"Why do you say that, Ellen?" Pa asked.

"Because the secret proceedings of the investigation wear the appearance of injustice and knavery," she answered.

A knock at our door brought Mr. Edward Thurber, Secretary of the Syracuse Musical Institute with news of their next meeting at Frazee Hall on the seventh. Pa was up for re-election as president and expected to win, but he still had to go to the meeting.

Uncle Horrace arrived after that, along with Moses Summers, editor of the *Standard*, to talk to my parents and anyone else who happened to be there.

"We all know that you used the entire police force to preserve the peace!" Summers stated emphatically to my uncle.

"They hold a different opinion at the *Star*, Moses," Uncle Horace, began. "They even accused *you* of being a prominent ringleader of the *mob* that attacked the police office! Then they said that if I'd done my duty, you'd have been arrested."

Summers responded, "They know darn well that I was in my office when the Police Office was attacked! I had no more connection with the *mob*, than the editor of the *Star*. I'm told that he was an indifferent spectator in the crowd when Jerry was carried off. He talks flippantly about traitors, knaves, ruffians, and ringleaders of mobs, and of the necessity of putting them down, but what did he do to prevent the outbreak and avoid the disgrace which he claims has stained our city?"

Uncle/Mayor Horace, replied, "I wonder if the editor of the *Star* is content to remain in a place so deeply disgraced as he declares Syracuse to be!"

Summers said, "I hope that he leaves in disgust!"

"Perhaps he will," my uncle responded hopefully.

Charles Sedgwick next appeared to join the conversation in our front parlor.

"What is treason?" the eminent lawyer began, "And who are these individuals who purport that defending a person from perpetual bondage is treason against the United States? Is there not a law of self-defense for a man to defend his life?

The administration in Washington labors to give character to the riot at Christiana, and make treason of it! But other occurrences similar to that have not been called treason—nobody supposed that war was levied against the United States when people prevented a slave from being dragged away into bondage."

Moses Summers replied, "I've read the law! Treason against the United States shall consist only in levying war against them, or in adhering to their enemies, giving them aid and comfort. No person shall be convicted of treason without the testimony of two witnesses or a confession in open court!"

Uncle Horace said, "Let the people read the Constitution and decide for themselves if war has been levied against the United States in Pennsylvania, here, or anywhere else. The administration will soon discover that it labored in vain to deceive the people!"

Ma listened quietly behind her grim expression.

The black community in Syracuse suffered a huge loss from the departure of the Reverends Loguen and Ward. Ma reminded me that Jerry Henry's freedom came at a cost, but what a price to pay! She encouraged us to frequently check on our neighbors who keenly felt their absence.

When Black George and I reached the local station of the underground railroad, unfamiliar faces were anxious for transport. Rev. Lyles conversed with Mrs. Caroline Loguen, who'd recently been promoted to stationmaster. Mrs. Loguen showed the obvious signs of her next child expected by year's end, while her daughters busied themselves. Rev. Lyles offered reassuring words to their mother.

"Always remember, Caroline, you're not alone! Even no matter how hard it seems."

"Thank you, John, I do appreciate you!" she replied.

Black George said cheerily, "Hello, Missus! Hello Suh!"

"Hello Mr. George and Mr. Edward! What brings two gentlemen here?" Rev. Lyles asked.

"Oh, we's just seein' dat everyone's alright, I s'pose."

"Thank you, George, you too, Edward!" Mrs. Loguen said.

Rev. Lyles asked, "Do anyone know where Jerry's at?"

"No, suh—I sho don't," Black George answered.

I rejoined, "Me, either, Rev. Lyles. My pa said that only a few people knew where Jerry went."

"Well, please let me know if you find out—lotta folks been askin'!"

"I will, sir," I assured him.

I found out the next day. Walking to and from school with the Cheney's, the silence was deafening both times that we crossed Orange Street.

"This is weird, Prentice—Davis must've lost his voice!" I said.

"Yeah—I can see 'im in there, but he's never this quiet," Prentice agreed.

"I'm just glad that he finally shut up," Si Cheney pronounced.

"I'm with you, Si, I'll see you guys tomorrow!" I said, leaving my friends at their turn-off.

Back home, we had another gathering of men discussing the rescue. Both of my parents, along with Rev. Raymond, Abner Bates, and John Thomas were listening to the Rev. May. As they were all members of the *Vigilance Committee*, I knew this wasn't a chance encounter.

Rev. May surprised me. "Ah, here's Edward now—I was just speaking of you!"

"Who, me?" I stammered.

"Yes, you! We couldn't decide what to do with Jerry until you provided the answer."

"What? When did I do that?"

"Don't you know? It happened when you told me how sick that Cale Davis looked."

"Uh, I don't quite follow, sir, but I was gonna ask you why you went to see him that night."

"It's simple, Edward—I asked Davis to hide Jerry, and he said that he would!"

I stood thunderstruck, mouth agape, while everyone laughed.

"Don't feel bad, Edward—everyone else reacted the same!" Rev. May reassured me.

Ma said, "Reverend May's right, Edward—I still can't believe it. We were about to hear the details."

Rev. May told an incredible story. "It happened like this, Ellen . . . according to the plan formed at Dr. Hoyt's office, we didn't attempt to take Jerry from the city that night. The driver was to escape all pursuers, if there were any, but not attempt to leave town as we knew all the roads were watched. About nine o'clock, he delivered Jerry into the hands of Jason Hoyt and James Davis. They led him not many steps to the house of Caleb Davis, who with his wife promptly provided shelter at their home on Orange Street."

I protested, "But Reverend May, Davis berates you in the streets—you and the abolitionists!"

Ma backed my petition, "We've all heard him, Reverend May, Davis is no abolitionist."

"No, but his wife is, and a stalwart Christian woman, too!"

I'd seen Mrs. Davis many times, but rarely heard her speak. A quiet woman, she spoke with a controlled, even voice, unlike her bombastic husband. It seemed she held significant sway over the butcher.

Rev. May continued. "When her husband returned shaken by what he'd seen, Mrs. Davis put her foot down. He's still a brawler, but he believes in what he calls *a fair fight*. Jerry's fight was anything but fair, being both handcuffed and outnumbered. After Davis heard that the militia might be called out, it put him over the edge—his encounter with Capt. Teall from New Year's, 1844, isn't a distant memory to him. Davis fought bravely in the War of 1812, and rejected the idea of the military condemning a fugitive to slavery. He told his wife, "If the militia comes out, I will come out, too! We'll see if the citizen soldiers will shoot us."

As I listened the truth began to sink in. I said, "So, Davis yelling in the streets for the past few days was all a ruse!"

"That's right," Rev. May affirmed, "I even encouraged him to pile it on! When I first arrived, he still looked as if felled by a pole, and didn't take much convincing. I told the Davises that we wanted to hide Jerry in plain sight. Their home would be the last place that anyone would look for an escaped fugitive.

"After receiving Jerry, his shackles were removed, then they provided refreshing food and put him to bed, but Jerry was utterly exhausted—he soon became feverish. A physician was called who dressed his wounds and administered such medicine as was applicable. But rest and sleep were what he needed, and he enjoyed them undisturbed for the next four days! Besides Mr. and Mrs. Davis, only four or five persons knew what had become of Jerry. It was generally supposed that he'd gone to Canada."

"What about Thomas Davis, Rev. May?" I asked, "He must've played a role."

"That he did, Edward—he was a tremendous help to Jerry in his recovery."

"Tell us how Jerry left town, Reverend!" Abner Bates requested.

"On Sunday evening, just after dark, a covered wagon with a span of very fleet horses was waiting near the door of the Davis's abode. Jason Hoyt and James Davis were seen to help a somewhat infirm man into the vehicle, jump in themselves, and start off at a rapid rate. Suspicion was awakened, and several of the patriots of our city set off in pursuit of the traitors. The chase was a hot one for eight or ten miles, but Jerry's deliverers had the advantage on the start, and in the speed of the horses that were bearing him to liberty."

Rev. Raymond added, "And they were assisted by a gate keeper on the plank road going north. The poor fellow was fast asleep and delayed the pursuers as long as he could!"

John Thomas, the current editor of the *Frederick Douglass' Paper*, remarked, "That's the best news I've heard since this all began. But let's be realists, *this affair is far from over!*"

HONEST CONVICTIONS | 257

Approaching mid-October, Ma had good reasons to worry—her husband could suddenly be arrested, charged with a crime punishable by death. Pa's confidence in this eventuality only made her feel worse.

"Edward, it's been ten days now without an arrest other than Lear's, but I've heard they're trying hard to get testimony for indictments! Treason has been talked of, also misdemeanor, but where it will end, nobody knows," Ma stated one evening before bedtime.

Forlorn, she said, "Good night, Edward."

On Tuesday, October 14, 1851, spirits ran high inside the noisy Weld's School for Young Men and Boys, emotions stoked with post-rescue excitement.

When Mr. William L. Crandal paid another surprise visit, the volume went up even further. Crandal said that he needed a break from publishing handbills. One announced *Death to the Whig Party* for their apparent support of the *Fugitive Slave Law*, another called for a mass meeting on the fifteenth for citizens opposed to the much hated decree. Crandal also wrote letters to the US District Attorney, James Lawrence, that were published in the local newspapers, which inflamed the law-and-order editors of the *Syracuse Star*. They began calling him Dogberry, and said that, 'Since Crandal has become the negro bell toller, let him stick to his occupation—every cobbler to his last!'

Prentice asked, "Mr. Crandal, do you care what they're saying about you in the *Star?*"

"Not really—publicity sells!" the advocate/reporter/salesman answered.

Bill Wallace joined, "I think that Rev. Raymond is their new favorite, Mr. Crandal. The *Star's* been blasting him even more than you lately."

"Yes, that's true, I read their *Preachers of Sedition* article."

Mr. Weld joined the conversation. "I read that, too—a very misguided piece. Their editors think little of Rev. Loguen. They welcomed his departure amongst the fifty or sixty other negroes who've fled since the rescue."

Crandal queried Parish Johnson next. "Mr. Johnson, what's new at the Police Office besides all the carpenters?" he asked.

"Well, sir, it's getting back to normal, but folks are still mad about how rough they were with Jerry, especially Officer Lowell. The police are still out making arrests, though. Shattuck, Hollister, and Lowell brought in some horse thieves this week; a pair of them were recognized as *state prison birds!*" Parish answered.

Will Stoddard interjected, "I have another legal headline for you, Mr. Crandal—Horace Conklin became the second fireman from Utica convicted of arson and sentenced to hang! It's said that Conklin was the ringleader, sir."

"That's tragic, Will—who'd ever suspect that firemen could become arsonists? Does anyone have any good news to report?" Crandal asked us.

Prentice's hand shot up. "I do, Mr. Crandal! The Syracuse Musical Institute re-elected Ed Wheaton's pa as president, and Rev. Raymond as vice-conductor, and the editor of the *Star* couldn't do nothin' about it—*Ha!*"

Alex McKinstry joined, "I have something, Mr. Crandal. The mines are still producing in California and the steamer *Ohio* just pulled in with another $2,000,000!"

"I could use some of that!" Crandal replied. "Anything else?"

Charlie Willard answered, "Yes, Mr. Crandal, the world famous Italian opera singer, Mademoiselle Teresa Parodi, will sing at Malcolm Hall tomorrow night."

"Ah, yes—I heard that, it's a great way to end the day after the County Rally. I can't wait for our city to celebrate the rescue and condemn the *Fugitive Slave Law!*"

"Well, half the city, anyways—everybody else wants to see people get arrested," I said.

The reporter replied, "Let's see what happens!" which made me eager to attend.

After dinner that night I asked to attend the rally at City Hall.

"Aw, c'mon Ma, please?" I begged. "Everybody who's against the Fugitive Slave Law should be there, don't you think, Pa? We talked about it at school today with Mr. Crandal—and he printed the handbills!" I implored.

"Yes, he did a nice job with it, too," Pa agreed.

"I like that man," Ma said. "I've read and agree with much of what he's written."

"So, does this mean I can go with you, Ma?" I asked again.

"Yes, since you asked, and because you're truly interested. I expect that the church will be crowded tomorrow . . . numbers of persons, who never felt any interest in the cause of the slave, before, now seem to have all their feelings roused, and their sympathies awakened, in his behalf, and this feeling is not manifested alone in words, but in deeds of a more substantial character."

Me and Pa nodded our heads in agreement. Cornelia and Ellen were already on the hook to watch the young'uns tomorrow.

# Chapter Nineteen
## (October 15 – 30, 1851)

Ma was in good spirits in the morning, getting out of the house always made her smile. While Pa drove the three of us downtown for the *Rally for Freedom,* she spoke of the *Women's Right's Convention,* the second one this year.

"It's happening today in Worchester, Edward. Reverend May wanted to attend, but the *Rally for Freedom* took precedence," she said.

"I heard a little about that, Ma—who's speaking?"

"Paulina Kellogg Wright Davis, Harriet Kezia Hunt, Antoinette Brown, and Wendell Phillips, among others—and, oh yes, Lucretia Mott will be there, too."

"Funny that it's on the same day as our *Rally for Freedom*—everything always happens at once!"

"That's true, Edward, next year they should have the *Women's Rights Convention* here in Syracuse—we're the convention city, right?"

"Someday women will get the vote, but not in my lifetime," Pa said.

Pulling up at our destination, I saw Charlie Pope among the people gathered outside.

"Ma, since we're early can I go talk to Charlie?" I asked.

"Yes, but I want you beside me when the rally starts."

"Yes, ma'am," I replied, jumping out to find Charlie. He hailed me on the approach.

"Hey, Ed, we're the first two from Weld's here today!"

"Yeah—we'll see who else turns up. Mr. Weld must regret all the history that happens around here."

"There's a lot happening out west, too, Ed. Besides all the gold, there's been Indian trouble between Salt Lake City & Sacramento. Some mail riders were attacked and lucky to have escaped! And the state government had two men executed in San Francisco, and another two in Sacramento. Then a man reprieved by the governor got dragged out of jail and was executed by the people, but it's all calm now."

"What a relief," I tartly replied.

"Hey, Ed—look over there—they're making an arrest!"

The news spread quickly when bystanders alerted that Jerry's rescuers were being arrested. Somebody ran over to the Congregational Church to ring the bell frantically. I thought that Daniel Webster's threat was happening again, but this time, without any attempt at rescue so far.

"More abolition convention arrests, huh, Ed?" Charlie asked.

Word of the first arrests for the Jerry Rescue further heightened passions at the *Rally for Freedom*. Even Ma was piqued, she said,

"From my limited opportunities of judging, it seems that the whole community is agitated concerning this matter—and a large number, if not the majority, are on the side of right! If they thought to insult the feelings of the people, they've done so—most wantonly. But we have a strong determination to stand by those arrested, to help them bear their heavy liabilities, and to comfort one another."

The rally commenced with Enoch Marks called to the chair, and George Boyer Vashon chosen as secretary. Few details of the arrests were given. US District Attorney James Lawrence charged eight individuals (five white—three black) with violating the *Fugitive Slave Law*. The accused were Ira Cobb, Moses Summers, W. S. Salmon, James Davis, Stephen Porter, Harrison Allen, William Thompson, and Prince Jackson.

United States District Court Judge Alfred Conkling had issued subpoenas the prior day, prompting US Marshal Bush to make arrests in the morning, then to bring the accused on the two o'clock train to the Federal courthouse in Auburn. Optimists at the rally took solace from knowing they'd stand before a jurist well-respected since his appointment in 1825 by President John Quincy Adams. The abolitionists approved of Conkling's recent ruling on the *Fugitive Slave Law*, but coming without a decision on treason, the gallows hovered over the accused. Many at the rally,

*Judge Alfred Conkling*

and across the country, expected federal prosecutors to act as they did in Christiana, but, thankfully, the present charges didn't include a crime punishable by death.

Adding to the suspense, I overheard talk that Marshal Allen had indicated that there'd be more arrests, but nobody knew who, where, or when, nor if treason charges would be filed.

Pa took the stage and stated that, given the recent arrests, the meeting's objective should be to unite against the Fugitive Slave Law and treason charges. Ever pragmatic, he proposed forming a finance committee to raise $500 for immediate expenses and another committee to secure legal aid, with himself, George Barnes, and Dr. Lyman Clary as members.

Ma relaxed after Pa turned the meeting over to Rev. Messrs. May and Raymond, John Thomas, and William H. Burleigh. They all supported Pa's proposal and his methods, emphasizing that it should never involve violence. Rev. May offered a stirring speech that began with,

"FELLOW CITIZENS: We have not come here to array ourselves against the government of our country, but to denounce a most tyrannous act of our government. We have come to speak as freemen may, and freemen should, against highhanded oppression, and execrable cruelty. And if we are not allowed to do this, what advantage is there in being freemen?"

He went on to offer resolutions that were unanimously adopted. Among them were:

"*Resolved*, That while we are irreconcilably opposed to the *Fugitive Slave Law*, we show that we are law-abiding citizens, by bearing patiently any evils that our government may implicate upon us, for showing our sympathy with our oppressed fellow man.

"*Resolved*, That we pledge our fortunes and our sacred honor, to stand by those individuals on whom the hand of government may fall, that we will help to bear with them any pecuniary losses to which they may be subjected, and manifest in every way we can, our sympathy for them, and show that we suffer as those who are bound with them."

After the resolutions were read, the chairman directed the *Vigilance Committee* to call for another county convention at their discretion. Patrons left satisfied, and many gathered at the train depot to encourage the *Jerry Rescuers* in custody, though no one resisted the Marshal. Supporters filled the train to Auburn, including ladies, some wearing bloomers! Pa also went, but not before telling me to drive Ma home, and to do whatever she says.

"I'll be back later tonight, Ellen!" he said, kissing Ma goodbye. Following orders to retrieve our horse and buggy, I encountered Austin Cook outside the bustling *Cook & Gay's* Coffee House. He said the Rescue Trial was good for business.

We weren't home for long before Mr. William L. Crandal surprised us at our door. At thirty-six, Crandal was only a year older than Ma.

"Hello, Ellen! I hope I'm not intruding, but would you like to accompany me on the morning train to Auburn? The railroad cut the fare in half for people to attend the hearing! I expect that Judge

Conkling will require bail tonight but the accused had more than enough supporters on the train to cover it, starting with your husband."

"Yes, I believe you're right, William, but this brood won't allow it."

I felt bad for Ma, but saw an opportunity. "I'll go with ya, Mr. Crandal—it's history, right?"

Ma answered for him, "Not on your life! You're not missing school again—two days in a row!"

I protested, "But Ma, the hearing is even more historic than the rally was, don't you think?"

"You just get yourself to school tomorrow or the next piece of history will read, *Here lies Edward Wheaton . . .*"

Crandal sighed, "Well, alright then, I'll let you know how it went!"

"Do you have to leave already, Mr. Crandal? Why don't you stay for supper?" I implored.

"Unfortunately, I can't, Edward—gotta print more handbills for tomorrow. I handed out everything that I had at the rally and the train depot. Now I'm off to find Chauncey Crofoot to start the presses humming at the Journal!"

After Mr. Crandal left, the wait for Pa to return on the last train from Auburn felt endless, everyone eager to hear what had happened. As soon as he walked in, Pa was surrounded; the rest of us piled on.

"Let your father refresh himself first, children! Charles, are you hungry?" Ma asked urgently.

"No, Ellen—we had dinner in Auburn."

"Well, you'll just have to tell us directly then! Come sit, and be comfortable."

Pa laughed, *"Yes, ma'am!"* taking a seat. The family gathered around.

"Tell us, Pa!" Cornelia urged.

"You surprise me, dear. I expected Edward to be the one most curious."

"I am, Pa, please tell us, sir!" I implored.

"Well, alright then! Despite our grim purpose, we were in good spirits inside the cars. Marshal Bush treated the prisoners gentlemanly for thirty miles on the rails, and afterward at the Auburn House. At five o'clock, he brought the accused before Judge Conkling, but it was only for the preliminaries—testimony begins tomorrow morning at nine o'clock. I think we surprised the judge with our numbers, there must've been at least one hundred of us! After he set bail, Judge Conkling must've been even more surprised when the Honorable William H. Seward stepped forward to sign his name upon the bail bond. I'm sure they'll be talking about this at the Capitol—a United States senator opposing the Fugitive Slave Law! Many followed his lead, and bail was quickly raised."

"Who else signed the bond besides you and Senator Seward, Pa?" I asked.

"Let's see, there was Alfred Cobb, George Barnes, Hiram Putnam, Rev. May, Rev. Raymond, Seth Haight, Abner Bates, and Charles B. Sedgwick, among others. There were so many people who wanted to sign that the District Attorney objected before we ran out of space on the bail bond."

"Then what happened, Pa?" Cornelia asked.

"Mr. Seward welcomed the accused, and all their friends, to his home where we enjoyed his hospitality until the next train to Syracuse!"

I could tell that Ma wished that she'd been there, especially upon hearing of the ladies in attendance. "Are you going back to Auburn tomorrow?" she asked.

"No, Ellen—I haven't been called to testify, and I have too many other things to do."

"Excuse me, sir, but, Mr. Crandal stopped to ask Ma if she wanted to go to Auburn tomorrow," I announced.

"*Really?* What did you say, Ellen?" he asked in surprise.

"I said that I'd love to were it not for housework and needy children."

"Oh, I see," Pa replied demurely.

Surprisingly, every seat was filled at Weld's School in the morning. I expected that at least one of us would be in Auburn for the hearing. Mr. Weld indulged us with conversation on the exciting current events.

"You're all here—I can't believe it! And the rail tickets are half-price for the hearing," Mr. Weld announced with surprise.

"That's because Teresa Parodi sang here again last night, Mr. Weld," Charlie Willard said, drawing laughter. "Laugh all you want!" Charlie retorted, "but it's universally acknowledged, that she's one of the best opera singers in the world. And if you're not familiar with that kind of music, you should hear it from the lips of Parodi."

"Who told you that, Charlie? The Malcolm Hall stage manager?" Billy Willard jibed.

Charlie barked to his brother, "Go haunt a house, would ya?"

"Yeah, but not ours again!" Flo Willard joined.

Mr. Weld interrupted, "All right, enough of that! Mr. Pope, what can you tell us of Col. Vandenburgh? He's become a feature in all the papers."

Charlie P. stood to answer—Mr. Weld called him knowing that militias were his niche.

"Mr. Weld, the colonel said the only guide to run his command were the laws of the state that governs the militia, and allowing them to turn out would have been a gross negligence of duty."

"How so, Charles?"

"Sir, the sheriff can request the militia to turn out, but first he has to get the okay from a county judge, and then the order is sent to the governor—but that never happened."

"Interesting! What else did he say?"

"Well, sir, he said that according to the *Fugitive Slave Law*, the marshal can summon by-standers to aid and assist—the whole county if he wanted to—but they're citizens, not the militia."

"And the colonel cleared my pa, too!" I avowed.

"That's right, Ed—he did. Col. Vandenburgh denied doing anything just because Charles Wheaton, or any other abolitionist asked him to. He said that Mr. Wheaton called upon him to ask if the military were coming out, and he replied that he didn't know about it. Mr. Weld, I was there when the colonel walked into the armory with Mr. Wheaton."

"Thank you, Charles—good reporting! I heard that the colonel denied saying that he'd do everything in his power to prevent the execution of the law. Is there anything else that we all should know about?"

Will Stoddard's hand shot up. "There is, Mr. Weld! There was a huge rally in Utica the other night about saving Orcutt from hanging!"

"I hadn't heard that, what was the result?" our teacher asked.

"A lot of upstanding citizens were there, Mr. Weld. After speeches were made by Messrs. Bushnell, McQuade, and Henshaw, strong resolutions were passed and a committee was sent to Albany to appeal to the governor."

"Did the people feel likewise for Conklin, the other condemned man?

"No, sir, they called him the ringleader, and he's not so young like Orcutt."

"I see, now it's time for arithmetic and science!" Weld said with enthusiasm.

Our groans were heard on Montgomery Street.

For the next few days, the papers were filled with courthouse testimony from Auburn. Witnesses were examined and cross-examined, names were dropped, accusations made and rebutted. In the end, the defendants were indicted for violation of the *Fugitive Slave Law*, and ordered to appear before the next Federal Grand Jury in Buffalo, the second Tuesday in November. I broached the subject at home after school.

"So, Ma—whatcha think of Judge Conkling's decision?" I asked.

"I wasn't surprised, Edward—the way that infernal law is written he didn't have much choice."

Cornelia said, "That's what Aunt Charlotte said at school, Ma—you're not sisters for nothing!"

Ellen joined, saying, "That's right, Ma, she said the judge's hands were tied."

"Ma, did you hear about the ladies on the train from Auburn?" I asked.

"No, please tell me!" she demanded as my sisters gathered around to listen.

"This is a good one, I heard it at the Journal Office with Parish."

"Oh, just tell us then," Ellen urged.

"Well, the story goes that there were a bunch of ladies who were friends of the accused, and they weren't happy with the judge's decision. And some of 'em wore bloomers to Auburn, Ma! Anyways, when they boarded the train for home they recognized District Attorney Lawrence, and they didn't want to sit with him."

"So, what did they do?" Cornelia asked.

"They all signed a request for him to find another car to ride home in!"

"Really? Now that's what I'd call spunk!" Ma exclaimed.

"But they weren't satisfied with that, so they took up a collection of thirty (three cent) pieces of silver and presented it to Mr. Lawrence as the price of innocent blood, but he only laughed."

"That's incredible, Edward, but I'm sure that not everyone sided with the ladies."

"No, they didn't. I heard that some guy on the train said only enraged women could conceive so cruel a punishment over a fancied wrong."

"Funny, Edward, so only women are cruel?" Ellen retorted.

"Not all women, Ellen, only the enraged ones—then you better look out!"

"Enough, enough!" Ma cried. "Listen, Edward—I have some news for you, and you, too, girls."

"Tell us, Ma!" Cornelia pled.

"After visiting Caroline Loguen, Rev. May stopped to tell me that he received a letter from Jerry in Canada."

"Tell us what happened after he left town!" I begged.

"Rev. May said that they took him twenty miles to the home of a Mr. Ames, a Quaker, in the town of Mexico. Jerry hid there for several days, then conveyed to the house of a Mr. Clarke, in the city of Oswego. Then it took several more days of diligent searching to find the right person for transporting a fugitive slave across the lake."

"Jerry must've been scared, Ma!" Ellen said.

"I'm sure he was—it's scary just hearing about it. But at length they found a friendly captain for the journey to Kingston, and once landed, Jerry soon plied his trade as a cooper."

"Ma, when Jerry wrote to Rev. May did he mention us?" I asked.

"Rev. May said that Jerry expressed in the warmest terms his gratitude for what the Abolitionists in Syracuse had done in his behalf. After pouring out his heartful thanks, he assured us that he had been led to think more than ever of his indebtedness to God, the ultimate source of all goodness—and that he had been brought to the resolution to lead a purer, better life than he had ever done."

In response to the *Rally for Freedom*, a counter-rally was called the following week by the law and order faction of Syracuse society. A call for a *Public Meeting* made the headlines.

"The citizens of Syracuse and the County of Onondaga who are in favor of sustaining the Constitution and Laws of the country, and who are desirous of expressing their abhorrence and reprobation of the late infamous proceeding in this city, by which the laws have been violated, the Government temporarily subverted, and disgrace fixed upon the town in which these lawless acts have been perpetrated, are requested, to meet at the City Hall in Syracuse, on Saturday the 25th day of October at 2 o'clock, p.m."

The call was signed by the highly renowned Major Moses D. Burnet, B. Davis Noxon, John G. Forbes, G.F. Comstock, Phares Gould, and Harvey Baldwin, along with eight-hundred other citizens of Onondaga County. A great number of them opposed the temperance movement, and scoffed at the idea of women's suffrage. There were plenty of Germans and Irishmen alike, including a mass of Salt Pointers who backed the Public Meeting on October 25.

Playing the history card, I obtained permission to attend with Prentice. Si looked ready to cry while he remained at home, grounded again for something. Approaching downtown, Prentice remarked,

"Hey, Ed—I read that Governor Hunt proclaimed that Thanksgiving will be on November 27th this year!"

"I read that too, Prentice—having it in December kinda ruined it."

"Wow, look at all the people waiting outside!" Prentice observed when City Hall came into view.

"Let's get there while there's still a chance of getting inside—all the late comers will be turned away!"

Joining the throng, we heard some interesting conversation. Apparently, my uncle had given permission for would-be disturbers of the Law-and-Order meeting to have use of City Hall from eleven till two, allowing them to pre-occupy the hall, and exclude the callers of the meeting! But he must've changed his mind or something because the building stayed locked until two. A large number of Jerry's supporters mingled with the Law-and-Order crowd, anxious to get inside. I overheard more than a few complaints from people who arrived early for the first meeting that never happened.

Upon opening, a tremendous funnel pushed toward

*Old City Hall*

the door, propelling bodies up the stairs to the meeting room that quickly filled to capacity. Signers of the call occupied the front, with a body of agitators seated at rear of the loud assembly hall.

The city's first mayor, Harvey Baldwin, called the Law-and-Order meeting to order, but things were more chaotic than orderly. After Baldwin nominated Maj. Moses D. Burnet as the presiding officer, the second mayor of Syracuse, E.W. Leavenworth, seated in the back with a heavy, thumping cane, nominated the city's third mayor, A.H. Hovey, for the post. Hovey took the stage to deliver a short address, then reclaimed his seat towards the rear. But nonetheless, Major Burnet took the chair with most of the crowd behind him. An impressive host of vice-presidents were elected, including B. Davis Noxon, Johnson Hall, Phares Gould, Miles W. Bennett, James Lynch, and Lewis H. Redfield, among others.

Led by former Mayor Leavenworth, the rowdy disturbers were having their way. Ex-Mayor Baldwin could hardly be heard over the boys in the back yelling out and thumping the floorboards. Somebody said that they'd never seen this much disorder outside of a New York ward meeting.

Then we heard "Yankee Doodle" being played in the distance by an approaching band of horn and drum, leading a procession of hard-fisted Salt Pointers from Salina. When they drew close we could see that they carried a banner with a full length likeness of Washington in the act of taking the oath to support the Constitution, a scroll, and the words, "Obedience to Law." At their arrival, the band started playing *"Hail Columbia."* There must've been a hundred of them who pushed their way onstage and planted their banner right next to the chairman.

I couldn't believe my eyes. "Hey Prentice, there's that two-faced thug, Ron Sheeney, up on stage. What's he doing at a Law-and-Order rally? I guess extortion's not illegal anymore!"

"I always said we should teach him a lesson," Prentice answered.

"Yeah we should, but it would take a bunch of us—*he's a brute!*" I replied.

I met Ron Sheeney on the same day that I met George Pfohl. It happened on a fishing excursion to Onondaga Lake when a few of us were accosted along the way by a legion of snot-nosed miscreants from Salt Point who awaited our next move. They had us surrounded, badly outnumbered.

*"Look at 'em all! They're climbing out of the kettles for us!"* Parish cried.

"What do you want?" our fishing ace, Milo Freeof asked.

A stern voice answered from behind the line of ugly mugs and brown teeth.

"That you, Freeof? I told you to pay the fishing toll before—Now it's double!"

"And I say that you don't own the lake, Ronald Sheeney."

"And I say that stuck-up strangers wearin' fancy clothes must have coins in their pockets," Sheeney answered.

Milo protested. "They're not strangers, they're my friends."

"Not mine, Freeof. But you was smart bringin' 'em to pay the toll for you."

Salt Point youth circled our flanks. I saw two options: complete surrender or make a mad dash for the lake and swim for it.

Our antagonists grew impatient, *"Time for show and tell, stiff necks!"*

A lone figure who hadn't seen the rocks fly approached with his fishing pole. He looked our age, and I mistook him for another Salt Pointer looking for free coins and tackle. Instead, it was yet another person who knew Milo Freeof. The newcomer entered the scene of a crime in progress.

"Hey, Milo! I thought that was you. I was gonna follow you to your spot," he said good naturedly. However, upon noticing the stern faces around us, he quickly reassessed the situation.

*"You guys in trouble?"* he asked.

Sheeney answered, *"No trouble if you pay the toll—you can pay right here!"*

Life went from bad to worse. A group of older teenage Salt Pointers appeared, hair growing irregularly from their faces in all directions. The one on horseback looked like a big creep.

"A fine catch, Sheeney! What bait?" the horseman asked.

"None—they hooked themselves!"

One of the elders recognized Milo's acquaintance.

*"Holy shite! Sheeney you idiot, don't you know who this is?"*

"Sure, Milo's friend come to pay the toll!"

"Right, then he'll tell his father, the Captain of the LaFayette Grenadiers, all about it. *You'll get us all killed!"*

The newcomer was George Pfohl, whose father, Jacob, commanded a German militia and wouldn't appreciate how his son was being treated. Envisioning certain annihilation in the young Pfohl's eyes, the elder Salt Pointers cleared the field. Ron Sheeney took complimentary thumps for almost bringing the Grenadiers down upon all their heads. Seeing that alone made it all worth it.

Disregarding the danger from Salt Point, Mayor Leavenworth's bunch resumed their interruptions at the *Law and Order* rally, but this time the most boisterous (except for the former mayor) were unceremoniously shown the stairs, then the door, by angry Salt Pointers who administered their own version of the *Higher Law*. After that, the meeting proceeded without much interruption.

Looking through the second-floor window at the crowds who couldn't get inside made me glad of our early arrival. Prentice said so himself when a heavy rain sent them all scurrying. Now able to be heard, Harvey Baldwin's oration lasted for about an hour. He declared himself opposed to slavery and the *Fugitive Slave Law*, but then spoke forcibly upon the danger of suffering the laws to be violated by force, and upon the necessity of defending them, and obeying them, whether we liked them or not. His remarks were well received, except to the ever-noisy opposition seated in the rear. Throughout the meeting, whenever a speaker asked the audience a yes or no question, the group in back always opposed everyone else.

After Baldwin concluded, a rousing call issued for the master of ceremonies, the Honorable Mr. James Brooks, editor of the *New York Daily Express,* and current member of the US House of Representatives for the 6th District of New York. Both the man and the meeting were backed by the *Syracuse Star,* which he gladly pointed out to the audience. Brooks called the *Syracuse Journal* the Whig Abolition, and the *Syracuse Standard* the Democrat Abolition—both abolition groups represented at the rear. The people in front all cheered, while hearty boos were heard from the back. He spoke of the history of the Compromise measures, and said the *Fugitive Slave Law* was rendered necessary to secure the peace of the country, and to preserve the Union. He spoke at length, mostly cheered, but hissed from all sides when he suggested that perhaps Congress should remove the duty on foreign salt, as a punishment to Syracuse for permitting the rescue of Jerry! Still, Brooks affirmed that *Syracuse* has now wiped out the blot that a few bad men had inflicted on her reputation, and would hereafter execute all the laws of the Federal Government.

*James Brooks*

George Comstock followed by reading a series of resolutions to which the people in front voted aye, while everyone in back voted no—but the ayes carried. Among the resolutions were,

"*Resolved,* That we, citizens of Syracuse and the County of Onondaga, deeply regret the commission of the aforesaid outrage upon the law. and would express our unqualified abhorrence of the infamous transaction.

"*Resolved,* That while we unreservedly condemn the conduct of those who actually participated in the riot of the 1st October, we repel the accusation that any large number of the citizens of Onondaga, were engaged in that disgraceful affair.

"*Resolved,* That the recent resistance to the law in this city, is the natural consequence of the teachings of these preachers of sedition; that they should therefore be held morally responsible as accessories before the act, and in consequence of such participation, as morally guilty of a violation of the law, and as such deserving of the severe reprobation of all good men."

The meeting adjourned with three cheers for the Constitution and the laws, while everyone in back cheered for Jerry. Depending on which side you were on, the late meeting was either a complete failure or an absolute success. But the organizers lacked a Charles A. Wheaton, so the meeting ended without a song.

The next day, after former Mayor Leavenworth denied accusations that he attempted to disrupt the meeting, the *Star* called him a convenient "fence man" who waited for the flood but caught the ebb. The *Star* next took exception to Mr. George Barnes' depiction of the delegation from Salina as a 'band of armed and infamous rowdies.' They named him an Englishman who insulted the hard working American, Irish, and German residents of Syracuse, suggesting they should do something about it. Friends of Barnes cautioned him to look over his shoulders, and not to walk alone at night across Division Street.

The Reverends May and Raymond became the object of pointed accusations in the *Star*, although the paper printed their lengthy rebuttals. Rev. May debated a writer called Ignoramus repeatedly in a battle of considered, articulate, yet conflicting values that inspired city wide discussion.

Outside the local press, tales of Rev. Loguen's crossing into Canada were bittersweet, but he arrived safely in St. Catharines across the Niagara River. When I heard from Black George that Rev. Ward was in Montreal, I bounded out the back door to ask Sam if it were true.

# Chapter Twenty
## (November 1851)

Sam asked me inside when I knocked at his door. The house felt empty with a lingering melancholy ever since Rev. Ward had fled. Sam confirmed the information I'd received from Black George, a man short on words but long on wisdom. A letter from Rev. Ward sat on the table, and though I feared its contents, I had to ask.

"I'm glad that your pa made it safe to Montreal, Sam. Did he say when he'd be sending for you?" I inquired, dreading the answer. Sam's response more shocked than surprised me.

"Probably when the next letter gets here, Ed—he's gettin' everything ready for us now," he said with reserve.

"I hoped your pa might change his mind since the grand jury indicted Lear and Allen for kidnapping," I said, hoping against hope. "My pa signed the complaint!"

"He mighta," Sam replied, "but my pa read what the Attorney General wrote to District Attorney Lawrence, about how President Filmore said to spare no efforts to bring the Syracuse offenders to justice!"

"But your pa didn't storm the building—he just addressed the crowd outside."

"Yeah, but a lotta people didn't like what he said—especially not from a fugitive."

"Too bad for them!" I protested.

"Everybody don't think like you do, Ed—half the country, I bet. Did you know that out west there's a law that excludes free blacks and mulattos? They just used it to kick a black man outta Oregon! And they got another law that says Indians can't testify against white people."

"I heard that, Sam—but Oregon's a long way from here."

"Well, in Philadelphia, the US Commissioner remanded a fugitive to an Indian owner, how's that for you?"

"I think it sucks! Did the commissioner say anything else?"

"He did, he told the fugitive's counsel that he wouldn't be guided by Judge Conkling's ruling on the *Fugitive Slave Law*—how it's only for slaves who run off after the President signed the law. The commissioner said that he thought Judge Conkling made a great mistake."

"That sucks, too, Sam."

"And if that ain't enough, the people arrested in Christiana could be facing the rope!"

The more I listened, the more I thought that if it were me, I'd head for Canada, too. It seemed wise while you still could, especially if your name were mentioned in court testimony or in the newspapers—better to live to fight another day. It was hard to act like things were normal when they weren't, but I tried.

I said, "Mrs. Ward, I should've brought some apples with me—George brought a barrel home! Can Sam come over to get some, Ma'am?"

"He sure can," Mrs. Ward replied, "But don't you go runnin' off, Sam—I need you here!"

"I won't Momma—I'll bring a basket home," Sam answered.

"Or maybe a bushel," I suggested.

"Let's go, Ed!" Sam said with conviction, and we did.

The late afternoon put a spring in our step, crunching the dried leaves underfoot. Barren trees presented a bleak outlook. Passing by the chicken coop, it hit me that our partnership was ending, and even worse, I was losing a friend. We both knew it. I left the inevitable words unspoken, dreading the thought of Sam moving away.

"Hey, Sam—you ready for some apple pie? I can almost smell it!"

"Oh, yeah! I gotta thank Mr. George for bringin' home the barrel."

"Me, too, but sometimes he looks at me funny when I do."

"Ha! That's George, alright."

We surprised Ma crashing through the back door, narrowly missing her. My siblings were everywhere, especially little Henry. By the look on the kitchen maid's face, I guessed that Black George was giving instructions again. Nonetheless, the delicious aroma of baking apples filled our house. Assorted Wheaton's approached Sam, excited for a new diversion. Things were way quieter at Sam's house.

"Hello all!" Sam greeted.

"Hello, Sam!" Ellen answered, pausing to add, "you, too, Edward."

"Yeah, you, too, Edward," Emma copied.

"You, Edward," two-year-old Henry babbled.

Ma looked intent on talking to Sam. Taking both his hands in hers, she spoke gently.

"Sam, I want you to know how deeply I regret your family moving away—I am both sorry and ashamed about it. May the Good Lord bless and protect you, my dear boy—you and your precious family!"

Then she hugged him as we quietly watched an unexpected moment of tenderness. Looking back at my spectacled mother, Sam's eyes glistened when he returned her embrace.

"Thank you, Mrs. Wheaton, I'll make sure to tell everyone, Ma'am."

"You're welcome, Sam, now come and see the apples that George brought home!"

A variety of large apples filled our table, with one giant specimen standing out. Black George took his queue, along with his due.

"C'mon over here, Sam, an tell me if you ever seen a bigger apple!" he insisted.

Without hesitation, Sam replied, "I never seen one that big, Mr. George. Where you get apples like that?"

"Deese from Mr. Munn Davis on Pleasant Hill—out toward Baldwinsville."

"What kinda apples are they, George?" I asked.

"Mr. Munn calls 'em Golden Russets—deys tasty too, but you gots to follow de recipe!" Black George answered with a warning glance at the frowning kitchen maid who found her voice.

"I knows what I be doin,' Mister, don't you worry none!" she responded, crisp like an apple.

"It smells great in here, Ma!" I said. "Mrs. Cook's gonna be worried about the competition."

"You can thank your sisters, Edward—they've been a big help with so many apples."

"Hey George—they make vinegar outta those big apples?" I asked.

"Sho do, but you best ask Mr. Freeof—he know more bouts it."

"You're right—and I haven't seen Milo lately, either."

Ma interjected, "Never mind about vinegar, Edward—you're helping Sam carry apples home with a fresh baked pie!"

"We baked one for Uncle Horace, too, Ma," Cornelia said. "Half the city's been after him since the *Jerry Rescue*, so we're sending him comfort food. Besides that, he's running to be the next State Canal Commissioner, and the election's on Tuesday!"

"He should get the county vote now that Uncle Horace has been cleared by the Law-and-Order committee," I stated.

"What are you talking about?" Ma asked.

"Major Burnet and the officers from the Law-and-Order meeting signed a letter that said the accusations against Uncle Horace were false, and he wasn't lettin' anyone use City Hall ahead of time."

Cornelia interjected, "Edward, I heard people talking about the banner from Salt Point at the *Law-and-Order* meeting—everyone liked the depiction of George Washington. Do you know who the artist was?"

"That would be Mr. Baumgras from the First Ward, Cornelia—even the disruptors sitting in the back liked it."

"That's what I heard, too—I expected you to say that Sanford Thayer drew it."

"Ha! I should tell Mr. Baumgras that you complimented him."

Ma joined, "Yes, that is a compliment! I loved the portrait that Sanford Thayer painted of Ossahinta."

"Who's Ossahinta, Ed?" Sam asked.

"He was Chief of the Onondaga Nation, Sam, and Thayer painted him in 1845 at his studio in the bank building."

"Sanford a nice fella—I sees 'im at market sometimes," Black George said.

"Does he want to paint your portrait, George?" I teased.

"Sho do—said to hang it yo room cuz you miss me."

*Chief Ossahinta*

"Don't pester George young man!" Ma directed. "Check in the kitchen to see if a pie's cool enough for Sam to bring home."

We lingered first, Sam enjoyed the attentions of nine Wheaton's aged sixteen on down. He liked talking to Black George, and we all liked how Sam would say *Mr. George*—little things like that. Sam enjoyed talking to Pa, too, but mostly about our fledgling chicken business. Everything went great until that man Lear arrived from Missouri, headstrong with ideas about stealing Jerry Henry.

Sam traded his basket for a larger one that fit the still warm pie on top, while I yelled to Ma that I'd walk Sam to the coop. Standing outside by the chickens, I found my nerve.

"Well, Sam, the way I see it, you still own half the coop but it won't help you none in Canada! I want to pay you for your half before you leave, though, you'll need it!"

"Thanks, Edward but I think your pa would call it *sunk costs*."

"Sunk? Sunk who? Sunk this, Sam—yer takin' the money!"

Sam smiled, and glancing around, he said, "You know, we all liked livin' here—right off I made lots a friends!"

"We liked havin' ya for neighbors, Sam, your pa's the most powerful speaker we ever heard—Ma said so herself."

"He's sendin' word soon, Ed—and we'll be leavin' next day!"

"I know—just don't like thinkin' bout it."

"Me neither. I'll tell everyone what your ma told me," Sam uttered, starting for home in the dark.

"Hey, wait a minute, Sam—I gotta tell ya somethin'."

"Yeah, what?"

"Oh, uh, I don't know—just that I'm gonna miss ya, I guess."

"I'm gonna miss you, too, Ed—we been like brothers, you and me."

"Yeah, we have," I agreed, following Ma's lead to hug him. Then he snatched his bushel of apples and pie off the ground, looking just like I felt, and turned for home.

Alone at night, out by our chicken coop, I sat down against a big elm tree. Then, as a canal boy might say, I cried like a bitch.

On the first Sunday in November, a sunny day kept us outside until dark, when the winds began to blow sharply from the east. Although Black George had lit the fireplaces, chilling gusts penetrated every crack that kept us drawn up close by the burning logs. In the morning, Ma said that the day looked dreadful compared to yesterday.

"Just look at those dark, heavy clouds, and the mud and water beneath—it's dreariness in full force!" she announced definitively.

"It sure is, Ma!" Cornelia agreed, then pressed for information.

"So, tell us about the letter from Aunt Emma yesterday, Ma! What she say?"

"Well, she said we're all invited to Pompey for Thanksgiving, but I don't think I'll go."

"Why not?" Cornelia protested.

"Cornelia, the roads are so dreadful this time of year that I consider it too formidable to travel with a load of children. Your sister, Florence, has been sick for a week with the measles, and I'm looking for its appearance among the rest of you. Perhaps you and Edward may go with Aunt Charlotte."

"What about me, Ma?" Ellen demanded.

Ma retorted, "You haven't had the measles, but they have, so you're staying home!"

The following Sunday in November, it snowed four inches, which ended all discussion of Autumn. Another downer came with the news that Rev. Raymond had resigned as Pastor of the First Baptist Church. Ma said she hoped that he'd keep lecturing even though he wasn't preaching anymore. The Democrats won big in the state elections, and although Uncle Horace lost a tight race for Canal Commissioner, he was appointed chairman of the Onondaga County Supervisors. John Boulding, the fugitive slave remanded from Poughkeepsie in August, had returned a free man. By the middle of November, there was lots more for us to talk about in newspaper class at school.

Mr. Weld got us started with, "All right, gentlemen, let's hear what you're writing about this week!"

Billy Willard was first to go, drawing playful chiding from his peers.

"Mr. Weld, the whaler *Ann Alexander* out of New Bedford got destroyed by a sea monster in the south Pacific! It happened right near where the whaler *Essex* from Nantucket was lost thirty years ago," Billy announced.

"Hey, Billy, you should ask the Fox sisters if dead whales can rap!"

"Yo, Willard, you figure them sperm whales have friendly ghosts?"

"Why you ask?"

"Cuz mediums burn the oil from a whale's head when they wanna talk to dead people!"

"How should I know?"

"You're the idiot—*you* tell *me!*"

"Mr. Weld, how much more a' this I gotta take?" Billy implored.

Our teacher stifled laughter with, "No more, I should think! Another word of provocation will result in dire consequences—*just try me!*" Mr. Weld threatened. Turning to Billy, he asked,

"William is there a real story here?"

"Yes sir, Mr. Weld! A giant sperm whale took out the small boats from the *Ann Alexander* before it made for the whaler. The captain said he saw it coming towards them at fifteen knots when it struck with force just two feet above the keel. Water rushed in at a fearful rate and she went down quick, Mr. Weld! The crew drifted in small boats until they were rescued by another whaler from Nantucket that took 'em all to Panama, sir."

"Thank you Mr. Willard—an interesting account! Someone could write a story about this someday, don't you agree?"

Austin Cook answered for Billy. "I do, Mr. Weld, but let's hope there's no sea monsters lurking off the English coast—they just laid a submarine telegraph cable between England and France and it could get chewed up before any messages arrive!"

Bill Wallace interjected, "Who cares about sea monsters when there's a real story, Mr. Weld? Daniel Webster is leaving the President's cabinet, and Filmore's replacing him with Attorney General John J. Crittenden."

Larry Sabine professed, "I can top that, Mr. Weld! The Hungarian exile, Lajos Kossuth is leaving England for New York City. They're preparing a tremendous reception, Mr. Weld—just like for General LaFayette."

Will Stoddard countered with, "But I have a story of life and death, Mr. Weld. Governor Hunt suspended Orcutt from swinging for arson until December the fifth. But there's no reprieve for his partner, Conklin—he's still gonna hang next week!"

Parish Johnson rose to speak next. "Mr. Weld, if it's life or death that you're looking for, then look no further than the men charged with treason in Christiana!"

Prentice said, "That's what worries the accused for the *Jerry Rescue*, Mr. Weld. They're takin' testimony this week before the grand jury in

Buffalo! Mr. D.D. Hillis and Charles B. Sedgwick are representing the long list of names subpoenaed."

Mr. Weld noticed my unusual silence as I sat thinking of what the *Jerry Rescue* trials meant for the Ward's and the Loguen's.

"What about you, Mr. Wheaton? You appear lost in thought."

"I was just thinking of what my ma said the other day about all this, Mr. Weld."

"And what was that?" he asked.

"Sir, she said that it's 'cheering to see how numbers of persons, who never felt any interest in the cause of the slave, now seem to have all their feelings roused, and their sympathies awakened in his behalf, and this feeling is not manifested alone in words, but in deeds of a more substantial character.'"

"That's beautiful, Ed, but what'll the Law-and-Order committee make of it?" Prentice challenged.

"Prentice, your mind runs about as deep as a puddle," I said in retort.

"But we're all in it together, Ed—and the top of the puddle is still in the mud," he replied.

Mr. Weld jibed, "Prentice, you just created The Puddle Theory—and it runs deep!"

Si Cheney enjoyed my rebuke of his brother, "Good one, Ed," he said.

On Monday, the seventeenth of November, all eight defendants charged for the *Jerry Rescue* returned on the train from Buffalo and nobody was smiling—they'd just been indicted by the grand jury for violating the *Fugitive Slave Law*, but so far, not for treason. While the grand jury continued their examinations, many supposed that additional indictments would be found. Trial was scheduled for January in Albany.

Running counter to the disappointing news from Buffalo, a second *County Rally for Freedom* occurred on Thursday, the twentieth, again held at City Hall. Unlike the *Law and Order* meeting, this assembly didn't include a band of protesters shouting their objections.

Having attended the first *Freedom Rally*, I was allowed to watch for a second time, along with Charlie Pope. From the packed audience, we saw Dr. Ephraim Leech Soule chosen as President, who brought the meeting to order and called for the singing of "Children of The Glorious Dead."

> *Children of the glorious dead,*
> *Who for freedom fought and bled,*
> *With her banner o'er you spread,*
> *On to victory.*
>
> *This is proud oppression's hour,*
> *Storms are round us; shall we cower?*
> *While beneath a despot's power,*
> *Groans the suffering slave?*
>
> *While our homes and rights are dear,*
> *Guarded still with watchful fear,*
> *Shall we coldly turn our ear,*
> *From the supplicant's prayer?*

After the group song, Rev. May read a portion of Scripture, then the Rev. Alfred Pinney offered a prayer. Pa was on the business committee along with Mr. William H. Burleigh and a few others who huddled to formulate resolutions. Mr. William Chaplin spoke in response to repeated calls from the house, as did Abner Bates, who urged upon the necessity of earnest and untiring efforts in the cause of human freedom.

When the business committee returned, Mr. Burleigh, then Pa, read their resolutions to a supportive audience that voiced approval. Two of which were,

"*Resolved*, That the same argument that proves *any* man's, proves *all* men's right to liberty.

"*Resolved*, That neither Constitutions nor Congresses, compacts nor conventions, but the Lord God Almighty, gave to man his inalienable right of Freedom."

During the evening session, it was hard to keep track of Pa's involvement. Already on the business committee, I heard his name mentioned on the Executive committee, then again on the Finance committee. I already knew how my mother would react, she was pretty used to it by now.

Rev. May spoke again, stating that . . . "the true enemies of the Constitution were the men who would endeavor to enforce the Fugitive Slave Law upon us." Dr. J.C. Jackson followed with an address upon the principals of self-government, and the force of public opinion upon persons in authority. Mr. George B. Vashon spoke forcefully, drawing from an "Address from the Freemen of Onondaga County."

"To our fellow-citizens of the State, and of the Union:

"We have fallen upon times of peril. The great principles of legal right and just liberty, which our fathers supposed to have been settled by them, after unparalleled struggles and toil are struck down by the Slave power in our land, and we, in Central New York, are threatened with a new reign of terror.

"A most stupendous outrage is now upon free institutions, and upon Christianity, perpetrated in the enactment of the Fugitive Slave Bill. The character of this Bill is well known, but let me remind you that it:

"Takes an individual, unaccused of crime, and free by our state laws—handcuffs and chains him in open day, and then by summary process forces him into irremediable slavery.

"That it commands all good citizens, upon pains and penalties, to aid and assist in inflicting upon such innocent, helpless persons, the cruelest of all wrongs.

"That it threatens with confiscation and dungeon, those who exhibit effective sympathy in behalf of the poor man fleeing for his liberty, from the power of the government; and it would even brand with a felon's doom our wives and mothers, should they shelter from the official spoiler, a slave woman fleeing from Southern lust.

"To carry out all these atrocities, the *Fugitive Slave Bill* further enacts that such trial of a man for his liberty, before a Commissioner, shall be summary and final; no appeal, no re-hearing, no arrest of judgment for error, or to procure needed testimony, is allowed by the law; and while the claimant (often an utter stranger, whose character is unknown to the Court) is permitted to swear away all the rights of a fellow—the poor man may not be allowed to testify in his own behalf. And all this, we need hardly say, is in utter derogation of the Constitution, and of the provisions of common law, which have been settled for hundreds of years."

Ira Cobb followed G.B. Vashon, alluding to the welcome of Kossuth by President Filmore, drawing further from the "Address from the Freemen of Onondaga County."

"And as though all this were not enough to test the law-abiding character and forbearance of Northern Freemen—we now see attempts of the Federal Government (at the moment they are preparing to welcome the great fugitive from Austrian oppression, Kossuth and his noble compatriots,)—to stretch the Law of Treason over men, who have done for the colored American, what those very dignitaries would glory in doing for the swarthy Magyar!

"That which the scarcely endurable government of Monarchial Europe might punish as a misdemeanor, our Federal Executives are now laboring to punish with the gallows!

"As we have hitherto declared, in deliberate, solemn Convention—so we now re-affirm—that we dare not, we will not, obey this thrice accursed statute, be the consequence to our persons and property what they may. An enlightened conscience can never be bound by it. It enacts wickedness into a duty, and punishes mercy as a crime. It is therefore no law. And we spurn it as we would any other mandate of a tyrant."

With the rally winding to its end, the audience called for a song, answered by none other than Charles A. Wheaton—who else? Charlie P. elbowed me and laughed when Pa stepped forward to favor the convention with a solo performance of "Freedom's Gathering."

> *Freemen! Freemen! Gather, gather, gather!*
> *Fill our ranks, fill our ranks, March on together!*
> *Hark! Hark! The call of Liberty!,*
> *Unfurl the flag that ever shall be free!*
> *Nerve every arm and strike a deadly blow,*
> *And lay in the dust proud oppressors low,*
> *Rushing at their ranks, scatter far the band,*
> *that dares to enslave Freedom's chosen land.*

After the rally, Pa felt more certain than ever that he'd be arrested. He admitted as much, confessing that he thought about it while singing on stage. Rev. May and Geritt Smith felt likewise—the trio had openly advertised their involvement in the *Jerry Rescue*, offering the authorities a complete and candid account if, and when, they were charged. Instead, Marshal Bush arrested four others for the crime, including L.H. Salisbury, J.B. Brigham, Montgomery Merrick, and William L. Crandal, adding their names to the docket for January. Pa expressed his gratitude that so many people gave to the fund for helping the accused and their families, like the Loguen's and the Ward's.

Sam moved away just before Thanksgiving. I was in school when he boarded the train for Albany with his mother and sisters. As Sam had mentioned, Rev. Ward's next letter signaled their departure and provided the means to accomplish it. From Albany, they'd travel north to Montreal—around two-hundred and twenty miles by boat, rail, and carriage. Given the uncertain future, I felt relieved knowing I'd provided Sam with his share of our business—he'd surely use it.

Around Syracuse, about a foot of snow fell over the two days before Thanksgiving, which made for excellent sleighing! As Ma had predicted, Cornelia and I would join Aunt Charlotte (aged 20) for Thanksgiving at the Birdseye home in the hills of Pompey. As she was close in age, we skipped the formality of title with Charlotte. I was happy to drive, the girls appreciative.

We left Syracuse heading east on the Genesee Turnpike, bound for turkey dinner in Pompey. Our sleigh pulled easily atop fresh snow, upping the ante of holiday spirit.

"So, Edward—have you read any good books lately?" Charlotte asked.

"No—but there's a new one coming out that Will Stoddard said he can get for me at his pa's store."

"Really? What's it called?"

"*Moby Dick*—it's about a crazy whaling captain and a giant sperm whale!"

"Where did you hear about it?"

"At school. The other week we were talking about how a whale stoved-in the *Ann Alexander*, and now this book comes out! But Mr. Weld said that Herman Melville wrote it about another whale from thirty years ago."

"I was down at Stoddard's shop myself this week, did Will tell you?" Cornelia asked as we slid toward Fayetteville.

"No—what he say?"

"He asked me if I read about the arsonist on the gallows at Whitestown," she answered as Charlotte grimaced.

"Yeah, he told everyone at school about it—had all the details, too."

"Why?" Charlotte queried.

"Cuz his pa sells fire insurance, and Will helps him get information. When all the fires broke out in Utica, he got sucked into the story."

"Oh, I see!"

"The way Will told it, after the governor denied his last appeal, Horace Conklin was calm, and used the time he had left to make his peace with God—he wrote a full confession."

"Now you've got me curious," Charlotte remarked, "What else did Will say?"

"He said that Conklin's account lined up with Orcutt's—and that Orcutt will be meeting Conklin next week unless the governor steps in!"

Cornelia asked, "Did Conklin say why he did it?"

"He confessed that all the fires started with him drinking, and he named the men who gave 'im the liquor! Then he begged for parents to restrain their children, and especially begged all young men to shun the resorts for drinking and dissipation."

"Were there a lot of people who watched the hanging?"

"About two-hundred including the Utica Citizen's Corps on duty. The Rev. Mr. Fowler declared that he couldn't conceive how anyone could act better than Conklin did since his conviction. Will said that he prayed right to his last breath."

"Then what?" Charlotte bade.

"Then they sprung the latch and launched 'im to eternity! After half an hour they cut 'im down and sent the body to his father's home in Utica."

Cornelia insisted, "Let's talk about something else—this is morbid!"

"Right, something more for the holiday," Charlotte agreed.

"How're the roads?" I asked, drawing their ire.

Thanksgiving dinner conversation at Grandpa Birdseye's was darker than Horace B. Conklin swinging for arson. The elders at table were gripped by the tragedy that claimed the lives of fifty schoolchildren in New York! Being a teacher at the Bradbury school, all eyes were on Charlotte for her reaction.

"Yes, I heard all about it!" Charlotte exclaimed, "How heartbreaking for the families!"

"What happened, Grandpa?" I asked.

"Edward, it happened at a large school in New York City—with about eighteen hundred students. Let me tell you about the building first, then you'll better understand what happened. The schoolhouse is a four story building with a winding staircase from the first floor to the upper landing. The stairway is not spiral, but formed of short flights of stairs winding around a square well. The ground floor was used as a playground and paved with flagstones. On the second floor was the primary department, with the females on the third floor, males on the fourth. All the school rooms are reached by the landings of the stairs. The outer side of the stairs was guarded by an ordinary wooden banister of no great height, and not firmly secured at the bottom where the balusters connected with the stairs."

"Uh, I kinda get it, Grandpa—so what happened?"

"Well, around two o'clock in the afternoon, a teacher on the third floor, a Miss Harrison, fell faint. Her students helped her out into the hallway and yelled for someone to bring water. Someone mistook this to mean that water was needed to put out a fire, and the cry of fire soon echoed through the building!"

"Wow, I hadn't heard that, Grandpa!"

"Many children panicked, which caused a rush for the stairs. The press against the balustrade was so great that it gave way, precipitating nearly one hundred children to the flagstones below—some may have fallen forty feet! At least fifty children died, and as many more badly injured."

Ten years senior to Charlotte, Uncle Lucien Birdseye applied his legal training and pronounced that new laws would result from the calamity.

"The wooden bannisters on the stairs should never have given way! If there wasn't a building code, there should be—and if there is one, it was either insufficient or just plain ignored!"

Despite the bounty of our table, I didn't feel grateful that Thanksgiving. I worried that Pa might be charged with treason, along with all the men on trial for rescuing Jerry. I imagined kids hurtling to their deaths and thought of an arsonist swinging for his crimes.

My mind wandered to the empty Ward house behind the chicken coop. I missed my friend and lamented that Rev. Loguen had to leave his family behind, including an unborn child. Grandma noticed me scowling.

"What's the matter, Edward?" she asked. "Eat something!"

"He ate, Grandma—he's just moody sometimes," Cornelia offered.

"That's right, Mom—teenage hormones," Charlotte agreed.

"Remember who's driving!" I rebuked.

Upon our return Friday morning, Lucie and Henry showed early signs of the measles. By Saturday both were fully broken out, looking progressively worse as the day wore on. Henry had frightful dreams that woke him in great terror! Ma said that he'd never been sick like this before and didn't know how to endure it. Everyone hoped that little Minnie wasn't next.

"What's the matter, Edward?" Ma asked, sounding much like Grandma Birdseye. "You've been moping from room to room!"

"You're right, Ma—I gotta snap out of it. I been thinkin' a lot about Pa ever since the trials for treason began in Philadelphia. I know that he's not worried, but I am."

"I read that two of the men charged escaped from jail," Ma said.

"Yeah—they vamoosed."

"Is there anything in particular that's troubling you, son?"

"Not really—just didn't seem like much to be grateful for this year. What did you all end up doing?"

"We went to Park Church to hear Mr. Sunderland preach a Thanksgiving sermon on the 'Signs of the Times.'"

"How'd you like it, Ma?" I asked. Her honest critique often surprised me.

"From his great reputation for eloquence, and sound learning, as well as piety, I had expected to hear something worth the trouble of going, but I was much disappointed!"

"Really? What irked you?"

"To my mind, he seemed to take a very superficial view of things in general, particularly of the state of society, and the evils which afflict it. The remedies he proposed were entirely inadequate! What society needs is for brave men to step forward, Edward."

"Brave men like Pa?"

"Yes, like your pa! How few men there are, at this present time, who have the moral courage to examine the great questions of the day calmly, and dispassionately, and having done so to act upon their honest convictions, without regard to what effect it may have upon their popularity."

"That's true, Ma—most politicians care more about getting elected than in showing courage.

"I saw plenty of courage a few weeks ago at the Unitarian Church from Miss Sallie Holley when she lectured about slavery and the *Fugitive Slave Law*. She delivered one of the best addresses that I've ever heard from anyone—either man or woman!"

"You must've really liked her."

"I did! She's graceful and dignified in her manner, and very impressive and elegant in her use of language. She spoke with great solemnity, and power, and it left a deep and abiding impression on the consciences of her listeners."

"I guess that settles it then," I responded. "So, who's next?"

"Next week Henry Ward Beecher will speak at the First Presbyterian Church, and I don't plan to miss it," Ma said emphatically.

I smiled at her, and said, "I'll go with ya, Ma!"

She had a way of cheering you up without even trying.

# Chapter Twenty-One

(December 1851)

At November's end, Ira Cobb became the latest person arrested for the *Jerry Rescue*, but no-one expected him to be the last. Gale force winds on Oneida Lake claimed three canal boats of the Oswego Western Line in tow of a steamer. Somewhere near South Bay, the cargo of wheat and flour went down with the boats, but thankfully, without human casualties.

At the Wheaton home, my mother battled the outbreak of measles amongst our youngest, but she still was eager to attend Rev. Henry Ward Beecher's lecture at the new Presbyterian church on December 3rd. I interrupted her departure for the "Franklin Institute Lecture Series" at the front door.

"Hey, Ma—what's the lecture about tonight?"

"It's called, *Precedence in Society*, Edward—I'll tell you all about it when I get home."

True to her word, she returned much invigorated, with a full account. My sisters joined me to hear her critique.

"What a noble lecture it was—and before a full audience, too!" she began with enthusiasm. "I wished for a double strength of memory to retain his grand and noble thoughts, and his beautifully expressive language."

"Tell us about it, Ma!" Cornelia urged.

"He opened his subject, 'Self-Precedence,' by relating the incident of when Christ was journeying up to Jerusalem with his disciples. A dispute arose among them as to who should be greatest, and Beecher claimed that the question is as far from being settled now as it was then. He said it was the only apostolic example that is faithfully followed today. Then he alluded to the different senses in which all men were to be considered equal. They are all alike, in the consideration of the law of God, possessed of equal rights, and, of equal value."

Ellen asked, "So how is it different in society, Ma?"

"Rev. Beecher said that in the estimation of society there is a distinction; there is a higher, a middle, and a lower class. But in our estimation of men, we ought not to be guided by mere outward show or circumstance, but by their intellectual and moral character."

"I don't quite follow, Ma," I said.

She elaborated, "According to Beecher, the animal part of man is lowest in the scale, next the intellectual, then the moral. The animal in our nature connects us with earthly things. The intellectual relates to, and connects us with the operations of the mind, in relation to science and the arts. The moral relates to the spiritual in our nature, and elevates us above all meaner things, to a knowledge of, and communion with our Creator. Accordingly, as these higher faculties predominate, does man take precedence in rank, not in station. His station is where he finds himself, his rank is where his character places him."

"Do you think the audience understood his message?" Cornelia asked.

"Yes, Cornelia, the lecture was filled with forcible illustrations of this great truth, Each department was honorable in itself, and in its appropriate place to be respected."

"Did he say anything about slavery, Ma?" I asked.

"Surprisingly not, especially since he denounced the *Fugitive Slave Law* in Rochester a few nights ago. Now, it's already late, and I'm tired—to bed everyone!"

The next day brought a surprise visit from Will Stoddard, bearing gifts and news.

"Here ya go, Ed—the copy of *Moby Dick* that you were waiting for."

"Thanks a lot, Will—you're alright!" I said, offering my hand.

Assorted Wheaton's gathered around to handle the hardcover book.

"Go easy, children, don' tear the pages! Edward, you'd better put that somewhere safe," Ma directed.

Will said, "I have some big news, Ed—Governor Hunt commuted Orcutt's sentence to life in prison!"

"Wow—he was supposed to swing for arson tomorrow!" I replied.

"Yeah—guess he won't be seeing Conklin for a while yet," Will agreed. Turning to Ma, he asked, "Mrs. Wheaton, do you think it's fair for one man to hang, and another not, for committing the same crime?"

She answered, "That's a hard question, Will—it's not so obvious as it seems. James Orcutt's youthful age was a factor, but I think it had more to do with how many upstanding citizens appealed directly to the governor."

"I think you're right, ma'am—goes to show the importance of having the right friends!"

Ma shrugged, then asked, "What else are people talking about at the bookstore, Will?"

"Well, ma'am, most of the talk is about Kossuth, but I heard a lot of concern for Henry Clay—he's in bad health, Mrs. Wheaton."

"He's supposed to argue a case before the Supreme Court, Will," I said.

"We'll see about that—he was too sick to attend the senate this week," Will answered.

"I suppose you'll be reporting this in school, huh?"

"You bet!" he responded.

Will's report in newspaper class was overshadowed by Kossuth mania. Mr. Weld joined the craze, even larger than for Jenny Lind. New York City erupted when his steamship arrived on December 6th, providing a welcome unseen since the arrivals of General LaFayette or George Washington. As Jenny's popularity waned, shrewd shopkeepers replaced her image with Kossuth's in the same picture frames.

Kossuth was seen as a patriot fighting for liberty, facing two formidable foes. While the exiled Hungarian struggled against the Austrians, the meddling Russians also sought Hungarian territory. Americans viewed Kossuth as a freedom fighter and welcomed him warmly. Invitations poured in from cities across the country, starting in Albany to meet the governor. Congress and President Fillmore requested his presence in Washington, but his appeal was less strong in the South, where Kossuth's speeches about liberty troubled the slave owners. Abolitionists like Garrison were also disappointed with him, not for what he said, but for what he didn't say. They believed Kossuth could have been a powerful voice against American slavery, but he feared losing support in the South.

In Syracuse, the Germans admired Kossuth far more than most Irish Catholics did. Local Indians and Blacks put their own struggles for liberty ahead of the Hungarians. Since both my parents liked Kossuth, that was enough for me. After reading his speeches, Ma said that he had great talents as a popular orator, which kindled into a glow by the fire of patriotism that burned so brightly in his breast.

In mid-December, Mr. Crandal appeared at school to extend his warmest regards of the season. Mr. Weld invited him to address our newspaper class after the *Syracuse Daily Standard* devoted page one to Crandal's latest periodical called the *Slave Law Examiner*. The first edition was to print on the first of the new year, with future editions dependent upon subscribers.

"You must be awful proud, Mr. Crandal, being front page news!" Prentice Cheney said.

"It's a good first step, Prentice—I hope that many others feel as you do."

"Are you writing the first edition now, sir?" Charlie Pope asked.

"Yes, Charles—and I'm happy to say that it will include the big news from Philadelphia."

"What's that Mr. Crandal?" Alex McKinstry asked.

"Haven't you heard? The jury returned a not guilty verdict against Castner Hanway for treason in the *Christiana Affair!* It's godsend for everyone charged in the *Jerry Rescue*—me included."

"That's great news, Mr. Crandal! How'd the trial end?" Bill Wallace asked.

"It was laughable, William—Mr. Theodore Cuyler opened for the defense by stating that treason shall consist only in levying war against the United States, then he asked if the facts of the case sustained the charge. Cuyler said to the judge, "*sir—do you hear it? That three harmless, non-resisting Quakers and thirty-eight negroes, armed with corn cutters, clubs, and a few muskets, and headed by a miller in a felt hat, without a coat, without arms, and mounted on a sorry nag, levied war on the United States? Blessed be God that our Union has survived the shock!*"

"What did the judge say, Mr. Crandal?" I asked.

"Judge Grier charged the jury that the case was not one of treason, and a verdict of not guilty was returned. The other indictments against Hanway were abandoned by the government."

"Tell us about the *Slave Law Examiner, sir* what are you planning to do with it?" Will asked.

"Will, I am under indictment for aiding Jerry. Better men have been indicted—better men imprisoned—for acts as glorious as that charged on me. I allude to this, only for the purpose of saying that if the United States Government shall have any use for me in jail, I will have the *Examiner* so organized that it will "whistle itself" while I am absent from the office!"

Si Cheney asked, "Do you think we're having another revolution, sir?"

"Yes, Silas! This revolution is the rebellion of the Spirit of Liberty against the Spirit of Slavery—but it should be wrought out by a clash of opinions, not of arms. Already, at Christiana and at Syracuse, this revolution has its Lexington and its Bunker Hill—affording conclusive proof that the principles of 1776 have not been extinguished from the American mind. The hour is come, when the State of New York will not be a hunting-ground of men—it is only a question of time."

Charlie Willard asked, "Why can't the slave law be repealed, Mr. Crandal?"

"The *Fugitive Slave Act* is despotism, Charles. It's an attempt by the Government of the United States to legalize human slavery! The majority of voters in our country are against it, yet that majority cannot repeal it. The Senators from fifteen Slave States represent one half of that body, and the few votes needed to prevent repeal can always be obtained for a consideration."

"Sir, what's the latest with the *Jerry Rescue* case?" Billy Willard asked.

"The latest is that a colored man, Enoch Reed, was arrested for his involvement, but Moses Summers and James Davis provided the bail of five hundred dollars," Crandal replied. "What other stories have you been following?"

Larry Sabine answered, "Mr. Crandal, I was tracking the story about Elizur Clark from the First Ward—he just won a contract to build a twelve-mile plank road in Nicaragua. He's leaving in January with about one hundred men, sir."

"He's the right man for the job, Lawrence! As the president of the *Syracuse and Bridgeport Plank Road*, he's a sound choice," Crandal replied.

"Yeah, there's lots of new plank roads!" I agreed.

"So, what else is happening?" Crandal asked.

Parish replied, "Sir, a fourteen-year-old German boy, John Wingel, fell three stories from the crockery store where he worked. He crashed down on his feet and one of his ankles was badly fractured along with bones in his other leg. Dr. White dressed his wounds and he appears to be doing well."

"That's good news, Parish, and a good place to end," William Crandal replied.

On Saturday the 13th, frigid temperatures had us all huddled around the fire. I helped Black George stoke the fireplaces, but you had to stand close to feel the warmth. Ma set us to work hanging curtains in the sitting room, and corking windows to stop the drafts. As I gazed out the window, the snow fell rapidly—Ma said it looked more like sleighing weather than at any time before this winter, which brought thoughts of Christmas from my ten-year-old sister, Emma.

"When can we hang our long stockings by the fireplace, Ma?" she asked.

"Very soon, dear, I know that you're all getting anxious!"

"Yes, we are—the toyshop windows are filling up!" Emma answered.

"So they are. When it warms up a little we can all go look together—how's that, Emma?"

My sister remained resolute. "It might not warm up, Ma—we'll just have to bundle up," she suggested.

Ma was right about the sleighing. The streets were crowded with all kinds of vehicles, that kept the livery stables busy. The Onondaga County Supervisors were seen in four large sleighs on Salina Street, heading to the County Alms House. Careless drivers, speeding and not using their sleigh bells, created a risk—Abel Cook saw a little boy nearly run over by the train depot. The sidewalks were icy, so property owners were encouraged to sprinkle ashes to prevent broken limbs.

The Cheney brothers slipped by the following week; both wanted me to join them at City Hall on Thursday night to watch the soiree of young ladies from Mrs. Hyde's Seminary.

"C'mon Ed, just think of all the pretty girls that'll be there!" Prentice urged.

Si added, "Yeah, Ed—here's your chance to see Mira Barker again!"

"That's right, I forgot that she went to Mrs. Hyde's school," I answered.

"You surprise me, Ed—I thought you were smarter than that," Prentice jibed.

"Why don't you stick to exploding steamers, Prentice?" I retorted.

Silas said, "Pretty soon he won't have to, Ed. Senator Fish just introduced a resolution to investigate what's causing the explosions!"

"Great—Prentice can volunteer!" I replied.

"Funny, Ed—but I bet your sisters are going to the soiree—our Frances is."

"Yeah, they're going, and I will, too—should be fun."

"Now you're talking, Ed!" Silas answered with glee.

Cornelia, Ellen, and I met the Cheney's at their door, everyone anxious to attend the soiree at City Hall. Mr. Cheney kindly gave us a ride, while Mrs. Cheney wished us a good time but warned her boys to stay out of trouble. When we arrived, many people were heading inside, adding to our excitement. Mrs. Hyde's students did a fantastic job decorating the Hall, tastefully adorned with paintings and drawings to showcase their talents.

Prentice exclaimed, "It'll be a great show if the performance is half as good as the paintings!"

Cornelia replied, "Yes it will—we've heard them sing before!"

The crowd was delighted by the sweet-sounding voices, which lifted spirits with renditions of the "Mignonette Polka" and the "Jenny Lind Polka." Miss Childs' performance of the "Low Backed Car" was so well-received that she was compelled to give an encore. Despite the audience's enjoyment, a few young troublemakers nearly ruined the show with their repeated stamping, whistling, and catcalls, reminiscent of the loudmouths at the back of the Law-and-Order meeting held in the same venue.

Prentice alerted, "Hey, Ed—there's your girl Mira onstage! She's a pretty one, all right—make sure to say hello after the show."

Following his advice, I made my way over after the final act. Mira looked great as usual, but suffered through the obvious effects of a bad cold, as were many others. She was part of a group of twenty girls who recited a reading that was hard to understand because so many of them were sick. I quickly paid my compliments but kept my distance to be safe. The Cheney brothers were disappointed.

"Hey sugar lips, no smooching tonight?" Prentice teased.

"Guess not," Si joined, "Looks like he'll be thinking about her alone in his room again!"

"Yeah, and God only knows what he'll be doin' in there."

"Oh yeah? I don't see either one of you with anyone—why's that?" I countered.

"We were gonna make our move but didn't want to catch any germs," Prentice answered.

Silas said, "I'd go for your sister, but you and Grove would kill me."

"That's about right, Si—and don't forget it!" I warned.

"Good thing it's Christmas next week, huh, Ed? Great opportunity to catch a beauty under the mistletoe," Prentice observed.

"What would you know about it?" I challenged. "If you saw a pretty girl under the mistletoe you'd run, scream, or call the police."

"Ed's right, Prentice, Officer Lowell could tell you what to do—just ask Emeline or Thankful Long."

Cornelia interrupted with conviction. "C'mon Edward—Pa said he'd be picking us up about now!"

I hurried to the front door, spying Pa to end the night.

On Sunday morning, the twenty-first, Pa took us to the Congregational Church to hear Rev. Hiram Wilson speak about the plight of the poor refugees in Canada. Later that afternoon, a smaller group assembled at the Loguen's home on Pine Street for an update on Rev. Loguen's journey to British territory. Black George was eager to attend, and Ma and I were excited to join him. Upon entering, Ma greeted Mrs. Loguen warmly.

"My, you look like you could have your baby any day now, Caroline!" she said.

"I hope so! But it's been so cold that I think he wants to stay inside," Mrs. Loguen replied.

Looking around the room, I recognized Rev. Lyles and Mr. George Boyer Vashon, both loyal supporters of the Loguen's. John Thomas was there, too. Black George and I approached to shake their hands.

"I can't wait to hear how Rev. Loguen is doing," I begged.

"That's why we're all here, Edward," George Vashon replied.

"Mrs. Caroline has a letter from him," Rev. Lyles stated.

"He be doin' alright if I knows Jermain Loguen!" Black George insisted.

When Mrs. Loguen called for order, everyone gathered round to listen.

"Jermain is safe in St. Catharines," she began. "He's boarding with the abolitionist, Hiram Wilson, who's been a strong ally of the fugitives from slavery. He's back in the pulpit, teaching school, and promoting temperance!"

"With a man like Jermain there, they must be having a revival," Rev. Lyles claimed.

Mr. Vashon asked, "What worries him the most, Caroline?"

"Jermain wrote that efforts were being made to have the Canadian government extradite him for allegedly advising the killing of a man during the *Jerry Rescue*," she answered.

Black George offered, "But anybody who knows Rev. Loguen knows he'd never advise killin' anybody!"

Mrs. Loguen answered, "Jermain resolved that if a "requisition" did come, that he and his friends would make it plain to the British authorities that the accusations were but a cover to punish him for challenging the *Fugitive Slave Bill*. He said if the government would put him on trial for rescuing Jerry, and that alone, he'd hasten back to meet the charge like a man."

"That sounds like him!" Rev. Lyles agreed, "He once said that to be considered a traitor or a coward was a fate worse than recapture or death."

"What he doin' bout comin' home?" Black George asked.

"Mr. George, he wrote a letter to Governor Hunt askin' for protection if he should come back to stand trial. He claimed that he was indicted on perjured testimony, and he never urged the killing of anyone. The *Fugitive Slave Bill* had so exposed him to slave hunters that he wouldn't be able to defend himself. Still, he expressed his loyalty to Syracuse and the United States."

Ma asked, "What else did he say, Caroline?"

"I'll read it to you, Ellen. He said that he'd resided long enough in Canada to become a British subject; but having lived for many years in the State of New York, at Syracuse, as a minister of the Gospel and a *"citizen of no mean city,"* I have never been able to produce any other certificate of freedom than the one which was indelibly written upon my constitutional nature, by the finger of the Almighty."

George Vashon responded, using words that I didn't understand.

"I'm sure that his benevolent activities have mollified his bereavement, and made his expatriation more endurable," he said.

"Uh, what's that mean, sir?" I posed.

"That means he's doing the best that he can, Edward," he said with a grin.

"That's better than Henry Clay is doing!" I answered.

"What do you mean?" Vashon asked.

"Sir, I read that he resigned from the Senate due to his poor health."

"I says too bad for Henry Clay!" Black George pronounced.

Mrs. Loguen placed both hands on her large belly and said, "I just want my next child to be free! If Jermain is returned to bondage they'll claim my children, too."

The Monday of Christmas week found my pa in the public eye again. A call had gone out for a meeting at City Hall to invite Lajos Kossuth to Syracuse, and when he invited me to attend I gladly obliged.

"We shouldn't be late returning, Ellen," Pa reassured just prior to departure, "I'll be surprised if another meeting isn't called after this one to iron out the details."

Ma replied sternly. "I sometimes wish that you men could learn to cut it short! Instead, you'll reconvene just to repeat yourselves."

"You're right, Ellen, some men like to hear themselves talk."

"And others can't avoid being on committees—let's see if you can surprise me!"

I made an errant attempt to reconcile them, and said, "Don't worry, Ma—I'll be there!"

"That's a relief," Cornelia scorned from the next room.

Ma had the last word. "It feels like Syracuse has more spirit for Kossuth than for Christmas!"

Pa put his hand on the door, saying "Time to go, son."

It was fun riding in the sleigh, just me and Pa. Gliding past the Davis butcher shop, I remarked that the place had a different feel about it since the *Jerry Rescue*.

Pa agreed, saying, "It's been much quieter, if nothing else!"

"I was surprised that you didn't know where Jerry was hiding, Pa."

"I didn't! Rev. May was extremely tight lipped about it—we all asked, but he said the less people who knew, the better."

"It must've been hard keepin' a secret like that."

"It was, especially when the Orange Street residents complained about Davis ranting."

"He sure had me fooled," I agreed. "Parish told me that Thomas Davis is still coming around the Police Office. He wants to join the force, Pa!"

"Well, we need strong men but it'll take the backing of the Common Council first. Since he helped to hide Jerry, some might think him a lawbreaker."

"I hadn't thought of that, Pa—guess he shouldn't expect Alderman Higgins' vote! Moses Summers knocked him to the ground when he tried to stop Jerry from gettin' away."

"That's what made Moses a defendant in the *Rescue* trials," Pa asserted.

"Mr. Crandal got it for ringing the bell and passing out flyers!"

"The trial's in a few weeks in Albany, Edward, but for now, let's get to the livery and over to City Hall. This should be a good meeting!" Pa said.

The hall filled with familiar faces, all eager to invite the great Kossuth to Syracuse. I quickly spotted the Cheney and Johnson brothers, along with Charlie Pope and Miles Bennett Jr.—their fathers were as keen as mine for the famous exile to visit our city.

Miles said, "Looks like it's about to start—let's grab seats before they're all gone!"

The meeting began when Mr. George Comstock, a vocal proponent of *Law and Order*, convened the large assembly. On motion, D.D. Hillis, who represented Jerry Henry, was appointed chairman, with P.H. Agan of the *Standard* as secretary. Right before my eyes, the opposing forces from the *Freedom Rally* and the *Law and Order* meeting had come together in harmony—Lajos Kossuth had bridged the great divide! I looked at Parish, who read my mind.

"Hey Ed—who'd a thought it would take a Hungarian to make the Germans and Irish get along, huh?"

"And the Democrats and the Whigs!" Prentice added.

"And the Salt Pointers and the humans!" Grove quipped.

Taking the chair, Mr. Hillis stated the object of the meeting, then appointed a committee to determine the officers. When the Vice

Presidents were announced, the names of Charles A. Wheaton, Miles W. Bennett, Charles Baker, and Thomas Spencer were called.

"Why you shakin' your head, Wheaton?" Charlie asked.

I laughed, "My ma's gonna be disappointed that Pa's on another committee."

"Ha! My ma will be, too," Miles joked.

As the meeting progressed, I felt more aligned with Pa's sentiments and found myself laughing again when plans for the next meeting were revealed. A Committee of Arrangements was formed, which included Mr. Quincy Johnson, Timothy Cheney, and Charles Pope—now all of our pa's were involved. I'd have to learn more about this Kossuth fellow.

**On Christmas morning, 1851,** Ma had Black George bring the sleigh around, then she loaded Ellen, Emma, and baby Minnie aboard for the journey to Pompey and Grandpa Birdseye's 69th birthday. Minnie appeared to be in a cocoon with one little hole to see and breathe from. Pa's schedule was overbooked as usual, the Pompey trip its first casualty. Cornelia and I were kept behind to keep an eye on Clara, Florence, Lucia, and Henry (aged 8, 6, 4, and 2) so Pa could get his work done.

Henry cried when our horses whisked them away, and Black George yelled, "Merry Christmas, Missus! You girls help yo mamma now!"

"We will, George!" they both yelled back.

"How long you think they're gonna be gone, Pa?" I asked.

"I'm not sure, Edward—that's why I stayed home."

Holding Henry, Cornelia said, "I suppose we'll just have to have our own Merry Christmas without them!"

"That we will, honey," Pa answered.

"I best check on de maid if we's gonna eat today," Black George announced.

"Be careful, George—she might ring your neck like one of my chickens!" I warned.

I felt certain that Pa skipped the Pompey trip to avoid missing the second Kossuth meeting, scheduled for Saturday, the 27th. The day arrived with the thermometer reading at twelve below, the latest in a string of sub-zero temperatures. Mrs. Loguen's unborn baby must have sensed it and wisely stayed home.

Nationwide enthusiasm for Kossuth temporarily waned with news that a fire in the Capitol had destroyed the entire Congressional Library! Everyone spoke of the loss to our nation, some called it beyond calculation.

I asked Black George if he was interested in the Kossuth meeting and he said, "Not me, but I do wants to hear Mr. William G. Allen. He gonna be at the Congregational Church on Sunday, Monday, or Tuesday talkin' bout the destiny of the African race!"

"I met him, George—maybe I'll go with ya."

"But more den dat, I wants to see Elizabeth Taylor Greenfield, the 'Black Swan,' on New Year's."

Cornelia jumped in, "Oh, I'd love to see her, too, George! Can we go with you? I've heard how good she is—some say she's even better than Jenny Lind!"

"Yeah, George, let's all go! The last show that we saw with you was the Nightingale's."

"Well, since youse asked . . . and I spose I'd like the comp'ny," he replied.

The second meeting to invite Lajos Kossuth to Syracuse was larger and more spirited than the first. Chairman D.D. Hillis called the meeting to order and expressed his satisfaction with the turnout. He noted that events in Europe were leading to a general uprising for the deliverance of oppressed people. Resolutions were read and unanimously accepted, emphasizing Hungary's independence as a barrier against Russian and Austrian despotism. Several speakers, including LeRoy Morgan, Harvey Baldwin, Alfred Hovey, Dr. Spencer, and Captain Yard, delivered eloquent speeches. A committee was formed to request the Mayor and Common Council to invite Kossuth to the city. Additionally, a motion was passed for the Ladies of Syracuse to form an association for the relief of Hungary. The meeting concluded with the power to call another meeting if necessary. It surprised me to see Major Burnet and D.D. Hillis, who were on opposite sides during the *Jerry Rescue-Riot*s, working together.

The next day, Black George and I walked to the Congregational Church to hear Mr. William G. Allen. Sunday's lecture was free, but the following two days would cost 12½¢, so we braved the cold. The first black professor in New York drew a respectable audience for his lecture entitled, "The Origin, Literature, and Destiny of the African Race." I wished that Ma had heard him—she missed a good one! His thoughts were orderly and well-articulated, making it easy to follow along. At the end, he said that he hoped to bring about the time when,
*Worth, not birth, shall rule mankind,*
*And be acknowledged stronger.*
At the lecture's end, we left with our minds brimming with interesting facts, unsure of how to use them. As we walked home, it grew noticeably colder, we both hoped it would warm up for the 'Black Swan' show on New Year's night.

Two days later on the thirtieth, Black George came home smiling ear to ear—Mrs. Loguen had given birth to a healthy son that she named Jarvin.

"Oh, George, that's wonderful, I can't wait to see the baby!" Cornelia cried.

"How are the Loguen's stores holding out, George?" Pa asked.

"All's good—I be keepin' my eye on it."

Cornelia said, "You're a good man, George!"

"Why thankee, Missy," he replied with a tip of his hat. "I do believes I is."

# Chapter Twenty-Two

## (January 1852)

Black George, Cornelia, and I had big plans for the Black Swan performance at Malcolm Hall. Despite the awful weather, we arrived early, as did a great many others, including families. Surprisingly, we heard remarks that the singer's talents were overrated, but as soon as she began all doubts were laid to rest. As Black George said, "Dat Elizabeth Taylor Greenfield sho can sing!"

The swan's voice spanned an incredible range—her highest tones were two notes higher than Jenny Lind's, her lower tones a deep bass.

From start to finish, Miss Greenfield's songs were met with loud applause, several encores were called for. We found it hard to choose our favorites—they were all good! Black George favored "Ah, I don't mingle," while Cornelia preferred "Where are now those hopes I cherished?" Miss Greenfield's final encore, performed in her melodious bass voice while accompanying herself on the piano, showcased her considerable talents as a musician. She truly brought down the house!

*Elizabeth Taylor Greenfield*

Afterward, as we stepped outside into the cold, Cornelia and I urged Black George to recommend the next good show for us to see together.

"I think it be right over there," he said, pointing toward the Syracuse House. "General Sam Houston's in there now makin' a speech!"

The hero of San Jacinto had arrived on the eight o'clock train after missing the afternoon express. A welcoming party met him at the depot, providing escort to the Syracuse House where many anxious citizens were eager to see the famous man from Texas. The host, Mr. Gillette, provided a sumptuous dinner that concluded around the time we arrived. Ex-Mayor Baldwin introduced the general to the company, remarking on the many important events of the past half century concerning Texas. He closed by comparing Columbus with the general—the former provided a new world to the crown of Spain, while the latter delivered a bright new star to the American Union. Baldwin's final words offered a toast to the health of the renowned statesman.

When the general rose to speak, a perfect storm of applause erupted which lasted for some time. Like Baldwin, Gen. Houston spoke of the history of Texas, including its annexation to the United States. He attributed the delay to the impression people had of the moral character of Texans. Everyone laughed when he said that the people of the United States regarded Texans as a set of desperadoes and plunderers, but seemed to forget the fact that their education had been received in the United States! In closing, General Houston offered a toast,

*"The city of Syracuse—it's prosperity is only equaled by the intelligence and enterprise of its citizens!"*

When the assembly broke up around eleven o'clock, many followed the general to

*Gen. Sam Houston*

the train depot for his midnight departure. Pa had expected us earlier, waiting impatiently for our return. When he looked sternly at me and Cornelia, we let Black George do the talking.

Ma and the girls finally returned in the early afternoon of the second day of the year. My mother was keen to hear New Hampshire Senator John P. Hale's lecture before the Franklin Institute that evening, where lady members could attend for free. When Pa returned home for afternoon tea, he brought Senator Hale with him! Having never met a Senator before, I expected him to be stiff and formal, but he was quite sociable and easy to talk to. I wanted to attend the lecture with Ma, but she said that I had my fill of society last night. When she returned from the address, she said the Senator spoke of National Morality, providing a sound argument without a foolish or unwise word. Shortly after we questioned her, the senator returned with Pa to spend the night, departing directly in the morning after breakfast. Ma embarrassed me when she said the eggs came courtesy of Edward Wheaton. Senator Hale winked at me and remarked that he found the *abolition scramble* quite tasty.

Following Senator Hale's departure, Parish and Grove arrived to ask if we saw the New Year's stabbing on Salina Street that claimed the life of an Irishman.

"You weren't far from where it happened, Ed—did you see or hear anything?" Parish asked.

"Not a thing, Parish—it was too cold to loiter, but you seem to know all about it!" Turning to Grove, I asked, "Were you gonna tell me about it, too?"

"No, Ed—I just want to say Happy New Year to Miss Ellen."

"How old you gonna be this year, Grove, ten?" I asked.

"No—eleven!" he protested. One year makes a big difference!"

"Well, she's in the next room—go and tell her," I suggested.

"Don't worry about Romeo, Ed—you gotta hear this!" Parish urged.

"Okay, then tell me."

"The story from the Police Office is that Enoch Reed got into a brawl with a bunch of Irishmen and one of 'em's dead! Reed's the colored guy who just got arrested for the *Jerry Rescue*."

"Where exactly you talkin' bout?"

"On Salina St. just over the Oswego bridge—it happened around midnight, Ed."

"Who got killed, Parish?"

"His name was Sylvester Hogan, and Patrick Slader and James Carroll got stabbed, too!"

"Where was this, again?"

"You know—it's the block called *Tipperary* for all of the Irish."

"Oh yeah, I know the place—so what happened?"

"Officer Shattuck told me that a few days ago there was a big disturbance at Tipperary, and a policeman asked Enoch Reed for assistance inside one of the houses. The Irish didn't like it, and when they saw him passing by on New Years they ran outside to confront him. Reed took off toward the bridge but they caught-up and started in! He's a big man, that Enoch Reed—he fought most of Tipperary. He got beat up pretty bad, but he managed to turn his knife on his pursuers—I heard they were carrying knives, too."

"So who got arrested, Parish?"

"So far, only Enoch Reed—and right after it happened. There was another colored man with him who got away. Coroner Marsh called his jury in the morning and by the afternoon they finished. Shattuck said the testimony was contradictory, and the jury's verdict read that Sylvester Hogan came to his death by being stabbed with a knife in the hands of Enoch Reed, while in the act of self-defense. Reed's confined to his bed at the penitentiary now from the severe beating that he took."

"What's next, Parish?"

"I heard they're gonna hold him until Justice House can examine the case. Reed's charged with killing Hogan and stabbing the other two."

"We'll have to wait to see what happens then, I suppose."

"That we will, Ed, but first we gotta get Grove away from Miss Ellen before he declares again."

A lot happened in early January, but nothing more significant than Pa selling our house for a move to Fayette Park! It wasn't a complete surprise, but it still shocked us that we were really moving, if only a mile down the road.

The excitement affected Pa, too. In the early hours of the eighth, he became so ill that we had to wake Black George for help. A doctor arrived at six in the morning to provide relief, but he still laid in bed till noon. Ma and the girls took care of him, even Aunt Helen stopped by to help. By evening, he felt much better, which allowed mother to attend the Horace Greeley lecture on his observations at the Crystal Palace.

"He's had every opportunity to see and hear all that's worth hearing, and his account should be extremely interesting!" she said in departure.

Upon her return a few hours later, Cornelia couldn't wait to hear about it.

"So how was it, Ma?" she asked.

"Well, he has an awkward manner, but his thoughts are forcible and just—and he often used a glowing and beautiful language!"

"Was it crowded, Ma?" I asked.

"Yes, Edward—quite crowded. Long before Greeley started, many went away unable to find seats."

I knew that Ma had always admired the Crystal Palace from afar, but hearing about it first-hand brought her to life. She seemed more cheerful than she had earlier.

"Do you feel better about us moving now, Ma?" I enquired.

"I'll tell you tomorrow, dear—you're going with me to see the new house!"

The next day, I pulled the sleigh around, leaving Cornelia and Ellen in charge of the other five girls and little Henry. Our first stop was Clarissa Dawson's home, where Mr. John Becker, the music teacher, played some fine music on his guitar. Pa met us there, and together we went for a tour of our future residence at the Burt house on Fayette Park.

Mr. Oliver Teall Burt, along with his wife, Rebecca, and sister, Eleanor, welcomed us to what would soon become our new, their former, home.

"Come in from the cold, everyone!" Mrs. Burt commanded, "I can't wait to show you around, Ellen, and this young man must be Edward!"

"Yes, it is—he's turning fifteen this month."

"Fifteen already? I bet he can't wait to get out to the gold mines!"

"Yes, Ma'am," I answered, drawing laughter.

Mr. Burt and Pa went into the study while we toured the home's interior. Ma liked it—she remarked that it would be easier living here as far as housework was concerned.

"Hey, Ma—this wing will make a nice family room, don't you think?" I asked.

"Yes, I do!" she answered. "Did you know that the house is lighted with gas and heated with a furnace, Edward?"

"No, I didn't. That'll save me and George lots a work! Is there anything that you don't like about the house, Ma?"

"Nothing about the house, Edward, but we're going to lose our garden, the shade trees, and our orchard. In the summer, we'll miss them exceedingly."

"Yeah, I guess you're right," I said with some despair.

At the end, the house on Fayette Park met with her approval. She smiled when departing, but arriving home, she looked tired—tired and dispirited at the thought of uprooting her family and the mountain of work ahead.

While we pondered our household move, the daily headlines kept our attention. Due to failing health, Henry Clay resigned as senator from Kentucky, effective the first Monday in September. He did have a private meeting with Kossuth, which was reported as cordial without consensus. In his address to the citizens of New York State, Governor Hunt's support of colonization faced opposition from many. The Queen of Spain pardoned the Americans taken prisoner for invading Cuba, and most importantly, Lajos Kossuth accepted the invitation to visit Syracuse.

In local news, Parish Johnson announced that Police Justice House cleared Enoch Reed of murder charges, siding with the coroner's jury that the outnumbered man acted in self-defense. Captain Yard lost his position at the penitentiary for not re-applying on time, and a new militia was created, named the Onondaga Light Guards. The year 1852 began with a fast start!

On the 20th, the *Jerry Rescue* trial resumed in Albany for five of the accused: Enoch Reed, Ira Cobb, Moses Summers, William Salmon, and James Davis. District Attorney Lawrence wanted to try Enoch Reed first, but he was late arriving due to the fearful beating and murder charges.

That same night in Syracuse, Pa led a concert by the Syracuse Musical Institute, filling the seats with the promise of a hundred well-cultivated voices, accompanied by a skillful orchestra. The Cheney's and Johnson's were there, then Charlie Pope appeared, followed by the Williard's and the Cook's. I spied Larry Sabine peering out from behind his spectacles, talking to Will Stoddard and the McKinstry's.

Then my eyes alighted on Mira Barker, my all-time favorite dancing partner from Rust's Hotel, and the prettiest girl on the north side. I decided to ask her out on a date after the show.

Mira saw me approach, while some of her friends elbowed her in the side and whispered incoherently. My friends followed behind, I felt tracked from all directions.

"Hello Mira, you look wonderful as usual!" I pronounced.

"Thank you, Edward, it's nice to see you, too," she answered.

"Say, uh Mira—my birthday's in a couple days, you know—I'll be fifteen!"

"Really? What do you want for your birthday?"

"Well, I'd like for you to go see Susan Denin with me next week at the National Theatre. Please say yes, Mira!" I implored.

"I will, Edward—everyone's talking about her!"

*Susan Denin*

"I know—from what I've heard, it should be a great performance."

"Her sister Kate's in the show, too, she's more our age."

"Right—and Susan's only a couple years older."

I had just started to feel good about life when I heard an unwelcome voice.

"*What about us?*" Prentice Cheney asked.

I flashed red when a girl named Margie echoed his aspirations. Apparently, our conversation was overheard. I thought to myself that the Navy got it wrong when they recently abolished flogging.

"You got money for tickets, Prentice? Box seats are fifty cents, but it's only a quarter for the Pit," I challenged.

Austin Cook answered, "I got the money but I ain't sure if I can get outta work."

Charlie Willard invited himself while aggravating his brothers. "I'll be there, Ed," he said with certainty. Glancing at Billy and Flo, he stroked his irregular whiskers in provocation, saying, "Too bad the National don't allow children!"

Preparing for my date with Mira, I noticed Cornelia looking glum.

"What's going on, Cornelia? You look ready to cry!"

"I feel like it! Ma signed me up to go to school in New York, and I'm leaving soon."

"Oh no! I heard Mrs. Wicks tell Ma that her sister goes to school there, and it's run by three Quaker ladies."

"I don't care! All my friends are here, even you, Edward," she said with regret.

"It'll be strange without you here—we'll all miss you!"

"Especially when you're doing my work, but thanks, brother. Are you ready for your big date tonight?"

I guess so—finally got this cowlick to lay down with some Macassar oil."

"Ha! It might freeze before you get to the National. Who else is going?"

"A whole bunch! Everybody wants to see Susan Denin and we're all meeting out."

Unbeknownst to us, Black George heard everything.

"I be sorry dat you leavin' us, Missy," he said.

"Thank you, George!"

"But I wants to know if Edward done wrote poetry for his gal up town. Wouldn't want dat little Johnson fella showin' you up now," he jibed.

"Uh, too late for that now, George. But I'll be extra nice to her, okay? I bought some candy from the Knipp brothers and I'm buyin' her ticket, too."

"You boys gonna meet da girls' daddy's tonight?"

I stood perplexed. "Why you askin,' George?"

"Ain't you pickin' 'em up fo da show?"

"Nah—we're meetin' 'em there—maybe walk 'em home after!"

"You a real smooth one, boy," Black George scoffed as Cornelia shook her head.

Standing outside the National with the guys, we soon spotted Mira approaching with her girlfriends. I thought to myself that Black George was right, next time I should pick her up at her door. Pleasantries were exchanged when we filed inside, I really liked the feel of her arm in mine.

"This is gonna be a great show, Mira!" I said cheerfully.

"It's starting now!" she cried.

With Levi Martin leading the orchestra, the Messrs. G.A and W.H. Hough's production opened with *Love's Sacrifice*, featuring Miss Susan Denin as Margaret Elmore. Like the Black Swan, Miss Denin won the audience from the start—the reporters in New York and Philadelphia didn't exaggerate her talents. Kate Denin, along with Mr. J. Winans, joined the dramatic company that delighted the audience. Following *Love's Sacrifice*, the renowned dancer, Miss E. Kendall, cavorted before appreciative spectators—the evening concluded with the entire cast performing in *Napoleon's Old Guard*.

When we stopped clapping after the final curtain fell, Mira smiled, squeezed both my hands, and exclaimed, *"What a show! I could see Susan Denin again!"*

"Yeah, me too! She'll be here for a week, Mira, why don't we?"

"Do you mean it? That's a lot of money for tickets."

"I do! Let's talk about it on the way to your house—I'd like to walk you home, okay?"

"Okay, Ed—you guys can protect us!" Mira affirmed with her friends nodding approval.

The guys jumped at the chance to walk pretty girls home—who wouldn't? It made me think of how Mr. Weld called us *gentlemen* in school, now here we were escorting ladies down Salina Street—I guess we proved him right.

Our group began to splinter after we crossed the Oswego Canal bridge, not far from where Mira lived on Salt Street. Walking past the Tipperary block, the conversation turned to the recent stabbing as Parish searched the road for blood. Many Irish were about, a stern voice hailed,

"Making new friends, Mira?"

Knowing the voice, she responded, "That I am, Ron Sheeney!"

"Too good for us now, I suppose! Who's that with you?"

"Ed Wheaton," I answered.

Sheeney scoffed, "Oh, the abolitionist singer's boy. Rather late for you, ain't it? Be careful, you might get your clothes dirty!"

Several unfriendly faces appeared around him, echoing remorse that Mira had left the fold.

"There she goes!" one yelled.

"Look at her puttin' on airs!" another followed.

*"Well, la-di-da!"* an inebriated young woman cried.

"C'mon, Ed—don't pay them any mind!" Mira said.

Walking the last few blocks alone with Mira, the affluence level declined with every step away from downtown. We were still on the safe side of Division Street, but close proximity to salt boilers often made me wary.

Approaching her doorstep, it presented much differently than our new home at Fayette Park. Afterall, the Barker's lived on a whitewasher's income.

"Mira, I really want to see you again! After we move, I'll live a lot closer to you," I said excitedly.

"I didn't know that. Where ya movin' to?"

"Just a mile down Genesee Street to Fayette Park."

Mira looked subdued.

"Oh, are you moving into one of those mansions?" she asked.

"Uh, it's a nice house all right, but I don't know if I'd call it a mansion. It's not like General Leavenworth's on James Street, or anything like that."

"Perhaps not, but there's nothing like it on Salt Street!" she said.

Viewing the neighborhood, I conceded her point.

"Even so, Mira, that's nothing to keep us apart! I really like you and hope you'll be my Valentine. Can I kiss you?"

I couldn't believe that I managed to say all that, hopelessly lost in the twinkle of her eyes. When I began to lean in, snowballs started to land all around us. Both of us were hit as I counted a handful of Salt Pointers, including their number one thug, Ronald Sheeney. They must've followed us from Tipperary. Outnumbered five to one, I wished this Salt Point Navy would join the search for Sir John Franklin, lost in the Arctic.

"I say she's my girl!" the bulky, young Irishman proclaimed, "And I'm ready to settle it!"

"I've already turned you down, Sheeney!" Mira yelled.

Ignoring Mira, Sheeney challenged, "What about it, stiff-neck?"

"If it's a choice between fighting you or giving her up, then we'll fight." I answered with resolve.

Getting right in my face, with spittle he demanded, "Any last words?"

"Yeah—your breath stinks worse in the cold!" I retorted with my own spittle. Then I hit him in the head as hard as I could, hoping he'd go *night-night* in the snow.

Instead, he remained erect, unhurt, and annoyed. When he growled, *"You shouldn't a done that!"* I believed him.

I braced for the onslaught; hard blows rained down. As Sheeney forced me to the ground, I recalled the time that I saw a young Indian subdue a much larger one with an ankle-lock, and how the bigger one howled. This was my last hope, but when I pulled off his boot he only got madder.

Standing over me he bellowed, "What the hell are you doing?"

I answered by flinging the boot toward his face with bad intentions. The heel struck him hard on the nose, allowing me to regain my feet when the gushing blood distracted him. Now he was *really* mad! His fellow thugs cried *"Oooohhh!"* as the blood poured out his beak.

Mira screamed when Sheeney bellowed, *"Now you die!"*

My next thoughts were visions of Ma suffering at my funeral. I wondered if they'd plant me at Rose Hill or Oakwood—I never asked.

To my great relief, the bells of a rapidly approaching sleigh interrupted the pending slaughter. I recognized my fishing buddy, Milo's cousin Ray, holding the reigns of two horses, with Parish Johnson pointing the way, and Milo Freeof and George Pfohl aboard. Now it's five against five—or six if you count the lug Sheeney twice.

"*Yo there!* Who disturbs the peace?" Ray barked in a commanding voice, feigning authority.

"Who the hell are you?" came the angry reply.

"Salina Street Committee!" Milo yelled back.

"We're keepin' the streets safe!" George hollered.

Like a knight in shining armor, Parish alerted, "There's a lady present! Don't worry, Miss!" he shouted, bounding to Mira's side which confused the north sider's.

"Mira's not in danger!" a particularly ugly one said.

"She's one of us, you stiff-necks!" another croaked.

"No, I'm not!" Mira cried.

Milo offered Sheeney his prognosis, "Best tilt your head back, Ronald, and pinch your nose for a minute—that'll make it stop."

"*Just step inside, Miss—you're safe now!*" Knight Parish directed at Mira's front door.

"Please get Edward out of here, Parish!" she implored.

For our opponents' benefit, George Pfohl remarked, "Hey Ray, let's get the Grenadiers' from around the corner—they're lookin' for a fight."

"Whoa there, Pfohl!" a not-so tough-guy said.

"Get in!" Ray directed, starting the sleigh moving as we piled aboard.

"This ain't over!" Sheeney raged.

I yelled back to the lonely figure on the doorstep.

"Good night, Mira, I think I love you!"

Parish blurted, "Did Grove tell you to say that?"

"What you expect? He almost died for her," Milo alleged.

I asked, "How'd you know to save me, Parish?"

"I hung around Tipperary after you left, and seeing that Sheeney was up to no good, I figured you were in for it! I didn't know what to do, but lucky for you, Ray, Milo, and George happened along in the sleigh. I waved 'em down and pointed Ray to the Barker's."

"Yeah, and we had a near miss with Grasshopper—almost ran 'im over!" Milo added.

"I owe ya, Parish, I owe all you guys!" I vowed.

Ray said, "No worries, Ed—you'd a' done the same for us."

"I hope my pa never leaves the Grenadier's—they're great friends to have," George remarked.

"Absolutely!" Ray pronounced.

"Ah, Mira," I sighed as the sleigh bells jingled.

## Chapter Twenty-Three
### (January – February 1852)

While Jerry Henry lived free in Kingston, Ontario, his rescuers faced trial in Albany, New York. The crowded courtroom included many ladies, including the famed advocate for women's rights, Lucretia Mott, and her daughter. Trial-goers included delegates to the *State Temperance Convention*, particularly men from Onondaga and Cortland Counties. Rev. May was present alongside other supporters from Syracuse when attorney D.D. Hillis motioned to quash the indictment. Leroy Morgan and Charles B. Sedwick backed the motion with lengthy arguments, while District Attorney James R. Lawrence forcefully opposed it. Both sides expected a yes or no answer, but the jurist surprised everyone by sending the case to the June term of the Circuit Court in Canandaigua where Judge Nelson would preside, starting with the motion to quash. Conkling's decision left many feeling that he shirked his duty, some even questioned his manliness and nerve. Disappointed abolitionists and other opponents of the *Fugitive Slave Law* were resigned to find solace that in Philadelphia, the Christiana rioters were finally released from murder charges.

Concerning spirited drink, the temperance movement suffered a defeat when the Rhode Island Legislature rejected the Maine Liquor Law by six votes, prompting the *Syracuse Standard* to claim that no great moral reformation was ever achieved by the passage of a statute. As Cale Davis celebrated Rhode Island staying wet, at home, without alcohol, Black George and I toasted the Black Swan. Her success in

Albany and Troy inspired P.T. Barnum to offer fifteen-hundred dollars for her first concert in New York.

As January drew to a close, the House of Representatives proposed a joint resolution to amend the US Constitution so that Senators were elected by the people, not appointed by State Legislatures. Meanwhile, the steamers *Prometheus* and *Cherokee* returned with another two million dollars of California gold!

With John Cook Jr. holding the door, the entire Cook family welcomed us on an impromptu visit to their popular eatery. Mrs. Cook embraced Ma and Cornelia while I shook hands with Mr. Cook and the boys. Ma beamed at John Jr. enough to make him blush.

"My, you've become quite the businessman!" she announced.

"Yes, he's learned a lot," Mr. Cook confirmed.

"Yeah—especially about givin' orders," Austin added as Abel nodded agreement.

Mrs. Cook made us feel at home with her arm in Cornelia's, directing us to our table.

"Come this way, everyone!" she said cheerily.

Elbowing me in the side, Austin suggested the popular winter drinks.

"For cheeks as red as yours, I recommend a warm *Tom and Jerry*, whaddya say?"

"Sounds great, except for the alcohol," I answered.

"Or your ma's not lookin'!" Austin quipped. "I guess that means no to a *Lambswool*, too, I suppose—ha ha ha!"

"You know my pa—it would end badly."

Mrs. Cook interrupted the chatter, "Boys, come talk to Cornelia—she's leaving soon for school in New York!"

John Jr. spoke first, "Congratulations, Cornelia! I know you'll do well."

"I agree," Mr. Cook affirmed. Then he hugged her and said, "We'll all miss *our* Cornelia!"

"Fare thee well, Cornelia!" Austin offered.

"Me, too, Cornelia!" Abel chirped.

Mrs. Cook began excitedly, "Say, Ellen, it just occurred to me that when you visit Cornelia you could see the *American Crystal Palace*. They're reassembling the original from London in New York City—with all the exhibits, too."

Cornelia cried, "Yes, Ma, we all know how much you loved reading about the World's Fair."

"Cornelia's right, Ma—and I'll go with ya!" I declared.

"Thank you, Edward," Ma answered with a smile.

"And bring the girls, too, Ma," Cornelia insisted.

Monday, February 16, felt like a normal day at school.

Mr. Weld said, "Alright, gentlemen, someone tell me what's happening in the country—Mr. Wallace, please attend!"

Bill answered, "Mr. Weld, they're still building the Washington Monument, all the blocks are being donated by different states, cities, and societies. There's lots of folks around here who want to see Onondaga County represented, too."

"Excellent! From which quarry and for what kind of stone?" Weld inquired.

"Split Rock quarry, sir. For the best specimen of limestone they can find."

"Good report, William, please keep us informed! Now, who's next?"

I answered, "I am, Mr. Weld! State Senator Beekman just introduced a bill to appropriate funds for blacks to colonize Liberia. He must've been listening to Governor Hunt, sir, but that's not all. The *New York Tribune* thinks that blacks would be better off trying to colonize a township in southern New Jersey, or a county in Nebraska, first. That way, they can see how they do before trying Africa."

Mr. Weld scoffed, "Ha! Did anyone ask Henry Clay what he thought?"

Alex McKinstry answered, "I don't think so, Mr. Weld, but a committee from New York presented Senator Clay with a gold medal made in his likeness. They said it was a testimonial for his great services to the nation, and to mankind."

"If I'm not mistaken, it must be a large medal," Weld answered.

"Yes, sir, it is. One of the largest ever made in this country, too. It's three and half inches in diameter, made from pure gold from California, and packaged in a finely engraved silver case," Alex replied.

"I see!" Mr. Weld answered. "Now, who can tell me the latest on Kossuth's travels?"

Parish Johnson responded, "I can, Mr. Weld. They loved him in Cincinnati, sir, but not in Louisville. In fact, they voted him unwelcome in Kentucky! It all depends on which side of the Ohio River that you live."

"Thank you, Parish, but don't you normally cover the police?"

"I still do, Mr. Weld. Two frail sisters escaped from the penitentiary, sir! Officer Shattuck caught one, and Lowell got the other. I heard they were first arrested at a disorderly house."

"What do frail sisters get arrested for doing at a disorderly house, Parish?" Flo Willard asked, causing alarm in our teacher. Before Parish could answer, Weld directed,

"That's a question for your father, Florello!"

"Huh?" Even Flo got confused by his real name.

"You heard me!" Mr. Weld proclaimed with the final word on the subject.

The next day, at four o'clock in the morning, Weld's School for Young Men and Boys burned to the ground.

Standing outside the charred remains of what once had been our school, heavy wooden beams smoldered among the live embers in the rubble. My classmates were all there, milling around and smelling the smoke. There wasn't much left.

"Now what, Ed?" Prentice asked.

"I've no idea, Prentice! What do you think, Si?"

"I think there's no school today, Ed!"

"That's for sure," I answered, as firemen Peter Ohneth and Phillip Eckle of the "Empire" Company examined their machines alongside the firehoses that needed rolling-up.

"The flames tore through that tinderbox like a windstorm, Peter!" Eckle remarked.

"Praise God that nobody lived there," Ohneth replied.

Mr. Weld looked downcast, but thankful that there were no injuries.

"Chin-up, gentlemen!" he uttered, as much to himself as to us.

Bill Wallace asked, "What are we gonna do, Mr. Weld?"

"I'm not sure, William, but I'll let you all know very soon—first I must reflect and pray."

Si Cheney's prediction of no school carried through the week, right past Washington's Birthday on Sunday. Out of respect for the Sabbath the holiday parade was held on Monday, the 23rd. A bunch of us rendezvoused at the Johnson's to join the fun, everyone happy with the new arrangements for school. Grove kicked up his heels.

Backed by Samsel's German Brass Band, Capt. George Saul led the Washington Riflemen on parade through downtown, past the local residents attired from smartly dressed to shabby, and everything in-between. At parade's end the militia planted their artillery in Clinton Square to fire a national salute in tribute to our nation's first President. As the boom of cannon carried down the canals and into the countryside, *Canal Loafers* turned-out in a show of respect. From their familiar haunts on the bridges, they watched the opportunistic Grasshopper hawking his wares for a handsome profit.

Outside the Police Office on the Clinton Street Bridge, I kidded Parish that we were on assignment from school, so he owed us an update on local crime.

"Hey Parish, what's the latest from your police friends? Ha ha!"

"It's not funny, Ed! When officers Dodge and James arrested a rough named Shel Webster, a bunch of his friends followed 'em to the watch house to set him free. They failed, but came back after dark to bust him loose, and they did!"

"How'd they manage it, Parish?" Prentice asked.

"It's easy when there's no police on duty after dark," Parish answered.

"Yeah, our leader's need to fix that—the city's left to take care of itself when most of the crimes and fires happen," Alex observed.

"You're right, Alex, if the Journal building ever caught fire at night there wouldn't be an officer there to let people outta the watch house—that old watchman's asleep half the time!" I said with alarm.

Charlie Pope looked at me and said, "Ed, You should tell your uncle—he's the mayor!"

"But not for long, Charlie—the charter election's next week," I replied.

"Anything else we should know, Parish?" Larry asked.

"Not really, Justice House saw another slew of Irishmen, but this parade didn't have a band—Ha ha!"

"Oh yeah? Like who?"

"Let's see, Dennis Harrington, Mary Cole, Patrick Slaven, and Thomas Quinn were arrested for intoxication and breach of peace, but House let 'em go after they promised to leave the city *immediately*. Then Michael Clary and Patrick Ryan got the same for being drunk and disorderly."

"Where do drunks go when they get run outta town?" Billy asked.

"Who knows? Can't imagine where anybody'd want 'em."

"I hear they like to drink in Ogdensburg," Larry offered.

"Oh, yeah—I heard that about the 'Burg, too." Parish affirmed. "Hollister told me there's nothin' else to do in the north country."

Class adjourned after the parade, the new curriculum was a big hit!

A few days later, it didn't escape Ma's notice when the Cheney brothers arrived to get me for school, grinning from ear to ear.

"What kind of boys are happy when their school burns down?" she demanded.

"Just the lucky ones, ma'am!" Si blurted, drawing laughter from me and Prentice.

"I heard that, Mister!" she retorted.

"What do you thinks gonna happen with Weld's School, Ma?" I asked.

"It looks like the end of Weld's School as we know it, Edward. He certainly won't continue with so many students, rather few I would think."

"Why do you say that, Ma?"

"Because he's going to teach from his home, which limits it considerably. I was going to tell you, Edward, but we were all busy with Cornelia."

"Oh, I didn't know," I answered, feeling dumbfounded like the Cheneys who stood mouths agape.

Ma continued with a bombshell, "We've decided to keep you out of school for now, Edward, but like your sister, we're finding a suitable college for you to complete your studies. How would you like to start this fall?"

"Er, um, uh I don't know, Ma. Good, I guess . . ."

Prentice couldn't contain himself. "What about us, Mrs. Wheaton? What's gonna happen to me and Si?"

"That's for your parents to decide, Prentice. But I think that most of you will join the public schools, at least for now."

"You think that pa will let us stay outta school, like Ed?" Si asked his brother.

"Not a chance, but we're off today so we gotta make the most of it. C'mon Ed, the sun's shinin'!" Prentice said with conviction, and we did.

Walking to the Johnson's, Prentice gasped, "I can't believe it, Ed, no more Weld's School for us—it's really over!"

"Yeah, and now Cornelia's gone, too! What's it like, Ed?" Si asked.

"It's weird, Si, Grandma Birdseye stayed with us for a few days, and she cried with Ma and the girls when Cornelia left. Grandpa Birdseye came to see her off, too. She rode the trains with the Ballard's, so that helped Ma feel less worried."

"Ballard has a clothes store at the Syracuse House, right?" Prentice asked.

"Yup, that's him! He and his wife were going to New York and provided escort. Pa told her not to worry, but Ma already can't wait for a letter from Cornelia sayin' that she's okay."

"Well, since we're all scattering to the wind, maybe now's the time to strike out for California!" Prentice surmised.

"Right—while the mines are still full of gold!" Si agreed.

"Yer kinda young for the mines, ain't ya, Si?" I challenged.

"Yeah, but maybe in a couple years, ya think?"

"I'm jealous of my cousin James Wheaton—he just left for California."

"That your Uncle Horace's son?" Prentice asked.

"Yeah—he's eighteen but all the ladies said that *he's* too young—especially my mother and Aunt Helen."

"Hey, what if you told your ma that you wanted to go to school in California? You think that might work?" Prentice suggested.

"Nice try, Prentice, remember what they said about James Wheaton, and he's eighteen."

"Did you hear that twenty guys from Fabius just left with Captain Holway? He commands a whaling ship that's been around Cape Horn a few times, but it's a few months journey by sail," Prentice stated.

"Yes, and on the same day, eleven men from Skaneateles left for El Dorado!"

"All the steamers leaving from New York are crowded with adventurers, Ed."

"Yeah, but I read they're getting stuck in Panama tryin' to cross the Isthmus, then they gotta wait for a ship to take 'em to San Francisco. I learned from the chicken business that ya gotta make good plans!" I said.

"Oh yeah? But your chickens ain't layin' golden eggs, are they? Ha!"

"Don't listen to 'im, Ed—he's always breakin' balls," Si pronounced.

By Saturday afternoon, campaign posters filled the shop windows, signaling the city election on Tuesday. For mayor, the Democrats nominated Jason C. Woodruff, the Whigs backed Hervey Seldon, and the *Friends of Temperance* proffered longshot, *Charles A. Wheaton!* Pa also made the ballot as a Democrat for the 4th Ward School Commissioner. When my mother found out she stated with certainty that Pa was already spread too thin, and the city didn't need another Wheaton in charge.

Normally a Democrat, William L. Crandal somehow became the Whig candidate for the 3rd Ward School Commissioner, drawing the ire of Whigs in the their own newspaper, the *Syracuse Star*. An editorial reminded its readers that Crandal was the Negro bell puller at the late riot, now under indictment for his crimes. Who could vote for such a man? Not one!

If the election weren't enough to charge the atmosphere, it was Saturday night, the twenty-eighth of February, and it was leap year. Mr. W.B. Smith promoted a *Leap Year Ball* which promised to fill the Empire Hall to capacity. It made me think of Philo Rust—he'd have been right in the middle of it.

But there was more to it. The chaotic weather didn't know if it wanted to rain or snow as the wind blew steadily. Anxious people over-drank as police began escort service to the watch house. I joined the Willard's and Cheney's standing outside the Empire Block.

"Hey, ain't that the Knipp's over there?" Prentice asked.

We all recognized our favorite confectioners, the Knipp brothers, following behind Officer Ormsby, who had their father, Freddy Knipp, in custody. Apparently, the elder Knipp had a premonition about leap year that mixed poorly with alcohol. Attired in stiff collar, jacket, top hat, and cane, Freddy Knipp appeared as a one-man parade, heralding the coming destruction.

"The ides of leap year are upon ye!" Freddy cried to no-one in particular.

"Be quiet, Dad!" John Knipp beckoned.

"Oh, ain't you the smart one? Yesh, ish LEAP YEAR! Better watch out!"

"I think the *watch house* instead, you old duffer," son George countered.

"Yesh, to the Washhouse!—ish LEAP YEAR! Don't bunk yer head."

"What's he talking about?" one brother asked.

"No one knows," said the other.

"Move along now, Freddy!" Officer Ormsby urged.

"The ides of leap year are comin'," Freddy Knipp slurred.

Billy Willard shared Freddy's conviction. "He's right Ed, just look at the skies! Maybe we'll get a thundersnow—Leap year can do that."

Starting to believe, I answered, "We'll see, Billy."

As night fell, the weather worsened, a sudden gust of wind hurried us home under a threatening sky. Freddy's prophesy came true at four in the morning when the spire of the Unitarian Church came crashing down! The heavy steeple fell directly onto the church roof, reducing the building to ruins and waking the entire neighborhood. Only a small portion remained erect. The rear wall collapsed onto an adjoining house, where the Northrup family narrowly escaped with their lives.

The next day, Billy suggested a spiritual connection between the falling spire and our school burning because they both happened at four o'clock. Although proof enough for him, he sought to consult Madame Blanche, just to be sure.

Sometime in the morning, the Knipp brothers had Freddy released, feeling vindicated for teaching him a lesson. Freddy should have felt vindicated, too, but he couldn't remember a thing.

# Chapter Twenty-Four
## (March – April 1852)

Talk of the church disaster spread like wildfire, with leap year omens and miracle escapes fueling the banter. I had to see the wreckage for myself; me and half the city. Viewing the catastrophe, I joined the believers in miracles and guardian angels—just ask the Northrup's! Working through the crowd, I encountered several former classmates among the curious locals. Ma was right about what would happen to my old school—Mr. Weld now taught a much-reduced number from home, while some of the older, *young gentlemen* went to work with their fathers, scattering the rest to public schools.

On Tuesday, the steeple crash took a back seat to the charter election between Democrats and Whigs vying for leadership of City Government. Pa stayed out late to follow the returns—a landslide win for the Democrats!

> **DAILY STANDARD.**
> WEDNESDAY MORNING, MARCH 3.
> OFFICIAL PAPER OF THE CITY.
>
> **CHARTER ELECTION.**
>
> **Brilliant Victory of the Democracy!**
> *A DEMOCRATIC MAYOR!!*
> **A Democratic Common Council!!!**
> **A Democratic Justice, Treasurer, City Attorney, Surveyor, and 9 Democratic Poor Masters.**
> **FOUR DEMOCRATIC SUPERVISORS!**

Ma showed little interest, more concerned with Cornelia's first letter home that eased her worry, but drew remarks about how lonely the house felt, and how Pa hadn't sung since she left.

When the votes were counted, my father was elected the 4th Ward School Commissioner as a Democrat, as did Oliver T. Burt for Alderman, but Alexander McKinstry lost his race by six votes to Harmon Ackerman in a rare win for the Whigs. Despite taking a beating at the ballot, many Whigs celebrated W.L. Crandal's defeat as school commissioner. They further blamed my father and the *Friends of Temperance* for splitting the Whig vote, assuring that Jason Woodruff became the next Mayor of Syracuse over Hervey Sheldon. Pa said that because Sheldon had aided the legal defense of Jerry Henry, it dampened the *Law and Order* Whigs' enthusiasm for his campaign.

That Friday, the Common Council entertained the election winners at the Syracuse House, but the official transition of power happened at City Hall on Monday. The outgoing Mayor, my uncle Horace, offered his heartfelt gratitude for the kindness he received during his tenure. He also encouraged his successors to enhance the efficiency of the current police system by moving the Police Office to the Market Hall building, and to always have an officer on duty, day or night.

The incoming Mayor, Jason Woodruff, remarked that *"no complaint is more general than that of over taxation,"* vowing *"not to incur a single new obligation unless it is clearly within the scope of the charter, and manifestly necessary."*

Syracuse's new Common Council hit the ground running, making many appointments on the first day, including the now *ex-butcher*, Thomas Davis, as Police Constable! Parish Johnson had foretold this occurrence, attending at the Police Office when Justice House swore him in. Parish said that Davis's fiancée, the widow, Charlotte Terpenny, along with her three sons, Henry (7), George (5), and James (2), were all there to celebrate the happy occasion. Parish called Thomas Davis the 'butcher with a badge.'

After the ceremony, Officer Davis's first task as a city policeman was to witness his fellow officer's, Lowell and Green, being served with writs for assault and battery on Jerry Henry during his recapture on the Lock Street Bridge back in October. Justice House rejoiced that it fell outside his jurisdiction, with the writs returnable to the state Supreme

Court for the next term at Oswego. In Syracuse, the *Fugitive Slave Law* remained as hated as ever, even more so, a year and a half since President Filmore signed it.

A mid-March snowfall made our sleigh the better choice than a carriage for the twenty-mile jaunt to Pompey—provided that a sudden rain didn't land our sleigh runners on barren ground. But for a smoother ride, the sleigh won every time. At Ma's direction, I would drive her to Grandma's for business and pleasure in my expanded role as the family helper—me and Ellen split all of Cornelia's work after she left for college. I also became the gopher at the hardware store where everyone constantly told me what to do and how to do it, behind a steady *go-fer* this, and *go-fer* that, all day long.

"C'mon, Edward, let's get going!" Ma ordered from outside the front door.

"I'm ready, Ma! Just getting' a snack for the road."

"Never mind the food—Grandma will feed you."

"All right already—your chariot awaits!" I answered, grabbing the reins.

"To Pompey, driver!" Ma cried as she climbed aboard, leaving my siblings in despair with Ellen and the ladies she hired to sew.

With her face aglow, she prodded, "It's a fine day for sleighing, eh, Edward?"

"Sure is, Ma. It's a good day for going west, too—all the way to California!"

"Do you mean that yawning grave of a mother's fondest hopes? I know a broken-hearted woman whose oldest son just left for California—she only learned of his intentions a short while before he departed, and that without her consent! She went to see him off at the train, and fainted when he left."

"You won't have to faint over me, Ma; I can meet up with Uncle John when I get there."

"Right—and when should we expect the first shipment of gold?"

"Funny, Ma—there's lots of other ways to make money outside the mines, and scores of Christians are heading west, too."

"Who told you that?"

"It said so in the *Syracuse Star!* There's Presbyterians from Iowa starting a colony in Oregon, and the Baptists from Indiana are heading west, too. There's so many young men leaving from the Western States that some of the small towns are being depopulated."

"Well, you won't be among them—you're going to complete your education first! We're thinking that Hobart College at Geneva could be the one for you."

Ma's revelation jarred me. Pa's involvement closed the deal—he was recently appointed president of the Board of Education. Accepting my fate, I fell silent to ponder the future. Ma waited for me to process the new information, after a brief pause she chose a lighter topic.

"So what else have you been reading besides the newspapers, Edward? The Hawthorne books are popular—if we find Diane Dodge at Grandma's, she may let me borrow her copy of *The House of Seven Gables.*"

"I asked Will Stoddard to get me the new Charles Dickens book, *Bleak House*—it's supposed to come out this month." I replied.

Ma said, "When I'm reading lately, I find it almost impossible to fix my mind upon my book. My brain has no energy, and my thoughts wander without aim or object."

"What's ailing you, Ma?"

"I believe I must be unwell, or else I'm growing old and wearing out in my prime."

It wasn't hard to guess the source of her angst.

"Have the little ones been tryin' ya, Ma?" I probed.

"Yes! Lucie used to be good, and would be again if separate from Henry, but that cannot be for long, for he's an accomplished torment—your brother. He's as restless a spirit as I've ever seen, and he's only quiet by means of strenuous exertions. Besides that, Minnie's been sick, and my nerves are suffering from caregiving and worry."

"Don't worry Ma—we're almost to Grandma's and she's got the kettle on!"

"With something for you to eat!" Ma agreed, sounding more cheerful. She's a vibrant soul, my mother—sometimes she needs to vent, but she never blows her boiler.

As expected, we found Diane at Grandma's, book in hand. Cousin Charlotte was also there, having arrived that morning from Uncle Victory's home in Manlius. After a pleasant time in Pompey, Charlotte returned with us, along with a large sack of food supplies. As we cleared the hills at evening time, just reaching the plank road, we witnessed a breathtaking spectacle of nature.

"Look at that!" Charlotte cried, "the evening star is shining on the road!"

"I see it!" Ma replied, "Just look how the rays of the moon are touching the treetops!"

"The whole landscape is lighting up!" I joined.

Charlotte proclaimed, "I love how this road winds though the valleys."

"And the sound of our horses' feet to the musical tinkling of sleigh-bells," Ma answered dreamily.

They were both right. We jingled along, grateful to witness such a beautiful scene. By eight o'clock, we arrived safely with everyone delighted to see us. Little Henry whooped for joy.

Will Stoddard had a brilliant idea for **St. Patrick's Day, 1852.** He reasoned that since we're both heading off to college in the fall, we're mature enough to attend the dinner ceremony at the Globe Hotel after the parade. With a business-like demeanor, he secured permission at home and urged me to do the same.

"C'mon Ed—you can do it! Talk to your pa like a man. Tell 'im you'll let your ma know when you'll be home so she doesn't worry," he boldly said.

Summoning courage, I followed Will's lead. Pa surprised me with his consent, saying it would be a good test of my resolve and character. I couldn't believe it, things unfolded just as Will had predicted, much like the chicken business. I then resolved to embrace Will's next idea, whatever it was, come what may. After that, I wrote Cornelia to brag.

The downtown crowd eagerly awaited the Irish National Guards, led by Captain Prendergast, uniforms pressed, and silver polished. This year's festivities promised to be the best one ever as prominent Syracuse Irishmen had taken hold of the arrangements. The entire city, including the non-Irish, was invited to celebrate, as evidenced by Samsel's German Band marching alongside the Irish soldiers.

A bunch of us gathered early to secure a good spot for the parade.

Will asked, "Did you guys know that out of the twenty-three million people in America, there's five million Germans and over a million Irish?"

"Yeah, the potato rot starved them out of Ireland," Prentice replied.

"Almost all the Germans settled in the free States," Parish added. "And I heard Mr. Saul say that Missouri has the most Germans in the South."

"My pa said that a lotta the Irish stayed in the big cities where they landed—like Boston, New York, and Philadelphia," Will stated.

Knowing the local history of Irish-German brawls, I questioned the mixing of nationalities. "How do you think they'll react to the German Band down at the Tipperary Block?" I posed to no one in particular.

Grove Johnson answered, "Can't we all just get along?"

Samsel's Band struck up their horns to start the parade. Drums beat, song erupted, spirits soared, Ireland's patron saint had triumphed. Somehow, the marching soldiers parched the throats of the faithful, prompting drinks to flow. The many non-Irish began to wish that they were.

Will and I went directly to the Globe Hotel after the parade, leaving our jealous companions behind. Ex-Alderman Lynch presided, with ex-Mayor Baldwin and Capt. Prendergast as vice presidents.

The German band squeezed in at table—I wished that Grove could have seen it! After supper was dispatched and the cloth removed, the president announced the *regular* toasts as follows:

The day we celebrate, Ireland, America, the President of the United States, the Constitution, the Army and Navy, the memories of Washington, Thomas Moore, Daniel O'Connell, William Smith O'Brien and his companions in exile, homage to the governor and lieutenant governor, the City of Syracuse, and finally, to its ladies.

The opening astonished me. *"Holy shite, Will!* They could fill the canal with all the toasts they're makin'."

*"Ha! They're just gettin' started—wait and see!"*

The chair then read from letters of dignified guests who were unable to attend, including a toast from Charles Tallman that read, "May St. Patrick's ghost haunt the British Queen until the Irish exiles are free!"

A note from Jerome J. Briggs offered, "The tree of American Liberty—Rapid has been its growth for it was watered by the blood and tears of unhappy Ireland."

Addresses were then made by former mayor Baldwin, D. D. Hillis, and several others, after which Mr. Hillis favored the company with several excellent songs, and Mr. Marron sang the *Star Spangled Banner* in good style.

Will joked, "Hey Ed—your pa's not the only one who can sing!"

"I know! But did *you* know that we're movin' next door to Mr. Hillis? Him and Pa could start an act."

Then the *Volunteer* toasts began. Man after man rose to speak and lift his glass. I liked the one by Mr. Marron, who offered, "The American Eagle and the Irish Greyhound—Together may they pursue the foes of Freedom!"

Mr. McKinstry toasted, "Syracuse, the Dublin of New York!"

The festivities carried on in like fashion till well beyond our normal curfew. Redmond Ryan, the Irish vocalist and comedian, entered the room at a late hour to favor the company with several excellent songs, given in his best style.

"This is great, Ed—I like stayin' out late!" Will remarked.

"Me, too—tomorrow night we should try to get into the Fancy Dress Ball."

"Listen to you!" Will laughed.

The evening passed amicably, our youth made us instant favorites, especially when we joined the endless toasting. In that company, it would've shown poor taste to abstain completely, so we were just being polite. I soon detected a lofty feeling from spirited drink, conceding that I found it not unpleasant. It sure loosened everyone's tongues.

On the way home, we attempted to mask the smell of alcohol by sucking on confections from the Knipp brothers, but to no avail—Ma's nose cut through it like butter, no Fancy Dress Ball for me. Pa heard the commotion and came down to investigate.

"So, did you learn anything, Edward?" he asked.

He didn't like my answer.

"Yes, Pa. I learned that you don't have to be Irish to get into trouble on St. Paddy's Day."

Following several days of restricted labor, the Johnson brothers happened along.

"I'll get it!" I yelled upon hearing the knock at the door.

"Hey Ed! We ain't seen ya in a while so we came to check on ya," Parish announced.

"And we heard you and Will got drunk with Irishmen!" Grove said excitedly.

"Yeah, and you're still alive!" Parish added.

"What your pa beat you with?" Grove asked.

"Nothin', but I can't leave home till I'm thirty-three," I replied dejectedly.

"Let the boys in and close the door!" Ma ordered.

Stepping inside, Parish noticed the clutter.

"What they got ya workin' on, Ed? Can't be cleaning—the place is a mess!" he pronounced.

Ma overheard in revolt.

"I heard that, mister!" she cried. "We're getting ready to move, and now you two can help."

"Sure, ma'am, what can we do?" Parish answered.

"You can help carry supplies to the Loguen's—we're cleaning out the root cellar."

"And I'se in charge!" Black George commanded.

"And don't forget it!" Ma emphasized.

"Right dis way now!" George ordered, pointing to the cellar stairs. By command, we started filling crates with edibles while Parish gave an update on current events at the Police Office, starting with Officer Davis.

"You know, Ed, that Davis ain't a bad guy after all—he's just got a natural smirk to his face . . ."

"So you don't think he'd cripple you anymore?" I asked.

"Nah—he's shaping up to be one of the best policemen that we have—just ask Mrs. Thankful Long—ha ha!"

"Oh yeah? What happened?"

"Well, first she had George Sims arrested for assault, then the next day Sims has her arrested for being a disorderly person. She didn't have bail money, so they jailed her, but the frail sisterhood chipped in to get her out!"

I jested, "How'd they raise money so fast?

"Maybe they had a bake-off," Grove answered.

"Ha! They ain't sellin' baked goods, but maybe they ran a special for quickies," I replied.

"Funny, Ed, but that wasn't the end of it!" Parish retorted. "After Thankful got outta jail her traveling husband reappeared, but didn't like what he saw, so he assaulted her, too. Then Thankful had him arrested, but he made bail."

"Tell Ed about Dan Rice, Parish!" Grove urged.

"Oh yeah—Dr. Spaulding won his slander case against Dan Rice for over fifteen hundred dollars, guess that'll cool Dan's tongue for a spell."

Black George interrupted, "Dat be nuff jawin', get totin' dese vittles down da street!"

Rev. John Lyles opened the door at the Loguen's while Mrs. Caroline helped the latest runaway slaves to settle in. A small apartment had been fitted out within the Loguen's home to become an *aboveground* stop on the underground railroad. Rev. May worked tirelessly with the Loguen's, providing care and guidance to the fugitives as they navigated their new lives. Many made Syracuse their home.

Rev. Lyles remarked at the bounty that we carried in.

"Looks like harvest time, but this be March! How'd you do it, George?"

"We done cleaned out the root cellar at the Wheaton's ahead a movin' to Fayette Park," was his reply.

"Well, please tell Charles and Ellen that we do appreciate it! The house be full-up again."

"I will, suh—wanna tell Mrs. Caroline that we won't forget her when we move down the street."

"I hear you, George!" Caroline Loguen said. "Thank you gentlemen for bein' so generous!"

"You're welcome, ma'am—we're glad to help," I replied.

"Can I get you all somethin'?" she asked.

Parish indicated a thirst, to which she offered milk, tea, or water.

Rev. Lyles said, "Say, George—you seen Gerrit Smith at the Wheaton's lately? I wondered if Charles asked him to write the governor to say he's against colonizing Liberia with free blacks."

"No, but I do know that he don't like how the governor never answered Rev. Loguen's letter from back in December."

Looking at me, Rev. Lyles asked, "Edward, did your pa say anything about Gerrit Smith losing twelve thousand dollars for William Chaplin forfeiting bail in Maryland?"

"Pa said that it couldn't be helped, sir—he didn't think Chaplin would get out of Maryland alive," I answered.

"He's a ballsy one, that Chaplin, tryin' to run off with the Congressmen's slaves like he did," Lyles replied.

With a mischievous smile, Black George said, "I hears dat gold medal of Henry Clay got stole!"

"That's right! It was in a carpet bag that somebody left on a carriage by mistake—they found the bag, but it was empty," Rev. Lyles answered.

"Maybe the folk in Liberia can make 'im a nudder one," Black George retorted.

Just then, Mr. George B. Vashon entered.

"Hey, what's so funny?" he asked. "I heard laughing when Caroline opened the door!"

"We be talkin' bout gold medals dat growed legs," Black George replied.

"Ha! I heard about that, too. You think maybe one of the filibusterers took it? The Queen of Spain liberated ninety-five of them from a Spanish prison for invading Cuba—they just landed aboard the ship *Prentice*."

"I wish she keeped 'em!" Black George replied.

"They got peculiar ways down South—keepin' slaves and wanting to send all the free, colored folks to Liberia," Rev. Lyles said.

Mr. Vashon answered, "They don't want the Indians there either! Senator Mallory of Florida called upon the government to remove all the Indians from that state."

Rev. Lyles joined, "And the governor sent General Hopkins with an armed company to investigate the recent outrages in Orange County—the white men seem determined to force the Florida Indians to emigrate."

Vashon answered, "I read that a delegation of friendly Seminoles was sent to Chief Billy Bowlegs to induce him to leave, but he's not going anywhere. It appears to me that the government wants to colonize the interior with replaced Indians."

Mrs. Loguen re-entered the room holding baby Jarvin, followed by daughters Elizabeth, Helen, and Sarah.

*Chief Billy Bowlegs*

"The only colonizin' I care hearin' bout is Jermain Wesley Loguen comin' back to Syracuse where he belong!" Caroline Loguen asserted.

Just a year older than Elizabeth Loguen, Grove said to her, "I'm sorry that your daddy's not here—I hope he comes home soon."

"Me, too," she answered, echoed by her sister, Helen.

"Don't you fret, child!" Black George proclaimed. "Yo daddy be comin' home, and we's here till he do."

"Yes, indeed," echoed G.B. Vashon while we all nodded our heads.

Mrs. Loguen smiled.

During an early morning at the end of March, the Tipperary Block became engulfed in flames. Many poor Irish families were affected, but most managed to save something from the inferno that destroyed the entire block. Mr. John Dunn suffered a significant loss for his uninsured grocery and dwelling. It was widely held that the fire started in the woodshed by an unknown arsonist.

Observing the aftermath with the Willard's, I asked, "So whatcha think'll happen to all the Irish folks? There were a lotta families livin' at Tipperary!"

Charlie answered, "I suppose they'll be emigrating to Wolf Street."

"Ha! There's already an Irish colony there!" Billy joked.

"Yeah, those people all stick together," I agreed.

"So, what're we gonna do now?" Flo asked.

"I don't care, but let's go somewhere!" Charlie answered. "The wind's been dryin' up the mud so it's easier to get around."

"Hey look—there's Will Stoddard," Billy cried.

"Hey, Will! You here on official business, or just being nosy like us?" I asked upon our approach.

"Both," Will answered, "It's a total loss!"

"But the sun's shinin' and the ice is off the lake!" I replied.

"Funny you say that, Ed—Milo Freeof just told me his theory that the big ones schooled up in the winter and if you got there right after '*ice-out*' you'd make a killing. Let's give it a try, Ed!"

Recalling my vow to follow Will's advice, I readily agreed. Getting there ahead of Milo would be a major feat.

"When we goin,' Will?" I asked.

"First thing in the morning—and there's a sailboat we can use, too!"

On a sunny but chilly morning I stood beside Will Stoddard on the shore of Onondaga Lake, both of us anxious to catch fish in numbers. I couldn't wait to see Milo's face when he sees what he missed. Before stepping off the seawall, Will reached down to test the water with his hand.

*"Oh my God—the water's freezin'!"* he exclaimed. *"Better not fall in!"*

*"Yes sir, Captain! No swimming today!"* I answered, loading our fishing arsenal aboard the trim craft.

A slight breeze carried us from shore, we had the entire lake with all its fish to ourselves. Will sailed westward, uncertain where to anchor until the dying wind made the decision for us. I lazily left the sail up as we hurried to send our bait down, expecting an instant response. After time passed without a single bite, Will stretched out in the stern to watch a useless line while I decided to try the other side of the boat. The sail was in my way, and I fatally tried to step around in front of the mast, rather than crawl under the boom. In an instant the boat began to tip, my weight and grip on the mast carried us over. Will had to abandon ship to avoid going in headfirst, upside-down. Engulfed in ice cold water I called out to Will. He told me to cut the anchor rope, which I did with my pocketknife. Then we tried to right the boat, but the sail was still up; it swung over and drove us both under again.

"Cut the halyards!" Will shouted.

"Okay, Will!" I croaked.

Through great exertion we brought our wreck to a level, but bailing was out of the question. Will still wanted to save the boat, claiming that land wasn't far off and that we were both good swimmers. Despite creating the fix we were in, I instantly forgot the lesson of living for others and desired my captain to go down with the ship. Will's desire prevailed, however, with one of us swimming in front pulling a bow rope, the other pushing and kicking from behind. My body screamed against the frigid water, I expected to soon go under for good.

Our mishap was observed onshore, bad news traveled fast. We saw a party of sportsmen who tried the water, but decided it was too cold to save us. They stood ashore, watching us struggle towards them. We arrived, so chilled that they had to pull us out of the lake, nearly insensible. They were good fellows to strip our corpses and rub us in the way prescribed for resuscitation. Prostrate on our backs, I turned my head toward Will, who looked like a carp with his purple lips twitching up at the sky. We were both stricken, but after a while regained our footing. Then a rowboat came along and we got into it while our rescuers followed with the sailboat. The exercise of rowing to Salina was good for us, once there we secured a cart ride home. Arriving at Will's house feeling as cold as the grave, we found and drank all that was left in his father's bottle of old Madeira wine. False rumors of our demise began to spread, but seeing us both alive put an end to it.

A knock at our door brought an unexpected visit from Mrs. Loguen, accompanied by lawyer George B. Vashon.

"Hello Caroline, hello George—come in, come in!" Ma greeted.

"Thank you, Ellen," Mrs. Loguen replied. Mr. Vashon nodded, saying "Ma'am" while he tipped his hat and followed Mrs. Loguen inside. The two Georges shook hands.

"So what brings you both here today?" Ma asked cheerily.

Mrs. Loguen answered, "We were going to George's office to write some letters, but when I saw you in the window I thought to stop—been meanin' to for bout' a week now!"

"I'm glad that you did," Ma answered. "What are all the letters about?"

"Well, we's tryin' to get the state officials to convince Governor Hunt to let Jermain come home."

"How is Jermain getting by in Canada, Caroline?" Ma asked.

"Better than most runaways, I suppose. His voice is heard from the pulpit, but his heart is home with his family, and the son he never met," Mrs. Loguen answered.

"I can't imagine how difficult it must be for him, Caroline—for *all* of you!"

"We doin' the best we can, but it sure be hard sometimes."

Mr. Vashon said, "The Anti-Slavery Association of Canada met last month in Toronto and they think that between five and six thousand refugees entered Canada in the past two years, comprising thirty-thousand colored persons living in that country now."

Using my experience from attending Syracuse rallies, I asked, "Mr. Vashon, they must've made resolutions at that meeting in Canada. Do you know what any of 'em were?"

"Yes, I do, Edward—they resolved their opposition to the *American Colonization Society* that's chiefly supported by slaveholders! They were grateful for the bravery of the American clergymen who exposed the atrocities of the *Fugitive Slave Law*, but they deplored the indifference of other church leaders. Lastly, they resolved that as British subjects enjoying the blessings of freedom, they rejoiced to offer shelter and protection to the poor, persecuted Americans flying from the grasp of their heartless countrymen."

"Wow—I'd call that a shot across the bow, Mr. Vashon!"

"And rightly so, the legislature in Pennsylvania voted to repeal the act of 1847 that prohibited the jails of the Commonwealth to be used for the detention of fugitive slaves."

Ma interjected, "But Senator Hale presented two petitions, numerously signed, for repeal of the *Fugitive Slave Law*—that offers some hope, doesn't it?"

Mr. Vashon answered, "Not when there aren't enough supporters behind it, but it's a start! State Senator Munroe just gave an excellent speech in which he maintained that the action of the *American Colonization Society* is:

- *To degrade the free colored people of the United States to prevent them from having and enjoying political and social advantages, and by doing so to drive them to consent to emigrate from their native land.*
- *To confirm the domestic slave trade.*
- *To perpetuate and give security to the system of slavery in this country.*

It takes a man of conviction to speak like that before the State Legislature," the lawyer pled.

"That's true, Mr. Vashon, but you forgot what's giving people the most hope for seeing an end to slavery," I stated.

"Do tell, sir," the big man replied.

"The new book, *Uncle Tom's Cabin*, is flying off the shelves! Pa got us a copy and we're all fighting over who gets to read it next."

"Henry Ward Beecher's sister Harriet wrote it!" Ma said, showing pride of her gender.

Black George said, "I don't reads a lot, but what I hears make me glad I ain't workin' a plantation some where's."

"It's a heartbreaking story, but I have enough of my own at present," Mrs. Loguen remarked with sorrow.

Ma encouraged, "Well, good luck with the letter campaign, Caroline—you have the right lawyer for sure!"

"Thank you, Ellen—Mr. Vashon's doin' God's work in helpin' us bring Jermain back home."

Listening to the conversation made me wonder whatever became of my friends, the Ward family. I sure hoped that Sam and everyone were okay.

At month's end, endless rain hindered our move to Fayette Park, a mile distant down muddy Genesee Street. Between loads, I suggested hiring canal boys, but Ma wouldn't hear of it. We soldiered on, sometimes caught by torrential downpours.

While distracted by our move, Kentucky Senator Henry Clay turned seventy-five, his feeble health of national concern. One day he's improving, the next day he's feeling worse, and so on. I suspected that the majority of Syracusans showed interest in Clay's health, certainly all of the Whigs did, and many Democrats, but definitely not Charles A. Wheaton.

"Henry Clay's the man to thank for the *Fugitive Slave Law*, Edward—it could never have passed without him!" Pa said with conviction at our new house. He recently took issue with an article in the *Daily Star* that scoffed at the idea of there being a *Higher Law,* and Pa hated the author's misuse of scripture, as he put it. Still, the paper printed his rebuttal. Pa wrote,

"Jerry likes the scripture that you quoted on Saturday. He told me he didn't care to be a slave, but chose freedom rather, and put to Canada! Don't you think that he acted like a man? If you sympathize with the slave catching business, or are inclined to sneer at the idea that God's law is "higher," or is to be obeyed when man's law conflicts with it, you are a more hopeless sinner than I expected to come amongst us, even from south of the Mason-Dixon line."

"So, I guess this means that you're not worried about Henry Clay, huh, Pa?" I asked.

"Not in the least—I'm more concerned with the safe return of Jermain Loguen."

"Yeah, we saw Mrs. Loguen right before we moved and she seemed kinda sad."

"I would expect so," he replied. "She carries many burdens."

# Chapter Twenty-Five
## (May 1852)

Half the family joined Ma for church on Sunday at the new Baptist church where the Rev. Mr. Sunderland preached from the text, "All Souls are Mine." Speaking for my siblings, we all loved him for keeping it short and sweet. Standing in the line of departing churchgoers, Ma shared her learned assessment.

"He reasoned it out very well, Edward, and he conveyed some good, sound, Anti-Slavery truth. I liked how he directed us to the story of *Uncle Tom's Cabin*, and I could tell that he heartily endorsed the views it contained."

"You're right, Ma," I agreed. "He made everyone feel bad that Rev. Loguen had to escape to Canada while his family struggles."

Ma said, "The other day, Rev. Sunderland told your father that he was entirely converted to the Anti-Slavery cause, and I should judge that he's going to work for it in earnest!"

Small groups gathered at the back of the church, where several side conversations were happening all at once. I tried to listen to as many as I could.

"Did you hear about of the shooting of a fugitive slave in Columbia, Pennsylvania?"

"Yes—I heard it was a policeman, not the slave owner's agent, who pulled the trigger!"

"I read that the Maryland House of Delegates voted to promote African colonization."

"True, and they want the State Treasury to fund it!"

"The 18th Annual Meeting of the *American Anti-Slavery Society* will be in Rochester this month because New York City's still closed to them."

"What will come of McGrawville College now that they're accepting blacks for medical school? It's said the next class will include some of *Jerry's Rescuers!*"

"Yes, and that an endowment was made to this *pet-negro* institution to establish a new department."

"Some editors feel bound to protest against the school's existence. One claimed that there's a scheme afoot to engraft upon the teachings of medicine with the doctrines of negro philanthropy."

"Take heart, gentlemen, perhaps Wendell Phillips will speak here after he departs from Rochester!"

I was content to linger and listen, but my siblings had other ideas.

We had many reasons to like our new house, but the best part was its proximity to Clinton Square—now only several blocks distant. The arrival of Packet boats crammed with passengers drew both spectators and speculators alike, creating fun opportunities to observe humanity. Pickpockets worked the crowd, preying upon the unwary.

With May half over and the sun shining, I joined the loafers on the Salina Street bridge to enjoy the show. Examining the crowd, I spotted the Cheney brothers, who hadn't seen me yet.

"Hey, Prentice! Hey, Si! What took ya so long?" I kidded.

"Hey, Ed! It's still a mile walk for us," Si answered.

"That's right, rich boy—we didn't move to Fayette Park like you," Prentice chided.

"You should have been here last week, Ed," Si began, "Captain Luther had the *Monterey* full-up—musta had about eighty passengers!"

"Yeah, the packet boat business is up so far this year—everyone's sayin' it," Prentice agreed.

"Yeah? And how's the steamer business going, Prentice?" I asked with a wry smile.

"Actually, Wheaton, it's been great! Senators Mallory and Stockton backed the resolution to build a war steamer for defense of the New York harbor!"

"That's a good one, Prentice! Got any more?"

"Sure, the US Mail steamer, *Crescent City*, arrived with $3,000,000 in gold dust!"

"Again? We gotta go west before all the gold is gone!"

Si stood quietly, so I asked, "How about you, Si—any good news?"

"No, Ed. Henry Clay's gonna croak in six weeks."

"Yeah, I read that too, and that President Filmore went to visit him."

"Hey, I have more good news," Prentice alerted, "Here comes Charlie Willard!"

I entreated, "Hey, Charlie! Tell us about the great performers in town—I heard that you saw Catherine Hayes and Lola Montez, too."

"That's right, Ed. Catherine Hayes sang beautiful, and she ain't so bad to look at either."

*Catherine Hayes*

"We heard that, Charlie, how was Lola Montez?" Prentice asked.

"Ha! That Lola Montez is nothing like Jenny Lind, Teresa Parodi, or Catherine Hayes—she's a dancer, and her show was a lot *seedier*," Charlie replied.

"What's that supposed to mean?" Si asked.

"If you saw the way she danced, you'd know! With her tight costumes and unique gyrations she had the Salt Pointers on the edge of their seats. Her dancing was peculiar, to say the least, but the audience left gratified."

"Tell us more, Charlie!" Si encouraged.

"Well, it was a one night only performance at the National Theater, Si. Mr. Hough's gamble to engage the *Countess of Landsfeldt* really paid off—the place was full! Twelve ladies and gentlemen from the Broadway Theatre accompanied Lola—brilliantly, I must say."

"I wished I was there!" Si answered.

"It really was a great show, but there were some who didn't like her smokin' cigarettes, saying it wasn't becoming of a lady. But from what I seen, Lola don't care none. When she was down at the Globe Hotel, she said that she'd never lodge at a Temperance House again because *all they got are bed bugs and Bibles.*"

*Lola Montez*

"What about the crowd, Charlie?" Prentice asked.

"It was a large one, all right, but maybe not so fashionable, like for Catherine Hayes. And like I said, the Salt Pointers loved her. A bunch of 'em saw her off at the station when she took the midnight train to Buffalo after the show."

"So what's next, Charlie?" I asked. "You're our local reporter for live entertainment!"

"Ha—you're right! The next thing is the return of the Black Swan—she's playing Malcolm Hall later this month."

"Really? I gotta tell Black George—we both wanna see her again!"

"I'll be there, Ed—she sings as good as anybody."

We soon tired of people watching from the bridge, opting to inspect the new location of the police office at the Market Building.

Police Justice Sylvester House beamed as he stood in his new *first floor* office. He'd always despised the Clinton Street location, especially the bridge. Ever since the Jerry Rescuers gutted the place he pressed to relocate, marshalling support at every opportunity.

Today, the judge shared his good humor. When Matilda Ryan was brought in for vagrancy, he released her on a simple promise to find work. Watching from the rear, a sobered drunk promised to leave town immediately, and the Judge told him to *start now*. The Police Justice reveled in having a night shift, hoping the rowdies took notice.

Officer Thomas Davis appeared, having just arrested J.R. Miller for passing counterfeit bills. Before that he'd made arrests for wife beating and public intoxication. I wondered if his butcher pa encouraged him to look the other way sometimes, but Parish Johnson was right; Officer Davis was already making a name for himself.

On our way out, we encountered Parish himself, quite surprised to see us.

"Hey guys! How'd ya like the new Police Office?" he asked with enthusiasm.

"It's a lot better than the old one, that's for sure!" Charlie Willard answered.

"So, did you hear if they caught the guy who threw the rock through the window at Graff's Tavern? Frederick Meyer got hit right over the eye."

"No, Parish, we didn't hear about that—just a vagrant, a drunk, and a counterfeiter," I said.

"Nothin' on Shel Webster then? He broke out of the penitentiary again with the *Canada Racer*."

"Never heard a no *Canada Racer*, who's that?" Prentice asked.

"His name's really Thomas Ashton, and they call him the *Racer* 'cause he gives "leg bail" to the officers who try to keep him in custody. He hung around the city after he busted loose, and stole six shirts from somebody's house. Officer James found him hiding in a barn wearing two of the shirts with the rest in his possession."

"He's a good one, that Officer James," I said.

Parish answered, "Yeah, and we almost lost him! When he was arresting a desperate character by the canal locks, the villain pulled a gun and took aim but it didn't fire."

"That was a lucky escape!" Charlie said.

"It sure was," Parish answered. "Justice House examined the pistol and found it charged with powder and ball—it's a miracle that nobody was killed!"

Losing interest in police business, Prentice asked, "Now what?" when the sound of brass horns and the pounding beat of drums answered his question.

"Oh yeah, I forgot about the fire department review! There's a short parade, then they're gonna test all the equipment at the canal basin," he announced.

"Ha—we just had a good spot on the bridge! C'mon guys, let's go!" I shouted

Today was the annual review of the Syracuse Fire Department, including all of the different fire companies and their machines. Kellogg's Brass Band led the uniformed firemen on parade, accompanied by Chief Engineer, B.L. Higgins, and several Aldermen. After the lively parade, the firemen set up on the northeast side of the Packet Basin to demonstrate their equipment. While the various machines exhibited great power, the firehoses didn't fare as well, with many bursting under the high water pressure. After a fine looking *gutta percha* hose yielded, an unseen voice uttered,

"I heard that kinda hose is useless in frosty weather!"

To which someone answered, "Don't appear to work when its warm, neither."

At the end, several fine speeches were made, including one from the Chief Engineer who addressed the hose breakage to the Common Council, insisting that the department deserved quality equipment to perform their duties. His speech was well received, and the crowd seemed satisfied with the annual review. Then, I noticed a spark of realization in Parish Johnson's eyes.

"Hey Ed, there's Peter Petrie and I gotta talk to him!" he blurted excitedly, stepping hurriedly toward the city's official dog killer. We followed behind to observe.

"Hello, Mr. Petrie," Parish began, "I wanted to ask you about the new ordinances for killing dogs!"

"Oh, I remember you," Petrie answered, "You're the kid who's always hanging around the Police Office."

"That's right, sir. With all the mad dogs roaming the city, people are afraid of getting bit and dying a slow, painful death from hydrophobia."

"Hydro what? I thought it was rabies," Petrie replied.

"Yes sir, it is—Doctor Hoyt told me it's the late stage of rabies and it hurts when you try to swallow water."

"I suppose that's what all the fuss is about then," the canine executioner pronounced.

"The new ordinance goes into effect on June 15th, Mr. Petrie, that's when all the street commissioners are ordered to kill, or cause to be killed, all the unmuzzled dogs they can find."

"That's right young man—and that's when they'll ask me to do it for them!"

"What about poison, Mr. Petrie? The council passed an ordinance on that, too."

"Yes they did, and it's a good thing! There's crazy people leavin' bits of poisoned cake around that a child could easily find. The Council authorized a ten dollar reward for the conviction of anyone poisoning a dog, and fifty dollars for anyone scattering poison."

"I'm glad, Mr. Petrie, there's been a lot of dogs poisoned around here lately!" Parish said.

"Anything else you wanna know, sonny?" Petrie asked.

"You're not worried about the street commissioners taking your business, then?"

"Nope, business has never been better," the hired executioner replied.

Starting around mid-May, Syracusans went nuts over the Hungarian exile, Lajos Kossuth. During a public meeting chaired by Mayor Woodruff, the details of his welcome were debated, including whether to fund it publicly or privately. Ultimately, the city treasury was chosen over private subscriptions.

Although nobody knew exactly when Kossuth would arrive, the best guess was sometime in early June. His persistent health issues made scheduling a challenge. Before his official visit, the hero made a short stop in Syracuse where a large crowd gathered at the train depot to catch a glimpse of him on his way to Niagara Falls to recuperate.

After Kossuth departed, I heard all about it from the Cook brothers. They were upset because he dined at the Syracuse House, but the overflow crowd landed at Cook's Coffee House, much to Mr. Cook's delight.

Austin said, "You should have seen it Ed! When Kossuth's train pulled up at the station, there were a whole bunch of people waiting, and when he stepped out of the cars, a loud cheer broke out! His wife was with him, and some of his entourage, but he was only in Syracuse while his train was stopped."

"So how'd he end up at the Syracuse House, then?" I asked.

"I guess that Mr. Gillette invited him, and the *Committee of Arrangements* escorted him there and back. But he looked pretty tired to me, Ed!"

"Yeah, I heard that Kossuth wrote a letter to the mayor saying that he's worn out and is hastening to Niagara Falls to rest and recover," I replied.

"And Kossuth won't say when he's returning until after he feels better," Austin concluded.

On Friday, May 28th, the headlines announced that Kossuth would visit Syracuse next Thursday! However, on Saturday, the papers reported that he'd arrive on Monday instead, leaving the *Reception*

*Committee* with just one day to prepare. Pa and Mr. Crandal were part of the large group working to accommodate the accelerated schedule. Syracuse's German residents were particularly eager to welcome the Hungarian nobleman, holding their own meetings to make their own plans. Mr. George Saul, of course, was right in the middle of it. The *Standard* announced that Kossuth would address the Germans on Tuesday night at City Hall.

At half past seven on the morning of Kossuth's arrival, the *Committee of Escort* proceeded to Auburn to conduct the distinguished exile to Syracuse. By nine o'clock, they were introduced to him at the residence of New York Senator William H. Seward, where Kossuth was staying. Then they all went to the train depot, Kossuth, the mayor, the committees, and the band, where more speeches were made at the crowded station. Everywhere he went it was the same thing—a full day of hearing and making speeches. He thought to himself in Hungarian,

"Ez a szar kezd megöregedn—*This shit is getting old.*"

As the party stepped aboard the Syracuse train, three cheers were given for Kossuth and Hungary, and when the train reached Geddes a salute of artillery sounded, which started the church bells ringing in Syracuse. Flags and streamers adorned the downtown buildings as the streets filled with people—everyone anxious to view the illustrious exile. When Kossuth at last made his appearance sporting his popular "Kossuth hat," the multitude sent up a shout that made the welkin ring.

*Lajos Kossuth*

Kossuth was immediately conducted to a stand erected in front of City Hall, where the city leaders had a full-grown bald eagle on display. Mayor Woodruff welcomed him, saying,

"Sir, it gives me great pleasure to receive you in the city of Syracuse, and as its Chief Magistrate, to tender you a heart-felt and cordial welcome, and to extend to yourself and suite, its hospitalities!"

Kossuth replied,

"Mr. Mayor—I must humbly and cordially thank you for the honor of this reception and for the consolation and joy which is connected with it! There is something stirring and emblematic in the associations of this reception. Here before me I have the Eagle of America with spread wings ready to soar up to Heaven (cheers) so I take it to suggest an idea that the people of America are about to soar among the nations of the earth in their power and might. I would suggest only one alteration . . ."

Then Kossuth took in his hand the eagle which stood at his feet, and raised it over his head.

"I would see this Eagle of America elevated above the head of humanity (cheers) with spread wing in protection of the law of nature and of nature's God! (cheers). Continue to ring that bell, gentlemen—we will add the ringing of cannon, and the triumph of Liberty must be sure!"

A procession including a large contingent of Germans then formed in prescribed order, proceeding up Genesee Street along the familiar parade route ending at the park where Kossuth was greeted by the school children of Syracuse. The mayor again welcomed and introduced Kossuth to the crowd, Kossuth spoke, followed by the local leaders of education who, in turn, were answered by the champion of freedom.

Then the procession reformed to deposit the governor at the Globe Hotel for a short rest before the three o'clock proceedings at the First Presbyterian Church. It all made me think that Kossuth was smart to lay low at Niagara Falls for a while.

Promptly at three, accompanied by the mayor, Common Council, and *Committee of Arrangements*, Kossuth proceeded to the overflowing church where admission could be purchased for one dollar. A sort of bond or certificate was given, declaring that the Independent State of Hungary, one year after being securely established, will pay to the bearer one dollar upon demand.

After stirring music by Kellogg's Band and the singing of the choir, ex-mayor Baldwin welcomed Kossuth at length, to which Kossuth replied in kind, frequently interrupted with sympathy and approval. At the close, a great outburst of applause and cheering ensued. Today's gathering netted $1,000 for the Hungarian cause—Kossuth had gained another $600 in Auburn.

The hero was then conducted back to the Globe Hotel, concluding the day's itinerary. His plans had changed again, however, now he'd be leaving on the morning train to Utica, but he did say that he'd receive his German friends at the hotel, not at City Hall as previously announced. First, however, there was a magnificent party planned in Kossuth's honor at ex-mayor Leavenworth's palatial home on James Street—the one with the big, white pillars and the streetlamp out front.

*"Absolutely not!"* was the answer that I got from Ma about going to the Kossuth party tonight.

"Why not, Ma?" I protested. "You and Pa are going — even Charlotte!"

"But we were invited Edward — who do you think you are?"

"I'm fifteen now, Ma, and ready to make my way in the world! Ain't that why you and Pa pulled me out of school till I go to college?"

*Leavenworth Residence*

"Yes, you're ready to learn the ways of the world, and it starts with this—*you weren't invited!*"

"Yeah, but they'd let me in if I was with you."

"Probably, but it would be rude of me to impose—case closed!"

I could see it was hopeless, but little Henry gave me an idea to lash out with.

"Hey, Ma—I bet that Kossuth picks his nose just like everyone else! Let me know if you catch him, won't you?"

For my ingenuity, she said, "And for that you're staying home tonight."

Hanging out with my seven younger siblings, Black George, and the kitchen maid wasn't my idea of having fun while a high society function happened without me. I should have been there with Kossuth, rubbing elbows with the politicians and all the local bigshots, half of 'em high on the booze.

It was after eleven when my parents returned with Cousin Charlotte from the Kossuth gala. Me and Ellen started right in with the questions.

"So how was it, Ma? Did you get to meet him?" I asked.

"We sure did, Edward! Mr. Leavenworth presented us to the governor and we all shook his hand," Ma replied.

Ellen said, "Wow—I'm jealous! Charlotte, did you meet his wife?"

"Yes, indeed, she seemed very kindhearted to me, Ellen!" Charlotte answered happily.

"Was it really crowded, Ma?" I asked.

"Of course it was—and a very fashionable crowd, I should add!"

"What do you mean? None of the ladies wore bloomers? Ha!"

"No indeed! There you go again."

"I thought it was all the rage for ladies' fashions."

"Not for society events on James Street."

Ellen asked, "Ma, did you have a chance to talk to Kossuth, or were you just introduced?"

"Yes, we spoke, and somehow the topic of discussion moved to religion. He said, As to the Catholic religion, I indeed am a Protestant, not only by birth but by conviction, and warmly penetrated by this conviction I would delight to see this conviction shared by the whole world. But before all, I am morally opposed to intolerance and to sectarianism. I consider religion to be a matter of conscience, which every man has to arrange between God and himself."

"He's a deep thinker, Ma—and he sure can talk. I lost track of how many speeches he gave."

"That's how he's raising money for Hungary's freedom, Edward—now go to bed!"

Despite Kossuth's seemingly endless oratory, the local Germans felt the hero was still one speech short. They'd raised over three hundred dollars for the Hungarian cause and wished to present it to him personally, *en masse*, at Market Hall. They believed that Kossuth would still address them, and so marched to the meeting place on Tuesday morning led by Samsel's band. I went down to watch and ran into George Pfohl and Milo Freeof amongst many unhappy looking Germans.

"Hey, guys! What's with all the long faces down here?" I asked.

"Hey, Ed—looks like Kossuth ain't gonna address us, that's what!" Milo said.

"That sucks! Why the hell not?"

George answered, "He said it's because of his ill health and busy schedule, but we don't care about how busy he was because he always said that he'd address us, even though he blew us off last night."

"Hmm, I hadn't heard that George, tell me!"

"So, you must know about the Kossuth party at the Leavenworth's last night," George began.

"Sure I do—my folks were there, and they met him," I replied.

"Well, if he was healthy enough for a party then he could've said some words to us, but he didn't have time. Then, back at the hotel after the party, he wouldn't acknowledge the serenade provided by Samsel's band with the singers from the German Musical Institute."

"Kinda hard to ignore a brass band, don't you think?"

"Not for Kossuth! He had Counselor D.D. Hillis fill in for him—you know this guy, Ed?"

"I hope so—just moved in next door to 'im."

Milo joined, saying, "So Hillis came out and addressed the crowd, sayin' that the governor would speak to them in the morning, but I don't expect that to happen."

"Why you say that, Milo?"

"Because he should've been here already! Mr. Saul and Dr. Elsner went to the Globe to ask Kossuth to come here to speak but they both looked doubtful when they left."

Milo's words rang true when all eyes alerted to the grim looking committee of two who'd just returned from the Globe Hotel. Mr. Saul ascended the platform to relate what had transpired.

"We found him on his feet, busy shaking hands, and told him our wishes, but he said that he was too unwell and engaged. I suggested that if he were well enough to stand and shake hands then he could take a short carriage ride to Market Hall and say a few words. Kossuth replied that he'd receive us at the hotel, but I repeated that it was the earnest wish of the German people to see him at Market Hall."

Dr. Elsner said, "That's when a Mr. Hammerer stepped forward and assured Kossuth that the greater part of the Germans will come here—at least the better part of them!"

"And if Mr. Hammerer is the better part of them, then it's no wonder that Kossuth has a bad opinion of us!" Mr. Saul announced with bitterness.

*George Saul*

Several speakers followed, each with great indignation at the treatment that the Germans had received. Mr. Saul spoke again, reminding the large gathering how the they'd been misused, how the Germans made up the greater part of yesterday's procession, that their band played the best music, but still, the German citizens were thrown back among the crowd.

Mr. D.D. Hillis spoke next, stating that Kossuth would receive them in the dining room of the Globe Hotel. George Saul responded that the Germans felt themselves too good to be received in the dining room like servants, if the Americans were received in the parlor. Besides that, the Globe couldn't accommodate their numbers.

Mr. Hillis departed to try again, but Kossuth remained firm about staying at the hotel. I thought I heard Mr. Saul remark that Kossuth can go to the devil! Then a murmuring began when a man unknown to me entered the hall.

"Who's that, George?" I asked.

"That's Mr. Hammerer! I'm surprised that he'd show his face here," George replied.

A loud hissing overtook the hall with shouts of *"Kick him out!"* echoing in the rafters. Hammerer wisely took the hint to depart with speed.

With calm restored, several resolutions were passed, with the meeting adjourned to June 12th. The Germans then marched through the streets again, but this time with their flags rolled up and carried upside down. Three cheers were given for Alderman Ackerman, who'd stood by them faithfully, and for the great music from Samsel's band. Mr. Saul vowed never to be fooled again, and instead of giving the money to Kossuth, they started a German newspaper.

# Chapter Twenty-Six

## (June 1852)

Though only here for a day, Kossuth remained the talk of the town. Accounts of his presence filled the newspapers, competing with headlines for the Democratic Party National Convention happening in Baltimore at the *Maryland Institute for the Promotion of the Mechanic Arts*.

Heading into the convention, Lewis Cass of Michigan, the Democrat's nominee in 1848, was again the front runner, followed by James Buchanan, Stephen A. Douglass, and William L. Marcy. Despite leading the first nineteen ballots, Cass failed to secure the required two-thirds majority. Each day, newspapers reported the official results and political maneuverings. On the twentieth ballot, James Buchanan pulled ahead, but still fell short of the nomination.

On the third day of the Convention (Thursday), Syracuse was asked to support another foreign hero. A public meeting at City Hall was planned to invite Thomas Francis Meagher, celebrated by the Irish for his role in the 1848 rebellion. Sentenced to death for sedition and high treason, Meagher's sentence was commuted to life at Van Diemen's Land, south of Australia. But the clever Irishman managed to escape, making his way to America where he received a hero's welcome.

Charlie Pope accompanied me to the Meagher rally, both of us anxious to learn how the city would respond to yet another foreign exile. Arriving early for the eight o'clock start, we joined the enthusiastic crowd hoping to welcome Thomas F. Meager to Syracuse. Mayor Woodruff was made President, with ex-Mayor Baldwin and James Lynch as vice presidents. Messrs. McCarthy, Hall, Gardner, Foran, and Bagg were chosen for the committee to draft resolutions. In their absence, Mr. Baldwin made an eloquent speech.

> **Enthusiastic Public Meeting FOR HONORS TO THOMAS F. MEAGHER.**

When the committee returned from deliberating, the preamble and resolutions were read amid much applause.

"Whereas, that distinguished Irish exile, Thomas Francis Meagher, has providentially escaped from a British penal colony, and arrived safely on the shores of our free Republic, And, Whereas, this escape is truly gratifying to his fellow-countrymen in America, as well as to every lover of Liberty. Therefore,

Resolved, That the Representative in Congress from this, the 24th district, the Hon. Daniel T. Jones be and he is hereby requested to urge immediately upon Congress the passage of a law granting to Thomas F. Meagher the rights and citizenship of this government, without the formality of the present law of naturalization and citizenship."

Charlie leaned over and said,

"Did you hear that, Ed? They wanna give Meagher the fast track to becoming a citizen!"

"Yeah—I bet there's a committee going out to Baldwinsville to see Dr. Jones about getting that new law written."

Mr. McCarthy, on call, then read Meagher's address upon his conviction for treason and before his sentence, to which the audience exploded with applause. Three hearty cheers were given for Thomas Francis Meagher and Liberty to adjourn the meeting.

"Well, Charlie—looks to me like the invitation's in the mail!" I proclaimed.

"Sure does—you think Meagher will accept?"

"I hope so—if he's doing a tour he probably will."

"I think you're right—but for now we'll just have to watch the Convention returns from Baltimore!"

The Democrat Convention in Baltimore struggled to nominate a candidate. On Saturday, day 5, Franklin Pierce of New Hampshire appeared on the 35th ballot with 15 votes. By the 40th ballot, Pierce had 29 votes, and by the 47th ballot he reached 55. On the 49th ballot, deafening shouts were heard as state after state changed their votes for Pierce, giving him the nomination with 283 votes, winning all but five. A national salute was fired and the convention adjourned until four o'clock.

At six o'clock, Mr. William R. King of Alabama was nominated for vice president on only the second ballot. When I mentioned the disparity to Ma she remarked,

*Franklin Pierce*

"That only shows how little people think of the vice president."

I asked her why, and she said,

"It seems the only time he's important is when the president dies."

"You mean like Filmore and Tyler?"

"Yes, like Filmore and Tyler—and I won't be surprised if the Whigs nominate General Scott instead."

"I won't be surprised either, Ma," I conceded.

On Wednesday, June 16th, the Whig Party began their National Convention at the same venue in Baltimore with General Winfield Scott slightly favored over President Filmore, and Daniel Webster a

distant third. Meanwhile, Syracuse focused on the *Fifth Annual Meeting* of the *New York State Temperance Society* at City Hall on Thursday and Friday. Pa was scheduled to speak, and the event was expected to be lively with female delegates like Miss Susan B. Anthony from Rochester, and Mrs. Stanton and Mrs. Bloomer from Seneca Falls. Charlie Pope and I attended.

On Thursday morning, the Society's President, Mr. Herman Camp, opened the proceedings, followed by a prayer from Rev. Mandeville. After an eloquent speech by Mr. Camp, Pa stepped forward to read the Constitution of the Society.

Charlie elbowed me and said, "Your pa's up next, Ed!"

As Pa began reading in his clear, commanding voice, I wondered if he'd be singing later. After he finished, Mr. Burleigh read the Annual Report that showed the temperance cause flourishing in New York State. The report advocated passing the *"Maine Law,"* backed by statistics that showed a great decline in pauperism and crime in Maine, and elsewhere, due to laws that suppressed the sale of intoxicating liquors.

After Mr. Burleigh sat down, the convention turned on its head from an objection to an allusion in the report to the *Women's Temperance Society*. The debate quickly intensified, but was adjourned until the afternoon session.

Stepping outside into the sunshine, Charlie said, "You know, Ed, it's kinda funny how they're having a big *Temperance Convention* and right down the hall the City Clerk's taking applications for new liquor licenses!"

"Ha! I never thought about that—I'll have to tell Pa," I replied.

"Well, he's right there," Charlie alerted, pointing directly at him.

"Yeah, he's getting' into our carriage now with Miss Anthony and Mrs. Bloomer. C'mon Charlie, I bet he's bringing the ladies home for dinner!"

Ma wasn't surprised to see us, she'd had Black George restock the pantry so there was plenty for everyone. It wasn't unusual for us to take in lodgers for a big event, this being no exception. Several guests had arrived last night.

After greeting Pa and the ladies, Ma said, "Hello boys! I'm going to attend this afternoon, did I miss anything good?"

Charlie answered, "Hello Mrs. Wheaton, I think the best part's coming up, Ma'am."

"Charlie's right, Ma—the *Women's Temperance Society* left 'em all flustered!"

Saying that got everyone's attention, they all leaned in as Ma remarked, *"Oh, really?"*

"Absolutely, Ma, things were heating up right before the break."

The ladies were amused by our analogy of the meeting. I think I embarrassed Pa when I said, *"Yeah, Pa got to speak at another convention—but so far he ain't sung yet'."*

I thought I heard Black George chuckle from the next room.

Ma quipped, *"Don't worry, Edward—there's still time!"* and everyone laughed.

The Convention reconvened at two o'clock when Rev. Mandeville moved to strike out that portion of the report which referred to the *Women's State Temperance Society*, offering a lengthy argument to support his position. Mandeville desired to keep females in their proper sphere and believed the cooperation of this Society would be an endorsement of the *peculiar doctrines* and notions of the *Women's Temperance Society*.

Mr. Burleigh replied that as the author of the report he desired to make an explanation, and to defend the allusion to the *Women's Temperance Society*, saying that it wasn't to endorse their doctrines, nor to dictate the proper course that females should take to aid the cause of Temperance.

W. C. Wisner, of Lockport, then opposed the paragraph referred to. He said that *if we cooperate with the Women's Society, we should be obliged to admit their delegates to seats upon this floor, and the right to vote and take part in the deliberations of the Convention.* This, he declared, would lead to bad results, and seriously impair the influence of the State Society.

Mr. Havens, of New York, desired to introduce an amendment which he thought would satisfy all parties, He read a paragraph, the substance being that *female influence is all very well in its proper place, but their action should be restrained to the family and social circle, where they can be more efficient than at the ballot box.*

Rev. Mr. Coles, of Allegany, objected, stating it was absurd for the Convention to dictate the sphere in which women should act. It was ridiculous to say that such females as Mrs. Stanton, Mrs. Gerrit Smith, and Miss Susan B. Anthony, were *unsexing* themselves by forming a State Temperance Society, and sending delegates to this convention. The friends of Temperance had always invoked the aid and influence of females, and now the first movement on their part was frowned upon, and their delegates excluded from a voice in the deliberations of this body.

Animated discussions ensued, but the amendment of Mr. Havens was adopted, and the paragraph was incorporated in the report. Just when things were calming down, Rev. May offered a resolution that the ladies present as delegates should be allowed to vote, and to take part in the deliberations of the convention, which started another round of excited discussion. In the midst of it all, Miss Anthony rose to speak, which increased the excitement tenfold! Half a dozen gentlemen jumped to their feet, as cries of *"Mr. President," "Mr. Chairman,"* were heard from every quarter of the house. Miss Anthony stood her ground nobly amid the noise and confusion. The chairman lost his temper, declaring that he would vacate the chair unless the gentlemen (and ladies) kept order. He then declared Miss. Anthony out of order, and she sat down.

"I never seen anything like this, Charlie!" I uttered.

"Me neither, Ed! Women's Rights are right up there with Temperance."

Then an appeal was taken from the chair, the ladies rose to vote, but they weren't counted. I sensed Ma's agitation when someone said that *for a Temperance Convention, this was about as intemperate as it gets.*

Before the afternoon session closed, Rev. May announced that Mrs. Stanton would deliver an address at the Wesleyan Methodist Chapel in the evening (while the convention reconvened for an evening session). Ma said that she planned to attend the church, as did my father. Considerable dissatisfaction was expressed at the unceremonious treatment of the lady delegates.

When the convention adjourned, Charlie said excitedly, "I'll meet ya here tomorrow morning, Ed, when Miss Anthony rose to speak it got so loud they mighta heard it in Brewerton!"

"That's for sure—I'll ask 'em at the Emmons' Store by the bridge!"

That evening, in company of my parents, I sat up front at the well-attended Wesleyan church to hear the ladies present the claims of their society. Unlike at the *Temperance Convention,* this audience couldn't wait to hear them.

Mrs. Stanton delivered boldly as promised, followed by Miss Anthony, who read a speech that she'd written especially for the convention. She ridiculed the idea that woman owes any alliance to man, demanding for her sex all the rights enjoyed by the sterner sex, even to the ballot box. She closed with a series of resolutions that re-affirmed those opinions. Once concluded, loud calls were made for Mrs. Bloomer, who rose to make a few remarks. After that, a song from Charles A. Wheaton ended the meeting!

Ma winked at me and said, "What did I tell you?"

*Elizabeth Cady Stanton with Susan B. Anthony*

Day two of the convention began at nine o'clock with the president seated. The Business Committee submitted several resolutions, including one that *invited persons of all classes, ages, sexes, conditions, and color, to cooperate with this Society in their efforts to promote the cause of Temperance.* Passions swirled around this point until the Convention adjourned for the dinner hour.

Restless and hungry, Charlie and I set off for Cook's Coffee House. At the street corner ahead, two men were engaged in animated conversation.

Charlie joked, "Hey Ed, ain't that your butcher friend, Davis up, there? Looks like he's fussin' with his son, the new policeman."

Charlie identified the pair correctly, drawing closer we overheard words about the temperance pledge being circulated ahead of the 4th of July.

"Ah, so you're a Star of Temperance now, is that it?" Cale Davis bellowed.

"Aye, that I am, so there it is! I'm tired of the endless parade of drunk and disorderlies," son Thomas responded.

"They never bothered you before," Cale persisted.

"True, but you get a different perspective at the watch house."

"Listen to you! Now your pals with Oliver Teall, I suppose?"

Recognizing me approaching, Cale Davis added, "Yes, I can see you sitting down to drink lemonade with Olly Teall, Rev. May, and Charles A. Wheaton!"

"Don't forget Stoddard, Bickford, Cobb, and Williston," Thomas retorted.

"A lot of good it will do," the butcher rang with sarcasm. "The world's gone upside down I tell you—women wanting to vote, and now Marshal Allen's on trial for kidnapping."

Thomas scoffed, "Please don't say that you're worried about Allen, Pa. You're the one who hid Jerry while the whole city was looking for him!"

"Aye, there's truth in that," the butcher resigned.

After a quick stop at Cook's we returned to City Hall for more excitement at the *State Temperance Convention*. Up for debate was the resolution to invite all societies, of every sex, kindred, people, tongue and color to cooperate with this Society to promote Temperance.

Mr. Platt said he hoped the advocates for the ladies would, for the sake of harmony, waive their claim. He believed that if female delegates took part in the proceedings of the convention, it would be seized upon by such men as James Gordon Bennett (of the *New York Herald*), as a subject of ridicule, and seriously impair the influence of the Society. He believed this would be a greater load than the Society could carry.

Mr. Hathaway then remarked that the load was already on the temperance car, and he desired to get it off. The convention, by their vote of yesterday, had undertaken to prescribe the particular sphere in which women should move in the temperance reform, and he regarded this as loading the temperance car with the question of women's rights. He agreed with other gentlemen that it was more than the car could carry, and he hoped that the Society would throw off the load and confine themselves entirely to the promotion of the cause of temperance.

During a lull, laughter broke out when the sounds of a hurdy gurdy and an organ grinder erupted from the street outside. The levity faded when the noise became a distraction that prompted several conventioneers to encourage the showman to perform elsewhere.

As the afternoon grew late, Charlie and I both had our fill of the Women's Rights debate at the *Temperance Convention*. I stepped toward the door when he nudged me.

Standing outside of City Hall, Charlie said,

"Well, that was somethin,' Ed, the ladies stole the show! And all kinds of ladies, too—everything from plain quaker bonnets to Mrs. Bloomer herself."

"Oh yeah they did—the radical *Women's Temperance Society!*" I answered.

"So what's the next big thing then?" Charlie asked.

"Gotta be the Marshal Allen trial on Monday, I suppose."

"Sounds good to me—why not?" Charlie answered.

With that, we both left for home.

On Monday morning, June 21, 1852, I walked alone to the State courthouse for the trial of US Deputy Marshal Henry W. Allen, charged with kidnap for arresting Jerry Henry under the *Fugitive Slave Law*. Charlie had to work, selling carriage and harness trimmings, and all the saddlery hardware in the world. Nearing the courthouse, my heart sank at the crowd size, doubting that I'd get inside. Spotting Parish Johnson, his expression showed he felt the same.

"Hey Parish—I knew you'd be here! You think we'll get into court?"

"I don't know, Ed—it'll be tough!"

"Be a shame to miss it, though."

"Yup, the county's gettin' all riled over the *Jerry Rescue* again."

"Yeah, I wonder what Jerry would say about it. Hey look, Parish—here comes Mr. Crandal!"

"I see him, Ed—and he's carrying a notebook, so he must be covering the trial."

"Good morning, Mr. Crandal—are you reporting today?" I asked.

"Good morning, gentlemen!" Crandal answered. "Yes, I've been hired by the *Star*, no less."

Parish answered, "The *Star* hired you, sir? They didn't like you so well when Jerry got rescued—I remember they called you the *negro bell puller*."

"Ha! There's irony for you—I believe the Whigs despise me less these days," Crandal remarked.

I earnestly pleaded, "Mr. Crandal, do you think you could get us inside the courthouse, sir? We're both dying to watch!"

"I don't blame you—this case is the first of its kind since the Constitution of the United States was adopted!" he answered excitedly.

"But can you get us in, sir?" Parish prodded.

"I can but try—stay close to me and we'll see what we can do," the reporter vowed.

Mr. William L. Crandal kept his word, including us in the press corps. I wished that Mr. Weld could see how his newspaper class had paid off, but I'd be sure to tell him. Once seated, Parish asked,

"Mr. Crandal, what do you think is really at stake here today?"

The reporter drew a breath and replied, "It would seem that the question in this case is, whether in the State of New York, any man has the right on any authority whatever, to place another person who has not committed crime, and is not charged with crime, or breach of contract, in *durance vile*, with impunity."

"Uh, what's *durance vile*, sir?"

"That means imprisonment for a bad reason."

"And that's what people think of the *Fugitive Slave Law*, right, sir?" I asked.

"Yes, but only in the North. Marshal Allen acted in conformity with the *Fugitive Slave Law* of 1850, but it seems that Federal law is inconsistent with the 1840 New York State law against kidnapping. The Grand Jury found a true bill against Marshal Allen for kidnapping when he arrested Jerry under the *Fugitive Slave Law*."

Nearing ten o'clock the case was called, Judge Richard Pratt Marvin presiding. For the prosecution were Onondaga County District Attorney, Rowland H. Gardner, attorney Charles B. Sedgewick, and attorney/politician Gerrit Smith. Defending US Deputy Marshal Henry Allen were US District Attorney James R. Lawrence, with attorney's George F. Comstock, and Stephen D. Dillaye.

Although the *Jerry Rescue* trials were postponed at Federal Court in Canandaigua, it felt like Syracuse was reliving the *Jerry Rescue* again—but this time Jerry was safe in Canada, forever free from the slave-catcher's grip. Parish and I both hoped for a fast-moving courtroom drama, but instead, the morning and afternoon were consumed by a defense motion to prove that Marshal Allen acted under the authority of the *Fugitive Slave Law*. After lengthy arguments, the judge disagreed. Most of the legal wranglings went over my head, and the courtroom drudgery left me restless. Mr. Sedgwick haggled with George Comstock as the first day concluded, with Gerrit Smith set to plead the prosecution's case in the morning.

"How are you two holding up—are you still with me?" Crandal posed into our sleepy faces.

"Yes, sir—just glazed over a bit!" Parish responded.

"Me, too, Mr. Crandal—it's pretty warm in here!"

Crandal replied, *"That it is!* But tomorrow Gerrit Smith will keep you on your toes."

"I hope so!" we both cried.

We arrived early on Tuesday with the city abuzz that General Winfield Scott had become the Whig candidate for President. The Whigs surpassed the Democrats 49 ballots, giving Scott the win on the 53rd tally—casting November's election between Winfield Scott and Franklin Pierce to become the 14th President of the United States. Like the Democrats, Whigs required two ballots to select William A. Graham for Vice President. Courtroom gossip suggested that Democrats were more excited about Pierce than Whigs were about Scott, leaving the many Filmore supporters disappointed.

At 8:10 with Judge Marvin seated, the jury was called but only eleven answered. The Crier called the sheriff, who sent for the absent William K. Blair, and by half past the hour Blair resumed his place on the jury.

*Gen. Winfield Scott*

All eyes focused on Gerrit Smith as he rose to argue against the constitutionality of the *Fugitive Slave Law*. With a strong, deliberate voice, Smith said that yesterday, "Mr. Lawrence hoped they could complete in one evening. In reply, I think that my own argument might occupy a whole day, which shows the difference in our estimation of the importance of the cause.

General Lawrence makes light of it. I do not.

General Lawrence thinks the case a very different one from what it would be, had one of his own children been seized and attempted to be plunged into slavery. I do not.

No doubt the children of General Lawrence are very dear to him and very dear to their mother. So were the children of Jerry's mother!"

Hitting upon the constitutional question, Smith said, "It must not be forgotten that an officer is sworn not to obey an act of Congress, but the Constitution of the United States! The Constitution provides for a jury trial in all criminal cases—Why?

There must be a reason for this—what is it? It is that a man's character and property are involved in the issue. But a man claimed as a fugitive slave loses his liberty for life—aye, more than that, sinks his manhood forever. To try a man for his liberty for life, without a trial by jury, is unreasonable. What is an unreasonable law, if to drag a man down to beast-hood be not one? It seems to me that this law is unconstitutional and void, to deny jury trial in a suit at Common Law."

Gerrit Smith spent hours attacking the constitutionality of the *Fugitive Slave Law*. He argued that commissioners under this law were not empowered by the Constitution to grant judicial powers. Judges are paid salaries to ensure impartiality, but Commissioners were paid fees, which could act as a bribe since they were paid twice as much for siding with the slavery over liberty. Smith declared there was never a more shameful act in the history of laws.

During his discourse he made sixteen points for the unconstitutionality of the hated law, amongst which were that it recognized slavery in the territories and the District of Columbia, suspended the writ of Habeas Corpus, all while denying testimony for the defense. Smith passionately defended the Constitution of the United States, asserting that it wasn't a monster with two heads, one liberty, the other slavery.

In Gerrit Smith's final words, he claimed that the fugitive clause did not refer to slaves.

"If the slave be not a man, if he does not own himself, he cannot *owe* any man anything—he is incapable of obligation. If the slave be unmanageable and lazy, you cannot look to the law for aid, any more than in the case of a horse or an ox. If a slave be property, he cannot be held to service and labor by law, any more than a horse or an ox."

It was hard to imagine how the defense could respond, but they did so ably, first by Stephen Dillaye, followed by George Comstock.

Comstock reminded the jury that "it is well known that on the first day of October last an attempt was made in the city of Syracuse to execute a law of the United States, obnoxious to the prejudices of some portion of our fellow citizens. It became the duty of the defendant to receive and execute a process placed in his hands for the arrest of a slave who had fled from the service of

*Gerrit Smith*

his master in the State of Missouri. He did so, and did no more! There is no complaint of any inhumanity or excess in the performance of his duty. It is also known that a large number of misguided and infatuated persons, ignorant, it would seem, of their simplest duty as citizens—that of obedience to law—assembled themselves together, erected the standard of rebellion against the Constitution and the law, invaded the sanctuary of justice, and forcibly rescued the prisoner in custody.

"An unsound and unwholesome sentiment appears to pervade the minds of many good men that the Union and the Constitution are in some indefinable way responsible for the existence and perpetuation of slavery, and hence not a few, I fear, are ready to see the Union sacrificed on the altar of anti-slavery agitation. I have said that the Constitution did nothing to weaken the institution of slavery as it existed in the States. I now say it did nothing to extend its domain or to guaranty its perpetuity.

"Let the Union be dissolved and a Northern and a Southern confederacy take its place, and what then? He, who supposes that two conterminous states could maintain peace with each other without some compact of this kind, has but slightly considered the subject. The necessity of preserving peace and order would so compel them to enter into treaty stipulations for the surrender of fugitives. Nor would it be strange if the free states should be the first to desire to enter in these stipulations."

Comstock's words carried weight; hatred of the *Fugitive Slave Law* alone would only lead to armed conflict, agreements were needed to keep the peace. Marshal Allen had followed the law as written, and no more.

Suspense grew in the courtroom as closing arguments drew to an end. Judge Marvin charged the jury, who acquitted Marshal Allen without leaving their seats.

# Chapter Twenty-Seven
## (July 1852)

My mother wasn't surprised by the verdict. Black George shrugged his shoulders while Ellen, Emma, Clara, Florence, Lucia, Henry, and Minnie couldn't have cared less. Once again, my father was off to parts unknown, which left Ma feeling sulky.

"What's wrong, Ma?" I asked. "Is Pa at another meeting somewhere?"

"Leave her alone, Edward," Ellen said in her defense, "Just tell us what your reporter friend said about the verdict!" she directed.

"Ellen, Mr. Crandal said that the Law-and-Order crowd should feel vindicated. He said they'd hail this as a good omen, the first victory over the public sentiment that took Jerry from the custody of the law."

"Ha! That sounds like something a reporter would say," Ellen scoffed, drawing my ire.

"Oh, really? I didn't know that you knew any!"

Unwilling to be drawn, she changed the subject.

"Ed, did you remember that the *Festival of the Rose* is coming up on the twenty-ninth? Emmie and I are both singing, so don't forget!"

"I won't, Miss Ellen. Grove Johnson will be sitting right up front, for you and Miss Emma."

"Grove's the same age as Miss Emma!" Ellen teased, making Emma blush.

Ma joined the conversation, saying, "Well, Edward, you're right that your father is off on a committee somewhere."

"What else is bothering you, Ma?" I asked again.

"Let's see," she began, "Besides your absent father, it's been over a week since my last letter from Cornelia. Then there was the telegraph that Cousin Louisa died suddenly, and finally, that the Congregational Church is coming apart. But besides that, everything's fine."

Assured of her well-being, it felt safe to complain.

"Ma, I'm bored!"

"Edward, I believe that you've been so long accustomed to unlimited freedom of thought and action, that you don't know what you want, only that you're determined not to be pleased with anything or anybody," she retorted.

"Huh? What I do now? I'm staying out of trouble, Ma—the city's fixin' to throw a great 4th of July party this year and I don't plan to miss it!"

"Don't forget the benefit for the Loguen's, it's on the same night as the *Festival of the Rose*," she reminded me.

Black George joined in, "Dat be right, missus—and I'se goin'!"

"I'll go with ya, George," I vowed, then began plotting a course for the holiday.

Syracuse planned a memorable 4th of July celebration, shifting the festivities from Sunday, the 4th, to Monday, the 5th, keeping the sabbath day holy. Despite the many signers of the holiday temperance pledge, partying and fireworks pervaded the city. The taps were flowing at John Greenway's new Ale House on Montgomery Street near Genesee.

At the Committee's request, the military, city firemen, and their counterparts from Oswego and Fulton, along with various civic societies, would put on a brilliant display. The one thing everyone wanted to avoid was another cannon misfire—just ask Grasshopper!

The Fifth of July celebration would commence with a National Salute and the ringing of bells at sunrise. *President of the Day*, Major Moses D. Burnet, would preside over thirty vice presidents. Music from three bands would accompany the event, with Mr. Dennis McCarthy's reading of the *Declaration of Independence*, followed by Rev. Sunderland's Oration.

The city's butchers joined the revelry leading up to Monday. Allen and Drew advertised a pair of four-year-old steers to be slaughtered for Independence Day. James Meldrum paraded four steers with ribbons and "Robinson's Band" of wind instruments. The next day, Luke Collins, landlord of the James St. House, ridiculed Meldrum's parade, claiming to have the tastiest beef in Syracuse. I looked for Cale Davis, but things were quiet on Orange Street ever since Thomas signed the pledge.

On June 29, a church bell rang unexpectedly on a Tuesday afternoon, soon joined by another until all the city's bells rang in unison. It wasn't the same knell as for a fugitive slave, though it was much louder at Fayette Park. From our front door, I hailed a passerby who informed me that Senator Henry Clay had died that morning in Washington.

"What's going on, Edward?" Ma asked when I stepped back inside.

"I just heard that Henry Clay died in Washington, Ma. The telegraph lines must be humming in every State and across the territories!"

"Henry Clay was born in 1776, Edward—did you know that?" she informed.

"No, Ma, but it's fitting, ain't it?"

"Yes, son, but please don't tell your father—here he comes!"

My father wore an uneasy look when he crossed the threshold, but after he didn't say anything, Ma broke the silence.

"Charles, what's wrong?" she asked.

*"Ellen, I'm being vilified!"* he answered.

"Why? What happened?"

"I told someone at the Congregational Church to stop ringing the bell."

"Told who?"

"I don't know who it was, but he wasn't a member of our church, so he didn't belong there."

"What did the man say after you made him stop?"

"He vowed to let everyone know what I thought of Henry Clay, but I told him that it's no secret. Then he headed toward the Square, *talking shit!*"

"Charles, *such language!*" she reproached.

"It's an apt description, Ellen," he replied.

"The Irish call it *shite*, Ma—is that any better?" I asked.

"Keep flappin' dem lips, boy!" Black George suggested.

For much of the afternoon, except at the Congregational Church, the bells of Syracuse rang in mourning for Henry Clay. This time, however, I doubted that Mr. Crandal was in the belfry of the First Presbyterian, standing on the trap door to pull the rope undisturbed. There was already talk of a public meeting to organize a proper send-off for the *Great Compromiser*, much like that for President Taylor.

After a hurried supper, I rapped on Black George's bedroom door, anxious to depart for the Loguen Benefit.

"Hey George, you in there?" I asked from the hallway.

"I'se here—what's yo hurry?" he answered, opening the door.

"Oh, no hurry George," I lied.

"Sho, you never come knockin' less you want somethin'!" he pronounced.

"I was just itchin' to get outta here, George—wonderin' who's at Market Hall . . . We're walkin' over together, right?"

"Yes, we is. You gonna be dis anxious to leave soons we get there?"

"No sir, the *Festival of the Rose* don't start till eight."

"Well, les get goin' den!" he said with conviction, and we did.

Rev. John Lyles hailed our arrival at Market Hall, acting as chief greeter for the Loguen family.

"Welcome to you both!" Lyles beamed, shaking our hands. "I expected you early, and here you are."

"Yes suh, Reverend, we's here for brother Loguen!" Black George affirmed.

"That's right, Rev. Lyles—George can tell you how I rushed him, too," I said.

Looking past Rev. Lyles, I saw Rev. May talking with Abner Bates and Mr. Raymond. It was strange to think of Mr. Raymond now as the *former* Pastor of the First Baptist Church.

"Hey George, I'm gonna go talk to Rev. May," I said, leaving the two hastily. As I approached, Abner Bates spoke to his friends.

"I expect a good showing tonight. Everyone knows how this man was driven from his home and his family!" Bates issued.

"Yes, courtesy of the *Fugitive Slave Law!*" Mr. Raymond answered.

Rev. May said, "Since then, Jermain has labored in Canada for the temporal and spiritual benefit of those who seek asylum from the government."

"True, but these people are poor, and unable to make him any return save their gratitude," Bates replied.

"And that justifies us to call upon our citizens to contribute for the support of Brother Loguen's family," Mr. Raymond pronounced.

"Food, money, and clothing gladly accepted!" Rev. May agreed.

I took my queue to join the conversation.

"I guess that an envelope will do, Rev. May!" I said, holding one out towards him. Pa had filled it good.

"Yes, most assuredly, Edward," he answered.

"There's a collection box over there on the table," Mr. Raymond advised, pointing to where Mrs. Loguen held baby Jarvin as the girls played nearby.

Mr. Bates said, "Thank you, Edward, and your folks at home, too!"

"You're welcome, sir," I answered. "Uh, Rev. May, I thought of you when all the bells started to ring but I could tell that it wasn't the same ring, like for a runaway."

Rev. May agreed, "You're right, the last time that so many bells rang was for Jerry's arrest."

Bates rejoined, "Today we rang the bells for the man who brought us the *Fugitive Slave Law*, and tonight we hold a benefit for a man who suffers from its effects—there's irony for you!"

Looking over at the Loguen's, Mr. Raymond said, "Poor Jermain, it must be hell for him to be away from his family and newborn son."

"Will Reverend Loguen ever come back, sir?" I asked.

"We pray that he will, Edward, but no-one knows when, and not soon enough for Caroline," Mr. Raymond answered.

I joined Black George in line to greet Mrs. Loguen. Along the wall, several tables were beginning to fill with baskets, jars, blankets, and clothing.

"Looks like it's off to a good start, huh, George? Lots of folks here already!" I observed.

"Sho is—I be helpin' to bring everythin' to the Loguen's later."

"Should be a cartful, George—maybe two!"

"Dat be good, Edward—Caroline's strugglin' without Jermain, an de railroad still bringin' strangers to her door."

"It ain't fair, George, is it? Henry Clay's a hero, while Reverend Loguen's a fugitive."

"Look dat way, don't it? Who know what he be walkin' into when he come back—police be lookin' for 'im, even if slavers gone."

"I think you're right, George, he's risking a lot to come home."

Mr. Bates overheard, adding, "More than that, Edward, he's risking life and liberty to leave Canada for America. How do you like that? I'm pretty sure that's not what the founders intended."

"No sir, Mr. Bates, it says so in the Declaration!" I replied.

"But not for da colored man," Black George said matter-of-factly.

I answered, "Yes, it does, George—but too many people don't follow what it says."

*Henry Clay*

Mr. Bates took issue, "The folks down South disagree, Edward—they say the Constitution supports slavery."

Just then, Black George reached the front of the line where Mrs. Loguen became emotional. Although Pa donated more monetarily, George's contribution came at a higher cost—like the story of the widow's mite from the Bible. Being a preacher's wife, Caroline Loguen knew her scriptures.

"Oh, George, you've been a brother to me!" she cried, throwing her arms around him.

"Jermain do the same fo me, Caroline!" he replied, returning her embrace.

I stood silent, and after she released George Johnson, I was next.

"Oh, thank you for coming, Edward—and for everything!" Mrs. Loguen said while she gave me a hard squeeze.

"You're welcome, ma'am—we're all glad to help."

"I know you are—may the good Lord bless you!"

"Thank you, ma'am. Uh, Mrs. Loguen, do you know when Reverend Loguen's coming home?" I bluntly asked, immediately wishing that I hadn't.

"Oh, if only I knew," Mrs. Loguen lamented. "He's afraid that the wrong people might read his letters, so he can't tell me. But I know my husband, and he won't be kept from where he's needed most!"

As Mrs. Loguen greeted the person behind me, a loud cry came from across the hall. Helen Loguen had slipped and hit her head while chasing her sister. The fall left a cut above her eye, bleeding freely down her face and staining her white dress with crimson. She presented a startling image, causing many to gasp, including the anxious Mrs. Loguen. Luckily, Dr. Hoyt took charge with his medical bag.

"Poor Mrs. Loguen," I reflected, "this is the last thing that she needs."

The more I thought about it, the angrier I grew because a good man like Rev. Loguen couldn't be where he was needed most, all thanks to the *Fugitive Slave Law*, just like Mr. Raymond said.

Meandering around City Hall, I recognized many faces from last October's *Rally for Freedom* after the *Jerry Rescue*. I saw Jerry's former employer, Mr. Williston, ex-Mayor Hovey, Moses Summers, Ira Cobb, and Washington Van Zandt, amongst many others who recognized me as Charles A. Wheaton's son, not someone returning from California with a trunk full of gold.

Leaving Black George, I headed to the *Festival of the Rose* at Malcolm Hall, passing Cook's Coffee House where Austin and Abel spoke with Parish and Grove Johnson outside. As I approached, Parish feigned,

"*Shh, Shh, here he comes . . .*"

"Yeah, right, Johnson—like yer important or somethin'!" I retorted.

Parish cried, "*Boo hoo!*" and everyone laughed but me.

Austin asked, "So where ya comin' from, Ed?"

"Just left the Loguen benefit at City Hall—turned out pretty good, too."

"Well, we been full-up here—lots of folks going to the *Rose Festival!*"

Parish said, "Hey Ed, anything good from the Police Office? You were just over that way."

"Like what? Anything in particular?" I replied.

"Anything unusual, I suppose—like when Officer Way brought in Cornelius Redding for marrying Michael Doyle's wife! Mike was furious, and they had to restrain him from attacking Mrs. Doyle and her new husband. Besides that, it's been the usual parade of wife beaters, drunks, and disorderlies—I like it when they get thirty minutes to leave town!"

Abel said, "Yeah, it's like the wild west right here in Syracuse, huh, Ed?"

"I suppose, but I care more about the 4th of July celebration."

"Me, too!" Grove answered. "When's the parade?"

"Starts at 10:30, Grove—goes down Salina Street to Jefferson, then around Fayette Park, right past my house."

"We can watch from your front steps, Ed, if you're not hoity-toity," Austin teased.

"Where's the parade end?" Grove asked.

Abel answered, "The parade ends at the Grove, Grove, right behind the Court House."

"Right—and they'll be speeches given from two separate stands, one in English and the other in German," Austin added.

"Then, there's dinner at the Globe Hotel and fireworks after dark!" I concluded.

Suddenly, John Cook Jr. emerged to retrieve his brothers.

"All right you two, break's over!" he directed. "Oh, hey, you guys," he said to the rest of us, quickly adding, "So if you're going to the *Rose Festival* then you should bring some roses for the girls, don't ya think?"

"It's John's latest idea, Ed, he's been sellin' flowers on the side," Austin advised.

"How many will it be, fellas?" John asked, closing the deal.

Long stems in hand, Grove surprised us, saying, "Hey Ed, we don't wanna be late for the show! C'mon, Parish, you're always holding me up."

"Ha! I guess it's your turn to be the anchor, Parish," I observed.

Parish retorted, "You shoulda seen 'im gettin' ready, Ed—he even combed his hair."

"Nothin' stays the same, Ed," Abel said, shaking his head.

"Except us working," Austin sighed as John Jr. held the door.

Reaching Malcolm Hall, we squeezed in next to Ma and cousin Charlotte.

"Oh look, Ellen—here's three young gentlemen come courting!" Charlotte announced. "Are those for me?" she kidded.

"Uh, sorry, cousin—they're for the girls in the show," I replied.

Parish said, "John Cook was sellin' 'em—said we oughta show our support."

"Are both of those for Miss Ellen, Grove?" Ma asked.

"No, ma'am, the other's for Miss Emma—one apiece."

"How was the benefit for the Loguen's, Edward? Did many people attend?"

"It was pretty good, Ma, except for when Helen Loguen fell and cut her head! She got blood all over her white dress and Dr. Hoyt had to stitch her eyebrow."

"Poor Caroline, what next?" she lamented.

"That's what I thought, Ma. And she don't know when Rev. Loguen's coming home, neither."

Grove asked, "Excuse me, Ma'am, but is Miss Ellen gonna sing a solo tonight?"

"You'll have to wait and see," Ma replied, "but hush now—the show's about to start."

This year's performance proved a success. Mr. and Mrs. Allen's production kept the proud tradition alive, and as Ma said, "The girls sang charmingly!" Martha Downer was crowned Queen amongst the Maids of Honor, and although Miss Bassett sang the solos, the Wheaton sisters had Grove Johnson making moon eyes at the stage.

At show's end we surprised the girls with our flowers, which grew into bouquets before we left for home. Ellen and Emma were thrilled, I felt happy for them as we relived the evening at home on our piazza with Pa and the others. Unfortunately, Ellen, Emma, and Charlotte fell ill in the middle of the night. Ma attributed the girls' malady to all of the bad air in the concert room.

Come morning, I slipped out to retrieve a newspaper, hoping to find a review of the *Festival of the Rose*. Instead, to my horror, I read an article in the *Star* that called out the abolitionist Charles A. Wheaton by name for silencing the bell at the Congregational Church, implying that he was a hypocritical fanatic. Pa wasn't home when I read it, but Ma's temperature went up a degree or two when I showed it to her in print. I tried to imagine how this would have gone over in Mr. Weld's newspaper class and shook my head.

That afternoon I accompanied Ma to the Arcade in the Bastable Block to view *Powers' Greek Slave*, the world-renowned sculpture by Hiram Powers.

At the entrance she said excitedly, "We're lucky to see this, Edward—the statue's making its way to Europe, never to return!"

"I heard that it could be the most viewed statue outside of Italy, Ma. Hey look—there's Sanford Thayer! I wonder if anyone's ever painted a portrait of *Powers' Greek Slave* before—*Ha!*"

*Powers' Greek Slave*

"I wouldn't be surprised. After Elizabeth Barrett Browning saw it at the *Crystal Palace* she wrote a sonnet named *"Hiram Power's Greek Slave."*

"Didn't Powers have a second statue at the *Great Exhibition*, Ma?"

"Yes, he named it '*Fisher Boy*'," she said as we entered the Arcade. At first sight, the statue's nudity shocked us, I could tell that Ma was taken aback. But the feeling soon passed, albeit the skills of the craftsmen.

As we stood beside the naked, chained, female slave in marble, Ma remarked "It's really a superb specimen of art, and it really does seem like life, don't you think, Edward?" she posed without averting her gaze.

"I almost fancy I can see the chest heave, and the lips quiver."

"It's cut from one block of pure Italian marble, son—and as a work of art, it seems wonderful. The limbs are beautifully shaped with every indentation, look at the knees and ankles! And there's an expression in the bend of her wrist, as she leans on the post at her side."

"You have a way with words, Ma—you shoulda been a writer!"

"Hmm—why was not I a poet? I feel the spirit of poetry, strong within me, but alas! it never shapes itself into words."

"You know, Ma, when I first saw the statue I expected the slave to be black."

"Well, it's white marble to begin with, but you're right about her face—she's from Greece, not Africa."

"Yeah, I guess I was only thinkin' of the slaves from Africa."

"Son, there's been slavery everywhere on earth going back to antiquity, but the chattel slavery on our southern plantations is an especially cruel variety."

"I saw the cruelty of it at the Loguen benefit. It ain't right how the *Fugitive Slave Law* is keeping a man away from his family!"

"No, it's not, but tonight the mayor called a public meeting for a tribute to the law's champion, Henry Clay," Ma reflected.

I answered, "All while Mrs. Loguen's at home alone with three girls and a baby because the law made her husband a fugitive."

"That's true, but don't forget that your grandfather served with Henry Clay in Congress and held him in such regard that he named my brother after him."

"What do you think he'd say about Powers' *Greek Slave*, Ma?"

"I think that my father would see the art for its beauty, excluding the nudity. After that, he'd want to know the cost of creating it. He says things like, *'Everything comes at a cost.'*"

"Grandpa's right, Ma—and I say the cost of resisting the *Fugitive Slave Law* is too high! Rev. Loguen and Rev. Ward both had to flee, and there's all those men on trial for violating it."

"But they didn't think so, Edward, they refused to see Jerry dragged off to perpetual bondage. They summoned the courage of their convictions to face the moment thrust upon them."

"Yeah, but now my friend Sam is gone with his family, and Rev. Loguen's family needs him at home!"

"We're all praying for his safe return, Edward."

"Yeah, that's what Mr. Raymond said, but nobody knows when."

"Man proposes, but God disposes," Ma pronounced.

Two days later, Black George invited me to visit the Loguen's to check on Helen. Recalling the bright red blood on her white dress, I needed to know she was okay. Despite George's assurance of a healthy prognosis, I decided to go anyway.

Walking toward my old neighborhood from Fayette Park felt strange, as I was used to the park as a destination. On Genesee Street, we passed a quiet corner at Orange where things had changed dramatically ever since Thomas became a policeman and went dry. I looked for the Cheney's around Almond Street, but they were gone. A new family occupied our old homestead, reminding me of Abel Cook's words that nothing stays the same.

Nearing the Loguen's, my thoughts wandered to Henry Clay.

"Hey George, did you hear what happened at the big meeting for Henry Clay the other night?" I asked.

"I don't care none for Henry Clay," he answered.

"Well, the city sure does, Mayor Woodruff was named chairman! Then they decided on sixteen names for the *Committee of Arrangements* and another five for the *Committee of Resolutions*."

Black George said, "I resolves dat Henry Clay be a bad fella for makin' de *Slave Law*."

"Ha—That's a good one, George! Don't think the committee'll like it, though," I scoffed in return.

No sooner had we knocked on the Loguen's door when Black George rang out, **"*Sweet Lord Jesus!*"**

There stood the Reverend Jermain Wesley Loguen, holding his son, surrounded by Mrs. Loguen and the girls. We stepped closer to touch him.

Rev. Loguen beamed, "Hello, George!" The two men clasped hands at first, then Loguen embraced him with one arm while still holding Jarvin with the other as he pulled George inside.

"I want to thank you, George. Caroline's told me how good you've been to my family—isn't that right?"

"That's right, George," Mrs. Loguen smiled to say.

"We love you, Mr. George!" cried the nine- and ten-year-old sisters, Helen and Elizabeth, rushing in while two-year-old Sarah spoke gibberish from the floor.

I thought I perceived a glisten in George's eye, when Rev. Loguen said,

"And you, too, Edward—your whole family. We're blessed to have friends like the Wheaton's, you tell your pa that I'll be round to see him soon's I can!"

"I will, Reverend, it's good to have you back, sir!"

Leaving Black George with the happy family, I rushed home to relate the good news.

"And what do you think, Edward?" Ma asked.

"I never heard of a round trip ticket on the underground railroad before—Rev. Loguen's the first!"

Ma observed, "How apprehensive he must have felt, not knowing if he'd be arrested on sight."

"I can't imagine, but he gave me hope, Ma. It made me think that even though there's a hard road ahead, somehow everything'll turn out right in the end."

"I see! Is there anything else?"

"Yeah, there is—I can't wait to celebrate the 4th of July! It's gonna be the best one ever, Ma, even if it's a day late!"

On Sunday, I squeezed into the AME Zion with Black George to hear Rev. Loguen recount his flight to freedom and back. As he gave thanks for being reunited with his family, I prayed that Sam Ward might soon follow. After all, today was the 4th of July, and the founders declared in writing that all men are created equal, that they are endowed by their Creator with certain unalienable rights, that among these are life, liberty and the pursuit of happiness.

They all signed it, too.

☞ Rev. J. W. Loguen will preach at his old p!ace next Sabbath (4th of July) at 2 o'clock in the afternoon and in the evening.

# Epilogue

**The Fugitive Slave Acts** of 1793 and 1850 were repealed by a congressional act on June 28, 1864.

**The 13th Amendment** to the U.S. Constitution abolished slavery and involuntary servitude, except as punishment for a crime, within the United States and its territories. It passed Congress in January, 1865, then became ratified by the states that December.

Having birthed twelve children, **Ellen Birdseye Wheaton** died suddenly from a seizure on December 17, 1858, aged 42. Tragically, it occurred on the night following her daughter Cornelia's marriage to Frederick Ayer.

**Cornelia Wheaton Ayer** had four children before she succumbed January 9, 1878, also aged 42.

**Charles A. Wheaton** struggled after Ellen's demise, moving to Northfield, MN, where he became publisher and editor of the Rice County Journal. He remarried and had five more children with his second wife, seventeen in total. When Wheaton purchased the interests of the local flour mill he may have economically saved the town. For some time, Wheaton's Northfield Mills produced "choice family flour." He died in 1882, aged 72.

**Edward Wheaton** didn't do well in college, but fulfilled his dream to live in California. Despite an illness plagued sailing voyage and never striking it rich, he ultimately became a bookkeeper for the US Mint in San Francisco. He died September 6, 1905, aged 68, survived by his wife Louise and their six children.

**Will Stoddard** went on to become a prolific writer and private secretary to President Abraham Lincoln. He passed in 1925, aged 89.

**Parish B. Johnson** was a captain in the United States Army before becoming editor of the Walla Walla Union from 1876 to 1890. He lived the remainder of his life in the state of Washington until his passing in 1906, aged 67.

**Grove Johnson** became a lawyer and followed his brother Parish out west in 1863. He was elected to both the California State Assembly and Senate before serving as a US representative to Congress. He passed in 1926, aged 84 in Sacramento, CA.

**George Johnson** "Black George"—remained in Syracuse after Charles Wheaton moved his family to Minnesota. In 1860 he hired on with the wealthy Cornelius Longstreet, living at Renwick Castle until 1867 when Longstreet traded homes with Alonzo Yates on James Street. George died in 1878 and is buried at Oakwood Cemetery.

**Jermain Loguen**—continued the struggle for freedom in Syracuse. In 1869 he became the first black man selected for the Onondaga County Grand Jury, the year that his daughter Helen married Frederick Douglass' son, Lewis. He died in 1872, aged 63.

**Samuel Ringgold Ward**—never returned to the United States, residing in Canada, then England, where he continued to speak publicly against slavery. He died in 1866, aged 49, after living his last 11 years of life as a minister and farmer in Jamaica.

**Caleb "Cale" Davis** remained on good terms with Rev. S.J. May. When Mrs. Waty Davis died in 1861, Cale, with son Thomas, held her funeral at Rev. May's Unitarian Church.

**Thomas Davis** was named Chief of Police in 1856, only four years after joining the force. He held the position several times, when not chief he partnered in a private detective firm. His last appointment in 1869 continued until his death in 1880. At his passing, Thomas received full honors from city leaders for twenty-five years of faithful service. The entire police force escorted their fallen leader to his well attended funeral at Oakwood Cemetery.

**William "Jerry" Henry** lived for two years in Kingston, Ontario where he made a hickory cane presented to Charles Wheaton in thanks for the role that he played. Jerry died from tuberculosis on October 10, 1853.

**Enoch Reed** was the only person convicted in connection with the Jerry Rescue. He died while his case was under appeal.

# Acknowledgements

First and foremost, I'm grateful to my wife, Sue, for her unwavering support. Countless times (out of the blue) I brought up people and events that she'd never heard of, always hoping for a big reaction. For your incredible patience, humor, and much more, I thank and love you.

Next, I'd like to thank my brother, Leo, for his editorial critique that was much used. No pain, no gain—it hurts to admit when your brother's right.

I wish to extend heartfelt gratitude to my friend, Barry Cronin, for being the first person to read the draft in its entirety. Your encouragement meant a lot, despite my knowing your fisherman's powers of exaggeration.

To Donna Frateschi, Maria DeAngelis, and Mark Reynolds, three people who encouraged me from the outset. It's great to have confidants that you're not afraid to bounce ideas around with! Thank you for honest feedback that kept me on track.

I'm grateful to the team at Barringer Publishing for putting it all together, especially to Linda Duider for the cover design and book layout.

I'd be remiss not to acknowledge these writers from the 1850s:

Thank you, Ellen Birdseye Wheaton! Your diary painted a picture of 1850s life that I tried to depict. I used your own words to let you speak for yourself. Likewise, thanks to Will Stoddard, Parish Johnson, Timothy C. Cheney, Charles F. Williston, Rev. May, Rev. Ward, and Rev. Loguen. Your recollections brought life and accuracy to this book.

I must thank the many unsung newspaper writers of the day, whose stories captured my imagination and inspired me to write/assemble this novel. I gleaned from press clippings to portray the real events as they occurred in order. There's magic inside all of those old newspapers—a veritable time machine.

Finally, a word of thanks to Bob Searing and the folks at the Onondaga Historical Association for providing me with access to Syracuse history! For those interested, I've given the OHA all of the research materials that I gathered/created for this project—a great resource to further explore the Jerry Rescue and Syracuse of the early 1850s.

www.ingramcontent.com/pod-product-compliance
Lightning Source LLC
Chambersburg PA
CBHW020047170426
43199CB00009B/198